DIGITAL

GAME

BASE

LEARN

Also by Marc Prensky:

Don't Bother Me Mom—I'm Learning! How Computer Games Are Preparing Your Kids for 21st Century Success—and How You Can Help!

Game Design Handbook
(Chapter on Games and Learning)

Collected Essays

Companion Websites:
www.games2train.com
www.socialimpactgames.com
www.twitchspeed.com
www.marcprensky.com

DIGITAL GAME-BASED LEARNING

Marc Prensky

FOREWORD BY SIVASAILAM "THIAGI" THIAGARAJAN,
PRESIDENT, WORKSHOPS BY THIAGI

Paragon House
St. Paul, Minnesota

Paragon House Edition 2007

Published in the United States by
Paragon House
1925 Oakcrest Avenue, Suite 7
St. Paul, MN 55113

First Edition 2001 by The McGraw Hill Companies

The text of this book was set in Opti Berling Agency by MM Design 2000, Inc.

Cover design by Aubrey Arago.

Library of Congress Cataloging-in-Publication Data

Prensky, Marc.
  Digital game-based learning : practical ideas for the application of digital game-based learning / Marc Prensky.
      p. cm.
  ISBN 1-55778-863-4 (pbk. : alk. paper) 1. Computer-assisted instruction.
2. Educational games. I. Title.

  LB1028.5.P695 2007
  371.33'4--dc22

2006019986

The paper used in this publication meets the minimum requirements of American National Standard for Information Sciences—Permanence of Paper for Printed Library Materials, ANSIZ39.48-1984.

Manufactured in the United States of America

10 9 8 7 6 5 4 3

For current information about all releases from Paragon House,
visit the web site at http://www.paragonhouse.com

Rie, my wife and love,
this book is dedicated to you with all my heart.
I have no words to thank you enough for all you have given me.

———————————————————————

CONTENTS

ACKNOWLEDGMENTS

I share one thing with Stephen King, although it's not—I'm sad to say—an ability to create scary stories. We both have written at and been inspired by the beauty of an incredible lake in Maine. For that wonderful opportunity, I most gratefully thank Rena Koopman, her children Zandy and Jordan, and their late and always remembered father, Rad Smith.

To Lil, Jim, Russell, and Tyler, as always, thanks for everything. I couldn't have done it without you.

Ann and Stephen Graham, you are among the most generous people I know, and have encouraged and helped me since the beginning. I humbly thank you.

And Jon Fabris, you have been the magician who made my ideas come to life. Thanks for all these years together.

I would also like to gratefully thank all of the following people who contributed generously of their time and ideas to make this book happen. My agent, Jim Levine; my researcher, Linda D. Paulson; the editing supervisor, Scott Amerman; and my editor, Michelle Reed, whose valuable contributions helped shape the book and make it what it is. Sivasailam "Thiagi" Thiagarajan, Noah Falstein, Ann Graham, Dr. Joan Levine, Dr. Patricia Greenfield, Paula Young, Joanne Veech, Rosemary Garris, Dr. Ray Perez, and Don Johnson read all or parts of the manuscript and made many helpful suggestions. My team at games2train—Jon Fabris, Rob Posniak, Aubrey Arago, Amy Faxon, Annette Bronkish, and John Ariz—were all very supportive, helpful, and understanding.

I am especially grateful to the following individuals who kindly spoke with me, wrote to me, or otherwise contributed ideas: Carlye Adler, Clark Aldrich, Dr. Michael Allen, Stuart Alsop, Dr. Dee Andrews, Aubrey Arago, John Ariz, Paul Asplund, Richard Barkey, Barbara Berke, Mark Bieler, Sheryle Bolton, Cappy Bray, Vicki Carne, Bryan Carter, Bart Casabona, Dawn Cassidy, Dr. Susan Chipman, Luyen Chou, Cathy Clark, Joe Costello, Chris Crawford, Tracy Carter Daugherty, Bob Dean, Bob Downes, Esther Dyson, Ethan Edwards, Win Farrell, Amy Faxon, Roger Faxon, Bran Ferren, Tom Fischmann, Sarah Fister, Patricia Franklin, Jim Freund, Cheryl Garcia, Rosemary Garris, Amy George, Lt. Gen. Paul Glazer, Seth Godin, Pete Goettner, Martha Gold, Eric Goldberg, Harry Gottlieb, Henry Halff, Trip Hawkins, Ed Heinbockel, Vince Henry, J.C. Herz, John Hiles, Danny Hillis, Kurt Hirsch, Barry Howard, Don Johnson, Michael Junior, Tom Kalinske, John Kernan, Andy Kimball, Cindy Klein, Victor Kluck, Kathryn Komsa, Sylvia Kowal, Donna Kush, Jaron Lanier, Amanda Lannert, Tom Levine, Ashley Lipson, Elliott Masie, Margery Mayer, Pete Mazany, Eric McLuhan, David Merrill, Jerry Michalski, Joe Miller, Kim Miller, Peter Moore, Nicholas Negroponte, Mark Oehlert, John Parker, Michael Parmentier, Anita Paul, Rob Posniak, Ted Prince, Kevin Oakes, Mark Rein, Marc Robert, Dale Russakoff, Paul Saffo, Corey Schou, Patricia Seybold, Doug Shuman, Sharon Sloane, Jeff Snipes, Cindy Steinberg, Peter Stokes, Ed Summers, Laine Sutten, John Sviokla, Don Tapscott, Hannah Tetens, Thiagi, George Thibault, Mike Trainer, Joanne Veech, Winnie Wechsler, Annette Wellinghoff, Johnny Wilson, Bob Wolf, Will Wright, Paula Young, Steve Zehngut, Andy Zimmerman, Michael Zyda, and Rob Zeilenski. Thank you one and all!

A special thank you to Rob Posniak, games2train's great low-level programmer, for always making everything work.

Last, but certainly not least, I especially thank Aubrey Arago, the extrememly talented Web designer and graphic artist who designed, built, and maintains the companion Web sites to this book, *www.socialimpactgames.com* and *www.twitchspeed.com*, and who is responsible for most of the look of *www.games2train.com* as well.

FOREWORD

Early in my life, my mentor explained to me the three paths that lead to the creation of knowledge: The analytical path, where philosophers reflect, meditate, and make sense of objects and events; the empirical path, where scientists manipulate variables and conduct controlled experiments to validate reliable principles; and the pragmatic path where practitioners struggle with real-world challenges and come up with strategies for effective and efficient performance.

In this book, Marc Prensky has followed all three paths to create and share knowledge related to education and training. He has systematically analyzed the contexts and events of training and has synthesized a logical framework for digital game based learning. He has reviewed and summarized major empirical principles from psychological and sociological points of view. Most importantly, he has practiced (and continues to practice) what he preaches: Marc has designed, implemented, and evaluated digital game-based learning. He has successfully presented the business case to management and managed game design projects.

During the past six years, I have watched Marc in action while he made keynote presentations at professional conferences. With the unerring intuition of a street performer, he attracts and holds the attention of the audience and explains complex concepts in plain language. With the charm and wit of a storyteller, he communicates clearly through the use of appropriate examples and meaningful metaphors. This powerful communication skill is apparent in Marc's writing style also. However, don't be misled by the readability of the book. It contains deep scholarship and profound messages. The style of the book invites you to take hyper-reading approach. Before you know it, you flip to random pages, surf the text, and become totally immersed in the content.

The book has several important messages and I won't attempt to summarize all of them. However, here are some specific topics that I find to be fascinating:

> As a corporate trainer, I see the significant implications of the chapter on how learners have changed. Although I was born before the Second World War (remember those antique days?), I have tried to pass myself off as a member of the twitch-speed generation ever since I decided to beat my son in playing a precursor of *Pong* on a Radio Shack Model I computer. Unfortunately, in spite of my second childhood behavior, I still have an immigrant accent when compared to my son and his age cohorts. However, knowing the 10 ways (plus "attitude") in which the games generation is different from my generation has made it easy for me to design my training materials and methods to appeal to the parallel processing, random-accessing, fantasy-focused, connected group.

As an instructional designer, I am impressed by Marc's explanation of how and why digital game based learning works. From the second part of the book, I have learned several strategies for making my training give the learners enjoyment, involvement, structure, motivation, action, flow, ego gratification, adrenaline, creativity, and passion.

As a business consultant, I am happy with the wealth of examples and case studies presented by Marc, especially in the third part of the book. I am no longer tongue-tied when a client says, "All of this sounds great. But can you give me examples of where this stuff is being used? And what results does it produce?" I can select the most appropriate example that makes sense to the client. I am also grateful to Marc for the guidelines and details that he has provided for convincing management and getting the bucks.

I don't believe (and neither does Marc) that the digital game-based learning framework presented in this book is the only or the best approach to education and training. I have been in the training business for a long period of time and in the interactive game design business for an equal period of time. The frightening and exciting thing about technology is that it is changing rapidly and we have yet to see the major changes. We cannot slow down or turn back the changes in the field of education and training. They are automatic consequences of the fact that the newer generations are growing up digital.

Let's accept the inevitability of things to come—and play with them!

Sivasailam "Thiagi" Thiagarajan
President, Workshops by Thiagi

Part One
INTRODUCTION/ BACKGROUND

When you think of computer games, there's lots of engagement but little content. Business has lots of content, but no engagement. Put the two together and you have a way to learn the business through computers that makes sense for this generation.
— Marc Prensky, quoted in the Economist Intelligence Unit's report on
  The Learning Organization

INTRODUCTION

Congratulations! By opening this book you have already made it to the high scorers' list of those who "get it" (or at least who *want* to get it). Get what? You get that business *learners* have changed as their *technology* has changed. You get that workers raised on a steady multiyear diet of MTV and video games, rather than books and filmstrips, just might not sit still for the old style of learning. You get that although learning methods and styles may vary among individuals, to be effective with *today's* learners, the "fun" component of *all* learning will have to go through the roof. And you get that Digital Game-Based Learning, in a variety of forms and price ranges, can be a big part of the solution.

We are fortunate to find ourselves at the beginning of something very new and powerful. Imagine, if you will, a book written on automobiles in 1890. Or a book on airplanes written in 1910. Or a book written on computers in 1950. The authors of such books would have been able to paint a picture of a phenomenon just getting started, with a lot of promise. They could have pointed out only a relatively few pioneering instances, several of which had failed. If they were especially clever, they might even have laid out a grand vision of the future—people traveling at *30 miles per hour,* on paved *two-lane roads; a fleet of biplanes* delivering mail to remote locations; solving complex math problems in *only weeks.* Any further predictions at those times would have been pure science fiction. Even the pioneers themselves saw limits: "I don't think the world needs more than 4 or 5 computers," Thomas Watson, CEO of IBM, is said to have remarked in the 1950s.[1]

Yet in each case, *within less than a single lifetime,* ordinary people— men, women, and children—were doing previously unimaginable things: controlling vehicles moving at over 60 miles per hour a few feet apart over vast interconnected highway systems; flying to anywhere in the world in only hours often on a minute's notice; accessing—in seconds, at no cost—the entire network of human information and knowledge from little boxes in their laps.

Henry Ford and Ransom Olds saw 65-mile-per-hour superhighways. (They died in the 1940s.) Orville Wright lived to see the jet plane. (He died in 1948.) Many of the people who built ENIAC, one of the first computers (where the computing power of today's giveaway calculator took up an entire room), were still alive in the year 2000, experiencing megaMIPS (millions of instructions per second) on desktops, and lots more power than ENIAC in their toasters.

I believe it will be the same with Digital Game-Based Learning, the phenomenon described in this book. Long before today's teenagers have grandchildren, Digital Game-Based Learning—or, more precisely, its infinitely more sophisticated successors—will be totally taken for granted as the way people learn.

There are three key reasons why I believe this is so:

1. Digital Game-Based Learning meets the needs and learning styles of today's and the future's generations of learners.
2. Digital Game-Based Learning is motivating, because it is fun.
3. Digital Game-Based Learning is enormously versatile, adaptable to almost any subject, information, or skill to be learned, and when used correctly, is extremely effective.

In 1994, Jay Ogilvy, co-founder and Managing Director of the Global Business Network, wrote that "we can see the convergence of Nintendo and Sega and interactive computer graphics and learning theory and pedagogy and developmental psychology and Gardner's work on multiple intelligences. All these are coming together like tributaries of a river. They aren't with us, but by 1997, 1998, they're going to be here." [2] He was off by a few years, but right on with the concept.

In this book I will show the following:

• Why today's learners and trainees have changed and therefore require something different than they are now getting
• Why and how fun will become an integral part of the learning and training processes
• How Digital Game-Based Learning will incorporate an amazing variety of subject matters, instructional approaches, and learner preferences to become an extremely effective and ubiquitous learning method, benefiting learners and instructors and the institutions in which they work

Although we are at the very beginning of the Digital Game-Based Learning phenomenon, we already see it sprouting, and in some case taking firm root, in a wide variety of places—in several of the world's most prestigious consulting firms, including The Boston Consulting Group, McKinsey, and PricewaterhouseCoopers; in industry leaders like Nortel, Ameritrade, Shell, Holiday Inn, Eli Lilly, Pepsi, Burger King, and Bayer; in smaller firms such as engineering and real estate companies; in service and manufacturing industries, in orientation, product training, soft skills, hard skills, marketing, and strategy; in many branches and levels of the public sector, and most of all, in the U.S. military and law enforcement.

In his book *The Tipping Point*,[3] Malcolm Gladwell describes three conditions that make an idea or thing spread like an epidemic: the law of the few, the stickiness factor, and the power of context. Among the readers of this book are the few who matter. The approach is sticky. The context is right. All the elements are in place for Digital Game-Based Learning to become a worldwide "epidemic" of better learning. So while the book *Digital Game-Based Learning* is aimed primarily at individuals concerned with learning in a business, professional, vocational, or military context—what is commonly called "training," the *phenomenon* of Digital Game-based Learning will eventually reach and affect a much wider audience of individuals involved in both education and entertainment, because its power goes far beyond training alone.

In the highly lucrative world of entertainment, the games business and the theatrical movie business have grown to roughly equal sizes and there is constant talk (although relatively little action to date) about their "converging." The learning business—education and training (an industry worth over $2 trillion worldwide at the turn of the millenium [4])—is in a huge phase of consolidation and refocus through a new delivery system, the Net. The *really* large and potentially far-reaching opportunity is the combination of the entertainment businesses with learning, education, and training. This outcome might seem anathema—or even absurd—to many educators and trainers who see learning as a "serious" activity. And it might seem a strange business proposition to those entertainment executives focused single-mindedly on the commercial mass market. *But it makes perfect sense to today's learners.* The key premise of this book is that by marrying the engagement of games and entertainment with the content of learning and training it is possible to fundamentally improve the nature of education and training for these students and trainees.

What I want to highlight in this book, more than anything else, are not just my own efforts in this area, or those of my former team and colleagues within Bankers Trust, or those of my current company, games2train, but the broad scope of what is being done in the field of Digital Game-Based Learning. I will describe some of my efforts as examples of particular approaches, and, because I know them intimately, I will try to speak as frankly as I can about successes, failures, and problems in getting them done. What is much more important for you, the reader, to take away from this book, however, is the realization that there are a growing number of pioneers—teachers, trainers, learners, and pioneering companies—who are creating more and more Digital Game-Based Learning each day, *out of the sheer frustration that it doesn't exist.* Many of these people are trainers and teachers, possibly much like you. More and more are frustrated learners. As I will show in Chapter 15, there is lots of opportunity for those who envision a fun, game-based solution in their own area of expertise to create it—alone or with a small team—much like individuals initially created the automobile, the airplane, the computer, and the $7 billion games industry of today.

So if you have ever dreamed of a better, more fun, more engaging way to learn, read on. You are not alone, and you can *absolutely* help make it happen. You won't even need much money to start, but you may, as many have, seek—and find—millions down the road. And one thing you can be absolutely certain of. *Do it well, and you will be a hero to your students and trainees and all who come after them!*

This book is intended to be at the same time visionary in outlook, theoretically grounded, and extremely practical. Although I have tried to present a cogent logical progression from beginning to end, one great advantage of the book format is that using the proven technology of "manual hypertext" you can skip directly to anywhere. So I would suggest the following:

- Readers who care about *why learners are different,* and why change is both necessary and difficult, can read Chapters 2 and 3.
- Readers who want to know *what Digital Game-Based Learning is,* should go to Chapter 6.

- Readers who are looking for ideas of *how Digital Game-Based Learning can be used* for a wide variety of training areas and subjects can go to Chapters 7 and 8.
- Readers who want to see *examples and case studies* can go to Chapters 9 and 10.
- Readers who are already convinced and seek *ammunition to overcome objections* and/or convince a boss or executive group can go to Chapter 12.

I have also tried to incorporate into the book a number of less usual and more innovative features, which are connected to what the book is about. There are games incorporated into many of the chapters, necessitating, because the games are digital, the use of a computer and Web browser. All are email games, requiring only the ability to send an email message in order to play.

Many games can be seen or played on the Web sites *www.social impactgames.com* and *www.twitchspeed.com*, which are an essential part of the book's experience. (*Twitch speed* is the accelerated pace at which players' thumbs move during fast-action or "twitch" games.) This book is incomplete without the site, which includes games (including the ones started in the book), links, examples, additional and updated information, quotes, research, references to products and companies, and especially opportunities for your discussion and input around Digital Game-Based Learning. I urge you to go to and especially to add to the site. As Tim Berners-Lee, the father of the Word Wide Web, has said: "What people put into the Web is much more important that what they get out of it." [5]

The book *Digital Game-Based Learning* is also incomplete without your getting to *see and experience* all levels of Digital Game-Based Learning *for yourself.* You can do so in a number of ways. Many low-end examples (i.e., games that are less complex functionally and graphically), can be accessed directly on the Web. Some good examples of Digital Game-Based Learning are commercial products that you can purchase. To experience high-end (i.e., complex and expensive) business examples, which are mostly on CD-ROM, you will have to make some requests for demos, but many are available. In the Further Reading section and on the Web site I list sources you can consult or access to see or obtain examples of

Digital Game-Based Learning. *I urge you in the strongest possible terms to do this, because just reading about Digital Game-Based Learning will give you only a small idea of its attraction and power.*

One final point. Learning is a big job. No one method works alone or by itself for everything. Digital Game-Based Learning is great in that it motivates and teaches in ways that other methods seldom do. But it is neither the unique solution to all training problems nor a panacea. Digital Game-Based Learning needs to be combined with other learning methods that work equally well. One complicating factor is that there haven't been a lot of other effective learning methods lately. But there are certainly some, and lively interaction among teachers and learners and among learners themselves is one of the most effective methods. So please take everything I say about Digital Game-Based Learning in that context.

You will find throughout this book that many of the key ideas are repeated and illustrated in different ways and examples. This repetition is deliberate. Winston Churchill counseled that "if you have an important point to make, don't try to be subtle or clever. Use a pile driver. Hit the point once. Then come back and hit it again. Then hit it a third time—a tremendous whack."[6] *Digital Game-Based Learning* conveys an important message. I'm hoping this book will be, if not a tremendous whack, at least a small jolt to your thought processes.

Have fun learning. May the games begin!

CAVEAT:
WHO DIGITAL GAME-BASED LEARNING IS *NOT* FOR

I strongly believe, based on all my experience and research, that the phenomenon I am about to describe—Digital Game-Based Learning—is a new and important way for many people to learn—especially, although by no means exclusively, for people from what I will call the "Games Generations," and for content that many perceive as "dry" or "boring."

But it is by no means the only way to learn, for the Games Generations or for anyone else. *There are plenty of things that people are motivated to learn without games, and plenty of people who do not prefer games as a way to learn.* What I am describing is not designed for them, although they might be pleasantly surprised by what has been accomplished lately.

Please bear in mind as you read through the book that Digital Game-Based Learning is *only one way*—albeit a fun and effective way—for people to learn.

1

The Digital Game-Based Learning Revolution

FUN AT LAST!

This generation is growing up in a revolution.
— Ryan Zacharia, 16-year-old Internet entrepreneur

Sure they have a short attention span—for the old ways of learning!
— Edward Westhead, former University of Massachusetts biochemistry professor

They said we could be a toy business, but we wanted to be a sex toy business!
— a trainee in a Wharton ebusiness simulation

E3, The Electronic Entertainment Expo in Los Angeles, is a mind-boggling affair. Now that video and computer games have equaled or surpassed movie box office in revenue (each around $7.5 billion in the United States)[1] marketing budgets are immense. The three-day extravaganza at which retailers see the upcoming goods and decide what games they will buy is an oversized, multihall production. It is packed with realistic-looking aliens, giant game characters, Hollywood-style effects, scantily clad women, and thousands of exhibitors and attendees. Game-style noises and lights assault your senses. The "booths" of the big three—Sony, Sega, and Nintendo—are immense fields measurable in acres—effectively kingdoms—with structures rising several stories up in the air, balconies and stages pulsating with go-go dancers, musicians, and entertainers. In the epicenter is Sony's continent; because of their new machine they are the year's biggest spender. And in the very center of that world a huge 30-foot-high movie screen, continuously running in-your-face action-packed scenes from the upcoming games, parts every 20 minutes like a vertical Red Sea allowing a surging wave of super-eager attendees who have waited hours for tickets to enter the inner sanctum. Inside, amidst a storm of SurroundSound and Laser Beams, the latest game console rises onto its pedestal like a God.

Elsewhere on the floor a slightly lesser-known game company, vying for attention in the madness, has brought in a full, two-story-tall half-pipe for stunt bikes, sponsoring shows every hour with name-brand cyclists doing competing 360s. Not far away is a full-size boxing ring with real sparring contests. Every exhibitor has a twist, an angle, a giveaway, something to draw you in. Wait—in very long lines—and you can have your picture taken with Lara Croft from *Tomb Raider* (a real girl with real guns on a real Harley, and don't try to sit in front); or with a huge oversized Simpsons family, or with the seminaked actual L.A. Lakers cheerleaders.

And everywhere, amid the sound, lights, music and dancing girls, shines the glow of thousands of the latest, largest, flat-panel computer screens with the newest, greatest, still-to-be-finished games set out like appetizers to be test-driven by attendees. Many games have waiting lines several people deep, despite multiple stations.

The crowd is young, almost exclusively in their twenties and early thirties, and full of energy. They are not skeptics, but participants—possibly even addicts—eager for this year's new dose.

This is *fun*! This is the *entertainment* world. These, ladies and gentlemen, are today's train*ees*.

WHAT IS THE AVERAGE
AGE OF A COMPUTER
GAME PLAYER IN THE
YEAR 2000?

What were you THINKING?
Don't you know Jack?

You are huddled in your office.
People are coming from everywhere.
Do this! Do that!
Get it out now! I need that report now!

WHAT DO YOU DO FIRST?

The category is statistics.
Please formulate your answer as a question.

THE MEDIAN AGE OF
A CORPORATE WORKER
IN THE YEAR 2000

BEEP!!

You have exactly 30 seconds to
put these words in the correct order:

TO SPECTACULAR THE BIGGEST
WITH PLANET OF E-COMMERCE
OUT TO BEST MORE SERVICE
IS COMPANY CUSTOMER
ON MISSION BE PRICES

BEEEEEEEH!!!

THE TOTAL NUMBER OF ATARI, NINTENDO,
SEGA & SONY VIDEOGAME SYSTEMS SOLD
WORLDWIDE SINCE 1980 IS _____?

How MUCH Of this week's salary
are you willing to risk?
Risk it all and answer correctly
and you could win a Porsche.
Answer wrong and you lose the pay.

(I'm just kidding about the Porsche,
but a real company might not be.)

Ok, game player, you've caught me.
Answer this right and I'll be your client:

WHAT PERCENTAGE OF PEOPLE
COMPLETE COURSES ON-LINE?

Don't know?
GO BACK TO B-SCHOOL!

1) 31 2) Do important first, then do urgent; 3) 39 4) Our mission is to be the biggest ecommerce company on the planet with the best prices and spectacular customer service; 5)300 million 6) 50 percent or less.

Dallas, just one week later. The American Society of Trainers and Developers (ASTD)'s annual convention. The total exhibit floor is less than one-tenth the space of E3—less than only one of E3's big halls. Most booths are the minimum 4 feet by 8 feet, and no booth is larger than eight or ten of the smallest ones. There is no music. No fancy lights. No noise. No lines. *Certainly* no dancing girls. The energy level is low — maybe one-fiftieth of that of E3. There are maybe one-fiftieth of the people as well, mostly in their thirties, forties and fifties, meandering at glacial speeds along straight aisles from tiny booth to tiny booth. Not a single line anywhere, only slightly larger groups at the two or three booths selling training "props"—funny pointers, noisemakers, koosh balls, etc.—which are the closest thing to any "fun" at the show. One single PlayStation (version 1, not 2) displays a racing video game—totally unrelated to the product being offered—in an out-of-place and seemingly unsuccessful attempt to draw people in. Another exhibitor draws some attention with a small climbing wall and an expensive setup of futuristic chairs and 3D electronic headsets. But when you take the trouble to sign up and wait your turn, all you get is a three-dimensional headshot of a guy standing in front of a movie screen, reading (badly) from a script. Plenty of coffee (you need it). Chocolate chip cookies. Comfortable shoes.

This is *boring*! This is the *learning* world. These, ladies and gentlemen, are today's train*ers*.

Exaggerated? Sure. And I'm not questioning the *dedication* of the ASTD or its members. Exceptions? Of course. There are training conferences like "Online" with a lot more computer equipment. But the overall story is the same.

Today's trainers and trainees are from totally separate worlds. The biggest underlying dynamic in training and learning today is the rapid and unexpected confrontation of a corps of trainers and teachers raised in a predigital generation and educated in the styles of the past with a body of learners raised in the digital world of *Sesame Street,* MTV, fast movies, and "twitch-speed" video games.

The two groups—trainers and trainees—are so different in their approach, outlook, style, and needs that they can hardly communicate. And the result is disaster. The trainees, which represent *fully half* of America's corporate workers (remember, the median age of a corporate worker is 39)[2] and whose numbers continue to grow daily, find today's training (and education) so incredibly boring that *they don't want—and often refuse—to do it.*

At Bankers Trust Company, where I worked for several years, workers continually signed up for "required" training classes and then just didn't show up. "Do you want me to go to training, or do my job?" they replied when questioned. This response is not unusual. Ask someone to describe a corporate training class. Chances are very good you'll hear some foul language. "People *hate* training," writes Roger Schank, head of The Institute for the Learning Sciences at Northwestern University. [3] And it's not only training people hate but practically *all* institutional learning. "There is, on the whole, nothing on earth intended for innocent people so horrible as a school," wrote George Bernard Shaw as far back as 1909.[4] "School days, I believe," says H.L. Mencken, "are the unhappiest in the whole span of human existence." [5]

And online training is worse! Most designers of computer training readily admit that after some movement toward multimedia on CD-ROMs, they took an enormous step backward when training moved online. Despite the increasing availability of training courses on intranets and the Internet, and even though they are almost all free to users (employers pay for practically all training), completion rates are terrible, often less than 50 percent.[6] A writer in *Training & Development* magazine says that the thing that keeps him awake at night is how to get people to stick with Web-based training long enough to learn something.[7] Most of it is *more* than soporific. And although there is great talk of things like "learning communities" and online tutors, in fact, online training has taken away from trainees the only thing universally *liked* about training—*the ability to get out of the office.*

There is a terrible vicious cycle going on, to the detriment and dismay of learners—most of whom do want to learn—in which purchasers of corporate training are convinced that this boring style of "learning" is OK and continually acquire more of it. So that is what is made and offered by vendors, many of whom are growing like weeds and going public to amazing multiples. It is as if they have totally adopted, in twisted form, the former Apple evangelist Guy Kawasaki's new motto about just getting on with it, "Don't worry, be crappy!"[8] And this, despite the fact that they have for the most part merely replaced their so-called shelfware (unused CD-ROMs) with forget-it-ware (uncompleted online training)!

But don't worry, learners, it will not always be thus. For as the need for *learning that people actually want to do* becomes more and more crucial in the blur of the quickly changing business world, and as business finally confronts the fact that the generations who are the customers of E3 and love to play computer and videogames to the tune of $7.5 billion annually[9] are also the workers who need to be trained, the training and learning process—in companies, homes, and last but not least schools—stands at the beginning of a huge revolution.

We have heard this before. But in my view the training and learning revolution is *not*—despite what many preach—the shift in training delivery to the Internet, although that is important and transformational. And it's not "distance learning," although that, too, is an important part of the process. It's not just more, faster, smaller computers in corporate classrooms, on desks and in laps. It's not wireless, or broadband, or just-in-time, or learning management systems, and it's *certainly not* computer-based training (CBT).

The true twenty-first-century learning revolution is that learning—training *and* schooling—is finally throwing off the shackles of pain and suffering that have accompanied it for so long. Within most of our lifetimes pretty much all learning will become truly learner-centered and *fun*—fun for students, fun for trainers and teachers, fun for parents, supervisors administrators and executives. The huge wall that has separated learning and fun, work and play for the last few hundred years is finally beginning to tremble and will soon come tumbling down, to everyone's benefit. And although it will continue to resist for a while yet, like the

Berlin Wall in the political world, when the wall finally falls there will be a stampede to freedom.

The reason this will happen, and happen soon, is that *learners will demand it, to the point that management, teachers and administrators can no longer resist.* The workers of the Games Generations will no longer accept, attend, or do training that is boring. So we will have to inject fun and games into training, as businesses, schools, and the military are already beginning, in places, to do.

And the *really* good news is that when we do it we will find—to the amazement of many (although certainly not the trainees)—that adding fun into the process will not only make learning and training much more enjoyable and compelling but also *far more effective* as well.

This book is about the coming together of two seemingly diametrically opposed worlds: *serious learning* in schools and in businesses, and *interactive entertainment*—computer games, video games, and, to a lesser extent, the movies.

On the "serious" learning side today there is an enormous, multi-billion-dollar training budget focused on the most "serious" kinds of adult learning—how to run businesses and improve processes, how to manage people and organizations, how to wage war and maintain peace, how to manage and avoid dangers and risks, how not to violate the law. This is what is usually called "training," in both business and the military, and is a particular subset of adult learning. Training is *very* big business these days, usually estimated at over $100 billion in the United States (counting the government),[10] part of a worldwide learning market of over $2 trillion.[11] Its computer-based elements, mainly online and distance learning, are growing at almost 80 percent a year.[12]

On the other side is the world of entertainment—music, television, films, and, increasingly, computer and video games, now equal to or bigger than the movies. Much of this entertainment is aimed at what Sony calls the "digital dream kids," but it also includes all adult entertainment from sports, to bridge and chess, to gambling. Entertainment is also a huge enterprise, also estimated in the trillions of dollars.[13]

The forces bringing these two worlds inexorably together, in Ogilvy's words "like tributaries of a river" are first, *technological change and generational discontinuity,* causing learners today to be different than in the past, and second, *the need for training and education to catch up* to be efficient and effective.

Although, as we will see, there is no consensus on exactly how people or adults learn, almost all theories recognize that learners must be engaged in the process. And although it is sometimes possible for learning *for its own sake* to be an engaging motivator, much of what people need to learn, particularly in a business setting, is *not* intrinsically motivating to most of the population. But this doesn't mean learning it can't be fun—on the contrary. *Digital Game-Based Learning* is precisely about fun and engagement and the coming together of and serious learning and interactive entertainment into a newly emerging and highly exciting medium—digital learning games.

Digital Game-Based Learning is already sprouting, and in some case taking firm root, in a wide variety of businesses and other places: in several of the world's most prestigious consulting firms, in industry leaders; in smaller firms; in service and manufacturing industries, in orientation, product training, soft skills, hard skills, marketing and strategy; in many branches and levels of the public sector, and especially in the U.S. military.

But despite some early successes, Digital Game-Based Learning is still a radical idea. It is based on two key premises that are still not fully accepted in the training and adult learning community. The first is that the *learners have changed in some fundamentally important ways*—the bulk of the people who are learning and being trained today, people who in the year 2000 were roughly under the age of 39 (the median age of the U.S. corporate worker),[14] are, in a very real intellectual sense, *not the same* as those of the past. As a result, while there is a great deal of discussion about "how people learn," there has been relatively little focus on how *these people* learn, with the exception of snide and generally unhelpful observations that often they do not (or at least not in the manner that some think they should).

The second "radical" premise is that these "under-40" individuals are of a generation that when growing up *deeply experienced, for the first time in history, a radically new form of play—computer and video games—* and that this new form of entertainment has shaped their preferences and abilities and offers an enormous potential for their learning, both as children and as adults.

In *Digital Game-Based Learning* I will show how the immense changes in technology over the past thirty years, of which video games are a major part, have dramatically—and, importantly, *discontinuously*—changed the way those people raised in this time period think, learn, and process information. Although to a surprising extent unremarked upon, the change has been so enormous that today's younger people have, in their intellectual style and preferences, *very different minds* from their parents and, in fact, *all* preceding generations.

Those raised on traditional educational and training theory need to realize that because this *is* a discontinuity, much, if not most of the data we have collected and the theories we have formulated in the past about how people think and learn may no longer apply. In fact, as anyone can observe, our whole learning system, which worked well for hundreds of years, is breaking down. Perhaps the most important difference is that the "stuff" to be learned—information, concepts, relationships, and so on—cannot just be "told" to these people. It must be learned *by* them, through questions, discovery, construction, interaction, and, above all, fun.

It is becoming clear that one reason we are not more successful at educating our children and workforce, despite no lack of effort on our part, is *because we are working hard to educate a new generation in old ways*, using tools that have ceased to be effective.

No less an authority than the late Dr. Albert Shanker, head of both the New York City–based United Federation of Teachers (UFT) union and later the nationally based American Federation of Teachers (AFT) union, claimed, as far back as 1988, that "only 20 to 25 percent of students currently in school can learn effectively from traditional methods of teaching." [15]

And in 1999 John Chambers, CEO of Cisco Systems, stated: "Technology is moving too fast right now for companies' traditional hire-and-train methods to work." [16]

Anyone who is barely awake knows that today's children, teens, and young adults—Generations X, Y, and Z—don't relate well to traditional teaching methods. "Every time I go to school I have to power down!" complains one student. Corporate education and training are even worse.

Many blame the students. But as Colin Powell said to the 2000 Republican Convention, "Our children are not the problem, the problem is us!" We are all living through an immense technological revolution, yet mainstream education and training have done precious little to accommodate the new learning styles of those individuals raised with such different inputs and influences. For a generation that *taught itself* computers, their approach is still the same old "tell-test" methodology as always. And despite the growing number of Web-based offerings, the dirty little secret of most Web-based training is that completion rates are appalling!

It's all so boring!

"The reason most kids don't like school is not that the work is too hard," says Dr. Seymour Papert, professor at the Massachusetts Institute of Technology (MIT), "but that it is utterly boring!"[17] Ditto, triple, and quadruple for most corporate training!

Why is this so? Why is most learning—whether in schools or corporations, whether instructor-led or computer-based—so incredibly *un*engaging? And does it have to be the case? Although there are many points of view on this issue, it is my view that if we want to improve education, whether in schools, institutions, or in corporate classrooms, it is incumbent upon us (and eventually upon the people from those generations) *to invent radically new ways of learning* that mesh with the new world, style, and capabilities of Generations X, Y, Z and beyond.

Digital Game-Based Learning is an important one of these ways. It is certainly not the only one, but it represents one of the first *effective and doable* means to alter the learning process in a way that appeals to, and excites, people from the "Games Generations."

Many people, especially from the older generations, think of learning as "hard work." Digital Game-Based Learning doesn't dispute this. What is changing in the term "hard work" is not the "hard" part—no one seriously disputes that effort and energy is involved in learning. The change is in the word *work*. Learning, as great teachers have known throughout the ages, does not *feel* like work when you're having fun. The MIT Media Lab folks have a term for this, "hard fun," taken from the comment of a third grader, searching for a way to describe the learning he had just done.[18] Digital Game-Based Learning can certainly be hard fun. But at its very best, *even the hard part goes away*, and it becomes *all* fun, a really good time from which, at the end, you have gotten better at something, through a process that Doug Crockford of LucasArts has referred to as "stealth learning."[19]

THE OPPORTUNITIES IN THE DIGITAL GAME-BASED LEARNING REVOLUTION

Digital Game-Based Learning is an alternative that is being used—with amazing and increasing success—in pockets and "skunk works" (small, often unofficial, innovative teams) around our corporations, schools, and institutions such as the military. From business simulators to preschool "edutainment" titles, a new learning paradigm—learning via play—is gradually emerging:

- Preschoolers learn the alphabet and reading through computer games.[20]
- Elementary students learn the kindergarten through sixth grade (K−6) curriculum on PlayStations; scores rise 30 to 40 percent.[21]
- Computer chess becomes a big part of kindergarten through twelfth grade (K−12) curriculums.[22]
- Typing games are among the top-selling software products.[23]
- High school students play a multiplayer online game to learn electoral politics.[24]
- Financial traders use computer games to hone their skills.[25]
- Policymakers play a Sim City–style game to understand the health care system.[26]
- Business executives play at running simulated human resources departments and oil refineries.[27]
- Engineers use a consumer-style video game to learn new computer-aided design (CAD) technology.[28]
- Military trainees fight realistic battles in video game–like simulators.[29]

Game-Based Learning, whose nontechnology roots go deep in the past, has become with the rise of computers the learning wave of the future. It will soon cut across the entire population, from "cradle to grave." My goal is to show you the following:

- What Digital Game-Based Learning is

- Why it is different and better
- Where it can be effective
- How you can create and use it

Not only is *Digital Game-Based Learning* a wide survey of what's happening in this exciting field and a manifesto of what can be accomplished, it's also a hands-on manual, because anyone—trainers, executives, educators, parents, *and especially you, the reader of this book*—can begin using Digital Game-Based Learning on some level much more quickly than you might think.

PRIMARY LEARNING—NOT JUST FOR REVIEW

A key point about Digital Game-Based Learning is that it is *not* just about using games for review and reinforcement. Although that is an important and useful component, it has been going on for a long time, and is not what has really changed. What is new and different and gets people really excited, as Sarah Fister points out in an article in *Training* magazine,[30] is that *computer games can now be used for primary (i.e,. the only) learning of really hard subjects*, including people management, difficult-to-learn software, complex financial products, and intricate social interactions.

Digital Game-Based Learning can play an important role in learning material that is *not intrinsically motivating* to anyone but which needs to be learned. We have all encountered material like this, from the multiplication tables, to typing, to vocabulary and language learning, to spelling, to rules and regulations—stuff that is, in a word, *boring*. (And by the way, just to keep you out of trouble, the "B" word is typically not uttered in "corporatespeak." The politically correct term for this type of material, as I was summarily informed one day, is "dry and technical.")

Despite what corporatespeak might dictate the material be called, companies in the business world are increasingly turning to Digital Game-Based Learning for:

- Material that is dry, technical and, yes, boring
- Subject matter that is really difficult
- Audiences that are hard to reach
- Difficult assessment and certification issues

- Complex process understanding
- Sophisticated "what-if" analyses
- Strategy development and communication

Let's look at two examples.

CASE STUDY 1
The Monkey Wrench Conspiracy:
How to Get 3 Million Engineers to Learn (and Like It)

In the spring of 1998, I sat waiting one morning at 7 a.m. in Fraunces Tavern, where George Washington gave his farewell address to his officers and reputedly the oldest restaurant in New York City. It is conveniently located right next door to Goldman Sachs, the investment bankers and financiers. Aside from the waiters setting up, I was the only person there at that hour, waiting for what I expected to be a routine breakfast meeting with a CEO interested in doing business with my company, games2train. At 7:15 in strode the man I was to meet. At a lanky six foot six, wearing a baggy, beige, unstructured suit and colorful tie, with shoulder length hair tied back in a pony tail and a big infectious smile on his face, Joe Costello was definitely not what I was expecting.

Costello, the CEO of a new company called think3, was bursting with energy—literally a man on a mission. A highly respected veteran executive in Silicon Valley, he had built Cadence Design Systems from sales of $50 million to over $1 billion. He had been tapped by Michael Milken to be CEO of Milken's new learning company, Knowledge Universe, and had started and quit within a week. Now he had just signed on to lead a small company with a terrific new 3D mechanical drafting CAD software product in its quest to capture the mechanical design market. "This market hasn't moved in a long time and is ripe for change," Costello told me, "and I like change." He was squeezing in his meeting with me before a (successful) request to Goldman for $25 million.

Think3's product, *thinkdesign*, was demonstrably better than the product that the vast majority of mechanical designers were using, known as AutoCAD. More like the rarified "high-end" CAD packages costing $15,000 to 20,000 per seat, thinkdesign allowed mechanical designers to work directly in 3D, instead of starting from the two-dimensional (2D) drawings of AutoCAD. Backed by impatient venture capital money from Goldman and others, Costello's business objective was crystal clear—to convert as many of the 3 million-or-so AutoCAD users to thinkdesign as quickly as possible. His first major obstacle, the traditionally large difference in price between 2D and 3D products, was removed by his board's agreement to lower the price of thinkdesign to match the price of AutoCAD. But another, even more formidable obstacle remained, Costello knew—ease of learning.

Despite all the great advantages of 3D drafting over 2D, most mechanical design engineers were loath to make a change. CAD programs are extremely complex and traditionally have a steep learning curve. The mechanical designers—almost all male engineers between the ages of 20 and 30—were extremely comfortable with AutoCAD, which they had been using for years, typically since engineering school. AutoCAD did the job for them—why change? Learning a new CAD system—especially a powerful one—would take a lot their time and effort. They would have to learn to draft, and even think, in a whole new way (hence the company name "think 3"). Focus groups showed that most of these engineers were reluctant—and even dreaded—going "back to school" to learn a new product, no matter what its supposed advantages.

"Why was this?" Costello wondered. "It just didn't seem possible that it could be or had to be that complicated." After all, these were professional people, many with advanced degrees, who had spent lots of time in school. Learning was nothing new to them. As an engineer himself, and a former training manager for Cadence Design Systems (the company of which he later became CEO), Costello finally concluded that the engineers dreaded the training *precisely because it was dreadful.* Whether delivered by traditional instructor-led training (ILT) in a classroom, or by newer computer-based training (CBT) on the screen, learning a new CAD product consisted of someone starting from the absolute beginning, taking you through all the lessons, no matter what you already knew or how fast you could go. "In this first lesson you will learn about the workplane" the traditional training began. It would take hours and hours—or, more likely, days—before you ever got to do anything interesting or work at the skill level you were used to. There was absolutely no fun in it. It was just too boring to bother.

Costello was not willing to accept this as *his* company's training. He was convinced there had to be a better way, and he set out to find it in the training marketplace. He soon became very frustrated. "We talked to lots of companies," he said. "We looked at the existing different kinds of training approaches and there was *nothing* out of the ordinary. It was essentially you had the old manual and instructor-led training kinds of approaches—get everybody in a classroom and bore them to death and hope that they stick around for lunch—and there were a few people who put the same boring stuff on CD-ROMs. A couple of those did what I call the 'dancing banana' effect, which is put a few animations around the same old boring dry material that has little to do with teaching anybody to learn anything. And so none of this looked particularly exciting." That wasn't going to cut it for Costello.

As serendipity would have it, I had just created a *"Doom"*-style game for Bankers Trust's derivatives traders and salespeople called *Straight Shooter!* that had attracted some interest from the training press.[31] Costello read about the game and called, saying, "Let's meet!"

So Costello and I began talking about training visions. After about half an hour of exchanging ideas we knew we were in synch. "I knew that this was the ticket," says Costello. "That this is the way to actually get the immersion, the excitement, the energy and get people sucked in long enough that they actually start absorbing some of the real material." We both realized happily we were on exactly the same wavelength. "Training should be as much fun as *Doom*," I had said to an interviewer five years earlier.[32] Costello and I decided we would make it so for think3.

We could already hear, in our minds, the "charge" to the learner:

Your mission is simple, Moldy: infiltrate Copernicus. If you attempt to disable the anti-matter engine before it has been repaired, the antimatter will become unstable and ". . . boom!" Unfortunately you cannot bring any weapons with you. Your only tool is this small, lightweight computer. However this computer has been loaded with the most powerful CAD program in the universe. It will allow you to construct whatever equipment you need.[33]

Costello and I saw our own mission clearly. We would create a way to:

- Engage jaded engineers
- Let them have a whole lot of fun while they learned
- Get the engineers to learn to use the 3D CAD software without feeling they were "in school" or even learning
- Challenge serious game players while also drawing in novices and nongamers
- Pull them all the way through to the end
- Be sure when they completed the game they were competent at using the software

How would we do this? We would build a fantastic game—one the target market couldn't resist starting or put down once they began. The learning would happen almost without the learners' realizing it, in pursuit of beating the game. We would give them "stealth learning."

The design process began within a week, with a small team from both companies. In our initial brainstorming, we arrived at five key principles. First, we would try to be as contemporary as possible. Second, we would keep the pace of the game and the learning fast. Third, it was easier to teach a user to fix something than to create something from scratch. Fourth, the learning tasks would follow a consistent format so that they could be easily replaced or the order changed. Fifth, the learning tasks would be progressive but not didactic.

Principle 1 led us to the theme of the game and the character of the main antagonist. (A future, outer space theme, with the player being a top secret agent on a mission to save the Copernicus Space Station.) This allowed for lots of futuristic looking parts to be designed and repaired. We hired Dub Media, an innovative consumer games graphics' house, to create a look that equaled that of the commercial games then on the market.

The "need for speed" of the audience dictated a fast-moving game. Therefore, we chose to create a "first-person shooter" à la *Doom* and *Quake*, because our audience was going to be almost all male and very familiar with this style of game. The player would run through the space station, encountering a series of tasks that had to be accomplished quickly in order to save the station, and requiring the use of the CAD software to accomplish them. We decided to make it a three-level game, with lots of rooms, puzzles, space-walks, and evil robots to eliminate, and to give the player only one hour of "game time" to get to the end. Miss this deadline, and the space station blows up spectacularly.

Our main antagonist had to be someone who broke things, so the player could re-create them using the software. Gilad Atlas, a relatively junior team member, suggested "throwing a monkey wrench into the works," and the main character quickly became "Dr. Monkey Wrench." Though an alien, he would sport the taped-together eyeglasses and pocket protector that all engineers could relate to. Our learning game became "The Monkey Wrench Conspiracy."

Fulfilling the final two principles—that the learning tasks would follow a consistent format so that they could be easily replaced or the order changed, and that the learning tasks would be progressive, but not didactic—proved far harder and more time consuming than inventing, and even making, the game. Our clients and partners at think3 were to a large extent teachers—the founder was a professor—from a very traditional background. Their idea of teaching was to start from the beginning: introduction to the interface, introduction to the workplane, simple lines and arcs, extrusions, fillets, and work their way through the "textbook," feature by feature. We challenged them to come up instead with 30 "tasks" which, if accomplished in order, would lead the player from being able to use the easy features to being able to use the hard features of the program. They also insisted upon showing the player the "concepts" before they started on a task, so a short "concept movie" in the "avi" format was created by think3 to introduce each task.

"Fire and Ice"

In only a matter of weeks, the models for the tasks were decided upon, the initial tasks created and the concept movies prepared. We integrated the pieces into our first prototype and proudly presented it to Costello. He looked at it and thought for a while. "Fire and ice," he said gravely, shaking his head. "Huh?" said the rest of us. "The mix of learning and entertainment isn't working," he explained. "The game is fire—it's fun, fast and engaging. Then you hit the first learning task. Suddenly you're back in school. It's boring."

Costello was right. We needed to make the "learning" parts as exciting as the rest of the game. How could we do this? The answer, it turned out, was *urgency*. You had to be made to *want* to complete the task as quickly and efficiently as possible in order to get on with the mission. How do you create urgency? It turns out there are professionals at this— they're called Hollywood scriptwriters. So we hired one. Immediately out went the "You will now learn the following three things," and in came "Come *on* Moldy, you've got to do this or we're *doomed.*" The words *objective, learn,* and *know how to* were banned, replaced with imperative action verbs like *build, get through, repair,* and *rescue.* The concept videos introducing tasks were cut from 3 minutes to a maximum of 30 seconds, and began with "OK, Moldey, here's what you need to know to do this." Wordy instructions were cut dramatically and spiced up with integrated video clips that showed how each thing was done. Later testing revealed that most users hardly ever read the text at all.

We knew we were on to something even before the field testing. People in the company were bringing the alpha versions home ostensibly to show to their girlfriends and spouses but really to ask their friends for hints on how to beat the game.

The Monkey Wrench Conspiracy was released in the fall of 1998, to critical acclaim from the engineering community. It was distributed as a separate training disk—the only training—with the thinkdesign product, under the educational heading "think fast."

Costello's strategy with *Monkey Wrench* was both a learning strategy and a marketing strategy. He was convinced that the game could, in fact, sell the product, especially to engineering students who were still forming their tool preferences. We created a demo version—two levels instead of three—that could fit on a single disk along with a trial version of the actual thinkdesign product. The demo disk was bundled into sixty thousand copies of *Cadence* magazine, the mechanical design industry standard. The next print run was two hundred thousand. Then another two hundred thousand, followed by translation into Japanese and other languages. A year later, there were close to a million copies of the game in print.

Built into the disk was a request for feedback, via the Internet, from anyone who completed the game. Think3 set up a special part of its Web site—The Monkey Wrench Zone—and posted all the returns along with comments, along with responses to all queries from Dr. Monkey Wrench

Some raved:

"I can't wait to play level three. The first two were so cool. Thank you once again," wrote Tim Davenport.

"Okay I am once again stuck. Yeah I can't play other games either sue me >;-) I have level 3 and I have 29 of the 31 parts. However the door is locked to get to the only part left that I can see.... How do I get through the locked door?? And will the 31st part show up after I get the 30th part?" wrote Mary Northrup. To which "Dr. Monkey Wrench" replied "The very last task is not available until after you defeat me, Dr. Monkey Wrench! In order to get by the locked door, you need to go to the bridge and look for 3 buttons on a wall. Choose wisely because 2 of those buttons are boobytraps. Muhahahha!."

How much like traditional technology training does *that* feel?

One of the most interesting postings was a letter from a father, who related the experiences of his 8-year-old son Aaron:

> A few weeks ago I received a CD containing Monkey Wrench and thinkdesign. I asked my 8 year-old son Aaron if he would like to try it out. Of course, he loves video games so he jumped at the chance....Well, we were not disappointed. Not only was the Monkey Wrench game a lot of fun, but the tutorial was excellent and Aaron was happy as a clam playing the game and learning how to design in 3D.... He became so excited, about learning to design whatever he could imagine, that he told me "this has changed my life." 8-year-olds have a penchant for over-statement, but it was obvious that he was hooked. [34]

One reason this is interesting, says Costello, is that "people said that 'this is too hard for my people to do.' If a third grader can figure it out, than probably anybody can figure out how to learn 3D. We've had that experience. We've had dyed-in-the-wool 2D draftspeople who've tried 3D products before without success, pick up *Monkey Wrench*, and within 30 days they're up and going. They're making progress in learning, having fun, feeling good about themselves, and learning a new way to do things." "Customer response has been universally positive to *The*

Monkey Wrench Conspiracy," says Art Ignacio, director of Educational Operations at think 3. "Whether it's in Japan, Italy, North America or Singapore, customers really like the idea of turning games into learning tools."

So what makes the game so successful? It is, as we shall see, the combination of the two powerful factors that make *all* good Digital Game-Based Learning a success. Those factors are the *motivation of the game,* which pulls you into the learning without your really realizing it, combined with a *learning methodology* that is fast, effective, and definitely *un*-school-like. "Let's face it, this is a far more inspirational and effective alternative to inches-thick manuals and tedious, text-heavy computer-based training manuals," says Costello.

For those interested in design, *The Monkey Wrench Conspiracy* is an example of what I call loosely-linked Digital Game-Based Learning (see Chapter 6). A templatized, task-based learning methodology makes it easy both for learners to learn the material and makers to change the learning tasks as the underlying product evolves. The "twitch-speed" video game part gets the player's adrenaline flowing, provides context and motivation for the tasks, and is a reward after each task has been done. What makes this format interesting is that both the tasks and the game can be updated separately. People inside and outside think 3 are continually creating new learning tasks using the game format, which can be easily integrated into the game. And as technology evolves and the initial game becomes less "state-of-the-art," the same tasks can easily be integrated into a new and better game. This Digital Game-Based Learning approach is ideal for open-ended, task-based content. But, as we will see in the course of this book, Digital Game-Based Learning can take a wide variety of approaches for different goals, content, audiences, and budgets. So let us examine another approach. (For more on *The Monkey Wrench Conspiracy,* see Chapter 9).

CASE STUDY 2

In$ider: How to Be Sure the People Who Audit the Books Get It Right (and Like It!)

Remember the old saw: "What's an accountant?—an actuary with a sense of humor!" Certified Public Accountants (CPAs) and auditors in particular, are not known historically for having fun. But to paraphrase Bob Dylan, *in these times, the* people *are a-changin'* (as I will show in detail as the book progresses). Today's average corporate auditor is 24 years old[35] and was possibly using a joystick before ever picking up a pencil. In fact, "sharpening your pencil" is a reference—much like "dialing" a telephone—that many of today's auditors might not even get.

The world of today's young accountants, like the rest of its generation, moves at "twitch speed." Changes in the ways corporations finance themselves and manage financial risks require auditors to have to learn whole new complex areas, often practically overnight. A great example is financial derivatives. Invented by, and long the exclusive province of the "rocket scientist" traders and marketers at the world's top financial institutions, in the 1980s and 1990s they began finding their way into more and more corporate financial structures, posing a series of difficult learning challenges.

First, people at the sellers needed to know more about these arcane and complex products, beginning with the marketers. Everybody inside companies like Bankers Trust—a derivative hotshot in the 1980s and early 1990s—was eager to learn more about them. But the knowledge was scarce, and the ability to teach it even scarcer. Pulling the "rocket scientists" off the trading floor to teach was unthinkable—they were minting too much money for the firm. So at one point in the 1990s Bankers Trust Company paid a consultant $10,000 *per day* to give one-week derivatives courses, offered several times a year to long waiting lists. Nice work if you can get it! It did the trick—this was an audience who *wanted* to learn the stuff—but at an enormous cost.

Next came the buyers of derivatives—typically corporate treasurers and Chief Finacial Officers. Derivatives are risky products, which can either lead to enormous profits if you bet big and guess right (e.g., on the direction of interest rates) or to enormous losses if you guess wrong. Used properly they can reduce risk; used improperly they are wild speculation. Relatively few corporate buyers had a sophisticated understanding of the way these products worked and their risks. So sellers, like Bankers Trust, tried hard to train their clients—traders at Bankers created gamelike simulations to illustrate exactly how derivatives could hedge corporate risks (see Chapter 9). Played by small groups of potential clients at corporate off-sites at fancy hotels, they helped, but they only reached a small audience, and derivatives were difficult products. The lack of buyer knowledge about derivatives eventually caused enormous losses, scandals, and pain for both sides. At Bankers Trust, stock selloffs as a result of lawsuits brought by customers literally halved the market value of the bank, and was a factor that led to the bank's eventual sale and demise. At the buyers, many financial officers lost their jobs. Finally—after eight years of study by the various regulatory agencies—in January 2000 the U.S. government finally stepped in, making it mandatory that derivatives be disclosed in all U.S. corporations' official financial statements in order to give a truer picture of risk.[36] Other countries have passed similar regulations. Derivatives must now be "on the books." Uh-oh! Here comes the third—and by far the biggest—derivatives learning challenge. All corporate *auditors* have to understand how derivatives work, and fast. It's scramble time at the accounting firms!

Fortunately, back in 1997, Paula Young, European leader for learning technologies at the global accounting firm PricewaterhouseCoopers (actually then just Price Waterhouse), saw this situation coming. She knew it would be a big problem for the company, because derivatives would be a really "hard teach" for many reasons. The number of people to be trained was large and decentralized, over fifteen thousand auditors scattered all around the globe. The subject matter was extremely complex, dry, and technical, and expertise within the firm was extremely scarce. Plus the time to prepare was relatively short—the regulations would be around in only a year or two.

Even more importantly, Young realized that the auditors who were going to have to know and apply the information on derivatives were not the company's 50-year-old partners but the 20-something men and women on the firm's auditing front line. Those employees were all from the "twitch" generation, highly competitive, and fast moving. Even if expensive rocket scientists *could* be found to teach classes on derivatives, those people were unlikely to sit still long enough to get much out of them. Not to mention that the *cost* of doing it that way—15,000 people / 20 per room x 5 days x $5,000 per day (let's be thrifty) plus the expense of flying people around—could potentially reach $20 million! The answer was clearly a technology-based solution, but Young had also seen her share of boring online training and had no intention of doing any of what she calls the "click and fall asleep" variety.

Mulling on this problem, Young—a near-Londoner schooled in Wales whose academic and professional background includes communications, psychology, television, film, and videodisc-based training—had an idea. In fact it was more than an idea, it was a vision. "The light bulb went off," she says. Young's vision was of computer games and movies, and of an engaged group of PricewaterhouseCoopers (PwC) auditors learning for hours, pulled forward by the factors that make those two entertainment media so compelling—challenges, storytelling, characters, music, "something at stake," and "inciting incidents" that you want to help resolve. In that moment of vision *In$ider*, PwC's pioneering Digital Game-Based Learning project, was born.

Young, now the excited evangelist, eagerly took her vision of the year 2030 3D world of Gyronortex, "an intergalactic mining company in the central zone," to the partners—to little effect. "I just had this idea in my head," she says. "Nobody I talked to had a clue of what I was going on about at all." Yet here's the story's ending: two years later, just as the new derivatives regulations were coming into effect, hundreds of PwC auditors a day were flying through Young's 3D world to Gyronortex, and loving the experience. The Digital Game-Based Learning application *In$ider* was a worldwide success, with 20,000 copies in print, orders coming in daily from offices from Bejing to Bermuda, and other companies—including sellers of derivatives products—purchasing it. This to be trained on some of the driest, most boring subject matter imaginable.

How did it happen? How did Paula convince the 50-ish partners in PwC to invest close to $3 million for "entertainment?" How did she combine the entertainment with the learning? And how did she get it done? Stay tuned (see Chapter 9).

THE PROMISE OF DIGITAL GAME-BASED LEARNING

Here, then, is the promise of Digital Game-Based Learning:

- Motivation can finally be found for learning the subjects and content that are the most difficult to teach or train—either because they are extremely dull and dry, or extremely complicated, or both, and to get people to train themselves.
- Small groups of trainers, teachers, content experts, and game designers working together can create experiences that will radically improve the learning, and ultimately the competence and behavior of thousands, and potentially *millions* of learners. Digital Game-based Learning audiences will include not only whole companies but whole industries, whole grade levels, even whole countries and populations. It will ultimately affect the market value of companies and perhaps even nations.
- The free market will create a phenomenon of highly effective learning "hits" that move through target populations at the epidemic speeds of best-selling novels, movies, or games, leaving a lasting educational impact. It will do so through a user-evaluated process of marrying the engagement-driven, experience-centered, "fun" approach of the interactive entertainment and games world with effective techniques for teaching the material, facts, concepts, skills, reasoning and behaviors that students and workers are required to learn.
- Eventually any individual trainer, teacher, or educator will have at his or her disposal the tools and colleagues to work with to *create* such phenomena. Talent at doing this will rise to the surface with successful, effective instruction no longer being confined to the audience a single fantastic teacher or trainer can reach in person but to all the learners in his or her entire potential target market, worldwide. Such target markets could be all salespeople, all managers, all third graders, all elementary school students, all math students, all college-level chemistry students, and so on.
- Consequently, there will be training and learning brands based not just on publishers but also on authors and designers, subjects and styles, as there are in books, movies, and games.
- This user-driven learning phenomenon will not only move from com-

pany to company and school to school nationally but will be world-wide, like movies and video games.

- The Web, the Internet, intranets, and successors, will not just be the conduit for boring education and training courses that people are forced to take or force themselves to suffer through. Instead, it will be a competitive forum—much like the games and movie businesses—where talent, creativity, and the ability to hold the audience and deliver a compelling experience is what wins. Learners will determine the best combinations of learning methodology, game play, and "eye candy."

- We will have a learning world, like the games and movies worlds of today, where there are both "classic" learning hits and exciting new-comers; where a plethora of magazines and reviewers cover what's in development and help learners choose the very best; where makers create their experiences with the goal of holding their audience and being successful in learning, and thereby making money and attract-ing capital; and where learners look forward to the next release as eagerly as they wait for an upcoming game, console, or movie.

All this is not only possible, but it is definitely coming. Some of it is already here.

THE KEY MESSAGES

To readers of this book, here are the messages about which you should be thinking as you leave this chapter:

- If you are a *business executive, school administrator*, or anyone involved in spending money to bring people—adults or children—to a higher level of learning, there *is* a newer, better way available. Although it is neither a panacea nor the only way, it behooves you to consider it seri-ously and invest a significant portion of your resources in this direc-tion.

- If you are a *trainer or teacher*, your students will *not* have short atten-tion spans for learning if the approaches you take really engage them. It is possible to get learners of *all* ages *totally* involved in learning *any* subject matter, and tools are increasingly available to help you do this.

Using them may, however, mean rethinking much of what you believe about teaching and training.

- If you are a *student or trainee*, don't despair; relief is on the way. The days of sitting bored to tears in classrooms or in front of a boring computer or Web-based training screen are numbered. If you want to make things better, faster, seek out and lobby for the approaches described in this book. You and your fellow learners will be glad you did!

But do we really need something so new and radical? Who are the learners of today, anyway?

2

The Games Generations
How Learners Have Changed

I've never lived in a house without a computer.
— Michelle Reed, 25-year-old editor of this book

Electronic toys were my first playmates.
— David Bennehum, 33, in Extra Life

I'm from the PacMan generation.
— a corporate worker

HOW LEARNERS HAVE CHANGED

I'm not so sure that we really have an appreciation of what this has done to our children.
— Dr. Ray Perez, Cognitive Psychologist, Department of Defense

At the turn of the millennium, the median age of the U.S. workforce was 39.[1] This means that half of all corporate employees were born after 1961. The oldest of this group were 7 years old when men landed on the moon; most were not even born. Most have never used a rotary dial telephone, never known a time when music wasn't totally portable or digital, never lived without hundreds of thousands of video images a day, never known a world without some kind of computer. (I will discuss older workers in Chapter 14.)

Sesame Street, the great television experiment that changed the way children around the world grow up, celebrated its thirtieth birthday in the year 2000, having begun broadcasting in 1970. Close to fifty percent of corporate employees (yes, we're talking about our colleagues, not our children) grew up with *Sesame Street* as a daily part of their intellectual diet. That program, as Malcolm Gladwell reminds us,[2] "was based about a single breakthrough insight: That if you can hold the attention of children, you can educate them." *Sesame Street* held their attention as it taught them, day after day, year after year. How? It *entertained* them. It was *fun*. This connection between fun and learning has been part of half of our workers' consciousness since their earliest days.

Pong, the very first commercial video game, appeared soon after *Sesame Street*, in 1974, just as the first of these 50 percent of workers turned 13. One of them, David Bennehum—then 6—deeply remembers his first encounter with this new phenomenon, which he describes in his book *Extra Life*:

> Holding the knob, I watched as my electronic paddle followed the movement of my hand. *Bonk*. I hit the luminescent ball. *Bonk*. It came back. *Bonk*. Faster now. *Bonk*. Too fast! It shot by. Several rounds later the game was over. I could lose privately. No one to laugh or yell at me for missing. I found another coin and played another game ... this was bliss.[3]

He was not alone. Millions of other kids were blissing out too.

Space Invaders, the first true game "hit," followed soon thereafter (in 1978). So the *oldest* employees from this 50 percent cohort—those that are now between 30 and 39—have been able to play, and for the most part *have been* playing, video games since their junior high school days. But the newest employee hires, just out of high school or college, have never known a world *without* video games. As older employees retire and are replaced by younger workers, the next wave of employees will never have known a world without the advanced gaming technologies of Sony PlayStations and multiplayer games on the Internet.

Star Wars, the first of the great, fast, special-effects films, premiered about the same time as *Space Invaders*, in 1977. The film series paralleled the initial growth of the gaming industry, with the next two episodes following at three-year intervals. The two are closely related, and this is not a coincidence, the special effects generated for the movies being the same ones used in the games. "Let's face it," writes J. C. Herz in her book *Joystick Nation*, "[the $100 million special-effects extravaganzas] are big screen video games anyway."[4] Soon after the George Lucas *Star Wars* films came the Lucas video games. LucasArts, the game producing part of Lucas' empire, produces constant revenue and cash flow in between the big hits of the movies.

Sony's Walkman made its debut in 1978. As of 2000, over 300 million of them (counting clones) have been sold.[5]

MTV began broadcasting in 1981, introducing a new style of fast-cut video that matched the speed of the games and movies. Recent high school graduates and B.A. hires in the United States *have never known a world without it*. Music videos with over one hundred images a minute have been part of their entire life.

The IBM PC was also introduced in 1981, bringing with it a whole new level of gaming. "When the PC came out and you could really start doing some thinking gaming, that's what hooked me," says Pete Goettner, 36, and now CEO of Digital Think. I wasn't doing that when I was 12 but I was doing it when I was 18 and as more product became available I got hooked on it."[6] One of the oldest of this cohort, he's been playing computer games for half his life.

Need I go on?

With these and many other radical changes and innovations in technology almost too numerous to mention (add the pocket calculator, the Atari, the Apple II, the VCR, the Handicam, the compact disc and Diskman, the wireless telephone, the Internet, the MP3 player, etc), young people's growing-up experiences and recreational interests in the last third of the twentieth century shifted radically. Today's schoolchildren, elementary through college, travel with their own personal Game Boys, Handicams, cell phones, portable CD and MP3 players, pagers, laptops and Internet connections, most of which are within their own personal budgets.

Each day the average teenager in America watches over 3 hours of television,[7] is on the Internet 10 minutes to an hour,[8] and plays $1^1/_2$ hours of video games.[9] By the time these people enter our companies as workers, we can conservatively estimate that they would have watched over twenty thousand hours of television,[10] played over ten thousand hours of videogames,[11] seen hundreds of movies in theaters and on video-tape, and been exposed to over four hundred thousand television commercials,[12] adding up to tens of millions of images. They've almost certainly read fewer books than their parents, but even if they were the most voracious of readers, they would not have spent more than three to four thousand hours at it. [13]

Since their earliest years, the workers now coming in to our companies have solved daily mysteries (*Blues Clues, Sherlock Holmes*); built and run cities (*Sim City*), theme parks, (*Roller Coaster Tycoon*), and businesses (*Zillionaire, CEO, Risky Business, Start-up*); built civilizations from the ground up (*Civilization, Age of Empires*); piloted countless airplanes, helicopters, and tanks (*Microsoft's Flight Simulator, Apache, Abrams M-1*); fought close hand-to-hand combat (*Doom, Quake, Unreal Tournament*); and conducted strategic warfare (*Warcraft, Command and Conquer*)—not once or twice, but over and over and over again, for countless hours, weeks and months, until they were really good at it.

And, of course, there's the Internet. The Internet and email have been an integral part of the lives of many if not most of our newest hires for at least six years, the entire life of the World Wide Web. Instant messaging has already been with them for a year or two, and for each succeeding class of incoming hires, this time will have been longer.

None of this stuff is "technology" for them. As Alan Kay reminds us, "technology is only technology if it was invented after you were born."[14] This is their world, just as much as cars or the telephone was the world of their parents. As Don Tapscott points out in *Growing Up Digital*,[15] "Today's kids are so bathed in bits that they think it's all part of the natural landscape."

So, *half* our current workers, and *all* our future workers (excluding the temporary effect of retirees re-entering our hot labor market) were raised with a very different set—a *digital* set—of key formative experiences. Their environment surrounded and literally "bathed" them in digital media. The members of this generation were assaulted continuously, during almost every waking hour, by multiple new forms of technological stimulation, from MTV to fast action films to the Internet, which was totally absent from previous generations. Anyone born in the United

States after 1961 almost certainly grew up with digital games in their life, either at home or at a mall or movie theater.

And these experiences have produced *major*, although largely undocumented and understudied, effects on these people. As a result of growing up surrounded by this incredible array of new technologies, the under-40 generation's minds have *literally* been altered. "Rewired" is the popular term often used by many whose frame of reference is technology.

"Kids for the most part are raised on media where everything is so vivid, graphical, fast, and intense," says cognitive psychologist Ray Perez. "I'm not so sure that we really have an appreciation of what this has done to our children."[16] J. C. Herz's wonderfully written history of video games, *Joystick Nation,* has as its subtitle *How Videogames Ate Our Quarters, Won Our Hearts, and Rewired Our Minds.*[17] As we shall see, this phraseology is not very far-fetched.

The "mind alterations" or "cognitive changes" caused by the new digital technologies and media have led to a variety of new needs and preferences on the part of the younger generation, particularly—although by no means exclusively—in the area of learning. Don Tapscott's research shows that these people are "learning, playing, communicating, working and creating communities very differently than their parents."[18] The result is a huge discontinuity, never before experienced in the history of the world.

Marshall McLuhan, who died in 1980 and never lived to see the Internet, nevertheless understood this discontinuity very well. In *War and Peace in the Global Village* he writes of the "pain and misery that result from a new technology."[19] This pain, he explains, is experienced by only two groups—those totally from the old technology, and those stuck in the middle—not by those who grow up with it. The "older technology" people (he designates people who grew up in a world dominated by print as this group) operate very much like blind people who for some reason regain their sight. "How they shrink, at first from the welter of additional stimulation, longing at times to return to the relative seclusion of their former world."[20] How often have people from today's older generation expressed this feeling of being overwhelmed?

The second group experiencing difficulty are those stuck in the middle—today's "Generation X." Having grown up with each foot in a different technological world, they are often extremely disoriented and depressed, as Copeland portrayed in his book. The *last* group though, those that grew up with the technology—the later genXers, genYers and beyond—are totally comfortable with it, not knowing any other way, and are excited by its possibilities.

The explanation for why those from the older, print-oriented generation don't "get it" is obvious to McLuhan: "The information environment and the effects created by the computer are as inaccessible to literate vision as the external world is to the blind."[21] The psychic and social impact of new technologies and their resulting environment reverses the characteristic psychic and social consequences of the old technology and its environment. In fact, he says, "Every new technology necessitates a new war."[22]

Don't believe me? Check out your kids.

BUT DO THEY REALLY THINK DIFFERENTLY?

Different kinds of experiences lead to different brain structures.
—Dr. Bruce D. Berry, Baylor College of Medicine

Baby Boomers, who include the vast majority of today's trainers and teachers, grew up with the clear understanding that the human brain doesn't physically change based on stimulation it receives from the outside, especially after the age of 3. "Ever since the 1950s one of the great themes in neuroscience had been that neurons in the cortex matured during a critical period in the first few years of life, and that the brain's organization did not change much after that," says neurobiologist Michael Merzenich of the University of California—San Francisco.[23] But it now turns out that that view is, in fact, *incorrect*.

Based on the latest scientific research and evidence in neurology, there is no longer any question that stimulation of various kinds actually changes brain structures and affects the way people think, and that these transformations go on throughout life. The brain is, to an extent not at all understood or believed to be when Baby Boomers were growing up, *massively plastic*. It can be, and is, constantly reorganized. (Although the popular term *rewired* is somewhat misleading, the overall idea is right— the brain changes and organizes itself differently based on the inputs it receives.) The old idea that we have a fixed number of brain cells that die off one by one has been replaced by research showing that our supply of brain cells is replenished constantly.[24] The brain *constantly* reorganizes itself *all our child and adult lives,* a phenomenon technically known as *neuroplasticity.* According to Paula Tallal, co-director of the Center for Molecular and Behavioral Neuroscience at Rutgers University, "you create your brain from the input you get."[25]

"It is clear that the brain is far from immutable,"[26] writes Dr. Marion Diamond of the University of California and one of the early pioneers in this field of neurological research. She and her team found that rat pups in "enriched" environments showed brain changes compared with those in "impoverished" environments after as little as two weeks. Sensory areas of their brains were thicker, other layers heavier. Changes showed consistent overall growth, leading to the conclusion that *the brain maintains its plasticity for life.*[27] G. Reid Lyon, a neuropsychologist who directs reading research funded by the National Institutes of Health, concurs. "The brain is malleable and continues to be plastic to and responsive to the environment to a greater degree than people have thought in the past," he says. "This is pretty promising information."[28]

In addition to Dr. Diamond's rats, other experiments leading to similar conclusions include the following:

- In a study done on ferrets, brains were actually physically rewired, with inputs from the eyes switched to where the hearing nerves went and vice versa. The brain changed to accommodate the new inputs.[29]
- Imaging experiments done on blind adults showed that when they learned Braille, "visual" areas of their brains lit up. Deaf people use their auditory cortex to read signs.[30]
- When researchers scanned the brains of people who were tapping their fingers in a complicated sequence that they had practiced for weeks, a larger area of motor cortex became activated then when they performed sequences they hadn't practiced.[31]
- Japanese subjects were trained to "reprogram" their circuitry for distinguishing "ra" from "la," a skill they "forget" soon after birth because their language doesn't require it.[32]
- Dr. Jay Hirsch and Dr. Karl Kim found that an additional language learned later in life goes into a different place in the brain than the language or languages learned as children.[33]

- Carefully designed intensive reading instruction experiments with students aged 10 and up appeared to create lasting chemical changes in key areas of the subjects' brains.[34]
- Harvard neurobiologist Mark Jude Tramano found that a comparison of musicians versus nonplayers using magnetic resonance imaging showed a 5 percent greater volume in the musicians' cerebellums, ascribed to adaptations in the brain's structure resulting from intensive musical training and practice.[35]

Brain plasticity research is being conducted by a large community of scientists. And we are only at the very beginning of understanding the implications of and applying this work. "Ultimately, says Dr. Merzenich, a founder along with Dr. Tallal of the education company Scientific Learning, this strategy will lead to neuroscience-based education."[36] Scientific Learning has created products that seek, based on brain research, to "reprogram" the brains of children with certain types of reading difficulties, with impressive results (see Chapter 7).

As if the news on brain plasticity from the neurologists and neurobiologists were not enough, there is evidence from social psychology as well. Western philosophers and psychologists have long taken it for granted that the same basic processes underlie all human thought. Although cultural differences might dictate what people think *about*, the *strategies* and *processes* of thought, which include logical reasoning and a desire to understand situations and events in linear terms of cause and effect, are the same for everyone. However this, too, appears to be wrong.

Research by many social psychologists—including work by Alexandr Luria[37] in the Soviet Union, who showed that collectivized versus noncollectivized peasants used different kinds of logic, and work by Dr. Richard Nisbett of the University of Michigan, who compared European Americans and East Asians[38]—shows that people who grow up in different cultures do not just think about different things, they actually *think differently*. The environment and culture in which people are raised affects and even determines many of their thought processes.

"We used to think that everybody uses categories in the same way, that logic plays the same kind of role for everyone in the understanding of everyday life, that memory, perception, rule application and so on are the same," says Dr. Nisbett. "But we're now arguing that cognitive processes themselves are just far more malleable than mainstream psychology assumed." [39]

So, people who undergo different inputs from the media and culture that surround them can, and do, think differently. However a person's thinking patterns do not just change overnight. A key finding of brain plasticity research is that brains do *not* reorganize casually, easily, or arbitrarily. "Brain reorganization takes place only when the animal pays attention to the sensory input and to the task," writes John Bruer in *The Myth of the First Three Years*.[40] "It requires very hard work," says Lyon.[41] Scientific Learning's Fast ForWard program requires students to spend 100 minutes a day, 5 days a week, for 5 to 10 weeks to create desired changes, because "it takes sharply focused attention to rewire a brain."[42]

Several hours a day, five days a week, sharply focused attention—does that remind you of anything? Oh, yes—video games! That is exactly what children have been doing ever since *Pong* arrived in 1974. They have been adjusting or programming their brains to the speed, interactivity, and other factors in the games, much as boomers' brains were programmed to accommodate television. This may not, in fact, be even the second time this "brain reprogramming" has happened. Some scientists suggest at least two other major "brain programmings" in human history—one dealing with the need to deal with radical change[43] and the other to deal with the invention of written language and reading[44] where the brain had to be retrained to deal with things in a highly linear way. "Reading does not just happen," says University of California—Davis neurology expert Kathleen Baynes. "It is a terrible struggle."[45] Neuroscientist Michael S. Gazzaniga at Dartmouth adds: "reading is an invention that is going to have a different neurology to it than the things that are built into our brain, like spoken language."[46] In fact, one of the main focuses of traditional school for the hundreds of years since reading became a mass phenomenon has been retraining our speech-oriented brains to be able to do reading. Again, the training involves several hours a day, five days a week, and sharply focused attention.

So here is the interesting and important part of the problem. Just when we've figured out (more or less) how to retrain brains for reading, they were retrained again by television. Now things have changed *yet again*, and our children are out furiously retraining their brains to think in newer ways, many of which, as we shall observe, are antithetical to older ways of thinking. This is one of the key tensions at the root of many of today's training and education problems.

"Linear thought processes that dominate educational systems now can actually retard learning for brains developed through game and Web-surfing processes on the computer," says Peter Moore, editor of the human resources newsletter *Inferential Focus*. [47] This may help explain the attitude of the high school student who complains that "every time I go to school I have to 'power down.'"

According to William D. Winn, the director of the Learning Center at the University of Washington's Human Interface Technology Laboratory, children raised with the computer "think differently from the rest of us. They develop hypertext minds. They leap around. It's as though their cognitive structures were parallel, not sequential." [48]

Moore reports that teenagers use different parts of their brain and think in different ways than adults when at the computer. We know now that it actually goes further. Their brains are actually *physiologically* different. But these differences, most observers agree, are less a matter of kind than a difference of degree. For example as a result of repeated experiences, particular brain areas are larger and more highly developed, and others are less so.

Patricia Marks Greenfield, professor of psychology at the University of California—Los Angeles, has been a long-time student of the effects of media on socialization and cognitive development. Greenfield reports that she became interested in this field when she realized that her son, then about 11, was developing thinking skills through playing video games that she didn't have.

Greenfield has studied and published extensively on the effects of video games on players' minds. She was one of the first to study this area, publishing her first book on the subject, *Mind and Media*,[49] in 1984. Many of her original ideas are just now finding wider acceptance. Greenfield has found that skills developed as a result of playing video games go far beyond the hand—eye coordination skills most often cited. "Videogames are the first example of a computer technology that is having a socializing effect on the next generation on a mass scale, and even on a worldwide basis," she wrote in 1984. "What is the person like who has been socialized by the technologies of television and video games? So far it appears that he or she may have more developed skills in iconic representation than the person entirely socialized by the older media of print and radio. The videogame and computer, in adding an interactive dimension to television, may also be creating people with special skills in discovering rules and patterns by and active and interactive process of trial and error."[50]

Among Greenfield's findings are the following:

- Playing video games augments skill in reading visual images as representations of three-dimensional space (representational competence). This is a combination of several competencies, including partnering with the computer in the construction of the representation, using the joystick (or other controller) as a "distanced" representational tool, working in real-time, multidimensional visual-spatial skills, and mental maps.

- Skill in computer games enhances, and is a causal factor in, other thinking skills such as the skill of mental paper folding (i.e. picturing the results of various origami-like folds in your mind without actually doing them). What is important, she finds, is this is a *cumulative* skill—there is no effect on mental paper folding from playing the game for only a few hours. These effects were found in other studies as well.

- Because no one tells you the rules in advance, video games enhance the skills of "rule discovery" through observation, trial and error, and hypothesis testing. In Greenfield's words, "the process of making observations, formulating hypotheses and figuring out the rules governing the behavior of a dynamic representation is basically the cognitive process of *inductive discovery* . . . the thought process behind scientific thinking." Computer games, she finds, require this skill.

- Video game skills transfer to and lead to greater comprehension of scientific simulations, due to increased ability to decode the iconic representation of computer graphics.

- Playing video games enhances players' skills at "divided attention" tasks, such as monitoring multiple locations simultaneously, by helping them appropriately adjust their "strategies of attentional deployment." Players get faster at responding to both expected and unexpected stimuli.

"Are these technologies in the process of creating a new person?" she asks. Her answer is that the cognitive skills are not new, but the particular combination may well be. That observation was made in 1984. Since that time, Greenfield's subsequent research has confirmed and enhanced her earlier findings.[51] It is clear that we now have a new generation with a very different mix of cognitive skills than its predecessors—the Games Generation.

DIGITAL MEDIA: A SECOND LANGUAGE

Many people have referred to young people's facility with computers as a second language, one that their elders do not speak, or at least not as well as the young people do. "For adults computer skills are a tool, but for teenagers using computers has become a second language," writes Moore. It is an apt metaphor. Citing the experiments of Doctors Hirsh and Kim, mentioned above, Moore suggests that "teenage facility with the computer, like language facility acquired in infancy, may well emerge from a part of the brain that adults do not use while doing the same computer operations."[52]

McLuhan also refers to these facilities in terms of language: "To educate the 'turned-on' teenager in the old mechanical style is like asking a three-year-old who has just learned English to talk pidgin-English or to use a heavy Scottish brogue. These things are not in his environment and therefore not cognizable."[53]

The Games Generations—others use the terms *N*-[for Net]-*gen* or *D*-for digital]-*gen*—are *native speakers* of the digital language of computers, video games and the Internet. Those of us who were *not* born into this world but have, at some later point in our lives, become fascinated by and adopted many or most aspects of the new technology are, and will always be, compared to them, "digital immigrants." (I am indebted to Sylvia Kowal of Nortel for sparking these ideas.)[54] And like all immigrants, as we learn—some better than others—to adapt to our new environment, we always retain, to some degree, our "accent," that is, our foot in the past. The digital immigrant accent can be seen in such things as turning to the Internet for information second rather than first, or in reading the manual for a program rather than assuming that the program itself will teach us to use it. We older folk have not been "socialized," to use Greenfield's term, in the same way as our children. Remember, a language learned later in life goes into a different part of the brain.

Contest 1: What are other good examples of the "digital immigrant accent?" Email your entries to *Contest1@twitchspeed.com*.

DIFFERENT FROM TV: MANIPULATING VERSUS WATCHING

As I mentioned earlier, television performed some "mind programming" of its own on the Baby Boomer generation and beyond. But to understand today's Games Generation learners it is key for us to distinguish and separate those mind changes that come from television from the mind changes of the next generations, influenced as well by *interactive* technologies such as video and computer games and the Internet. The key difference is that the Games Generations are *active participants* rather than passive observers. Greenfield calls video games "the first medium to combine visual dynamism with an active, participatory role for the child."[55] "They want to be users, not just viewers or listeners," reports Tapscott.[56] Janet Murray refers to this as "agency;" "the satisfying power to take meaningful action and see the results of our decisions and choices." [57]

While the difference betweeen watching and participating is *very* important, it is, of course, not an either/or proposition. As anyone can observe, many people, children and adults, both play video games and watch television. Even game designers concede this, with some regret. "I don't believe that interactive entertainment will dominate other forms of entertainment this coming century," says Scott Miller of Apogee. "I think, for the most part, people prefer passive entertainment, like TV, watching sports, and attending movies, where you can veg out and just enjoy what's in front of you. But there's little doubt that digital gaming will continue to grow."[58] Adds Brett Sperry of Westwood Studios: "We will always have books, movies, magazines, and television. Passive forms of entertainment are here to stay. However, we will see an incredible array of new interactive options, delivered in a few different ways. Everything you do now for entertainment purposes will become interactive in some way."[59] Although they use both active and passive media, Games Generation members often *prefer* video games and the Internet to television because of their interactivity. A 9-year-old girl commented to Greenfield, "in TV, if you want to make someone die, you can't. In PacMan if you want to run into a ghost you can."[60]

The point is that although both forms of entertainment will continue to coexist, the Games Generation now lives much more in an *interactive* world—with the emphasis on the "active." So when trainers or teachers from the Baby Boomer generation bring in passive video, in any way, shape, or form—as they love to do—they many think they are doing their learners a favor. But what today's learners crave is *interactivity*—the rest basically bores them to death.

SO WHAT ABOUT ATTENTION SPANS?

When I present the idea at training conferences that the interactive media-influenced Games Generations "think differently," I get a lot of "pushback" (training jargon for disagreement.) The reaction I have heard many times, often with a great deal of anger, is "you're just talking about traditional Myers-Briggs distinctions" (Myers and Briggs created a widely used test of thinking styles). About the only consensus I hear is that younger employees are generally rude and that their attention spans are shorter. In fact "the attention span of a gnat" has become such a common cliché that it just rolls off the tongue. But is this really true? Is it that they *can't* pay attention or that they *don't*?

"I don't buy that these kids have short attention spans," says Dr. Edit Harel, author of the book *Children Designers* and founder of MaMaMedia. "They think in different ways than adults. Sometimes they are multitasking. Other times they can get into something and spend many hours on it if it makes sense to them."[61] "I always believed that kids didn't have short attention spans," says Todd Kessler, Nickelodeon producer of *Blues Clues*.[62]

Older-generation folks often watch younger employees lose patience and tune out to traditional training. Management and trainers may conclude that their attention spans must be short, but it just isn't true. I contend that the people who hold these short attention span views have not been watching or listening to younger people closely enough. In the words of Edward Westhead, a former biochemistry professor at the University of Massachusetts at Amherst,, "Sure they have short attention spans—for the old ways of learning."[63] Their attention spans are *not* short for games, for example, or for music, or for rollerblading, or for spending time on the Internet, or anything else that actually interests them. Traditional training and schooling just doesn't engage them. It isn't that they *can't* pay attention, they just *choose not to*.

Concerning attention spans, there are two relative newcomers to the medical lexicon, widely discussed in the last decade or so: *attention deficit disorder* (ADD) and its sister, *attention deficit hyperactivity disorder* (ADHD). (The whole thing used to be known as *hyperactivity*.) This so-called disease is diagnosed in an enormous number of children, who are often treated with Ritalin and other drugs. Dr. F. Xavier Castellanos, who heads the attention deficit hyperactivity research unit at the National Institutes of Health, says: "Everyone knows people with attention deficit who can concentrate well enough to play computer games for hours."[64] Some researchers say ADD comes from an inability of a person's brain to produce extended beta, as opposed to theta, waves.[65] Determining whether a child's attention deficit is a result of illness or of boredom is not always easy, and we don't always get it right. But even when we do, interestingly enough, it is video games—the holders of even *these* children's attention—that are increasingly used to retrain children's brains and help them concentrate, as we shall see in Chapter 7.

In his book *The Tipping Point*,[66] Malcolm Gladwell cites research done for *Sesame Street* that revealed that children do not actually watch television continuously, but "in bursts." They tune in just enough to get the gist and be sure it makes sense. The assumption before the research involving sophisticated eye measurements was that children sit there like zombies, attracted by all the "eye candy"—the glitz and glitter of the medium. But that was not what they found. "The idea [was] that kids would sit, stare at the screen and zone out," said Elizabeth Lorch, a psychologist at Amherst College. "But once we began to look carefully at what children were doing we found out that short looks were actually more common. There was much more variation. Children didn't just sit and stare. They could divide their attention between a couple of different activities. And they weren't being random. There were predictable influences on what made them look at the screen, and these were not just triv-ial things, not just flash and dash."[67]

In one key experiment, half the children were shown the program in a room filled with toys. As expected, the group with toys was dis-tracted and watched the show only about 47 percent of the time as opposed to 87 percent in the group without toys. But when the chil-dren were tested for how much of the show they remembered and understood, the scores were exactly the same. "We were led to the con-clusion that the 5-year-olds in the toys group were attending quite strategically, distributing their attention between toy play and viewing so that they looked at what was for them the most informative part of the program. The strategy was so effective that the children could gain no more from increased attention." In another experiment, sequences were presented out of order, and the children lost interest, despite the same flash and characters.[68]

This ability to choose selectively what counts for us and to learn through distraction is perhaps not a new phenomenon, but is vitally important in an age of bombardment by digital media. It is the phenome-non that will later be observed in children doing their homework with televison, working listening to music, and is a key, as we shall see, to improving and speeding up learning and training.

REFLECTION: THE DISAPPEARING SKILL?

Maybe, just maybe, I have begun to convince you that many of those new skills and ways of thinking that the Games Generation learned growing up are different, and even that many of them are positive. But what about all the criticisms that we constantly hear from teachers about problems with reading and thinking? What, if anything, has been *lost* in the "pro-gramming" process? This is certainly an area of great importance to us as trainers, teachers, and educators.

As I read and spoke to people during the research for this book, one key word began to come up over and over again—*reflection*. Reflection is what enables us, according to many theorists, to generalize, as we create "mental models" from our experience. It is, in many ways, the *process* of "learning from experience." The ability to stop and reflect is what distin-guishes reading a book—where one can pause and think whenever one chooses—from a twitch-speed video game, or an Internet-speed business, for that matter, where if you stop, you die. In our twitch-speed world, there is less and less time and opportunity for reflection, and this development concerns many people.

Says J. C. Herz: "I think that attention spans are shorter in large part because the culture is much less formal than it was, and the idea of sitting down and concentrating is ultimately a spiritual issue among other things, as much as it is a psychological issue. And if you live in a consumerist society where it's about grabbing something new, or acquiring another object, or just being able to toss references back and forth, contemplation is not really valued or valuable in that space—it doesn't do anything for you. Although of course we actually need it to actually ground ourselves. Which is what's ignored."[69]

Clifford Stoll, a self-appointed contrarian from whom we shall hear much more in Chapter 14, thinks that learning games "substitute quick answers and fast action for reflection and critical thinking."[70] Jane M. Healy writes that "fast paced, nonlinguistic and visually distracting television may literally have changed children's minds, making sustained attention to verbal input, such as reading or listening, far less appealing than faster paced, visual stimuli."[71]

One of the most interesting challenges and opportunities in Digital Game-Based Learning is to figure out and invent ways to *include* reflection and critical thinking (either built into the game or through a process of instructor-led debriefing) with the learning *and still make it a fun game.* There are many genres of games that already allow for this (think of chess.) It is something that many users of simulation games, such as the military, have been doing for a while. Some of the Digital Game-Based Learning examples that I will discuss in Chapters 9 and 10 have taken interesting steps in the direction of building reflection and critical thinking into the software. But we can and must do more in this area.

TEN WAYS THE GAMES GENERATION IS DIFFERENT

Exactly *how* is the Games Generation, who grew up in the last quarter of the twentieth century, different from other generations? Here's one example. Growing up on twitch-speed video games, MTV (more than 100 images a minute), and the ultrafast speed of action films, the Games

Generation's minds have been programmed to adapt to greater speed and thrive on it. Yet when they go to school or go to work, educators and trainers typically give them all the "nontwitch" features of the past: "tell-test" education, boring corporate classrooms, poor speakers lecturing at them, talking-head corporate videos, and, lately, endless "click and fall asleep" courses on the Internet.

Speedwise, we effectively give them depressants, and then we wonder why they're bored! This is no doubt a big part of what the student means when he complains about having to "power down" at school.

Below are ten of the main cognitive style changes that I have observed in the Games Generation, all of which raise a number of important and difficult challenges for education, training, and business in general:

1. Twitch speed vs. conventional speed
2. Parallel processing vs. linear processing
3. Graphics first vs. text first
4. Random access vs. step-by-step
5. Connected vs. standalone
6. Active vs. passive
7. Play vs. work
8. Payoff vs. patience
9. Fantasy vs. reality
10. Technology-as-friend vs. technology-as-foe

Let's examine each of these in turn to see why the change represents a break from the past, and what it implies in terms of new learning needs.

Twitch Speed vs. Conventional Speed

The Games Generation has had far more experience at processing information quickly than its predecessors and is therefore better at it. Scrolling rapidly through a huge genetic database for matches to a gene he believes is involved in diabetes, Dr. Gary Ruvkun, a thirty-ish medical researcher, comments "You learn how to read these as they are ratcheting by. I think MTV is good training."[72] Of course, humans have always been capable of operating at faster-than-"normal" speeds, as airplane pilots, racecar drivers, and speed-reading guru Evelyn Wood can attest. The difference is that this ability has now moved into a generation at large and at an early age, as Professor Greenfield noted early on. A big problem the generation faces is that, after MTV and video games, they essentially hit a brick wall (short of piloting a jet, little in real life moves that fast)—hence the "depressants." In the workplace, we see the Games Generation's need for speed manifesting itself in a number of ways, including a demand for a faster pace of development, less "time-in-grade" before promotions, and shorter lead times to success.

An important challenge for today's business managers is how to speed up their assumptions around how quickly things can be done, while still keeping sight of other key objectives, such as quality and customer relationships. They need to create training and other experiences that maintain the pace and exploit the facility of twitch speed while adding content that is important and useful. Digital Game-Based Learning is one of the ways they can do this.

Parallel Processing vs. Linear Processing

The mind can actually process many tracks at once. Much of the Games Generation grew up doing homework while watching television and doing almost everything while wearing a Walkman. They often feel much more comfortable than their predecessors when doing more than one thing at the same time. Although some argue that parallel processing limits attention to any one task, this is not necessarily the case—the mind typically has quite a bit of "idle time" from its primary task that can be used to handle other things. "There is no question that people can learn to do quite a bit of parallel processing in certain job situations, such as a lot of military jobs," says Dr. Susan Chipman, a researcher at the Office of Naval Research. Whether parallel processing is what is going on when one focuses on homework, television and Walkmen all at the same time still, she thinks, needs to be proved: "One would have to do experimental testing to determine that."[73] Nonetheless, today it is common to see young computer artists creating complex graphics while listening to music and chatting with co-workers, young businesspeople having multiple conversations on the phone while reading their computer screens and email, and securities traders managing multiple screens of information simultaneously. Professor Greenfield cites parallel processing as a "cognitive requirement of skillful video game playing."[74]

In fact, as we saw previously, non-parallel thought processes may actually *retard* learning for brains developed through computer games and Web-surfing.[75]

This growth of parallel-processing ability appears to have been acknowledged by Michael Bloomberg in creating his *Bloomberg TV News*, in which the anchorperson takes up only one-quarter of the television screen, the remainder being filled with sports statistics, weather information, stock quotes, and headlines, all presented simultaneously. It is quite possible, and even fun, for a viewer to take in all of this information and receive much more "news" in the same amount of time.

"Does this mean we are taking in more but at a lower depth?" ask some. Maybe. But it's a fact of life that this is how information is presented and received and we have to find new ways to get depth. This may be one reason why more and more people get their news from the Web. More depth, if and when you want it, is only a click away.

Managers, trainers, and educators need to be thinking of additional ways to enhance parallel processing for the Games Generation to take advantage of this now more highly enhanced human capability. We can, whether in training or elsewhere, feed them much more information at once than has been done in the past. Watch any of them surf the Net—they'll have dozens of windows open simultaneously. Having all the information needed to do their job at their fingertips—numbers, video feeds, links, simultaneous meetings, and the ability to move seamlessly between them—is the Games Generation worker's nirvana.

Random Access vs. Step-by-Step

The Games Generation is the first to experience hypertext and "clicking around," in edutainment, in CD-ROMs, and on the Web. The result is the "hypertext minds leaping around" that William Winn speaks of.[76] Tapscott reports that the N-gen child takes in and outputs information differently. "It typically comes from multiple sources and occurs in a less sequential manner."[77] This new, less sequential information structure has increased the Games Generation's awareness and ability to make connections, has freed them from the constraint of a single path of thought. In many ways it is an extremely positive development.

At the same time, some argue, with justification, that unbridled hyperlinking may make it more difficult for these workers to follow a linear train of thought and to do some types of deep or logical thinking. "Why should I read something from beginning to end, or follow someone else's logic, when I can just 'explore the links' and create my own?" young people might, and do, say. Although following one's own path often leads to interesting results, understanding someone else's logic is also very important. A difficult challenge is how to create experiences that allow us to link anywhere and experience things in any order yet still communicate sequential ideas and logical thinking.

Yet what has been lost in linearity may have been made up for by a greater ability to perceive, and think in, structure and patterns. Says Marshall McLuhan: "Our electronically configured world has led us to move from the habit of data classification to the mode of pattern recognition. We can no longer build serially, block-by-block, step-by-step, because instant communication insures that all factors of the environment and of experience coexist in a state of active interplay."[78] At least one young person interviewed reports that because of his experiences with today's technology he thinks in terms of structures and sees conceptual structures very quickly.[79]

Graphics First vs. Text First

In previous generations, graphics were generally illustrations, accompanying the text and providing some kind of elucidation. For today's Games Generation, the relationship is almost completely reversed: The role of text is to elucidate something that was first experienced as an image. Since childhood, these people have been continuously exposed to television, videos, and computer games that put high-quality, highly expressive graphics in front of them with little or no accompanying text.

The result has been to acutely sharpen their visual sensitivity. They find it much more natural than their predecessors to begin with visuals, and to mix text and graphics in a richly meaningful way. A well-known exploiter of this capability is *Wired* magazine, whose intensive use of graphics makes it highly appealing to Games Generation readers yet difficult for many older folks to digest. "Why can't they just give us the plain text?" is a complaint I heard often from colleagues, particularly at the magazine's inception.

Professor Greenfield has documented these increases in representational skill and iconic understanding, citing a worldwide rise of "performance" or "nonverbal" IQ, which she terms *visual intelligence*.[80] Technology, and particularly video games, figures importantly in her explanation for this phenomenon. It is linked to other changes we are discussing as well, since, in her words, "pictorial images, in general, tend to elicit parallel processing."

This shift toward graphic primacy in the younger generation does raise some extremely thorny issues, particularly with regard to textual literacy and depth of information. The challenge is to design ways to use this shift to enhance comprehension, while still maintaining the same or even greater richness of information in the new visual context. Computer and video games designers are specialists in this area, which is a great advantage of Digital Game-Based Learning.

Another potential opportunity to use this heightened visual perception is to speed up learning by allowing the user to take in a great deal of information at once. Already, as we have seen, makers of MTV-style videos often include hundreds of images a minute, showing each image for a few tenths of a second. But a few *thousandths* of a second is all it actually takes for an image to register. In an experiment at Massachusetts General Hospital (MGH), Paul Whelan, Dr Scott Rauch, and co-workers found that humans could perceive images that activate their fear circuitry without even being aware of it. The MGH researchers used an approach known as *masking*; they showed subjects in an magnetic-resonance imaging (MRI) machine photographs of fearful faces for a mere 33 milliseconds, followed by a longer, masking exposure to expressionless faces for 167 milliseconds. The subjects had no conscious memory of seeing the fearful faces, yet their brains unequivocally did; the amygdala lighted up even during the brief flash of a fearful face but not during the similarly brief exposure of a happy face. Whelan feels this super-quick exposure is a "very fast and preferential way" to get information.[81]

Connected vs. Standalone

The Games Generation has been raised with, and become accustomed to, the worldwide connectedness of email, broadcast messages, bulletin boards, usegroups, chat, multiplayer games, and instant messaging. Although the previous generation was linked by the telephone, that system is basically synchronous and expensive. The Games Generation's connectedness is both synchronous and asynchronous—anytime, anywhere, at almost no cost. The asynchronous part—email, newsgroups, bulletin boards—is now their preferred means of communication in many cases. The synchronous part—multiplayer games, instant messaging, voice telephony—use of which is now increasing because of bandwidth, is different because cost is no longer a factor. People can be contacted, spoken to and played with—somewhere in the world—24 hours a day.

Some argue that this leads to "depersonalization," because people meet, chat, play, and even work on the Web without ever seeing one another or knowing the other people's names or genders. But people who do this often find it enormously liberating and fun to be freed of all the effects of "lookism" (a term discussed by William Safire in his New York Times column "On Language"[82]) and other prejudices. Clark Aldrich of Gartner Group cites the situation of *Star Trek* fans banding together on the Web to create new types of spaceships for the game *Starfleet Command* in order to get around a licensing agreement between the maker of the game and Paramount which limited the number of ship types in the game. Teams self-organized over the Internet and created all the necessary parts: wireframe models, outside "skins," specifications and armaments, and even the stories around these ships, without ever meeting in person at all. Says Aldrich, "people say classrooms are great because people can see each other. That's sort of a characteristic of our [i.e. the older] generation but not the next one, who are very comfortable working with people they've never met, frankly never even knowing how old they are, not knowing or caring about their background, just nothing. Its simply what can you produce, and if you're not producing something good than I'll move on to the next person."[83] It's a different world, and we'd better get used to it.

As a result of their "connected" experience, Games Generation people tend to think differently about how to get information and solve problems. For example, if I need a question answered, I'll typically call the three or four people I think might know. It might take me time to get to them, and take them a while to get back to me. When my 32-year-old programmer wants to know something, he immediately posts his question to a bulletin board, where three or four thousand people might see it, and he'll probably have a much richer answer more quickly than I would get via the phone. It took me a while to get used to using the Net for research, but the quantity and variety of material I found available was staggering. The Games Generation takes this availability for granted—just as I took the Forty-Second Street library for granted growing up in New York.

The challenge for all business managers, trainers, and teachers who are *not* from the Games Generation is to invent ways of taking advantage of this connected mode in their interactions with those people, as the Games Generation people do among themselves. (How many trainers, for example, instant message with their trainees, particularly outside of formal training?) The more we help connect all employees "mentally" as well as physically to one another—and to customers—the quicker *they* will invent positive ways to take advantage of this cognitive change. Digital Game-Based Learning is one way to do this.

As we saw, the "connectedness" of the Games Generation has also made them much less constrained by their physical location and more willing to work in the so-called virtual teams that are becoming more useful in a variety of businesses and industries. Workers who have grown up online tend to be much more comfortable with seeking out and working with the best, most knowledgeable people, wherever they may be. Such virtual teams often recruit one another via messages on the Internet, operate smoothly from widely scattered parts of the world, and many never physically meet their clients or one another. As they finish their day, software developers around the globe often electronically forward their work to a colleague in another country who is just waking up. Trainers, teachers, and managers need to become more adept at managing these connected capabilities and directing the acquisition, enhancement, and appropriate deployment of information, knowledge, and intellectual capital in schools and companies and around the world.

Active vs. Passive

One of the most striking cross-generational differences can be observed when people are given new software to learn. Older folks almost invariably want to read the manual first, afraid they won't understand how the software works or that they'll break something. Says Joanne Veech of PricewaterhouseCoopers: "The 40 and 50 year old group that have seen *In$ider* ask how to use it. They are very afraid to push the buttons on the [virtual] elevators. You know how much more careful our generation is when we turn the computer on, whereas my 12 year old just goes zing, zing, zing, zing, zing—fearless. So that generation of newcomers to PricewaterhouseCoopers, those 20-somethings that have grown up over 20 years with this fearless environment, when they get to this, it's very natural for them. It's a gaming environment—it becomes second nature, they don't think twice about clicking on a plant or clicking on an elevator or seeing what the buttons do."[84]

Games Generation workers rarely even *think* of reading a manual. They'll just play with the software, hitting every key if necessary, until they figure it out. If they can't, they assume the problem is with the software, not with them—software is *supposed* to teach you how to use it. This attitude is almost certainly a direct result of growing up with Sega, Sony, Nintendo, and other video games where each level and monster had to be figured out by trial and error, and each trial click could lead to a hidden surprise. Games are almost all designed to teach you as you go.

We now see much less tolerance in the workplace among the Games Generations for passive situations such as lectures, corporate classrooms, and even traditional meetings. As the Games Generation progresses up the managerial ranks, it is likely that such old-fashioned managerial standbys will be replaced by more active experiences such as chat, posting, surfing for information, and Digital Game-Based Learning, where employees not only more are active but also have more control over what happens. The processes of "designing for doing," and "designing for learning" (i.e., designing systems and experiences that employees can actively use to learn, instead of things they need to listen to or be afraid of doing wrong) may become the new generational equivalent of the industrial "designing for manufacture," where making the product is an important consideration in the design process. Nike's "Just do it"" slogan (which began in 1988!) hits this generational change squarely on the head.

Play vs. Work

Members of the Games Generation are often derided in the press as intellectual slackers, but in reality they are very much an intellectual-problem-solving-oriented generation. Many types of logic, challenging puzzles, spatial relationships, and other complex thinking tasks are built into the computer and video games they enjoy. Their spending on such electronic games has surpassed their spending on live movies, and PCs are now used more for running entertainment software than for anything else, including word processing. Although some have argued that play and games are simply preparation for work, I think that, for today's Games Generations, play *is* work, and, as we shall see in Chapter 5, work is increasingly seen in terms of games and game play. The fact that the real-life games are very serious does not make the player's approach any different than the way he or she approaches game software. Achievement, winning, and beating competitors are all very much part of the ethic and process.

As the Games Generations enter the workforce, their preference for the computer as the medium of play is already beginning to have a profound impact on how work gets done. Game interfaces are appearing in work software. Financial companies are inventing gamelike trading interfaces in which winning the game means making an actual profit. And more and more workers are learning to do their jobs through Digital Game-Based Learning.

One difficult challenge for managers and trainers is to be willing to let the younger generation's play attitude enter the "real" world of business as quickly and smoothly as possible. Instead of resisting play by removing or banning all games in the workplace, for example, they could be supporting and funding the development of new game interfaces that help the younger generation work and learn in their own cognitive style. Managers and trainers should reconsider their resistance to such changes carefully.

As we shall see in Chapter 9, the Games Generation's play preference has resulted in Digital Game-Based Learning being used for a great many functions in the workplace beside training, including employee recruiting, strategy communication, and customer support.

Payoff vs. Patience

One of the biggest lessons the Games Generation learned from growing up with video games is that if you put in the hours and master the game, you will be rewarded—with the next level, with a win, with a place on the high scorers' list. What you do determines what you get, and what you get is worth the effort you put in. Computers excel at giving feedback, and the payoff for any action is typically extremely clear.

A key outcome of this feedback is a huge intolerance on the part of the Games Generations for things that don't pay off at the level expected. Why, they ask, should I finish college when elementary school kids can design professional Web sites, 20-year-olds can start billion-dollar companies, and Bill Gates, who left Harvard to do something with more payoff, is the world's richest man?

Games Generation people make these payoff-versus-patience decisions every minute and sometimes in ways that are counterintuitive. For example, it was at first strange to me that the same people who prefer twitch games often have great patience with slow Internet connection speeds and the sometimes long waiting times in games like *Myst* or *Riven*. I suspect it is because they have decided, or realized, that the payoff is worth the wait. The challenge for managers, trainers, and teachers and is to understand just how important these payoff-versus-patience tradeoffs are to younger people, and to find ways to offer them meaningful rewards *now* rather than advice about how things will pay off "in the long run."

One clear business manifestation of this requirement for payoff is the increasing demand for a clearer link between what employees do and the rewards they get, leading to the growing trend toward pay for performance. Another result is the increasing use of equity as a component of compensation, along with the replication of equitylike compensation structures to reward workers with a "piece of the action" for their own initiatives and efforts. The growing realization that this generation wants its payoff now has also led to an increased willingness on the part of many businesses to provide seed capital and to spin off internal startups, allowing workers to potentially cash in more quickly and allowing the firm to benefit long term through an equity position.

Fantasy vs. Reality

One of the most striking aspects of the Games Generation is the degree to which fantasy elements, both from the past (medieval, *Dungeons & Dragons* imagery) and the future (*Star Wars*, *Star Trek*, and other science-fiction imagery), pervade their lives. Although young people have always indulged in fantasy play, the computer has by its nature made this easier and more realistic, in many ways bringing it to life.

Sociologists might say that some or all of this fantasy play is due to a desire to escape the realities of today's life: fewer good jobs, more alienation, and a degrading environment. Whatever its cause, the fantasy phenomenon has certainly been encouraged by technology. Network technology allows people not only to create their new fantasy identities but also to express them to others and join in fantasy communities and games such as *EverQuest*. The fantasy card game *Magic, the Gathering*, according to J. C. Herz, "is one of the largest closeted communities in America,"[85] with national and worldwide tournaments offering tens of thousands of dollars in prizes.

Some people distinguish between the genders in this area, claiming that many of these fantasies are more "male" oriented (although there are plenty of women at *Star Trek* conventions and many avid female *Dungeons & Dragons* and fantasy game players). The whole gender area is a controversial topic that will be discussed later in this book. But fantasy is a large part of the adult Games Generation's lives in ways that Disney, for example, is not part of the Boomers' lives.

So rather than admonish Games Generation workers to "grow up and get real" and abandon their rich fantasy worlds, trainers, educators, and managers might be better off searching for new ways to combine fantasy and reality to everyone's benefit. One place this is happening already is in the design of workspaces. Spaces designed by the younger generation are very different from those of their predecessors and from those designed for them by the older generation. Companies already run by Games Generation individuals generally have much more informal settings, and often have special rooms for games, miniature golf, and "fun" activities. Microsoft's "campus" is full of indoor and outdoor play opportunities.

The younger generation's fantasy preferences can also be seen in the growth of new off-the-wall job titles, such as Yahoo's Chief Yahoo or Gateway 2000's chief imagination officer. Young workers may be willing to go a lot further with their imaginations—Gateway decorates its shipping boxes as cows. We are also seeing an increasing debureaucratization of systems and procedures in many organizations. Perhaps it is not too far off when some companies will sport their own Klingon, Borg, or Wookee divisions doing serious business while decked out appropriately. Fantasy-based Digital Game-Based Learning is another opportunity for this, particularly if both genders are taken into account.

Technology as Friend vs. Technology as Foe

Growing up with computers has engendered an overall attitude toward technology in the minds of the Games Generation that is very different from that of their predecessors. To much of the older generation, technology is something to be feared, tolerated, or at best harnessed to one's purposes. Some, no matter how easy we make it, don't ever want to program their videocassette recorders or surf the Net. [86]

There is, of course, an increasingly large segment of the non–Games Generation workers and retirees who have learned to adopt many of the tools, technologies, and even attitudes of the Games Generation, Whether these "digital immigrants" come to the new shores willingly or are forced by circumstances to learn and accept a new, changing culture (i.e., digital technology), they will never be as entirely comfortable and trusting of the new environment as are their native-born children.

To the Games Generation, the computer is a friend. It's where they have always turned for play, relaxation, and fun. For many in this generation, owning or having access to a computer feels like a birthright. Being connected is a necessity. The huge generational reversal in technical skill, where parents must turn to their children for help in using their expensive equipment, is now legendary—Don Tapscott refers to it as the *generation lap*, as in "lapping" competitors in a race.[87] The answers to the questions, "What kind of computer will I have?" and "Will I have my own high-speed Internet connection?," are very often key factors in a young worker's decision about what job to accept.

How can an older generation of trainers, educators, and managers relate to and help employees who see computers and related technology in this way? One way is to empower them to create *their own* new business elements—computer applications, structures, models, relation-ships, Web pages—that make sense for their generation, or at the very least, enlist them as part of the teams creating these things. An additional approach is to continually seek ways to communicate, transfer needed information, and build desired skills via the media the younger genera-tion willingly engage in, such as computers and games, that is, via Digital Game-Based Learning. This was the approach of Sylvia Kowal at Nortel (see Chapter 9).

"Attitude"

In addition to all of the above, a defining characteristic of the Games Gen-eration is "attitude"—an irreverent, often sarcastic, tell-it-like-it-is, don't-try-to pull-the-wool-over-my-eyes way of looking at things. It is probably best captured by Jellyvision's wildly successful game series *You Don't Know Jack*, in which the announcer berates you quite personally for not knowing the answers. ("What were you *thinking?*"). This may be a reac-tion to all the "bullshit" commercials and other television that kids grew up with. In any case "attitude" is certainly now part of their language ("Duh!") and almost a *sine qua non* for communicating with them effec-tively, even in—or especially in—in training. "It's got *lots* of attitude," says Paula Young proudly of *In$ider*. In fact, *not* having attitude—or, worse, doing it wrong—is definitely part of the "digital immigrant accent" and is sure to be mocked.

So in all these ways—and I'm sure there are many others—the native Games Generation is *cognitively different* from its predecessors, whether digital immigrants or not. With this in mind, let us return once more to the "attention span" question and ask "What has happened?"

To a huge, underappreciated extent in our training and education we offer the Games Generations *very little* worth paying attention to from their perspective, *and then we blame them for not paying attention.* Many of the people accustomed to the twitch- speed, multitasking, random-access, graphics-first, active, connected, fun, fantasy, and quick payoff world of their video games, MTV, and Internet feel *bored* by most of today's approaches to training and learning, well meaning as it may be. And, worse, the many skills that new technologies *have* actually enhanced (e.g., parallel processing, graphics awareness, and random access)—which have profound implications for their learning—are almost totally ignored by education and training.

So, in the end, it is *all these cognitive differences*, resulting from years of "new media socialization" and profoundly affecting and changing the generations' learning styles and abilities, that cry out for new approaches to learning for the Games Generation with a better "fit." And while certainly not the only way, computer games and video games provide one of the few structures we currently have that is capable of meeting many of the Games Generation's changing learning needs and requirements. This is the key reason why Digital Game-Based Learning is beginning to emerge and thrive.

3

Why Education and Training Have Not Changed

I got into what was supposedly one of the best colleges in the country for technology. The professors were all from MIT. But in class all they did was read to us from their textbooks. I quit.
— A former college student

We learn more from a three-minute record, baby, than we ever learned in school.
— Bruce Springsteen, *"No Surrender"*

What does the average employee get out of training? Frequent flyer miles.
— A Corporate Training Executive

In what is almost a cliché, many writers on training, learning, and education have stated that if observers from 200 years ago came to the United States at the start of the twenty-first century, they would be amazed and uncomfortable with changes everywhere, *except* in a school or corporate classroom. So what? Is this so terrible? After all, the same time travelers would certainly recognize that we still all wear shoes, eat food, and go to sleep at night. Maybe education and training *should* stay the same. After all, "if it ain't broke, don't fix it" is a practical American approach, and just plain common sense.

But, the truth as we all know, and most of us admit, is that our learning and training system *is* broken. Seriously broken. The evidence comes from reading and math scores, boredom, dropout rates, and lack of skills in the workforce. The evidence also comes from standardized tests being "dumbed down,"[1] from colleges and businesses doing remediation of basic skills,[2] and from the fact that greater than 45 percent of American adults scored at levels 1 or 2 in the 1992 National Adult Literacy Survey, which means that they "lack a sufficient foundation of basic skills to function successfully in our society."[3] Parents are desperately seeking to move their children to places that parents perceive *do* work, through vouchers and other plans. Additionally, a growing percentage of parents don't bother with schools at all, preferring to educate their kids at home.[4] In their book *The Monster Under the Bed,*[5] Stan Davis and Jim Botkin argue that business is taking over by default many of education's roles. This is in some ways laughable, because, as Roger Schank, noted trainer and author, points out, the thing that is *worst* about business training is that it is just like school![6]

So what's going on? Is it the system? Is it society? Is it the environment? Is it the parents? Of course, each plays a role, but in almost all the analyses that appear, one point of view is surprisingly absent—*that of the learner.* What is it actually *like* to be an elementary, high school, college, or business-training student today? The answer, overwhelmingly, is that it's BORING! Boring compared to television, boring compared to computer games, boring compared to movies, boring compared even to work! Most teachers or trainers will tell you that it's difficult to "compete" with what's out there. Outside of the classroom, today's kids and workers are empowered and stimulated. Yet corporate training is almost always an unwelcome burden, and school, according to Jon Katz, a writer on technology, is "a nightmare, dull and claustrophobic and oppressive..."[7]

Does this *have* to be the case? Why is school and corporate learning so incredibly *un*engaging? What, if anything, can be done to make a difference?

The answer to the first question—does school and training *have* to be boring—is an absolute and emphatic *no!* School and training do not have to be boring at all. There are lots of instances—mostly isolated, unfortunately—in which learning isn't boring. If our training or school is boring to our students, it is entirely our fault as educators. Blaming anyone else—especially our students—is like a doctor blaming his patients for getting sick. While our students certainly have done some things that have contributed to the situation, such as play video games, this is not something that we can blame them for. People live in the world into which they are born, and do the things of their time that appeal to them. Because of the outside forces around them as they grew up, and because of normally living their early life in the last third of the twentieth century, learners' habits, preferences, and needs have radically changed. So, despite school's hundreds of years of "tradition" it is now time for our education and training to finally change, or else to continue to fail us. Why? Because it no longer holds the interest of its students, even under duress. While there are still many students who succeed at learning, in most places, they learn in spite of, not because of, their schools and training.

A favorite book of mine is called *How to Play the Piano Despite Years of Lessons.* [8] Its premise is that most piano teaching is based around what the "classicists" think you should know, and is taught through exercises that fit players of eighteenth and nineteenth century music. While some learners clearly enjoy this repertoire, many more would like to be able to just play their favorite songs, and improvise and accompany in the styles not of the eighteenth century, but of today.

So what, if anything, can be done to make a difference? My answer is that Digital Game-Based Learning can make a huge difference. But to understand *why* this is so, we must examine the second question carefully: Why is school and corporate learning so incredibly unengaging to today's learners? Interestingly, the answers are not so radical as to make solutions impossible. On the contrary, ways to fix the problem are clearly within our means.

CONTENT-CENTERED VERSUS LEARNER-CENTERED APPROACHES

You might think that learning is about learners. But to many trainers and educators, learning, training, and education are *not* about the learner; they are primarily about *content.* It is about "what" to teach or train, rather than about "why" or especially "how." A majority of the educational discourse taking place in our society, schools, and companies, centers around *what* to teach—what is known, in the beloved Latin of academia, as the curriculum,—rather than *how* to learn it. What I mean by "content-centered learning" is treating learners as if they were, in the words of

Luyen Chou, "receptacles for knowledge that is stuffed down into them, whether by a teacher or a computer."[9]

AFTRB

I once asked a colleague who had just returned from a training course how it had gone. "AFTRB" she replied. "What's that?" I asked. "Another *%$#! three-ring binder," she snickered. Anyone who has ever been to a training course knows precisely what she means. The training was done with slides and handouts, copies of all of which are contained in the 3-inch binder, between gobs of tabs. Many training veterans still have walls of these binders in their office, each stamped with its own acronym for the name of whatever course it was.

When an executive requests training, it is typically a "what," rather than a "how" request: "My people need to know this;" "My sales force needs to know that," and so on. The trainers are supposed to know how—after all, that's why there *is* a training department—and so they run out to create or find a solution, which generally takes the form of an "intervention" or course. Their first priority is to find the right content. Only secondarily, if they have time or if they have a choice, do they consider *how* the content should be delivered. And, typically, there is little variety in the alternatives; instead, it is a rather limited "bag of tricks" ranging from lectures with slides, to handouts with a few exercises to fill in, to making or renting a video, or, increasingly, licensing an online solution. Occasionally, they will commission something completely new. In such cases, there is some hope for more learner-centered training—but only sometimes.

Many times training purchasers care only that the required content be available to people. This "CYA" approach was the reason that so much "shelfware" was purchased in the 1990s, especially in the Information Technology (IT) area, making a few training vendors very successful and starting a stampede into the IT area. (*Shelfware* refers to courses, typically on CD-ROM, that are bought but never used—they just sit on the shelf.) Now much of this training is quickly moving online. Organizations still sign large, multiyear contracts giving their employees access to the same, or, because of the technical constraints of the Web, an even less interesting, "tell-test" version of the curriculum. The content in the shelfware has just been replaced by the same content in what Paula Young of PricewaterhouseCoopers refers to as "click and fall asleep"—ware.[10]

Contest 2: What is the online equivalent of AFTRB? Email your entries to *Contest2@twitch speed.com.*

Don't get me wrong—I'm not saying we *shouldn't* think about what we want our people to know. However, figuring out the content, putting it onto slides, and reading the slides to people is not the same as people learning the content. Of course, most trainers would say the same thing. They often search for ways to "spice up" training sessions, as evidenced by the crowds around the booths of the companies selling "training props" at ASTD.

But even these props, like the Internet, are just forms of *delivery*. As anyone who has ever sent a FedEx package knows, having even the best delivery system in the world doesn't help if the person isn't home to receive the package. Increasingly, our trainees just "aren't home," when it comes to receiving training. So the package of content either gets left on the doorstep unopened, or—via bored looks, people getting up to get coffee, and scores on tests—gets "returned to sender." All trainers may *say* and even *think* that they consider the learner and want to have him or her involved as an active participant in the learning process. But it is amazing how many courses I have attended, often at the largest and most progressive companies in many industries, where the training consisted of showing and *reading every bullet point* on slides, slides often not even written by the person doing the training!

The online version of this exact same approach is found in almost every course available on the Internet. One company even touts as its great interactive invention that it inserts a slide show every so often among its printed text! The famous "anywhere anytime" is really, says Paula Young, "nowhere, no time," to which I would add "no thanks!" This is what Elliott Masie is talking about when he says the "e" in elearning should stand for the user's experience.[11] What is this experience, typically?

TELL-TEST

I never try to teach my students anything. I only try to create an environment in which they can learn.
— Albert Einstein

Boiled down to its core, most of what is billed as training, school, and learning consists of being told information, via lectures or reading, and then taking a test to "measure" whether the information "went in." I have found many other critics of the practice who have used similar or other terms for the same thing. John Holt used the term *tell-'em and test-'em* in the 1960s.[12] Don Tapscott uses the term *broadcast learning*.[13] Others, like Luyen Chou of Learn Technologies Interactive, talks about *the sage on the stage*.[14] ("Oh yes, we have a *lot* of sage on the stage," says one IBM employee.) The idea is the same. Someone who supposedly knows more than you (at least about the matter at hand), tells you about it, either live, through a lecture, or through readings such as textbooks, handouts, or online text.

Despite there being many creative trainers and teachers, the majority of our education has become a series of informational or logical presentations or readings, followed by some sort of quiz or examination. Tell-test is the basic teaching method used in corporations, schools, colleges, and, worst of all, in almost all the new "e-learning" experiences being offered with increasingly competitive frequency on the Internet, even when touted with such marketing hype as "the new way to learn"—a trademarked phrase.[15] Other than coming to you through a browser, it is not new at all; it is merely tell-test to be read onscreen.

Tell-test education is especially ineffective with today's younger workers; it just bores them to tears. It's not exactly working great with older workers, either.

Of course, many trainers and teachers point to all the various things they do to make the telling more interesting to their students. And they are right. Nevertheless, there are two problems. First, most attempts to make learning more interesting than plain tell-test are haphazard, relatively infrequent as a percentage of the total learning time, and not at the core of what is going on. This is not a guess. I have sat through course after course at investment banks and world-class companies, that were almost all slide shows, with a very occasional cartoon or joke thrown in. Questions? Often none at all—questions only slow the process of getting out of there.

A second, and more important problem, though, is that even when instructors and instructional designers *do* try to engage learners, they often miss the mark. How many of the so-called engaging "tools" or "tricks" trainers use are actually like the things that really engage people—fast-action-based or high-emotion-based movies and MTV (as opposed to just video), and video games (as opposed to *Bingo* or *Jeopardy!*)? Some of this may be due to the instructor's thinking "what would engage *me*," which may be fine for students from their own age cohort, but not for twitch-speed learners.

THE LINEAR/LOGICAL APPROACH

There are several reasons why tell-test is used so often in teaching and training.

A certain amount of its use can simply be chalked up to inexperience. Lao-tse tells us that "the novice teacher shows and tells incessantly." I can still remember my first days of teaching and consulting when I thought that the best way to communicate something was just to lay it out as logically as I could.

A second reason may be, as Paula Young says, that "some people are attracted to training and teaching because they love to stand up and story tell."

A third reason might be that the means or knowledge to do anything else is lacking. Roger Schank quotes John Dewey, writing in 1916 in *Democracy and Education* asking, "Why is it that, in spite of the fact that teaching by pouring in, learning by passive absorption, are universally condemned, that they are still so entrenched in practice? ... [E]nactment in practice requires that the school environment be equipped with agencies for doing ... to an extent rarely attained."[16] As Schank argues, we need other available alternatives. Even the hurdle of other alternatives is surmountable however, because, as this book shows, we can and are inventing and creating these alternatives.

But there is another, more profound reason for tell-test, which is linked to the way schools developed over the past 300 years. It has to do with the technologies of literacy—printing and reading.

A BRIEF HISTORY OF LEARNING AND TECHNOLOGY

In the view of Robert McClintock, Frank Moretti, and Luyen Chou, the evolution of, and transformations in, teaching and learning goes hand-in hand with the evolution of technology.

Originally, education and training was a process of imitation and coaching—"pick up rock and throw at animal." If you can't do it the first time, practice until you can. "No, do it this way." To make this repetitive skill-based learning both bearable and memorable, practicing became, even in animals, a form of play. This apprenticeship-type of learning—demonstration and practice—which is still with us, requires good coaches, typically in a one-to-one relationship. It is how people learn to do sports, to play musical instruments, and to master other physical skills. At its most basic, even language is not necessary, which is why athletes and musicians are often expertly trained by people who barely speak the same language as they do.

One early technical addition to this process was pictures and symbols. I don't have to physically show you; I can draw, in the sand or on a wall, a picture (or several) of a man throwing a spear, and a crude map showing you how to cross the river to get to the hunting grounds, and you can "get it." Cave paintings may contain some of this learning. Today, we use it every time we actually heed the flight attendant's directions to "remove the card from the seat pocket and follow along."

Undoubtedly the next great technological innovation in learning was the development of spoken language. Now I can describe to you, or tell you how to do something, even if you are not doing it. To help you remember, I can invent stories and parables that help you see points and make the learning memorable. This happened so long ago that it is wired into our brain. Many of the great teaching stories of the past, such as the *Iliad* and the *Odyssey*, are in meter and rhyme so that people could memorize them more easily. With spoken language, I can also ask questions and see whether you answer them in a way that shows understanding. This form of dialectical oral learning purportedly reached its peak with

Socrates. The so-called *dialectical* or *Socratic method* of questioning is still used, for example, in law schools. The requirements of this type of learning are good storytelling, excellent memory, and the ability to think on your feet.

Next, sometime around the time of Socrates, came the invention of literacy: writing and reading. While Socrates told his stories and asked questions, Plato wrote them down. Plato's *Dialogs* do not have to be retold or memorized (although maybe they should be). They can be read repeatedly. Ideas and learning could now be codified in other ways than just in stories and in questions and answers. Learners could read the thoughts of others on their own. These thoughts could be collected in libraries. Thinkers of one time and place could read what others wrote and build on it. The concept of the scholar arose as one who spent time reading many learned books. However this form of written knowledge and learning was both rare—limited to the few who could read and write (mostly clerics)—and fragile—a single fire in ancient times at the library at Alexandria, Egypt, eliminated a high percentage of the world's stored knowledge, making it difficult for scholars to learn. This type of learning required knowledge of reading and writing. Meanwhile, the other types did not die; they flourished in other parts of the general population.

We now come to the next-to-last great technological change—the invention of the printing press. Now educational materials could be distributed to anyone who wanted them. They could be posted on bulletin boards, such as Martin Luther did with his thirty-six theses, and translated into the vernacular, as Luther did with the Bible, giving access to learning to many people. Printing led to the art of logical expository writing of speeches, essays, and books.

It also led to a need to teach more people to read and write. Our modern mass education, according to Neil Postman, the distinguished New York University communications professor, author, and social commentator, began essentially as a product of the printing press, and was designed to bring everyone to a basic level of literacy. School was developed, he argues, primarily to teach people to read books.[16] The mass distribution of the book, says Luyen Chou, gave the ability to standardize education. "Within 200 years of the invention of the printing press in the West," he points out, "we had all the trappings of the modern educational system—division of learners into age groups, division of knowledge into disciplines, and, especially, textbooks."[18] But more was involved than just literacy. School, Postman says, is intended to equip us to *read* and to *think* along the lines of books; that is, linear, reasoned thinking. Book-based learning favors logical exposition and presentation. While at its best logical exposition can be riveting and compelling, relatively few of our teachers are capable of making it so on the fly. So, over time, much of teaching has been reduced to pre-prepared lecturing, and learning has turned into merely reading or listening. Hence the *telling* part, which stems principally, I think, from schools' desire to be logical.

Then came the industrial revolution and industrial competition, which led to further standardization of the school system ("school factories" says Seth Godin, in *Permission Marketing*[19]) and to the need for testing to put people in the correct jobs quickly. Standardized testing actually grew out of World War I military needs.[20] Hence, the *testing* part, which is even more recent.

Thus, tell-test education is in reality a "tradition" that is less than 300 years old. Now that may be longer than anybody's living experience, but it's a very short time in the history of human education, learning, and training.

Tell-test actually worked pretty well through the late nineteenth and the early and mid twentieth centuries, and wasn't changed much by other new technologies that came along such as the telephone, radio, and television. One argument to explain this is that these were less transformational technologies than language, literacy, or the printing press. But another reason that these technologies didn't have much influence on education, according to Luyen Chou, was that the education system made a concerted effort to keep them out. "I wonder," he says, "if there had been a telephone on every student's desk for educational purposes, how much it would have changed things."

Perhaps the literacy-oriented, industrially standardized tell-test system could have gone on longer, but, again, a major technological change intervened.

That change, as we all know, is computers, interactivity, and their associated technologies—the great technological revolution of the late twentieth century and beyond. Compared with the other changes, this change was a massive one. Bran Ferren, former head of research and development at Disney, calls multimedia computing "the most important technical innovation since the invention of language. It makes the print-ing press look small."[21]

Seemingly gradually to those living through it, but extremely quickly compared to the past, a number of extremely important changes happened:

- Written language became less dominant (Ferren goes so far as to pre-dict that reading and writing will eventually disappear, after having been a 300- or 400-year "fad"[22]).
- Linear organization was supplemented with a random-access (hyper-text) organization.
- Passive media, such as books and TV, were supplemented with active ones, such as interactive games and the Internet.
- Speed in general increased to twitch speed, leaving far less time and opportunity for reflection.

Probably the biggest reason that tell-test is failing to do the job it used to do is that the world of the learner has changed so dramatically. Conse-quently, learners no longer see themselves as receptacles to be filled with content; instead they see themselves as creators and doers. That these changes happened so quickly is a primary reason why education and training hasn't changed to keep up. Even in normal times, education is slow to change. But now there is the phenomenon in which kids have totally outpaced their parents and elders in the new ways of the world.

Learners have access to and experience with so much before they ever hit a training or education classroom that they are rarely "empty ves-sels" (or tabulae rasae) when they get there. In business, it is extremely rare to find an audience that knows *absolutely nothing* about the subject matter at hand. *Everyone* knows something about it—we just don't know who knows what. So, by telling everything, we end up boring all the peo-ple most of the time. Even online, the supposed advantage of technology-based learning—go at your own pace, skip what you already know—often is more of a slogan than a reality. While people may choose to listen in their cars to commercially produced "great lectures" about art, literature, or music (or even business) in order to learn more about such subjects, I've yet to meet anyone who *wanted* to hear a tape—audio or video—of any organization's internal business training class; it's almost

always worse than being there. There once was a company that specialized in reducing the length of corporate tapes so that they it would take
less time to listen to them. The company was typically able to reduce a
60-minute lecture or speech to 5 or 10 minutes of real content.

That's the kind of improvement we need to be working toward. In
terms of learning methods, we are all desperately in need of new
approaches to replace tell-test. *We have to stop telling, because almost
nobody's listening.* Who is working to invent these new methodologies
that speak to this highly technological generation? Precious few, but
some are, including the creators of Digital Game-Based Learning. But
even among the people trying to invent new ways there is no consensus;
in fact, there is a lot of internecine criticism, largely because people have
very different ideas about how people actually learn.

THE GREAT "HOW DO PEOPLE LEARN?" DEBATE

We know more about how to improve the use of diapers than of brains.
— Stan Davis and Jim Botkin, *The Monster Under the Bed*

Asking the question "How do people learn?" is a lot like asking, "What is
the true religion?" Every religious person is convinced his or her religion
is the true one, and yet there are, according to the Religions of the World
Organization, "literally thousands" of different religions in the world.[23]
The truth is that learning is a highly complex phenomenon with a huge
number of variables. While we know many things about learning, we
don't completely know how people learn. In fact, we really can't even
define what learning is with a measurable degree of precision, although,
like many things, we know it when we see it or feel ourselves doing it.

There is a whole branch of science, known as epistemology, that is
devoted to the topic. Inside and outside this field there is much heated
discussion, lively debate, and research on the topic of learning. But not
nearly enough.

In *The Monster Under the Bed,* an excellent book about corporate
learning, Stan Davis and Jim Bodkin point out how relatively little
research is actually done in this area. Nationally, they say, "less than .1 percent [yes, that's one-tenth of 1 percent] of our school budgets is destined
for educational research—the lowest figure for research spent on any

major budgeted activity. Compared with health, defense, space, energy, or new products, new knowledge on the learning process is definitely a poor relation.... The federal government spends three times more for agricultural research, twenty-one times more for space research, and thirty times more for research on health. We know more about how to improve the use of diapers than of brains."[24]

So, absent more research, we are left with a variety of theories of learning, each with its own self-proclaimed experts, each with a particular theory of learning to champion. Let's look at some examples:

Learning happens when one is engaged in hard and
    challenging activities.
Learning comes from observing people we respect.
Learning comes from doing.
Learning is imitation, which is unique to man and a few animals.
Learning is a developmental process.
You can't learn unless you fail.
Learning is primarily a social activity.
You need multiple senses involved.
Learning takes practice, says one. No says another, that's "Drill
    and kill."
People learn in context. People learn when elements are
    abstracted from context.
We learn by principles, says one. By procedures, says the other.
They can't *think*, says the one. They can't *add*, says the other.
Everyone has a different "learning style."
We learn X percent of what we hear, Y percent of what we hear,
    Z percent of what we do.
Situated learning, says one. Case-based reasoning, says another.
    Goal-based learning says a third. All of the above, says a fourth.
Learning should be fun, peeps the girl in the corner. Learning is
    hard work, answers another.
We learn automatically, from the company we keep, says another.
People learn in "chunks."
No, "chunking" removes context.
People learn just in time, only when they need to.
People learn aurally, visually, and kinesthetically.

People learn through feedback.
People learn through reflection.
People learn through a loop of doing and reflecting.
People learn through coaching.
People learn through failure.
People learn from constructing things for themselves.
People learn from models.
People learn from mistakes.
People learn from stories and parables.
People learn by constructing their own knowledge.
People learn when they're working.
People learn by playing.
People learn through games.
People learn when they're having fun.
People learn when things are relevant.
And on, and on, and on.

For all the books published on this subject, do we know how people learn?

Behind the theories of most trainers are the researchers, doing studies. Most are academics, each taking a tiny piece of the puzzle, and doing very small experiments. Their research, while potentially helpful, is often reported in ways that only an academic audience can understand or even tolerate reading. Unfortunately this academic style is often what is fed to our budding teachers. There is an urgent need for researchers on learning to present their findings in more easily comprehensible ways, both to teachers and to the general public, so that we may use as much of it as possible in our designs, as well as understand what areas have *not* been researched, which are many. Some reconcile the variety of theories of how people learn by saying people are different—everyone has his (or her) own "learning style." Learning styles are big these days, and certainly important, but they are also problematical in designing learning. How many styles are there? (Again, differing answers.) If they are really different for everyone, how does this help us? Do I need different learning for all of them? Psychology has the "fundamental attribution error," which is the tendency for humans to explain human behavior in terms of the traits of individuals when powerful situational forces are at work. Could our need to think of ourselves as individuals be blinding us to other powerful forces? While learning styles are an important *piece* of the learning picture, they do beg the question of whether there are fundamental ways in which we *all* learn.

I think there are. And it seems to me, from my experience as a trainer and teacher, that there is another way of looking at all of this, a way that is, surprisingly, often missing in this debate, and that is: *How do they learn* *what?* It turns out that this perspective is very useful, because it helps us a great deal in constructing new ways to learn, including (but not only) Digital Game-Based Learning.

There is a variety of materials or content to be learned by students, ranging from information/facts, to tasks, to processes, to skills, to theories and more—all of which are best learned differently. So, it seems to me that the first cut is not by type of learner, but by type of material to be learned. Learning style, or type of learner, can still be, and should be, a second cut.

To illustrate what I mean, take a budding doctor in medical school. Among other things, he or she needs to learn the English and Latin names of all the parts of the body (facts); learn the ways the body systems behave (theory, observation, dynamics); learn how to perform procedures (physical skills); learn to diagnose (process, judgment, reason); learn to talk with patients and manage time (behavior, skill); learn to present cases to other doctors (language); learn to do research (organization, discovery); and so on. While we hear a great deal of "this is how people learn," and, more recently, "this is how this style of person learns," we rarely, if ever, hear "these are ways that people learn *facts*. These are ways that people learn *skills*. These are ways that people learn *theory*. These are the ways people learn *judgment*. These are ways that people learn to *reason*. These are ways that people learn to *create* new things. These are ways that people learn to *change their minds*." Once people begin to view things with this perspective, some of the problems in creating learning begin to sort themselves out:

- We learn *facts* through questions, memorization, association, and drill.
- We learn *skills (physical or mental)* through imitation, feedback, continuous practice, and increasing challenge.
- We learn *judgment* through hearing stories, asking questions, making choices, and getting feedback and coaching.

- We learn *behaviors* through imitation, feedback, and practice.
- We learn *processes* through explanation and practice.
- We learn *about existing theories* through logical explanation and questioning.
- We learn to *create and test theories* through experimentation and questioning.
- We learn *reasoning* through puzzles and examples.
- We lean *procedures* through imitation and practice.
- We learn *creativity* through playing.
- We learn *language* through imitation, practice, and immersion.
- We learn *programming and other systems* through principles and graduated tasks.
- We learn *observation* through examples, doing, and feedback.
- We learn *speeches or performance roles* by memorization, practice, and coaching.
- We learn *the behavior of dynamic systems* by observation and experimentation.
- We learn *grammar* through—how *do* we learn grammar?

This list is by no means complete or exhaustive, but is meant to illustrate that the same learning methods are not used for every type of thing we learn.

Even the old "learning by doing" saw, "we learn x% of what we hear, y% of what we hear and see, and z% of what we do"—which is sometimes filled-in with numbers that I'm almost certain are apocryphal, but which are heavily skewed toward the doing—is not *always* true. There are things all of us have heard or seen that we'll never forget, and lots of things we've done (like put our car keys somewhere) that we can never remember.

As anyone who has a menial job will tell you, there is certainly such a thing as "boring doing." Doing by itself does not make anything interesting, or make you necessarily learn it. It has to be doing *what.*

Performing and using this kind of analysis does not make us content-centered. On the contrary, it allows us to focus more directly on the learner. Each of these types of learning is important to a learner, and each has its place. To return to our doctor example, he or she needs to use many different means of learning to master all the different information and skills that he or she has to learn. Some argue that memorization, which is one way to learn facts, is not important. Would you want a doctor who didn't know what the tibia is? Or didn't know that *x* drug interacts with that *y* drug? There are other ways to learn facts besides memorization, such as questions, association, and mnemonics, but some variation of good old flash cards often works fine. No need for a complex simulation or learning-by-doing project here. Nor do you need to actually *do* unethical or illegal behavior (even in simulation) to learn that it is wrong. Different types of content to be learned require different skills, learning tools, and methods.

Of course, *within* any of these ways of learning there is considerable room for style, age, gender, and other individual variations. We must fit the "how do people learn?" question to "what it is they are learning."

What is so exciting to me about this is that it leaves us lots of room and opportunity to invent new ways of learning things. In fact, people do this all the time. It's called creative teaching.

INSTRUCTIONAL DESIGN—HELPING OR HURTING?

There is a field known as Instructional Design, which is supposed to be helping us out here. How is it doing in getting us away from content-centered, tell-test learning? Unfortunately, not too well, in my observation.. Much instructional design is done very "by the book," and the book (a system known as ISD, or Instructional Systems Design) is not very creative. It tends to have a lot of "these are your learning objectives," "in this module you will learn to. . . ," and so on. This may seem logical to the instructional designers, but I'm not sure it really helps people learn, especially people whose approach to everything may, in fact, be less logical.

"Nine times out of ten, if you see a great training program," writes Thiagi in "The Attack on ISD,"[25] "you'll find it wasn't created by someone schooled in ISD and following that process." In the same article, John Murphy of the consulting firm Executive Edge, observes, "The idea of learning styles seems to consume an enormous amount of time and concern in what the ISD people claim is their 'technology.'" Murphy goes on to say that there is very little concern or focus on business results, outcomes, or the learners. My own experience leads me to agree. I would hope that by adding an instructional designer to a design team a project would get the invention and creativity it needs. But I'm not sure that the opposite is not more often true: in the name of their own doctrinaire think-ing, instructional designers too often create what Thiagi calls "boring, cookie-cutter outcomes." Designing effective learning does not, I believe, require any formal instruction or specialized knowledge. Rather, it takes a thoughtful and creative approach to reaching the desired outcomes.

Now I'm sure that there are many instructional designers who con-sider themselves highly creative, and I'd love to hear from you about any exciting Digital Game-Based Learning projects that you have designed. I encourage you to contact me at the book's Web site: www.twitch-speed.com.

THE ROLE OF PRACTICE

This is really important. Almost all training, and to a lesser extent school, tends to take place in bursts. If business people don't know something, an "intervention" (read *interruption*) will be designed to teach it to them. This is fine if what they don't know is a fact, such as "tomorrow is a holiday," or other less useful but important things. However, much of what we want people to learn are skills and behaviors—things that are learned and acquired slowly, over much time, often an entire lifetime. The *only* way to make this happen is through *practice.* "How do I get to Carnegie Hall?" asks the tourist in the old joke. "Practice, practice, practice" is the answer. Musi-cians know it, athletes know it, and surgeons know it. We *all* know it—who wouldn't want the more experienced surgeon to do our operation? Prac-tice makes perfect. (And, say the neurobiologists, permanent!)

But there is almost no recognition of this in training. To learn the skill of making music, we take lessons (often all our lives) and we practice. Who practices the skills of conversation, leadership, or language? Smart learners, that's who. But with rare exceptions, such as the 2-year-long case method at Harvard Business School, people mostly have to do it on their own. Training doesn't help. It stops.

A few training programs have tried to address this. Some provide mentors. Others have created immersion-type courses that try to put the learner into the equivalent of a "foreign country" environment and let them try things out. However, this is usually limited to the length of the "course". Maybe you'll get an hour or two of practice in a 6-hour program. But what do you do next week?

Of course, practicing can get boring, as any schoolchild or musician knows. I remember that as a lute player, I would invent games to help me through all the technical work I had to do. "OK, now I have to be able to do this ten times in a row without a mistake, or I have to start over. Can I do this with my eyes closed? Can I do it four times as fast? Can I do it in a different rhythm?" Much of the tedium went away in the act of playing the games.

Pretty much everything we need to know has to be practiced—from the alphabet, to the multiplication tables, to calculation, to reading, to speaking with people, to negotiating, to leadership, to objecting in a courtroom, to working in teams. It needs to be done over and over every week, or every day, especially, but not only, right before we will use the skill (it does you only limited good to practice a language only a day before you go somewhere.) Unless we are either incredibly disciplined (like those people who keep toothbrushes at work) or masochists, we need some incentive, some fun way to make us practice—to *want* to do it. This is one reason why games are an important piece of learning. When Jim Freund was using computer games to teach secretaries computer skills at Citibank in the 1980s, he wouldn't say "OK, here's the training." He would say, truthfully, "Now for the fun part of your day." Any teacher worth his or her salt uses practice games with kids, but very few long-term, engaging, practice opportunities exist for adults. This is a big mistake.

WHY IS CHANGE SO DIFFICULT?

We *know* things aren't working:

> Faced with crippling skill shortages employers are spending sky-rocketing amounts of money training workers. The problem? Many programs just don't work. $5.3–16.8 billion is wasted annually. Training problems: 1. Employees aren't motivated. 2. Programs are poorly designed. Companies may unwittingly support unimaginative or dull programs that employees find deter learning. 3. Trainers lack expertise—those providing training may not know their audience, or they lack teaching skills.[26]

It certainly isn't hard to get nods and agreement that our corporate education and schools need help and change. In fact, it would be hard to find any really staunch defenders of the status quo. Yet, aside from isolated classrooms and pockets of innovation, very little changes. Why aren't we doing anything about this problem? Why is training and education still so content-centered, tell-test, and ineffective? Why is change so difficult and slow in training and schools?

The first thing to note is that in both the education and the training worlds, some change is happening, and some of it is happening quickly. Infrastructure is changing—the majority of business workers *and* classrooms are now wired to the Internet. Businesses, colleges, and universities are moving increasingly from instructor-led training to technology-based and Web-based training.

Unfortunately, aside from some increased ease of access (mitigated in business by the fact that you often must do it at your desk or at home) most of the changes that are happening have made learning no less content-centered or tell-test than it was before. It's still something that most workers don't want to do.

Reasons Why

Some of the reasons training and education is still so content and tell-test-oriented are:

Money. In the words of Kevin Oakes, CEO of Click2learn, "Corporations have a defined training need. Tell-test meets that need at its lowest level and it's the cheapest, and so that's why you see that being most prevalent. Doing a sophisticated simulation or a game costs more money, takes more time—it provides a better learning experience, but the corporation's got to be willing to say that that better learning experience is really what I'm going for. Most corporations are looking for quick solutions to their immediate problems rather than long-term better educational benefits."[27]

We don't know what today's learners want and need. While it is clear to many or most that today's learners need something different, even if it were free it is not at all clear what that alternative should be. The political debate on education focuses on getting better teachers, smaller classes, and more parental involvement through programs such as vouchers. These are not bad ideas, but they really don't address a key part of the problem. The issue is that most of our educators, coming from a previous generation and set of experiences, generally don't understand the new generation's needs or learning methods. Ditto for trainers.

Even if we have some idea of what it is, we don't know how to do it. Think about it. If you were (or are) a teacher or trainer, and you had to, starting tomorrow, do all your training in an incredibly engaging way without telling anybody anything, could you do it? How? There certainly isn't any "right way"—we have to experiment. Even the best way to experiment is not at all clear. When I arrived at Harvard Business School in 1978, having previously been a very non-business—oriented musician, I just assumed, naively, that business school would teach me *how to do business.* I was very wrong. What I soon discovered—pretty much to my complete shock—is that they *couldn't* teach us how to do business, because *nobody knows!* Business is much too complex and fast moving, and has far too many variables to figure out "how to do it." In fact, "the very best that we can do," said the Harvard professors, "is to let you read a lot of little stories (i.e., 'cases') about how various things in business were done in the past, and talk about what lessons they teach us. We expect these lessons will be of some help to you in the future, although we can't be sure."

Training and teaching is a lot like the rest of business—there is no formula for doing it right. We are all trying to figure it out. Given the changes in the world, we will probably need the help of our students to do it. Today's generation, as Don Tapscott points out repeatedly, is the first to know more than their elders about a key technology—computers.[28] How did today's kids learn so much about computers? Not through tell-test in a classroom, but in their own newly acquired learning style.

We are in desperate need of new ideas and methodologies that will engage these new generations and help them learn. We can no longer tell them anything, because they're not listening. We can't drill, because it does often kill. Who is working on inventing new methodologies that speak to this highly technological generation? Not enough of us, I'm afraid.

It's a big, fragmented system. The training and education system is huge. In the United States, there are 53 million K-12 students.[30] Add in college and training and there are probably closer to 150 million in the training and education system—more than the entire population of all but a handful of countries in the world. It's also a highly fragmented system. Unlike France or Japan where education is national and every student in every classroom learns the same thing on the same day, U.S. education is local. Each state or school district, and, in many cases, individual schools or teachers, decide what will be taught, when it will be taught, and how it will be taught. In business, every company does its training slightly differently, with the differences sometimes being only a matter of words, but very important to the people in the organization. What are *workers* in one company are *employees* in another and *associates* in a third, and this seems so important that training people will spend unbelievable amounts to conform to it.

Like all big systems, training and education are slow to change. "If the cure for cancer were offered to schools," said one observer who preferred to remain anonymous, "in 20 years they would still have cancer. Not because they think cancer is good, but because the decision and change process is so long and hard." But change is sorely needed. Almost half of U.S. adults are classified as illiterate or near illiterate.[31] Corporations are experiencing an influx of workers who don't have basic skills.

One of the saddest stories I remember from my time teaching high school in New York City's East Harlem is of one-on-one tutoring with ninth grade nonreaders. One activity we did daily was to read the headlines in the *New York Daily News*—pretty much the most basic paper you can get. One day, the front-page headline (and in the *Daily News* it is the *entire* front page) read something like "DA SEEKS LIFE." I was offering, as was my custom, 5 cents per word, and so a young lady tried her hardest: "dah" she began. She did know her phonics, but she totally missed the context. We must, and can, do better.

Reform of big systems *is* possible, with good leadership. In the summer before Harvard Business School, I was given a book to read, *My Years at General Motors* by Alfred P. Sloane. He figured out a new way to organize a large company that hadn't been tried before, and it was extremely successful. Obviously, what worked for GM in the 1930s will not work for the future of education. Let us hope, however, that the leaders working on the problem today incorporate into their solutions the very real issues of generational change.

The reformers are fragmented as well. It would be great if there were just *one* reform party, but as we saw earlier, there is little agreement among educational and learning reformers, and much infighting and jockeying for both intellectual and, increasingly, financial superiority.

We need to get the infrastructure built first. Clark Aldrich of the Gartner Group thinks that infrastructure is where people's focus will be until around 2002. After that, they will concentrate on meeting learners needs by making better content. "What Gartner is saying is that 2003-plus will be the 'content is king' stage. That will be when really great stuff comes out because there'll be good standards, there'll be good systems out there, there'll be machines that can run it in terms of graphic cards and having DirectX. I think around 2003 and 2004 is when the great content is going to come out."[30]

It might mess with the system. Schools, and to a lesser extent training, are big, big bureaucracies, and like all bureaucracies, they are very entrenched in their ways. Sometimes innovations require changes. At the Dalton School, Luyen Chou designed a terrific new way to learn, but to get it to work effectively longer class periods were needed, which involved changing the entire school schedule. "Schedule is one of the hardest thing to change at any school," says Chou. "It's like written in stone. People die on their swords." There are lots of "system" obstacles to innovation. Teachers' roles change. The amount of time they have to put into things changes. Evaluation changes. Assessments have to change. Change creates disruption. Think about changing length of the school year, or of a school day, or of summer vacations. In training, think about changing the "course" as the basic unit of instruction. Companies are already finding it hard to move to the paradigm of computer training at your desk—people at their desks are expected to be working. "The real test," says John Parker of First Union Bank, "is will the floor manager accept it—even with the 'don't disturb me, I'm training' sign on the back of the chair."[32]

It sort of works. If it ain't broke, why fix it. Students at prestigious schools that have the money and brainpower to innovate, are still "succeeding" from the administration's point of view by, for example, getting into good colleges. Similarly, top colleges and companies that still draw "the cream of the crop," feel little pressure to change. The issue is more with the other 99 percent. As Alcoholics Anonymous and other recovery programs have taught us, it is impossible to fix a problem until we admit it exists. Most people do not think we have a problem in methodology. If you listen to the politicians' speeches, all they want is "a good teacher in every classroom." The cry is always for more "good" teachers—if we only had that, along with smaller class sizes, all our problems would be solved. Unfortunately, what politicians (or parents, or educators) mean by "better" teachers or trainers, is better in the old, nineteenth century tell-test sense. That just isn't going to cut it with the Games Generation.

Retraining the trainers and teachers is hard. Of course it is, because we don't yet know what to train them to do!

Accountability is harder. We certainly know how to measure tell-test—use the test scores; but measuring innovative programs is harder. With 53 million K-12 students in the United States,[33] multiple-choice exams are the easiest tests to administer. Nevertheless, they are a very poor measure of process-oriented learning. As soon as you move away from standardization, measurement is difficult. So, accountability is a big problem, just as it is in business, where the task of matching training efforts with business results in a very complex system is so difficult that people tend to fall back on scores as their only "gettable" metric.

Clearly, there are a lot of problems to overcome. But there is hope. As I said earlier, solutions to the content-centered, tell-test problem are not impossible. There are solutions that are already being tried and that are clearly within our means. High among them is Digital Game-Based Learning.

4

Digital Game-Based Learning
New Hope for Learner-Centered
Training and Education

The future has arrived; it's just not evenly distributed.
— William Gibson

The "e" in e-learning should stand for the user's experience.
— Elliott Masie

Anyone who makes a distinction between games and education clearly does not know the first thing about either one.
— Marshall McLuhan

LEARNER-CENTERED EDUCATION

As we have seen, until the present, almost all training and education has been tell-test, either content-centered or instructor-centered. In this form of learning, the learner has no choice in the curriculum, and no choice in the way it is presented to him or her. Not that the people who decide these things have any harm in mind. They have a goal—getting people through the material—and they do their best to achieve it using, as McLuhan says, "the patterns that they find convenient to themselves."[1] As most of us have been taught all our school and training lives as learners, it is our job to absorb whatever is thrown at us, however much we may not like it or the way it is presented, because we will surely be tested and "measured" on our ability to retain it. The traditional way to get people's attention in a content-centered and tell-test environment is to announce "this will appear on the test."

Yet, there are other effective ways of learning besides tell-test. Educational and training reformers from John Dewey, Maria Montessori and Johan Heinrich Pestalozzi, to Seymour Papert and Elliott Masie, have been crying out for years for a new type of education that begins with the learner's experience—combining what the learner enjoys, with what the learner needs to know (or know how to do), and asking how he or she can learn it in the shortest, most effective, and most engaging fashion possible. A number of approaches have been proposed for creating more learner-centered education from "learn at your own pace," to "learn in your own style" (visual, verbal kinesthetic, or various Myers-Briggs-based categorizations), or "learn according to your own mix of intelligences," to "select only the learning objects that you want." Other approaches have centered on users' selecting and solving problems that they find relevant or interesting, and allowing users to follow any path they choose through hypertext. "Adaptive" systems, which change according to users' responses, as well as various forms of just-in-time learning, show great promise as well. All of these have their advantages, particularly over content or instructor-centered learning.

So that we continue to bear it in mind, it is worth repeating that the type of education we now think of as traditional—the current content-centered classroom—has no particular legitimacy to it as a way to learn. It is but a mere 300-or-less years old, created as part of the mass distribution of books and the Industrial Revolution. Before the time of printed books, learning was done primarily through questioning, storytelling, imitation, practice, and play.

As we now enter an era in which relationships and communication technology are changing radically, and where more and more of our communication is taking place by means other than the printed word, it is appropriate that our educational methods change accordingly. Whether, as Bran Ferren seriously suggests, reading and writing will eventually disappear after having been a 300- to 400-year "fad" is not clear.[2] What is clear is that reading and writing have already been seriously supplemented—and in some cases almost completely supplanted—in a number of areas of our lives, such as the way most Americans get their news and entertainment. This shift is already having its consequences. As we have seen, literacy rates are appalling!

LEARNING TECHNOLOGIES—A DOUBLE-EDGED SWORD

The current, potential technology-based solution to all of this, the net-worked multimedia computer (which is principally what is meant by "learning technologies") is, in fact, a double-edged sword. Even when there is a computer in every classroom—or even a laptop for every learner—these computers, even with the Internet, will not by them-selves produce a better-educated population, at work or in school. The issue is not even training the teachers or trainers. What would we train them to do today? Surf the Web? Critics rightly point out that it takes a very short time—often less than an hour—to learn to manipulate a com-puter. The issue is the software—and the ideas and approaches to learn-ing that it encodes—for which the computer is only the vehicle. It is often forgotten that while computer hardware gets old very quickly, good soft-ware lasts a long time. Many people are still using programs written 5, even 10, years ago. The problem is that in terms of learning software there is relatively little out there, other than things that provide better access to resources, for teachers or trainers to learn how to use to improve learning. (There are, of course, a few notable exceptions, such as the Archaeotype project and other examples, which are discussed later.)

While learning technology has not progressed very far at the school level, more has been done inside companies, which, as Stan Davis and Jim Botkin point out, are typically far ahead of education in their use of tech-nology.[3] We now have literally thousands of business-oriented courses available over the Internet, with many companies competing to offer them. We have "learning technology specialists" in companies, and sev-eral magazines and newsletters that cover the field.

But the problem with most companies' use of learning technologies from the *learner's* point of view is that they are used today primarily to make things easier for the *trainer.* "OK, these 50 or 100 courses are avail-able. We've done our job," training departments often say, or imply. The so-called learning technologies rarely improve things for the learner; in fact, they often do just the opposite. Training—even on the Web—is still a distasteful chore, to be done in the *dis*comfort of your desk or home. While some progress was made in the CD-ROM era toward more learner-centered approaches, the Web has brought us "two giant steps backwards," in the words of Kevin Oaks, CEO of Click2learn,[4] at least temporarily. Most of what exists so far in terms of Web and other technology used for learning is so elementary or old-fashioned in its learning approaches that, apart from remote delivery, it adds little to learning and often subtracts from it—chat rooms and email tutors notwithstanding. People do it because they *have* to, or because it helps them reach a goal. But it is not something most people *want* to do.

ENORMOUS POTENTIAL

CBT is on the coma end of the engagement spectrum; computer games occupy the other end.
—Bob Filipczak, *Training* magazine

Yet—and this is the other edge of the sword—the *potential* for learner-centered learning through technology is enormous, far greater than most of us think. (One comment often made by observers of technological change is that we tend to overestimate the short-term effects of new technologies and underestimate long-term ones.) At the same time as we have made such little progress on the learning-software side of technology, we have made unbelievable progress on the entertainment side. In less than 30 years, we have produced a brand new from of entertainment, the computer and video game, that kids, and increasingly adults (the average game player in 2000 was close to 31 years old [5]), are practically addicted to.

While writing this book, I invited some friends and their two children, ages 6 and 9 years, to visit for a weekend. The place was a spectacular setting on a beautiful lake in Maine, complete with private swimming area, raft, canoes, kayaks, woods to explore, and so on. The kids spent the entire weekend playing computer games (I had plenty for them to try) except when they were literally forced by their parents to go outside to canoe and swim, or to eat. The boys awoke each morning before 6 a.m. to play, and were huddled over the computers when the rest of us came down for breakfast; they were also the last to go to sleep at night. And I'm not talking about *Doom* or *Quake* here: these games were reasonably educational, including *Freddi Fish 4* (a detective-style adventure) and *The Logical Journey of the Zoombinis* (a series of logic puzzles designed as a quest) for the younger boy, and *Age of Empires II (The Age of Kings)* and *Starship Command* for the older boy.

Of course, we need to give children a more balanced life than just games (this weekend as part of my research team was an exception for the boys), but my point is that *this is powerful stuff*. It has the holding power of television, and it is far more powerful than television in its ability to teach. With the proper approach, as I will show in the remainder of this book, it can strongly motivate and help adults as well as children to learn.

How can we waste this opportunity?

Television is a worthwhile comparison because some of the same things were said about television way back when. Unfortunately, despite having created thousands of slow-paced documentaries on nature, space, and other topics, and despite the pioneering work of shows such as *Sesame Street* and *Blues Clues*, we have hardly realized any of television's potential as a learning tool, except in the realm of advertising. It has been · excluded from the formal education establishment exactly as McLuhan predicted it would be.

I believe that we have done pretty badly with television's entertainment potential as well, despite the *millions* of hours of entertainment programming created (and this from a self-avowed fan of good sitcoms). This is due, I think, to two factors. First, as in movies and books, there is a shortage of true writing talent. Unfortunately, for the dreams of all those with stars in their eyes, script writing is quite difficult, and there are relatively few great or even good writers in the world. (Good sitcoms often go sour when the original, highly talented writers move on to a new project.) Second, like shooting movies, shooting television is an expensive, labor-intensive undertaking. The combination of these two reasons explains why so much money can be spent—today's movies cost an average of $50 million[6] for only 100 or so minutes of entertainment—without producing very many good movies.

So, television has failed us as an educational medium. But are computer games the same as television? I don't think so. Not that the best games aren't hard or inexpensive to make—they are. Although the days of "one programmer in a garage" are pretty much gone, and game development costs have risen dramatically (to an average of over $5 million in 2004),[7] with the inclusion of better graphics and sound, most computer games are produced without big crews and without multiple takes on location or in a studio, but on, you guessed it, computers! This dramatically reduces costs. Although some games require shooting film or video, most do not, and the tendency is to use more realistic animation than live video. (For some of the reasons behind this, read Scott McCloud's *Understanding Comics,* [8] a book to which I will return later.) If we compare the number of people it takes to make a commercial game with the number of people that it takes to make a movie or TV show, it is no wonder that the movie costs are ten times higher!

But there is also another factor. I believe that it is easier to make a good, educational game than it is to make a good, educational movie or TV show. It may be easier because a great game can start with just a small captivating idea, or because tools exist and it is possible to reuse code and assets, or because successful entertainment models can be repurposed relatively easily, or because small teams have produced excellent learning games. Not that the edutainment industry has done it so well, but numerous successful examples do exist. Some will certainly dispute this, and I do not deny that making a good game is hard, nor do I take the slightest bit away from the true genius of the best game designers such as Shigero Myamoto, Sid Meier, and Will Wright. But making a decent or good educational game is easier, I think, than making a decent or good educational TV show. This is particularly true for Digital Game-Based Learning, because unlike commercial games, these games do not have to be either completely original or extremely long to be effective.

Of course, the number of *great* learning games, like any great creative work, will always be limited. But an individual with a good game idea and access to some resources is much more likely to produce a good learning product than a similar individual with a good movie idea and the same amount of resources. This may change over time, but it is certainly possible to make a good, reasonably polished training game today for well under $1 million, and people have done it with much less. As I will show later, the very simplest Digital Game-Based Learning can be produced for almost nothing, and many shells on the market enable one to achieve professional-looking results with no game programming at all!

It is important to note that I am not talking about huge visual extravaganzas such as the LucasArts *Star Wars* games or *Riven*, or complex story lines like the Ultima series. Obviously, these take time and resources. You need 2 years to make a good game, says designer Peter

Molyneux.[9] Yes, you do, if you want to make a game as original, long, interesting, and complicated as his *Black and White*. But the learning and training games we need to create are often much simpler, at least initially. They essentially involve putting some good gameplay around interactions that are helpful to learning. They can revolve around practicing a certain type of interaction or reflex skill, such as typing or communications or language. They can take one simple idea and drive you to happy madness, such as *Lemmings*. They can involve you in a story with plot and characters such as *In$ider*. The key, as Ashley Lipson says, is to start from the perspective of gameplay, rather than learning: "It must first of all be a great game, and only then, a teacher."[10] In fact the best example of this is Lipson's *Objection!*, a fun, useful, and highly successful legal-training game, designed by this professor of law in his spare time (see Chapter 9).

So, to return to learner-centered learning, we have at this point in time an enormous opportunity to mix the never-before-seen engaging qualities of games with the content of business and education to create truly learner-centered education and training in several senses:

- It will be training and learning that people *want* to do (or, when we really succeed, *rush* to do).
- It will take a wide variety of forms, just as games do, from the more physical (e.g., *Mindstorms* and other products by Seymour Papert), to the more cerebral (*Strategy Co-Pilot*).
- It will combine the appropriate learning methods for each type of content with a variety of game styles, giving players a wide choice.
- It will be "stealth learning" so that players enjoy themselves while doing it and realize that they have learned after.
- It will be combined with reflection and other types of learning where appropriate to produce a total result.

Clark Aldrich of the Gartner Group suggests that we are in a period of putting together the infrastructure for Digital Game-Based Learning.[11] As our businesses and universities, schools, and homes become wired so that broadband connections are available to everyone, the infrastructure to fully realize this new type of learning will be in place. These are all in the process of happening. One thing that is certain, is that the games industry is waiting for this infrastructure with saliva dripping from its mouth and betting hundreds of millions of dollars that it will happen soon. [12]

TOWARD A LEARNER-CENTERED ENVIRONMENT: WHAT IF THE TRAINING AND EDUCATION WORLD WERE LIKE THE GAMES WORLD?

Game designers have a better take on the nature of learning than curriculum designers.
— Seymour Papert, MIT

The games world is an example of a totally user-centered (i.e., consumer-centered) environment. To get some idea of what a learner-centered training or education environment might feel like, I thought it would be useful to describe the games world, and let you make the leap to training and education. I will do this from three points of view: the viewpoint of the player, the designer, and the seller. These correspond roughly to the learner, the teacher, and the vendor worlds of education and training.

Different Point of View 1: The Player

If you are a game player, a whole lot of people are catering to you. They are trying to get you to spend your $49 for *their* game, and they know they have to work hard to do it. They bombard you with advertising and information about their games. They package their products in an appealing way. They provide free demos, available via download from the Web whenever possible, or else bundled in your favorite magazines. They feed you information about each new game coming out, and you anticipate it for months. You upgrade your equipment—PC, console, or both—as often as you can afford to.

Nobody chooses your games for you; you pick them yourself. And there is information galore about these products at your fingertips. There are over a dozen paper-based magazines, and an equally large number of Web sites, that provide you with reviews of every game with star-based ratings, side-by-side comparisons, chats with other players, previews of games in development, interviews with creators, tricks, codes, cheats—

anything you might want to know to make an informed choice. When you buy a game and use it, you have access to tech support, which is essentially coaching about the installation and use of the game.

You expect a lot for your 49 bucks. You expect this game to be better than the last one you bought—better graphics, better and faster AI (artificial intelligence), more exciting game play. You expect it to be networked so you can play with others over the Internet. You expect that the learning curve will be progressive and easy, and the game will keep you "in the zone" for its entire life. You expect to receive upgrades, patches, and even unexpected surprises from the publisher. You expect the game to give you at least 30 and maybe even up to 100 hours of play and fun. You expect it to be part of a series, so that you can go on to greater challenges when you finish. (With arcade games, where you pay by the quarter, you actually expect the fun, and the challenge to be able to go on forever.)

What if all this were true for training? For education?

Different Point of View 2: The Designer

If you are a game designer, you are always thinking about your audience: "How can I keep a maximum number of players on the edge of their seats for hours and hours?" is the problem you're always trying to solve. This is different from a movie scriptwriter, who is trying to elicit the maximum amount of emotion in 90 or 100 minutes. It's somewhat like a fiction writer who will take the audience on a journey for days, but with much less absolute control—because games are interactive, the player has a big say in what happens. So as a game designer you are thinking a lot about the kinds of interaction the player will have with your game—its "interactive structure." Now, of course, you have chosen a topic or subject for the game, and you are thinking about how you will introduce everything you can about that topic via the gameplay, with an absolute minimum of telling (gamers hate telling).

You have, as George Broussard of Apogee/3D Realms says, "a passion" for your job.[13] You love to help create new games for yourself and others to play. In fact, you are designing something that *you* would want to do and that you would want all your best friends to do with you. It needs to be an experience that people will not just like, but that will cause people to actually leap out of their seats saying, "Man, is this cool." In the words of game designer Chris Roberts of Digital Anvil: "I think that we all strive to push the envelope, exploring new areas and making the rules as we go."[14] Designer Scott Miller of Apogee/3D Realms adds, "Making a better game absolutely does not matter. Instead, what matters is making an *innovative* game that does something new and revolutionary.... Innovative thinking, and risky, noncloning game design should be the most important priority."[15]

What if training and curriculum design were like game design? Wouldn't it be a lot more fun and interesting?

Different Point of View 3: The Seller

If you are a publisher or seller of games, you are always thinking about your audience. What do they like? Do they like simulation games? Do they like action games? How can I make a better one? Is there one they already love? How can I improve on it? What's a good mix of experiences? What experiences can I give them that they haven't had or can't get elsewhere? What additional aspects of the player's life can I relate to with a game? How fast can I incorporate the latest technologies? In short, what will *sell it to the player?*

You'll also ask yourself how you can make a game that will draw in an entirely new audience, one that you haven't even touched. What about a hunting or fishing game? A game that will attract female players? A skateboard game? A business game? A game about mediaeval warfare? You are trying to anticipate the market, hit the shelves just as interest peaks and technology upgrades, and, especially, to align the player to your own brands, getting them to demand product upgrades and new products to buy. In short, have them *clamoring for more.*

What if the goals of training departments and vendors were more learner-focused than content-focused? Wouldn't that be different?

Contest 3: What other things would make learning more like games? Email your entries to *Contest3@twitchspeed.com.*

MOTIVATING TODAY'S LEARNERS

A lot of this is about motivation. Today's learners are truly different, and training and education have not kept pace with them. Moreover, training and education are largely nonmotivating or demotivating to the Games Generation. So, we should ask, how *can* we motivate today's learners? What will get their juices flowing and their minds in gear? What will cause them to learn the things that we need them to learn? What will cause them to return for more whenever we need them to? Why do we need to bother? Can't they just motivate themselves? Can't training and learning be intrinsically motivating?

The primary reason we need to provide motivation is because learning takes effort. As Seymour Papert says, "learning is essentially hard. It happens best when one is engaged in hard and challenging activities." [16] In the real world, learning is often motivated by our real needs: to survive, to earn money, and all the way up Maslow's hierarchy. In the artificial situation of training and education, providing motivation has been a traditional role of the teacher. A teacher is often evaluated and remembered by how good a motivator he or she was. And whenever there *is* a teacher, this should never stop being the case. But wouldn't it be nice if the learning method *itself* could also motivate the learner to work hard? Even if the teacher wasn't with them, either at all, or for that moment?

POTENTIAL LEARNING MOTIVATORS

What can we use to motivate learners? Will the traditional motivators work? If not, what can replace them? Let's look at the potential alternatives one by one.

- *Self-motivation through the content.* There is a lot of talk today in the training world about self-motivated learners, and of a new paradigm of people "taking responsibility for their own learning." Wouldn't it be great if everyone were motivated to learn whatever we wanted him or her to know?

I doubt whether many of the people saying these things actually work in corporations. Unfortunately, given what we expect people to know, the completely self-motivated trainee or learner is an unattainable myth. We typically don't train on the things that people want to know, or that are easy to learn—people pick these up on the job. Sure, all of us are self-motivated some of the time to learn things, mostly things we want to know anyway, and some folks are truly motivated just because they enjoy the process of learning (mostly academics). But the vast majority of us— from kids, to medical students, to corporate workers—need some form of extrinsic motivation to learn what others want us to know, and to make the learning effort a higher priority than the rest of our lives. Motivation has traditionally been a primary role of the teacher. But teacher or no teacher, what motivates people, especially today's people, to learn what they don't want to know?

The basic human motivators to do anything are relatively few, and come down to essentially two categories. On the one hand are the proverbial "sticks," which are basically some form of fear. On the other hand are a variety of "carrots," including love, greed, power, lust, anticipation, ego-gratification, winning, and pleasure or fun. All of these are found in learning to varying degrees.

- *Fear* is traditionally an important learning motivator. As anyone who has ever brought home a bad report card or poor grade knows, *not* learning can have painful consequences. Corporal punishment in schools is still legal in 23 states! Fear as a learning motivator goes back to our animal roots: if you didn't learn to hunt, you starved; if you didn't learn to avoid predators, you died.

While the fear of physical punishment is no longer a factor for most of today's learners, other types of fear certainly are. Fail to learn and you can lose your job, promotion, status, ability to drive, and so on. It is fear that leads students to cram all night; it is fear that causes us to cheat. Most of us can remember teachers we were afraid of. Fear is a powerful motivator.

But the problems with using fear as a learning motivator are several. First, fear leads to stress, and stress is not the best way to produce effective, long-term learning. As anyone knows who has crammed all night for a final, most of what we learn goes out the window the second the test ends. Second, for fear to be effective, threats have to be carried through. This is not always easy or effective in a corporate setting, and people know this. "Do you want me to go to class or do my job?" is a question frequently heard. Most importantly, fear only works when people have no alternatives. While this may be true in schools, it certainly is not in the corporate world of today, where job choices are so abundant that the problem is more one of making people stay. It is now managers, in many cases, who are afraid to discipline their workers. In many of today's environments, "Do this training or you're fired" is likely to lead to "I quit!" [17]

- *Love*, a leading "carrot," is an important motivator because we often do things to get approval from people we care about, be they our parents, our bosses, or our teachers. We rarely, however, want approval from our trainers. In corporate training, this form of motivation is only useful if the *bosses* really want the employees to do it. And although to support the company line managers may *say* they want their employees to go to training, unless it's *their* training, managers would often prefer that their employees just stay on the job.
- *Greed* is also powerful motivator. Long before the Web, I remember a very corporate CPA who quit his job to start a telephone-based gambling company based on the serial numbers on dollar bills. He was convinced that he had tapped into the mother lode because greed was the key motivator of people. Unfortunately, in his case, it was only a motivator for him, and I'm pretty sure he lost his shirt.

But greed *can* work as a learning motivator. In the year 2000, *Greed* was actually the title of a popular TV show, a nastier rip-off of *Who Wants to Be a Millionaire?* People who went on the show as contestants studied like mad and learned (at least for the moment) all sorts of facts and information, with the goal of winning money. Greed can occasionally work in a corporate setting. As we will see later, Yoyodine took advantage of greed motivation with its Digital Game-Based Learning sweepstakes, H&R Block's "The We'll Pay Your Taxes Game." The effective technique of getting people to do something by offering prizes or other rewards is a form of greed motivation. Pepsi gives out merchandise gift certificates for completing its online orientation training (see Chapter 9).

Because the marketplace often rewards learning with dollars, greed is very often a learning motivator in the business world outside training. Doctors command high fees because of all the time they put in at school. Teachers' salaries may vary by the number of degrees they have earned. Having more skills can get you a better job and a higher salary in almost any field. Today's young people are making greed-motivated decisions all the time: "I want to learn PhotoShop [a graphics software package], but I know I can earn more as a systems guy, so I'll learn Windows 2000," an employee told me recently. Employers who pay employees more based on courses they've taken or what they know are using this form of motivation (along with fear if they require a minimum grade).

The trouble is that it's hard to pay people to learn at the "micro" level of training. Not only is paying people to go to training tough to implement, it's sort of against our morals, and it's not clear how much it would take!

- *Power* is of course a big motivator in the world of work, but it's hard to think of any training that would confer more of it. Even getting a Harvard MBA doesn't grant you much corporate power until you earn that power.
- *Lust* is also a powerful learning motivator. Witness all the things that people know about film stars and supermodels. For obvious reasons, lust is rarely, if ever, used as a motivator in corporate training. It is used widely, though, through advertising, to motivate consumers to learn about a company's products.
- *Self-actualization* is the motivator highest on Maslow's hierarchy of needs. Certainly, people do self-actualize through learning, getting degrees, and starting new careers. To a small extent, corporate training might fill these needs, but not very much.

My sense is that few, if any, of the above traditional motivators will help us create learner-centered corporate training. Fortunately, that is not the complete list. There are at least four additional important motivators:

- Ego-gratification
- Winning
- Pleasure
- Fun

The first two have been traditionally used as motivators in corporate learning through comparative scores and contests. The second two have been used less by businesses in the past, but that is changing rapidly for the Games Generations. It is these four motivators, particularly the last two, that we will harness and combine with other powerful elements of games to create truly learner-centered training through Digital Game-Based Learning.

Part Two
HOW GAMES TEACH AND WHY THEY WORK

Games can be used to teach anything to anybody at any time.
— Thiagi

5

Fun, Play, and Games
What Makes Games Engaging?

Children are into the games, body and soul.
— C. Everett Koop, former Surgeon General of the United States

When I watch children playing video games at home or in the arcades, I am impressed with the energy and enthusiasm they devote to the task. . . .Why can't we get the same devotion to school lessons as people naturally apply to the things that interest them?
— Donald Norman, CEO, Unext

You go for it. All the stops are out. Caution is to the wind and you're battling with everything you have. That's the real fun of the game.
— Dan Dierdorf

Computer and video games are potentially the most engaging pastime in the history of mankind. This is due, in my view, to a combination of twelve elements:

WHY GAMES ENGAGE US

Games are a form of **fun**. That gives us *enjoyment and pleasure*.

Games are a form of **play**. That gives us *intense and passionate involvement*.

Games have **rules**. That gives us *structure*.

Games have **goals**. That gives us *motivation*.

Games are **interactive**. That gives us *doing*.

Games have **outcomes and feedback**. That gives us *learning*.

Games are **adaptive**. That gives us *flow*.

Games have **win states**. That gives us *ego gratification*.

Games have **conflict/competition/challenge/opposition**. That gives us *adrenaline*.

Games have **problem solving**. That sparks our *creativity*.

Games have **interaction**. That gives us *social groups*.

Games have **representation and story**. That gives us *emotion*.

Nothing else provides all of these. Books and movies, which perhaps come closest, have many of these characteristics, but they are not interactive, and are typically experienced alone. Games, at their best, are highly social, highly interactive experiences.

In this chapter, I look at each element to see how it contributes to the unbelievable engagement of the best games. Of course, not all games have all of these elements and not all games are great. But when they do have all of these elements and are great, watch out!

FUN—THE GREAT MOTIVATOR

People rarely succeed unless they have fun in what they are doing.
— Dale Carnegie

What *is* fun, anyway?

Microsoft's *Encarta World English Dictionary* (2000) defines *fun* as:

1. *amusement*: a time or feeling of enjoyment or amusement. *Just for fun, we wore silly hats.*
2. *something amusing*: something such as an activity that provides enjoyment or amusement. *Skiing is fun for the whole family.*
3. *mockery*: playful joking, often at the expense of another. *What's said in fun can still hurt.*

It goes on to define *fun and games* as:

1. activity, difficulty, or trouble (*informal*) (*used ironically*). *A broken sprinkler in the stockroom overnight gave us some fun and games in the morning.*
2. carefree amusement (*informal*)

make fun of somebody or something to make somebody or something appear ridiculous.

poke fun at somebody or something to mock or ridicule somebody or something. [1]

The venerable *Oxford English Dictionary* (OED) defines *fun* as:

1. A cheat or trick; a hoax, a practical joke.
2. a. Diversion amusement, sport; also boisterous jocularity or gaiety, drollery. Also, a source or cause of amusement or pleasure.
   b. *to make fun of, poke fun at* (a person, etc): to ridicule. *For or in fun*: as a joke, sportatively, not seriously. *(He, it is) good, great fun*: a source of much amusement. *Like fun*: energetically, very quickly, vigorously. *What fun!*: how very amusing. 1 *for the fun of the thing*: for amusement; to have fun with: to enjoy (a process); spec. to have sexual intercourse.
   c. Exciting goings on. Also *fun and games*, freq. used ironically; spec. amatory play. Colloq. [2]

Right away there is a major duality: On the one hand, fun is amusement, but on the other hand, it is ridicule, or a cheat or trick, or even sexual. Of course, no executive wants his or her training to be "ridiculous," "sexual," or even just "amusing." Yet, there is a further division that is far more relevant and important. Note carefully that the above definitions tend to lump "enjoyment" and "amusement" into the same category. This, I am sure, is wrong, at least in terms of the modern use of the word "fun," and is what leads us to confusion and conflict.

Although *amusement* may be frivolous, *enjoyment* and *pleasure* are certainly not. We enjoy and take pleasure from many of the most serious things in life—our families, our passions, our work. The enjoyment, pleasure, or fun that we derive from these activities is the principle source of what makes us return to do them again and again, and there is increased fun when the more that we do them, the better we get, the easier they become, and the more goals we can achieve.

Fun in this positive sense is not passive, and can include real exertion, as in sports or other competitions. In fact, the learning crowd at the MIT Media Lab are fond of calling their type of learning "hard fun."

So the real issue is that the same simple word *fun* can connote both enjoyment and pleasure (good), and amusement and/or ridicule (bad). This dichotomy, which we will see repeatedly, lies at the root of resistance by business people and educators to new learning approaches based on any connection to fun (and, by extension, to play and games). In some

respects, it's only a matter of semantics, but with important consequences. Proponents of fun learning relate fun to enjoyment and pleasure. Opponents relate fun to amusement and ridicule. They use the
same word but don't speak the same language.

You might think this would be obvious enough not to belabor the
point, but when a business executive or CEO purchasing training says, as
they often do, "I don't *want* my training to be fun!" it is important to
understand that he or she is (hopefully) telling us only that they don't
want it to be frivolous, not that we should take the enjoyment out.

Some people, such as game designer Noah Falstein, go even further,
associating fun with survival. "It is my belief," he says, "that the main purpose of 'fun activities' is to practice useful survival skills." [3]

However, there is another factor. Many people relate training and
learning, not to fun—in any sense—but rather to its opposite, pain. This is
well expressed by Benjamin Franklin's aphorism: "The things which
hurt, instruct." Thiagi (aka Sivasailam Thiagarajan), the great proponent
of game-based learning in companies, says "I think people *want* learning
to be painful. If you look universally at every language, every culture has
the equivalent of 'no pain, no gain' as a proverb. I think it's partly due to
the survival need of human beings that usually suffering results in learning. Unfortunately, human beings took the *converse* of that also to be true;
that is to say, if you don't suffer you're not going to learn." [2] In this view,
learning *can't* be fun in the same way that pain is not fun.

Of course, there is no theoretical or practical reason why this converse should be true. In fact, it is patently *not* true. People, starting as
babies, learn all the time without suffering. Sure it hurts to touch a hot
stove and get the painful lesson not to do it again, but does it hurt to say
"dada" and get a huge smile, hug, and kiss as a reward? So, while we do
learn from pain, learning doesn't *have* to be painful. These ideas are learning shackles that certainly have no relevance for today's learners, and we
trainers and educators should all throw those shackles off.

To make matters worse, there is a strong religious tradition involved.
Remember the story of Adam and Eve? How happy they were before
they ate the fruit of *which* tree? In this extreme biblical view, the cause of
man's suffering is knowledge. *All* learning is painful, knowledge is sin, and
learning is merely a form of suffering. It is worth remembering that for literally thousands of years the church controlled schools and learning.

Many of its precepts live on in the minds of educators. While religious thought has many positive things to offer us, the link between knowledge and evil, fun and sin is not one of them. It is certainly time to throw these learning shackles away as well.

An additional concept with religious overtones that may inhibit a positive relationship between fun and learning is what some have referred to as the "Madonna/whore" complex, whereby people do not want to mix the "pure" with the "unholy." J.C. Herz in *Joystick Nation* cites this as a reason why the computer and the television are unlikely ever to merge—the computer is "serious" and the TV "a plaything," "whose first duty is to amuse us." [4] Anyone who sees learning as serious, and fun as frivolous or sinful, is experiencing this quasi-religious double standard.

An interesting fact about fun is that, according to Johan Huizenga in his *Homo Ludens*, there is not an exact equivalent of the word *fun* in any non-English language. [5] Maybe we do have something special going on.

As I said earlier, people at the MIT Media Lab are fond of using the term *hard fun*. In his landmark book *Being Digital*, Nicolas Negroponte, director of the Media Lab, explains how the term originated. In 1989, at a Media Lab news conference in which kids demonstrated their LEGO/Logo work, a reporter asked one 8-year-old whether it was "not just all fun and games." (*See?*) He replied, "Yes, this is fun, but it's *hard fun*." [6]

FUN AND LEARNING

People with the notion that learning cannot and should not be fun are clearly in an archaic mode.
— Mark Bieler, former head of Human Resources, Bankers Trust Company

So, what is the relationship between fun and learning? Does having fun help or hurt? Let us look at what some researchers have to say on the subject:

"Enjoyment and fun as part of the learning process are important when learning new tools since the learner is relaxed and motivated and therefore more willing to learn." [7]

"The role that fun plays with regard to intrinsic motivation in education is twofold. First, intrinsic motivation promotes the desire for recurrence of the experience....Secondly, fun can motivate learners to engage themselves in activities with which they have little or no previous experience." [8]

"In simple terms a brain enjoying itself is functioning more efficiently." [9]

"When we enjoy learning, we learn better." [10]

Fun has also been shown by Datillo and Kleiber (1993), Hastie (1994), and Middleton, Littlefield, and Lehrer (1992), to increase motivation for learners. [11]

It appears then that the principal roles of fun in the learning process are to create *relaxation* and *motivation*. Relaxation enables a learner to take things in more easily, and motivation enables them to put forth effort without resentment.

Next on our journey to understanding the power of games, let us consider *play*.

PLAY—THE UNIVERSAL TEACHER

Play is our brain's favorite way of learning.
— Diane Ackerman, *Deep Play*

While fun, despite its dualistic nature, is a relatively simple idea—a state of being—play is a much more complex phenomenon. There is relatively little written on fun, but the phenomenon of play has been studied and written about extensively. There are a number of classic books on play, including Johan Huizenga's *Homo Ludens*,[12] and Roger Caillois' *Les jeux et les hommes* (translated as *Man, Play and Games*),[13] both of which relate play to anthropological and sociological concerns.

So, what *is* play?

The OED, which allots *fun* less than a page, devotes more than ten of its tiny-print pages to defining play, with thirty-nine numbered definitions, each with many subcategories. With such a wide variety of meanings, ranging from sword fighting to staged representation to an activity of children to sexual intercourse, it is no wonder that there is sometimes controversy and misunderstanding over the meaning and value of play.

In the case of play, though, the dictionary is less useful to us, because what we are concerned about here is not *all* the many ways in which the word is used, but a particular activity that we all pretty much recognize. So, let us turn, instead, to the theorists.

Johan Huizenga, in his book *Homo Ludens*, characterizes play as a free activity that is consciously outside of "ordinary" life and is "not serious." Play, he says, absorbs the player "intensely and utterly." It has fixed rules and order, does not have any material interest or profit, and encourages the formation of social groupings.[14] Roger Caillois, in *Man, Play and Games*, defines play as an activity that is not obligatory, has its own space and time, is uncertain in its outcomes, creates no material wealth, is governed by rules, and has elements of make-believe and unreality.[15]

From these definitions of play several factors merit emphasis in our context.

- Play is something one *chooses* to do.
- Play is *intensely and utterly absorbing*.
- Play *promotes the formation of social groupings*.

PLAY AND LEARNING

Play is the original way of learning things.
— Danny Hillis

Some people assume that because children do it play is trivial and unimportant. In fact, in the view of many scientists, quite the opposite is true. Play has a deep biological, evolutionarily important, function, which has to do specifically with learning. It is "one of the cultural universals, something every single culture does," says Danny Hillis, founder of Thinking Machines and a former Disney Fellow. "Of course this has to do with learning."[16] "Play is our brain's favorite way of learning," writes Diane Ackerman in her book *Deep Play*.[17] "Children are expected to play because we recognize (perhaps unconsciously) the fundamental utility of games as an educational tool," adds Chris Crawford, noted game designer.[18] And Robert Fagan, a child psychologist, defines play as "optimal generic learning by experimentation in a relaxed field."[19]

Proponents of play as enhancing children's learning have much evidence to cite. Many point to young animals, such as bear or lion cubs, learning to fight and hunt by nipping at each other, and by sneaking up and pouncing on butterflies. Alison Gopnick, author of *The Scientist in the Crib*, cites the extended human childhood, which is longer than any other animal's, during which the child's needs are taken care of so that the child is free to play, explore, and learn.[20] Other evidence includes children's fascination with many forms of learning play, including the alphabet song and counting rhymes. Children's TV shows, such as *Sesame Street* and *Blues Clues*, provide strong evidence of the value of combining learning and play. Research into children's learning by MIT's Media Lab (see below) and its many offshoots, such as Edit Harel's company MaMa-Media, supports this view as well.

PLAY AND WORK

Great adults are driven to [play], too.
— Danny Hillis

But what about adults, the workers we are supposed to train? Do they play? Is there any value in it for them? And what is play's relationship to work?

Of course, adults play—they play with their children, they play games, they play in many of the senses of the earlier definitions. But unlike children, adults also have a serious, work, or real-life side that is often construed to be in conflict with, or even the opposite from, play. The definitions cited earlier define play as "outside of ordinary life," "not serious," and "unproductive." Some authors attribute this work/play distinction to industrialization or to social-class distinctions. We speak of executives who "work hard and play hard." But are play and work really that separate?

Certainly not for the most creative adults, including musicians, actors, and scientists. Musicians "play" for a living—it's the fun part of what they do. Actors, too, play for a living. (It is interesting that musicians and actors "practice" first, and then "play" as the end product. Doctors and lawyers on the other hand, study first, and their end product is called "practicing.")

Many scientists think of much of their work as play, often linking the idea of play with high creativity. "I've been really lucky," says Danny Hillis, "that I've had a chance to work with…people like Marvin Minsky, Claude Shannon, Jonas Salk, Richard Feynman. The thing that all those people have in common is that even as adults they have an extreme sense of play."[21] Alan Kay, the well-known pioneer and visionary of Xerox PARC, Apple, and now Disney, recalls "hours of play" at Xerox. "Play did not interrupt work," he says, "it just provided another venue for thinking. People often have more brainstorms on the jogging path than at their desks."[22] And Einstein, who was wiser than all, is reputed to have commented: "If A is a success in life, A equals x plus y plus z. X is work, y is play, and z is keeping your mouth shut."[23]

According to Professors William H. Starbuck and Jane Webster, "Work and play have always been overlapping categories."[24] Many people become very involved with and derive great pleasure from work activities, and play activities may create results of lasting value. A modern concept that they use to unite the two is the notion of "playful work," that is, work that is both productive *and* pleasant and involving.

In business, work and play mix regularly, starting at the highest executive levels. Deals are done on the golf course. Businesses have been bought and sold on bets. At Harvard Business School my fellow students played daily games of "who gets called on bingo" and would shoot the person talking with water guns while the teacher was looking the other way during the classes. They would, I have no doubt, do so as eagerly again 20 years later, many as multimillionaires. Many of the most successful adults, in business or in the professions, will tell you that they think of their work as playing, and that that is a big factor in their success.

Michael Schrage describes in his book, *Serious Play*, how many businesses are using a form of play to create models that are extremely useful in helping businesses to prepare for the future.[25] War gaming is another form of play that has been used successfully in business, and executives often get into this form of play completely. In one instance, for a particular business war game the company president ordered all his top lieutenants to dress in camouflage gear and created an olive drab painted war room, complete with camouflage contact paper on the computers.[26]

That play can be a valuable part of the learning and training process is not, of course, a new revelation. The best trainers and teachers have *always* tried and succeeded in making learning fun and playful. This is probably a big part of *why* we think of them as the best teachers.

Yet, one thing that often happens in companies is that as you go lower and lower into the depths of an organization, seriousness of purpose somehow gets translated into seriousness of demeanor. Playfulness is excluded, and this is often reflected in training. Outside observers of business can often see what the insiders can't or won't. Nicholas Negroponte is quoted in *Inside Technology Training* magazine as saying, "Sometimes I want to tell people who are in the training business to lighten up, that your customer will appropriate the knowledge much more quickly if playing is at the root of what you are doing."[27]

Negroponte should know. The renowned Media Lab he directs at MIT has created a whole research division, funded by Sony, Lego, Nintendo, and other major corporations, to investigate play and learning. With the decidedly nonplayful name of The Epistemology and Learning Group, the group is led by two well-known researchers in the field of learning and play, Seymour Papert and Mitchel Resnick, who have brought us terms such as *hard fun* and *lifelong kindergarten*. The group mixes learning, play, and work, through what they call constructivist learning, which is largely derived from the work of Piaget. Kids learn to create their own knowledge by playing, experimenting, and constructing with certain kinds of physical objects, such as LEGO blocks and necklace beads with built-in computer chips. While the group's research focuses exclusively on children's learning, many of their play-oriented constructivist ideas are being extended to by others through computer games such as *Roller Coaster Tycoon*. It is worth noting that the children they began working with in the 1980s are fast becoming today's corporate workers.

Just adding the labels "work" and "play" to something can affect our whole attitude, reports Thiagi in his newsletter *The Thiagi Games Letter.* In a word-association survey that he conducted, Thiagi found that the words most typically associated with work are pressure, boredom, deadlines, chores, office, salary, drudgery, nine-to-five, overtime, and goals. The words strongly associated with play are fun, enjoyment, game, laughter, choice, spontaneous, and relaxation. People enjoy difficult tasks more when presented as play rather than work, and their minds wander less.[28] What you think is what you get.

Current research in the areas of stress, anxiety, creativity, self-efficacy, and neuroscience shows that more play will *improve* our learning and performance.[29] While "more work and less play" has been touted for a long time as the way to improve human performance, there is much evidence that such thinking is wrong. When you are enjoying yourself and laughing, changes in the chemical balance of your blood boosts the production of neurotransmitters needed for alertness and memory.[30] When you feel threatened, tired, and helpless you lose your ability to recall information, notice things around, ask questions, and think creatively.[31]

An academic study of play at work comes from William H. Starbuck and Jane Webster in an important paper entitled "When is Play Productive?"[32] After reviewing the definitions in a number of other studies of play, Starbuck and Webster boil play down to two common elements: "playful activities *elicit involvement* and *give pleasure.*" They then seek to discover the consequences of play at work. Starbuck and Webster found the following things, among others:

- People play at work to seek competence, stimulation, challenge, or reinforcement.
- People who perform very playful tasks enjoy what they are doing. When they judge those activities appropriate, they switch to them readily and try to continue doing them.
- They tend to concentrate more and increase their persistence.
- They become less aware of the passage of time and are reluctant to change activities.
- They become so absorbed that they may neglect other things, such as long-term goals, nonplayful tasks, and social relations.
- Their learning is enhanced because the pleasure and involvement of playful activities induces them to expend time and effort.
- Through different forms of play they can broaden their behavioral repertoires incrementally, discover or invent radically new behaviors, and polish their existing skills through repetitive practice.
- Playful tasks foster creativity. If the playful tasks are new ones, they will put much effort into learning them and exploring them, usually trying to control their own learning.

So, the same attraction that children have for play carries on into the world of work, where people prefer, and are drawn to, playful tasks. In fact, as we observed in Chapter 2, the distinction between work and play is quickly becoming moot. The Games Generations *expect* their work to also be fun and playful. In Tapscott's words, "Fun, working and playing are all the same to them."[33] Many high-tech startups are changing their environments to make them more playful. At i-belong, a company near Boston, there is an indoor miniature golf course. At excite@home there are winding slides to get from one level to the next (unfortunately, down only.)[34] Interestingly, while this may be news at the dot-coms, or when corporations do it, the games companies have been doing it for decades. Play has always been a big part of their environment—after all, it's what they do. The change with the growing up of the Games Generations kids is that that environment has now moved outside of the games companies and into more mainstream business.

Again, this is largely the result of changing technology. Starbuck and Webster attribute much of the erosion of the distinction between play and work to the introduction of PCs into the workplace, because they are "simultaneously fun to use and serious tools."[35]

Although some people still claim that play in the workplace is just escapism designed to displace or avoid work, managers are increasingly realizing that making work playful reduces stress, and actually increases productivity.

GAMES—ADDING THE STRUCTURE

One of the most difficult tasks men can perform . . . is the invention of good games.
— Carl Jung

So fun, in the sense of enjoyment and pleasure, puts us in a relaxed, receptive frame of mind for learning. Play, in addition to providing pleasure, increases our involvement, which also helps us learn.

Both fun and play, however, have the disadvantage of being somewhat abstract, unstructured, and hard-to-define concepts. But a more formal and structured way to harness (and unleash) all the power of fun and play in the learning process exists—the powerful institution of *games*. Before we look specifically at how we can combine games with learning, let us examine games themselves in some detail.

Like fun and play, *game* is a word of many meanings and implications. How can we define a game? Is there any useful distinction between fun, play, and games? What makes games engaging? How do we design them?

Games are a subset of both play and fun. In programming jargon, games are a child inheriting all the characteristics of the parents. They therefore carry both the good and the bad of both terms. Games, as we will see, also have some special qualities, which make them particularly appropriate and well suited for learning.

So what is a game?

Like play, game has a variety of meanings—some positive, some negative. On the negative side there is mocking and jesting, illegal and shady activity such as a con game, as well as the fun and games that we discussed earlier. As noted, these can be sources of resistance to Digital Game-Based Learning—"we are not playing games here." However, much of that is semantic. What we are interested in here are the meanings that revolve around the definition of games involving rules, contest, rivalry, and struggle.

WHAT MAKES A GAME A GAME? SIX STRUCTURAL FACTORS

The *Encyclopaedia Britannica* provides the following diagram of the relation between play and games: [36]

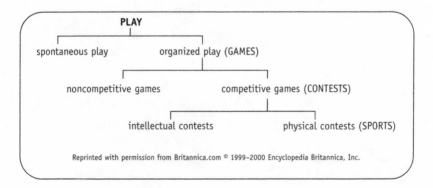

Reprinted with permission from Britannica.com © 1999–2000 Encyclopedia Britannica, Inc.

Our goal is to understand why games *engage* us, drawing us in, often in spite of ourselves. This powerful force stems first from the fact that they are a form of fun and play, and second from what I call the six key structural elements of games:

1. Rules
2. Goals and Objectives
3. Outcomes and Feedback
4. Conflict/Competition/Challenge/Opposition
5. Interaction
6. Representation or Story

There are thousands, perhaps millions of different games, but all contain most, if not all, these powerful factors. Those that don't contain all the factors are still classified as games by many, but can also belong to other subclasses, which are described below. In addition to these structural factors, there are also important design elements that add to engagement and that distinguish a really good game from a poor or mediocre one.

Let us discuss these six factors in detail and show how and why they lead to such strong engagement.

Rules. *Rules* are what differentiate games from other kinds of play. Probably the most basic definition of a game is that it is *organized play*, that is to say rule-based. If you don't have rules you have free play, not a game. Why are rules so important to games? Rules impose limits—they force us to take specific paths to reach goals and ensure that all players take the same paths. They put us inside the game world by letting us know what is in and out of bounds. What spoils a game is not so much the cheater who accepts the rules but doesn't play by them (we can deal with him or her), but the nihilist who denies them altogether. Rules make things both fair and exciting. When the Australians "bent" the rules of the America's Cup and built a huge boat in 1988, and the Americans found a way to compete with a catamaran, it was still a race—but no longer the same game.

While even small children understand some game rules ("that's not fair"), rules become increasingly more important as we grow older. The rules set the limits of what is OK and not OK, fair and not fair, in the game. By elementary school, kids know to cry "cheater" if the rules are broken. *Monopoly* and *Trivial Pursuit* have pages of written rules, and by adulthood we are consulting Hoyle, hiring professional referees to enforce rules, and even holding national debates—for example, about the designated hitter, the two-point conversion, the instant replay rules—over whether to change them.

In card games, board games, and other noncomputer games, the rules are written down and generally managed by the players, in extreme cases using an "impartial" third party (e.g., a "ref"). In computer games, the rules are built into the game. It is interesting that in business one often hears talk about "changing the rules of the game" as a way of beating the competition. This has particular implications for games used in business, such as simulation, which may have the rules built in.

Some computer game designers, Noah Falstein among them, call this *metagaming*, which is not just playing by the rules, but manipulating the rules and circumstances surrounding the game to your advantage. Children arguing about the specific rules of a game before they start is a kind of metagaming. Often the metagaming itself is a more satisfying way to play, and the game itself is anticlimactic. Richard Garfield, the creator of the fabulously successful *Magic: The Gathering* card game designed it with metagaming in mind, and in fact a large part of its success can be attributed to the card trading, selling, listing, and tournaments that are associated with the game itself.[37]

Goals or Objectives. *Goals or objectives* also differentiate games from other types of play, as well as from other non-goal-oriented games. In some designers' eyes, if your game doesn't have a goal but is something that can be just played with in many ways depending on your whim, you have what they refer to as a toy. Toy in this sense is a technical term, because they use it to refer to things as complex as *Sim City* and *The Sims*, and even an airline simulator. These goal-less simulations, however, are generally known as games, at least by the people who market and play them. In speaking to this, Will Wright, the designer of *Sim City*, says, "I'm not sure there's a real firm distinction. I think of our models as something you can either just play with, purely kind of Zen-like, un-goal-directed, or in fact you can pick a goal and turn it into a game at any time."[38]

In a game, achieving your goals is a big piece of what motivates you. "They are," says Wright, "what you measure yourself against." The goal is often stated at the beginning of the rules: Your goal is to get the highest score, to reach the end, to beat the big boss, to capture the flag, to get the best hand, and so on. Goals and objectives are important because we are goal-oriented as a species. Unlike most animals, we are capable of conceiving of a future state and of devising strategies for achieving it, and most of us enjoy the process. The rules, of course, make this harder, by limiting the strategies at our disposal. Goals push us to achieve and to win.

Outcomes and Feedback. *Outcomes and feedback* are how you measure your progress against the goals. The classic games are ones you either win or lose. "Games seem to want to have a win-lose state, or at least a goal state that you can measure yourself against," says Wright. Obviously winning and losing has strong emotional and ego-gratification implications, which is a big part of the attraction of games.

Feedback comes when something in the game changes in response to what you do—it is what we mean when we say computers and computer games are *interactive*. Feedback lets us know immediately whether what we have done is positive or negative for us in the game, whether we are staying within or breaking the rules ("Tilt"), moving closer to the goal or further away ("Hot or Cold"), and how we are doing versus the competition (high-score tables). Feedback can take a variety of forms, from an outside referee, to the other players, to the computer, but its main characteristic is that in almost all games it is *immediate*. I do something; I get a result. (This does not preclude a number of actions combining to produce longer-range feedback, such as an outcome, as well).

Feedback can come in the form of a numerical score, but it can also come in many other forms as well. Feedback can come graphically, like the size and condition of your cities in *Sim City* or *Age of Empires*, or seeing yourself ahead in a racing game. It can also come orally, as from characters in the game who talk to you, or the wisecracking announcer in *"You Don't Know Jack."* In computer games, it is increasingly coming to us through other senses as well, such as the tactile rumble felt in "force feedback" joysticks or other controllers when you are (figuratively or literally) on bumpy ground.

It is from the feedback in a game that *learning* takes place. Even in games that are purely commercial, and not at all what I call Digital Game-Based Learning, there is a great deal of continuous learning going on. The player is learning constantly how the game works, what the designer's underlying model is, how to succeed, and how to get to the next level and win. Via the feedback you either get rewarded for mastering something, or you get word that you have failed at something, and have to try again or seek help, until you can do it. Depending on the game, feedback can be spectacularly dramatic (crash landings, whole galaxies blowing up, or the "dead patients and big booms," that Sharon Stansfield creates[39]), or amusing (the Sailor in *Monkey Island* who says "No!"), or more subtle (the music in *The Sims*) but its goal is always to enhance your experience and move you along in the game.

The art of providing feedback in a game is extremely important and complex because either too little or too much can lead quickly to frustration for the player. This leads to another important characteristic of computer games—they are *adaptive*. This means that the level of difficulty goes up or down automatically depending on what you do. This is the way computer games keep players in the "flow state."

These first three categories—at their simplest: rules, a goal, and winning or losing—are the classic "well-accepted, thousands-of-year-old definition of a game," according to J. C. Herz, author of *Joystick Nation*.[40] There are also three additional elements that are usually thought of as part of the structure of a game—or at least as part of the structure of a computer game—by many game designers: conflict, interaction, and representation.

Conflict, Competition, Challenge, and Opposition. *Conflict, competition, challenge, and opposition* are the problems in a game you are trying to solve. "A computer game is nothing but a problem that we're selling," says Will Wright. "And basically your solving that problem is playing the game."[41] The conflict or challenge that produced the problem to solve does not necessarily have to be against another opponent, real or AI (artificial intelligence). It can be a puzzle to solve, or anything that stands in the way of your progress (How *do* I get this Sim married off?) Conflict/competition/challenge or opposition is what gets your adrenaline and creative juices flowing, and what makes you excited about playing the game. While not everyone likes head-to-head competition, and some people shy from conflict, most of us enjoy a challenge, particularly if we get to choose it and set its difficulty. Keeping the level of conflict/competition/challenge or opposition in synch with the player's skills and progress is called "balancing" the game, and, as we shall see, is a key skill in game design.

Some argue that competition is part of our basic nature as human beings. Whether or not this is true, as game designer Eric Goldberg notes, "the people who naturally gravitate to games tend to be competitive."[42]

So, can there be games that are noncompetitive or even cooperative? Sure. However, most games involve some kind of conflict, challenge, or problem solving, even if it is done through cooperation and teamwork. One of my favorite "cooperative" games was done on a kids' Web site where each of four simultaneous players could control only one of the four directions (left, right, up, down) that the spaceship could move. Getting that ship to go anywhere in a reasonably direct manner was *definitely* a challenge!

An oft-cited game quality is that games are safe and nonthreatening because they are "only games." Game players are thus in some sense "protected" from the dangers of the real world. While this is certainly true physically, it does not necessarily apply to players' *emotions* while playing the game, which are very real indeed.

Interaction. *Interaction* has two important aspects: The first is the interaction of the player and the computer, which we have discussed under feedback. The second, though, is the inherently *social* aspect of games—you do them with other people. As we saw earlier, play promotes the formation of social groupings. While you can play alone, it is much more fun to play with others. This is why in precomputer games, the category of solitaire games, although not insignificant, is tiny compared to games that are played with others. Despite the industry's initial (prenetworking) focus on single-player games or games played against the machine (an era in which we are still involved), just about *all* of today's computer games have become multiplayer in one form or another. Players recognize that while game designers are attempting, through increasingly better AI, to make computer-based opponents or collaborators more realistic, they are still very far from being able to create anything with the true wiles of the real human mind. Gamers generally prefer human competitors, and critics who see computer gaming as an isolating activity, should be aware of this. Like the Internet, computer games are bringing people into closer social interaction—although not necessarily face-to-face.

Representation. *Representation* means that the game is about something. This can be abstract or concrete, direct or indirect. Chess is about conflict. Tetris is about building and recognizing patterns. *The Age of Empires* is about the history of the art of war. Representation includes any narrative or story elements in the game. There is a difference of opinion among various computer game theorists regarding representation. Some theorists think that representation is the essence of what makes a game, while some think it is just the "candy" around the game. In any event, consumer games are becoming more detailed in their representation, and story and narrative are becoming a bigger part of games. This is raising a number of issues, both about narrative and games, because the integration of the two is neither obvious nor easy.

Representation also includes the element of fantasy, which some people, like game designer Chris Crawford, place in a game's definition. While there is a preponderance of games about a small number of types of fantasy—such as space, medieval times, and "modern" war—games actually represent an enormously wide variety of subjects. When I told my classic "business has lots of content but no engagement; games have lots of engagement but no content" story to J. C. Herz, she took quick issue. "Games *do* have lots of content," she countered. "It's just not content that's immediately useful in the 'real' world." Of course, as we shall discuss, putting content that *is* useful in the real world is what Digital Game-Based Learning is all about.

The Concept of "Flow"

There is a mental state—often reported by game players, but certainly not limited to this area—of intense concentration, often to the point where previously difficult tasks become easy and whatever you are doing becomes enormously pleasurable. Most of us have experiences it in one area or another. Researchers, notably Mihaly Csikszentmihalyi, refer to this state as "flow."[43] In the flow state, the challenges presented and your ability to solve them are almost perfectly matched, and you often accomplish things that you didn't think you could, along with a great deal of pleasure. There can be flow in work, sports, and even learning, such as when concepts become clear and how to solve problems obvious.

The trick with flow is to keep someone in the state. Make things too easy and the players become bored and stop. Make things too hard and they stop because they become frustrated. Well-designed games are especially good at maintaining this flow state in players, and game designers have developed specific techniques to do this, as we will see in a moment.

In Digital Game-Based Learning, one of the biggest challenges is to keep players in the flow state in the game and in the learning simultaneously; no easy task, but enormously rewarding when successful.

OTHER TYPES OF INTERACTIVITY BESIDES GAMES

To prepare us for designing Digital Game-Based Learning, it is important to briefly discuss several categories other than games that make up the object world of possible computer interactions. In a "grammar" of digital interaction, these are the "nouns." (I am indebted to J. C. Herz for introducing me to these theories.) Besides games, there are *toys*, *stories*, and *tools*. These categories can be, and often are, combined in a single work.

Toys

Toys are interactions that have *neither* goals nor objectives. They are meant to be "played with" as you explore the "phase space" of whatever they are about. To people who use this terminology, *Sim City* and *The Sims* are toys. So is *Microsoft Flight Simulator*. A toy, according to Herz, doesn't necessarily have rules; it's more open ended, and its identity really has to do with the material qualities of the object. In this sense, airplane and other equipment simulators are toys, as are economic simulations, if you are only playing and exploring rather than "playing to win." Laurie Spiegel—a lute player and brilliant composer of electronic music—programmed a "toy" (in this sense) called *Music Mouse* for the Macintosh when it first came out, in which by moving the mouse in various directions you can create different sound structures.[44] I remember playing with it for hours. As Wright says, it is easy to turn a toy into a game at any moment—just add a goal. So as soon as you say, "I want to land my plane safely at JFK," the toy becomes a game. In terms of play, some people prefer toys and some games. Corey Schou tells the story of how the pilots rejected a multiplane simulation he built for FedEx because there was no goal and therefore no competition.[45] As we shall see in Chapter 10, the military is experimenting with making some of its very expensive simulation "toys" more game-like.

Story (Narrative)

Narrative, or story, is another kind of possible computer interaction. At its least interactive, a story is merely put onto the screen in words and/or images from start to finish, and your interaction is clicking through it. This was done for example in the "Living Books" series for children, where part of a story is given on each screen and the kids can click to hear it or advance to the next page (there are toy elements as well, in terms of things you can click on.) Nonlinear hypertext can also be a kind of story in this sense.

Narrative has a long and important history in entertainment (and in learning as well—remember Homer?). Those who believe in the entertainment and learning power of narrative do so passionately. "I live and breathe storytelling," says Bran Ferren of Disney.[46] "I contend that linear narrative is the fundamental art form of humankind," says Alex Seiden, of Industrial Light and Magic.[47] Many, especially those who come from a literary or cinema background, are convinced that narrative is by far the strongest way to engage people. The reason it is so engaging is because it is a terrific way to stimulate our emotions. "In order for it to be emotional it has to be story-based," say Jeff Snipes of Ninth House Networks.[48] Stimulating emotion is the "prime directive" of fiction writing, as any screenwriting book will tell you.

A big issue facing both the "narrative" people and the "games" people is how to *combine* narrative with games. Digital computers have introduced consumers of entertainment and stories to interactivity. And interactivity—getting immediate feedback to your actions—is a very powerful way of engaging people. Large and varied groups of creative people are struggling hard to find ways to put narrative and interactivity together, creating interactive stories that can, for example, be included in games. I use the word *struggling* because it isn't at all obvious how to do this, and many attempts to create interactive stories have failed. When, in the first bloom of computer games, the people from Hollywood (who see themselves as the masters of narrative) tried to combine and work with the gamers of Silicon Valley (who see themselves as the masters of interactivity) the initial results were disappointing. Many referred to this as "Silliwood."

At the heart of the issue is the fact that narrative or story has always been something that is *completely controlled by the storyteller*. The author is uniquely in charge, feeding the story to the reader or viewer in the exact manner and at the exact pace that he or she chooses. Whether the author of a movie is an individual or collaborative effort, after the film is "in the can" the viewer, like the reader of a book, can't change the story, except in his or her imagination.

In a digital, interactive world, however, the receiver of the narrative *wants* and *needs* to interact with and influence that story on the fly. How to make that happen while still preserving the kinds of emotional impact that good writers know how to elicit through effective structuring and organization of the material is the big question. Many of the tools they use to do this—plot twists, surprises, things coming together at certain moments—depend on the author's, not the user's, making the choices. A great number of highly creative people are working hard on this problem, trying to invent what effective interactive storytelling will look like, and to merge this into games more effectively than has been done. They are trying many different approaches, from highly branching, but occasionally converging, decision trees, to generating story and video on the fly, to endowing characters with particular qualities and letting them interact with each other according to certain rules. Their results are highly important to digital gaming and Digital Game-Based Learning, so it's an area worth staying in touch with.

Tools

Tools are interactive programs that are used to make other things. A word processor or spreadsheet program is a tool. So is a graphics program, a programming language, or an authoring system. Tools can be included in games either as an integral part of the game play (e.g., the tools that you use to build your theme park in *Roller Coaster Tycoon*) or as supplements (e.g., the tools that you use to design your character in *EverQuest*, or to design new levels in *Quake*).

Simulations?

Although some might expect simulations to be included as one of these "interactive noun" categories, they are really more of an action, or, in Herz' terms, a "predicate." "Depending on what it's doing, a simulation can be a story, it can be a game, it can be a toy. If it's a role-playing simulation, ultimately it's a story. If it's a simulation of trading, it's a game. If it's a sim of an airplane, it's a toy. It's an analogy to a real-world situation. But what that situation is can be anything," says Herz.[49]

There is more discussion of games and simulations in Chapter 8.

"DIGITAL" GAMES

Games and computers are one of the great marriages out there.
— Eric Goldberg, Game Designer

In the preceding discussions, my focus has shifted (subtly, I hope) from games "in general" to computer games. Let me now be more explicit. What is different about playing a game on a computer? Why do so many other people, including the Games Generations and many adults, find the combination so attractive and satisfying?

The biggest difference is that computers enhance the "play experience," which is what people want most out of games. In many noncomputer games, points out Eric Goldberg, a long-time game developer and CEO of Unplugged Games,[50] much the time in the game is taken up figuring out and administering (and often arguing about) the rules. One thing the computer does well is to take care of all the boring little rules and details, freeing the player to enjoy more of the game experience. The computer handles a lot of the tedium. For example, it knows automatically what moves are illegal, and won't allow you to make them. In war games before the era of computers, every time the competitors moved their forces a time-out had to be called while the referees looked up all the individual unit damage consequences in a large book of tables. Now the computer, in what appears to the players to be instantaneous, does this, enabling the creation of so-called real-time war-strategy games such as *Command and Conquer*.

Why do more and more people prefer to play their games on computers? That is, why do so many people prefer *digital* games? There are many reasons:

- Digital games take care of the boring stuff.
- Digital games are typically faster and more responsive.
- There are fun things that digital games can do easily that noncom-

puter games can't do at all, such as simulating the physics of shooting in space, or combining all the factors in flying an airplane, or considering the millions of possibilities in puzzles or strategic contests.

- Digital games are capable of more, better, and far more varied graphic representations.
- Digital games can be played against real people or, if none are available, against AI (i.e., the computer). That means that multiplayer games can be played at any time.
- The whole world (i.e., anyone online anywhere) is available as a potential player.
- Digital games can generate and allow huge numbers of options and scenarios.
- Digital games can deal with infinite amounts of content.
- Digital games can play at differing levels of challenge.
- Digital games can be updated instantly.
- Digital games can be customized to and by the desires of each player.
- Digital games can be modified and added to, making the player part of the creative team.

The list goes on. For the reasons we have seen, most of the traditional games moved quickly to computers and the Web and were wildly accepted by players of all ages. Millions of people play computer chess, computer bridge, computer *Jeopardy!*, and computer *Wheel of Fortune*, to name just a few. The classic solution for increasing traffic to your Web site is to add a game.

GAME TAXONOMY—CATEGORIES OF GAMES

Is there a taxonomy of games? Can all games be broken down and classified into a limited number of specific categories?

Writing in precomputer-game 1958, Roger Caillois, in *Man, Play and Games*, divides games into four classes: competition, chance, simulation, and movement. He then further subdivides them by their degree of agitation vs. restfulness.[51] In his 1982 book *The Art of Computer Game Design*, game designer Chris Crawford identifies five major types of games: board games, card games, athletic games, children's games, and computer games.[52]

Today computer games are generally recognized as falling into one of eight "genres," which often overlap. Alphabetically, they are action, adventure, fighting, puzzle, role-playing, simulations, sports, and strategy.

- *Action games* began with the classic "twitch" games of the arcades and home video consoles: *Super Mario, Sonic the Hedgehog,* and so on. The category includes the old "side scroller" games, maze games (*PacMan*), platform-jumping games (e.g., *Gekko*), falling things that you have to shoot (*Missile Command*), car races, and chases. Obviously, this is the category of the shoot-em-up games such as *Doom, Quake, Duke Nukem, Half-Life,* and *Unreal Tournament.*
- *Adventure games* are the "find your way around the unknown world, pick up objects, and solve puzzles" games. These are among the earliest of computer games; *Adventure* was played on mainframes. *Zork* is a classic of the genre. Present-day adventure games include *Myst* and *Riven* on the PC and *Zelda, the Ocarina of Time* on Nintendo.
- *Fighting games* are a lot of what you see in the lobbies of movie theaters. Two characters, drawn from a stable of hundreds, battle each other until one is wiped out. All these games are really doing is matching up two "moves" at the same time, to see which wins. But the speed is intense, and the moves are athletic, balletic, and fantastical. Motion capture sensors on dancers and real martial arts fighters typically capture them, and the goal appears to be to combine outlandish fantasy in the characters with realism of the computer graphics. The classic example is *Mortal Kombat; Virtua Fighter MMMCIII* is a modern example.
- *Puzzle games* are just that. Problems to be solved, typically visual, stripped of all story pretense. The classic example is *Tetris; Devil Dice* is a modern example.
- *Role-playing games* (RPGs) are generally some form of *Dungeons and Dragons* brought to the computer screen. They are mostly mediaeval in their imagery and involve quests, usually to rescue someone or something. You play a character, who has a "type" (human, orc, elf, wizard, etc.) and a set of individual characteristics you assign it. You acquire equipment and experience via action and fighting. Things such as spells are a big deal. The classic example is the *Ultima* series; a modern example is *EverQuest.* RPGs are most often played online with others.

- *Simulation games* are about flying or driving things (often military) or building worlds, such as *Sim City* and *The Sims*, or, increasingly, running companies (*Start-up*).
- *Sports games* are the one category in which the content, rather than the game play is the determining factor. Most are action games where you can control one or more players at a time. Sports games are getting so photorealistic that on the latest consoles you'd almost swear you were watching real players on television. There also exist less action- and more statistics-oriented sports games such as fantasy baseball, as well as action sports games, especially in arcades, where you control the game via a realistic piece of sports equipment, such as skis, a surfboard, or even—but only in Japan—a rotating kayak paddle.
- *Strategy games* are typically about being in charge of something big— an army, or an entire civilization—and making it evolve the way you want, either on your own or more often against opponents. The classic example is *Civilization*; a modern example is *Roller Coaster Tycoon*.

COMPUTER GAME DESIGN

Game designers have a better take on the nature of learning than curriculum designers.
— Seymour Papert, MIT

Computer game designers are an extremely interesting group of people. Were you to attend the Computer Game Designers Association Conference (CGDC) in San Jose each spring, you would find yourself surrounded by thousands of what might look to be "ur-geeks"—guys, mainly, in ponytails and t-shirts. If you really knew nothing about them, you might take them for a group of high-energy dropouts, but you would be dead wrong. This group might actually beat the entire Ivy League in brainpower. The group certainly includes some of the most talented—if unsung—creative people of our generation.

In his address to the 2000 CGDC, Danny Hillis, the renowned creator of Thinking Machines, and at the time a Disney Fellow, said:

> I really believe that this is a really important group of people. I
> get to talk a lot to politicians and scientists and entertainers, and
> they all assume that they are the center of the world, and that

they are making the decisions that are going to control how things come out. I actually think they are overestimating how much they are really influencing how things are coming out, and I usually give as an example people whom I think are really influencing the world—game designers."[53]

Game designers are often unknowns, even in their own industry, typically performing their magic in the shadows. In an industry that rivals the movies for revenues, their name rarely goes on boxes in the way authors' names go on books and director's names go on movie marquees. There are but a few superstar designers whose reputation is known to gamers at large: Shigeru Miyamoto of Nintendo, creator of *Mario 64* and *The Legend of Zelda: The Ocarina of Time*; Sid Meier, Creator of *Civilization*, *Railroad Tycoon*, and *Alpha Centauri*; Robyn and Rand Miller, creators of *Myst* and *Riven*; Peter Molyneux, creator of *Black and White*; Richard Garriott, creator of the *Ultima* series; and Will Wright, creator of *Sim City* and *The Sims*. Forgive my omission of anyone else who should be here, but for the most part, this world-transforming force travails in anonymity.

How do the game designers describe what they are trying to do? In December 1999, on the eve of the millennium, several game designers were interviewed by Geoff Keighley of *Game Spot*, the online affiliate of *Game Developer* magazine.[54] Here is what some of them had to say.

Brett Sperry of Westwood (Half-Life) said, "I'm fascinated with the concept of fun, constantly pondering what makes one game pleasurable and another one drudgery. I'm always puzzling about how to kindle more adrenaline-filled moments outside the twitch realm. How is it possible to create extreme emotional involvement with a game? What causes a player to have a peak experience? And how can I do that without requiring that the player have the dexterity and coordination of a 15-year-old?... Should my game have a fixed story with scripted plot points and sacrifice replayability? On the other hand, should it have lots of random elements and less compelling story elements?"

George Broussard of Apogee thinks about making "fun games . . . that make you want to finish them . . . that make you laugh, scream, and jump out of your chair when you play . . . that make you call your friend on the phone and tell him he *has* to see this new game."

Lou Castle of Westwood thinks about creating characters and phenomena that impact our worldwide culture in the same way as Lara Croft, Mario, and Pokemon.

Justin Chin of The Infinite Machine thinks about adding irony, subtle foreshadowing, restraint and good writing—"something I think we in the game industry must take to heart if we want to have compelling stories in our games."

And Bruce Shelley of Ensemble Studios *(Age of Empires)* thinks about "problem solving. . . . Interesting decisions in a competitive environment, that lead to a satisfying conclusion, and making virtual combat as interesting and fun as chess."

How's *that* for a set of challenges to spend your day on?

THE PRINCIPLES OF GOOD COMPUTER GAME DESIGN

Computer-based training designers could learn a lot from the people who build computer games.
— Bob Filipczak, *Training* magazine

Is game design an art or a science? The answer is important to us as we sit down to create Digital Game-Based Learning.

In 1997, *Next Generation* magazine undertook, in a special report, to answer the question "What makes a good game?"[55] It was not trying, as we did before, to distinguish games structurally from any other phenomena, but rather to see if it could determine what separates the "bad from the good" in this "modern day art." *Next Generation* came up with six elements "found in every successful game throughout history":

- Good game design is *balanced*. Balance leaves the player feeling that the game is challenging but fair, and neither too hard nor too easy at any point.

- Good game design is *creative*. Creative here is the opposite of formulaic. Good games are not merely clones of other games, but add something original.
- Good game design is *focused*. Focus is figuring out what is fun about *your* game and giving the player as much of it as possible, without distraction.
- Good game design has *character*. It's a game's depth and richness. Both the character and the characters in a game, if fully developed, are what are memorable.
- Good game design has *tension*. Every good game does it in its own way. The classic way is to make the player care about the goal of the game, and then make it hard to achieve.
- Good game design has *energy*. This comes from things such as movement, momentum, and pacing. The game's energy is what keeps you playing all night or rejuvenates you after a hard day.

OTHER IMPORTANT DIGITAL GAME DESIGN ELEMENTS

While those six elements are important to a good game, they are, according to Noah Falstein, more the *results* experienced by a reviewer or player than the processes used to create the games. Some, though by no means all, of the more process-oriented principles and elements that designers use to create good games include (I am indebted for many of these principles and elements to Falstein, who is a master game designer):

1. *A clear overall vision.* As in any other artistic endeavor, a clear vision is key to making a good game. It is generally a good idea that one individual (designer, project leader, or producer) be the "keeper" of the vision, but the entire team must *share* the vision. This requires good and frequent communication.
2. *A constant focus on the player experience.* Because most of the creators of computer games are players as well, they often make a game that they would want to play. This is good, but they must also focus on making the game accessible to their entire audience, including new players who might find challenging what has become trivial to the designers, and not make it too hard at the start.

3. *A strong structure.* Classic game structures take many forms, from having what Crawford calls a "very bushy tree" with as much branching as possible, to what Falstein calls "convexities," which means starting out with a small number of choices, branching out into many, and funneling back into a few. Some game structures are fractal, with "convexities of convexities," but the structure must be carefully thought out up front.

4. *Highly adaptive.* The game must be fun for a variety of players. One way that this is accomplished is through a series of levels of increasing difficulty, so that experts can find their challenge later on in the game, while novices are challenged at the beginning. Another is to have user-controlled "difficulty levels" or "cheat codes" that provide varying levels of invulnerability or resources.

5. *Easy to learn, hard to master.* The best games are often the ones that can be learned in only a few minutes, but provide hours or even lifetimes of challenge. Will Wright's favorite game, *Go,* "has only two rules," he says, "one of which is seldom used. Yet, from those two simple rules is derived this incredibly rich, complex strategy—it's much richer than chess, and the rules are far, far simpler." Think of *Rubik's Cube.*

6. *Stays within the flow state.* A successful game needs to constantly walk that fine line between not too hard and not too easy, and do it for a variety of players. One strategy used to accomplish this is "negative feedback"—that is, when you fall behind, the game gets easier; as you get ahead, it gets harder. In Sid Meyer's *Civilization,* for example, if a player does well and grows a civilization quickly, the cost of maintaining the civilization increases and so does the money that must be devoted to keeping the citizens happy.

7. *Provides frequent rewards, not penalties.* Rewards are an incentive to go on. Finishing a level is one reward, but there are often many small rewards, such as things to find and collect, along the way. While early on points were often subtracted for failure or bad moves, people generally do not like this. A better way is to have rewards that decrease with time, or to have players who "fail" start over from some recent milestone, rather than losing points or dying.

8. *Includes exploration and discovery.* While not typically a part of puzzle or sports games, players like to explore their turf, and uncover progressively various portions of the landscape.

9. *Provides mutual assistance—one thing helps to solve another.* Clues about one puzzle or task can be embedded into another puzzle or task, providing mutual assistance. In sophisticated games, these can be made to disappear when no longer needed, giving the player the illusion that less help was available than was actually the case.

10. *Has a very useful interface.* What is important for a successful game is *not* a simple interface, but a highly useful one. It must have a built-in learning curve so that beginning players know what to focus on and don't get confused, yet advanced players have plenty of power options and interesting ways to control the game.

11.*Includes the ability to save progress.* Most games have a "save game" button that stores all the pertinent information about the exact state of the game at the moment it is saved. The player can at any time choose "load saved game" to continue again from that point. This is pretty much of a *sine qua non,* although, says Falstein, some games are starting to lean away from that structure.

Contest 4: What are other good game design elements? Email your entries to *Contest4@. twitchspeed.com.*

A particularly interesting and specific set of game design principles have been put together by Harry Gottlieb, CEO of Jellyvision, the company that created the fabulously successful trivia games *You Don't Know Jack* and *Who Wants to Be a Millionaire?* Called the "Jack Principles," they reflect Gottlieb's unique approach to making computer games feel more like a TV show that you are actually in. They include techniques for maintaining pacing, creating the illusion of awareness, and maintaining the illusion of awareness. More information about the Jack Principles can be obtained directly from Jellyvision.[56]

"Eye Candy" vs. "Game Play"

Game designers often make a distinction between the way a game actually plays and the way it looks. In the early days of video and computer games, when the technology was still very new, there was not very much that could be done with graphics. So designers concentrated on making the game as exciting as possible. Even if the spaceship, for example, was only a greater than sign (>), or the character only a disc with a mouth, you enjoyed the game because it provided a lot of challenge and fun.

As the display characteristics of computers improved, however, designers began to add more and more "eye candy" to games—the eye-popping landscapes of *Myst* and *Riven*; the ultrarealistic characters of the sports games; the ultradetailed cars and track of the driving games; and, in many cases, movielike video. While this has obvious attraction to people, it also often had the unfortunate consequences of dramatically increasing costs and distracting designers from good game play. This has been disappointing to may old-time game players.

"I think it always boils down to the interaction design, whether that's single player or multiplayer," says J. C. Herz. "It's always possible to make a game prettier—just add money. But the games that wind up having a real impact always have incredibly well-designed rule structures, and the game play itself is well-thought-out interactions. Initially, when someone makes a breakthrough in graphics it will sell a game, because we love eye-candy, but that gee-whiz value only lasts so long." [57]

Many game designers think that we are fast approaching diminishing returns in improving graphics. After they are photorealistic, where do you go? Many designers are excited, because they believe this will mean a renewed focus on game play. And despite the raised bar on eye candy, it is still possible to make a really fun game without great graphics, as Ashley Lipson's legal game *Objection!* illustrates. The ultimate example of the primacy of game play over graphics is, of course, *Tetris*.

What comes out of a good game design—and a lot of hard work to actualize it—is the player's experience. Gamers' connection to these experiences and to their games is an extremely passionate one. Digital Game-Based Learning should evoke similarly strong passions as well.

DIGITAL GAME PREFERENCES:
CULTURE AND INDIVIDUALS

Some people, such as J. C. Herz, who reviewed computer games for several years for the *New York Times*, are omnivorous in their gaming preferences. Others are very specific. Think for a moment about the games (computer or not) that *you* like. Why do these games, but not others, appeal to you and?

Games, it turns out are extremely culture and age specific. They reflect the overall culture we grew up in, the specific milieu in which we were raised, our own particular culture and ethnicity, and even our religion. Because many games are learned and played in our youth, the games we like often reflect what was going on in our environment when we were at an impressionable age, usually teenagers (e.g., boomers and Jeopardy!), and what we actually experienced (e.g., the sports of our particular culture and choice). Thus knowing as much as possible about your intended audience is crucial to successful game design.

Digital Games and Age

Unlike children who see it as a challenge or just natural to learn a new game, adults sometimes shy away from learning new games, because to play any game well takes effort and practice. Many of us are embarrassed not to be good at something. Today many adults over a certain age are reluctant to try the "twitch games" of their kids, particularly if anyone is watching. Yet, as I discovered with *Straight Shooter!*, given a little privacy to practice, adults will often take to even those types of games.

I suspect our teen years are when we become addicted to many games. There is currently a nostalgia boom going on among young professionals and others for the games of their youth. Old hand-held games from the 1970s, such as *Frogger* and *Ms. PacMan*, are selling for sky-high prices.

Try this. Take your birth year. Go to the table and find, in the first column, the years closest to it. See if you don't like the games listed in that year and the ones close to it more than others.

Your Birth Year	Game	Year Game Introduced
Pre-1949	*Monopoly*	1935
1949	*Jeopardy!*	1964
1959	*Pong*	1974
1963	*Space Invaders*	1978
1964	*Asteroids*	1979
1966	*Battlezone / Defender*	1981
1967	*Frogger / Trivial Pursuit*	1982
1971	*Super Mario Brothers*	1986
1973	*Sim City*	1988
1974	*Tetris*	1989
1976	*Sonic the Hedgehog*	1991
1977	*Mortal Kombat*	1992
1979	*Doom*	1994
1981	*Quake*	1996
1984	*Roller Coaster Tycoon / The Sims*	1999

Age, however, is not a barrier to learning and playing computer games. Often, when one finally realizes what a particular game is about, there's a big "aha."

"I watched my 60-year-old father have his 'ah-ha!' moment a couple of years ago playing *Wing Commander,*" says Gabe Newell of Valve Software.[58] "Now, he spends a lot more time playing computer games than he does watching TV. He and my half-brother spend more time playing games together, talking about games, or arguing about games than they do playing, watching, or discussing sports."

Digital Games and Violence

There's so much comedy on television. Does that cause comedy in the streets?
— Dick Cavett

Although there are, of course, many violent games, games *in themselves* are not violent. Sure, those that are violent get most of the press attention, especially after incidents such that at Columbine High School in Colorado. But the vast majority of digital games are not at all violent, and that includes many of the bestsellers: *Sim City; The Sims; Roller Coaster Tycoon; Tetris; Myst;* and *Riven.* Action/fighting games are only one genre (or two depending on how you count) of video and computer games. Adventure, puzzle, role-playing, simulations, sports, and strategy games are all primarily nonviolent (although some of them do simulate war or have "combat"—but so does chess.)

Obviously, violent games are not the best choice, nor do I advocate them for Digital Game-Based Learning. But it is important to note that what is at the core of even these games is not the violence but the action and the game play.

It is often possible to take an action genre, extract the violence, and still make an exciting game, as we shall see with *Straight Shooter!* (see Chapter 9).

Digital Games and Gender

With the exception of violence, few game topics inspire so much passion as computer games and gender. The issue is whether computer games are only "boys toys," or whether females will play in equal numbers, either because there are games that appeal to both sexes or because there are games that appeal directly to them. Gender is an issue very much on the minds of game makers. Gender is certainly an issue that we will have to keep in mind as we create Digital Game-Based Learning. There has been and continues to be (and no doubt will continue to be for some time) much heated discussion and debate about computer games and gender. Yet, the truth is far from clear and is, in fact, a moving target.

One component of the issue is computer use in general by girls, which, while once clearly behind boys, appears to have reached parity, at least in the United States. "There isn't much of a difference between boys and girls anymore, and that's true in all age groups," says Nicholas Donatello, President of Odyssey, a research company.[59] But the kinds of sex differences that marketers and social scientists have long observed, such as boys preferring competition and girls preferring relationships, can manifest themselves on the computer as well. Both resulting from and fueling the computer-fluency of girls has been a huge rise in the number of computer games designed for girls ages 6 to 12.[59]

If males and females are at parity in their computer use, and the number of computer games aimed at women has risen extraordinarily, we need to ask, "Do females play computer and video games as much as males?" and "What games do they play?" While no one disputes that video and computer games were initially an overwhelmingly male experience, there's plenty of evidence that female attitudes toward games are changing. "We're seeing far more unashamedly nerdy girls today than we saw in the 1980s," says Idit Harel of MaMaMedia.[61]

At a 1995 *Killer Instinct* tournament in San Francisco, three of the eight winners were girls, surprising even the organizers, the public relations agents for Nintendo of America. "All our research told us girls don't like these fighting games. But they had to be playing *Killer Instinct* in the arcades or they wouldn't have been that proficient," said vice president Don Varyu of Golin Harris.[62] At the same time, Sega and Nintendo game counselors, who field thousands of calls daily from players, reported that girls and young women accounted for 35 to 50 percent of the phone traffic, up from 90 percent to 10 percent in favor of boys.[63]

Although Mattel's *Barbie* games are by far the biggest sellers to girls,[64] 13-year-old Kate Crook, a semifinalist in the Blockbuster World Game championship made a point of saying that *Barbie Super Model* is "stupid." "There are plenty of girls who like fighting games and role-playing adventures," she said.[65]

Many adult women are gamers as well, although not always playing the same games as men. According to J. C. Herz, *Tetris* "is more popular with women than any other game and notoriously addictive among female professionals."[66] Why? Because it appears to provide elements that females need and like. "Tetris is about coping," says Herz. "It's about imposing order on the chaos. It's not about blowing thing up; it's about cleaning things up." Herz, for one, thinks that the game gender gap has disappeared, at least in the United States.[67]

The following can safely be said about games and gender:

- Initially, many fewer girls than boys played computer games—computer games were "boys toys." Many people, including the computer games makers—girls after all represent half their potential audience—have been trying to do something about this for some time.
- Few dispute that things are changing and that more women play computer games—the issues are how much are they changing and how

fast.
- Many observers think the proportion of women playing computer games has changed considerably in the last several years, as girls have more access to, and are more comfortable with, computers and video consoles.
- There have always been girls and women who like or love computer games. I have personally observed women playing, in a highly engaged way, a variety of video games from *Devil Dice* to *Golden Eye* to *Unreal Tournament* and loving every minute of it. One of the top game champions who travels the country challenging players is a girl.
- Some well-researched and well-funded attempts, such as *Purple Moon,* to make games specifically based on what are supposedly girls' preferences, such as interaction rather than action, received positive reviews but floundered commercially.
- An exciting game is an exciting game. While certain games such as *Tetris* are reported to be played preferred by women, and others, such as shoot-em-ups, are reputed to be disliked by them, I know many women in their twenties who *love* shoot-em-ups. We used a shoot-em-up format at Bankers Trust (shooting ideas out of a cell phone) and found that the competitive-type females at the bank were just as into it as the males.

So, whether or not there is still a "games gender gap" is hard to say. Game *preferences* are sometimes different, which clearly has implications for the design of Digital Game-Based Learning. Nevertheless, it's safe to conclude that a large and steadily growing number of girls and women appear to be finding satisfying types of computer games to play. It's also safe to say that finding *more* of these types of games is a quest that is being pursued vigorously on many fronts.

THE "LANGUAGE" OF DIGITAL GAMES

Every medium of communication has its own language—sets of meanings and shortcuts that are taken for granted by those used to the medium, but which have to be learned before it can be fully enjoyed, or even, sometimes, understood very well. Language has grammar: there are doers, actions, and things acted upon. Written communication adds the logic of relationships: chapters and subchapters; forms of emphasis: bold and italics; forms of reference: quotations and footnotes; and so on. Movies and TV have their own language of cuts, transitions, close-ups, and blackouts to indicate the passage of time and other things. Professor Greenfield of UCLA studied these media languages and showed that children (or others new to the media) must gradually learn them over a period of time.[68] There are no courses for this (except in film and communications schools). People learn by doing and making inferences, and getting help from others along the way.

There is also a language or rhetoric of computer games, which is shared between all players, that is learned by early experiences, and that is often opaque to non-computer-game-players. This is part of the great generational difference that was described in previous chapters.

Among the things that all digital-game-players tacitly know, do, and look for are:

- All things can and should be clicked on (actually, this is more subtle, with what is or isn't clickable often indicated by very small design elements.)
- Things are "built" by clicking on an icon and dragging it to where you want it.
- People move by selecting them and clicking where you want them to go.
- There are hidden combinations of keys that do interesting things.
- There are hidden surprises, commonly known as "Easter Eggs," to find.
- There's almost always more than one way to do something.
- Something may have to be tried many times before it works.
- There are usually "cheats" or ways to get around something. These codes, which at the origin were ways for programmers and testers to get further ahead in the game, are coveted and passed from player to player and even reported in magazines. Some "cheat codes" introduce funny and incongruous elements. You can, for example, create a fleet of machine-gunning twentieth-century Ford Cobras in your mediaeval *Age of Empires II* scenario, with predictable effect. [69]
- Games can always be saved and reloaded later.
- Games are "fair." They don't kill you off without giving you a chance and they don't require resources that you cannot get (although surviving or finding the resources may not be easy).

The language of video and computer games is important because for those familiar with the language certain things are extremely obvious and transparent; but for outsiders, they are often hard to guess. This is *very* important, as we shall see in the next chapter, in designing Digital Game-Based Learning.

SUMMARY: WHAT MAKES DIGITAL GAMES SO ENGAGING?

The reasons that computer games and video games are so engaging for hundreds of millions of people are that:

1. They give us *enjoyment and pleasure.*
2. They give us *intense and passionate involvement.*
3. They give us *structure.*
4. They give us *motivation.*
5. They give us *doing.*
6. They give us *flow.*
7. They give us *learning.*
8. They give us *ego gratification.*
9. They give us *adrenaline.*
10. They spark our *creativity.*
11. They give us *social groups.*
12. They give us *emotion.*

It is time now to see how we can use and apply this level of engagement to create something new and really worthwhile for training and education: Digital Game-Based Learning.

6

Digital Game-Based Learning
Why and How It Works

I believe learning comes from passion not discipline.
— Nicolas Negroponte, MIT Media Lab

One wonders whether there's any limit to what can be done in merging the addictive elements of computer games with effective instruction.
— Bob Filipczak, *Training* magazine

Learning through games—yes!!!
— A Potential User

We've seen how and why the training and education process is typically so incredibly *un*engaging due to its focus on content and "telling." We've explored why digital games are so engaging. It is time now to talk about how the two worlds—computer games and learning content—can be put together by creating Digital Game-Based Learning. We need to answer three key questions:

- *What* is it?
- *Why* does it work?
- *How* does it work?

Most simply put, Digital Game-Based Learning is any marriage of educational content and computer games. The premise behind Digital Game-Based Learning is that it *is* possible to combine computer and video games with a wide variety of educational content, achieving as good or better results as through traditional learning methods in the process. So, let us define Digital Game-Based Learning as *any learning game on a computer or online.*

What does Digital Game-Based Learning look like and feel like? Ideally—and I'm not sure that anyone has fully realized this ideal as yet—it should feel *just like a video game or a computer game, all the way through.* But the content and the context will have been cleverly designed to put you in a learning situation about some particular area or subject matter. For example:

> You are agent Moldy, sent on a top-secret mission to save the Copernicus Space Station and keep the evil Doctor Monkey Wrench from blowing up half the galaxy. Your only tools are your wits and the new CAD program that has been programmed into your computer. As you look around you, you discover a weapon—but the trigger's broken. You have only a few minutes to learn to use the CAD program to make a new trigger, beam the evil robots into outer space and complete your mission ... [1]

The primary focus of this book is Digital Game-Based Learning for business and government, including the military. But I will also touch in Chapter 7 on some interesting Digital Game-Based Learning applications in pre-school, K-12, and higher education. This is important because the experiences of people as they come through these institutions will strongly influence the needs, preferences, and desires they will bring with them when they enter our businesses.

An immediate piece of good news is that the process of bringing Digital Game-Based Learning into business has already begun without us. No longer confined to pure fantasies, consumer computer and video games are beginning to contain content that we might want trainees or students to know. A small but growing number of commercial games, such as *Start Up, Aviation Tycoon* (or, if you prefer, *Pizza Tycoon*), *Wall Street Trader 2000*, and even *Sim City,* are filled with content that can be very useful for certain types of business training. And games like *Age of Empires* have much historically correct content that can potentially be used in schools. Of course, most consumer games would still require almost total revision to make them useful as either training or education vehicles. But the process of combining real computer games and learning has begun, *because Digital Game-Based Learning works.*

WHY DIGITAL GAME-BASED LEARNING WORKS

Digital Game-Based Learning works primarily for three reasons:

1. The first is the added *engagement* that comes from putting the learning into a game context. This can be considerable, especially for material people are loathe to learn.
2. The second is the *interactive learning process* employed. This can, and should, take many different forms depending on the learning goals.
3. The third is *the way the two are put together* in the whole package. There are many ways to do this, and the best solution is highly contextual.

Of course, an important part of the picture is also *how it is used.* In most cases, Digital Game-Based Learning isn't designed do an entire training or teaching job alone. As indicated in the case studies in Chapters 9 and 10, many Digital Game-Based Learning instances are part of larger initiatives and approaches, often including instructors or teachers and other types of learning. But increasingly, the game portion is taking up a larger, more up-front, and more primary role in the learning process.

A final requirement—and this is no different than in any learning—is that the content and the learner be well matched. If they are not, little or no learning will happen with any method.

Dr. Robert Ahlers and Rosemary Garris of the Navy's NAWCTSD Submarine Lab have their own theory of why games work after a 3-year-long study of computer and video games.[2] They conclude that opportunities for success (from the game's goals, rules, and control of one's destiny) lead to a sense of purpose; that curiosity appeal (from surprise, complexity, mystery, and humor) leads to fascination; that simulated danger (from conflict, sound, graphics, and pace) leads to stimulation; and that social reinforcement, (both real, from online conversations, and game chat rooms, and simulated, from scoreboards and game interactions) leads to a sense of competence.

They describe a cycle of *initiate>persist>succeed* that leads players of training games to remain involved as they initiate game play, adopt a role, control game play, practice skills, solve problems, persist to the end, and strive to win (which translates as "learn").

Digital Game-Based Learning also fits well with current "theories of intelligence." In his *Thiagi Game Letter*, Thiagi has examined several of these theories and found that they all support games-based and experiential learning.[3]

How is it possible to create learning that has all the engagement of games *and* all the content required by business or education? And how do we make it successful? In other words, how do we design and make Digital Game-Based Learning that works?

You might ask, for example, "The picture you paint sounds great, but isn't it *hard* to create Digital Game-Based Learning?" Of course, just as it is not easy to create a successful video game, creating successful, complex Digital Game-Based Learning is not an easy task. There is definitely a whole lot more involved than throwing up a few PowerPoint slides. But,

- You can start small and grow.
- The people who've done it have really enjoyed the process and been successful.
- It's getting easier all the time.
- It's definitely worth the effort

Quite a few trainers, educators, and their teams have successfully created Digital Game-Based Learning applications, and these can serve as models of what to do and what not to do. In the remainder of this chapter I discuss a number of approaches, issues, and difficulties in creating Digital Game-Based Learning. I will then move on in future chapters to present and review a great many examples in business, schools, and the military, at many different levels of complexity and cost—at least one of which, I'm certain, can serve as a model for any project that you might want to do. In the book's final chapters I will discuss implementation—how to get a project funded and started in your organization.

As we go through this process together, I ask that you please try, as I will, to keep an open mind to a variety of approaches, and not to jump too quickly to critical conclusions. We are at the very beginning of the Digital Game-

Based Learning phenomenon. In our quest to get better we will gain much more by observing what does work than by harshly criticizing what doesn't.

HOW DO YOU COMBINE COMPUTER GAMES AND LEARNING?

How *can* two so seemingly disparate phenomena as computer games and effective, rigorous learning (because that's what we want, of course) be combined? The answer, happily, is *in a great variety of ways*. But anyone looking for one standard solution will be disappointed, because the answer is also highly contextual. The best way to do it in any particular situation depends on:

- The audience
- The subject matter
- The business and political context you are in
- The technology available
- The resources and experience that can be brought to bear
- How you plan to get it out there (distribution)

I have always found it useful to think of Digital Game-Based Learning along the two principal dimensions of why it works: *engagement* and *learning*.

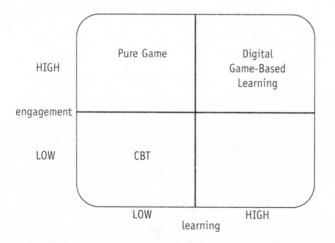

DIGITAL GAME-BASED LEARNING COMES ONLY WHEN ENGAGEMENT AND LEARNING ARE BOTH HIGH.

CBT (computer-based training), for all its hype, is basically low engagement/low learning (lower-left quadrant). Games, of course, along with some edutainment are high engagement/low learning (upper-left quadrant.) Digital Game-Based Learning occupies the high engagement/high learning upper-right quadrant. I have yet to see something, online or elsewhere, that is really high learning with low engagement; I think it is a "null" category that just doesn't exist.

But even within the Digital Game-Based Learning quadrant, there can be a lot of variation. Each dimension is a continuum, and each project has a different amount of both learning and engagement. Ideally, you want to move out continuously on a 45-degree line balancing the two. Although there might be reasons in a given case to lean more toward one or the other, I'm not sure this is a good idea (although I have always thought it would be nice to have a slider, so the user could choose his or her own mix between learning and engagement based on their mood at the time).

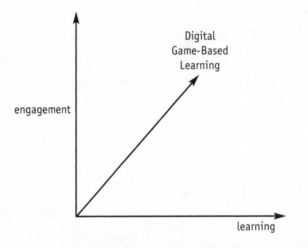

GOOD DIGITAL GAME-BASED LEARNING DOES NOT FAVOR EITHER ENGAGEMENT OR LEARNING, BUT STRIVES TO KEEP THEM BOTH AT A HIGH LEVEL.

The reason this is important—and it is—is that as we design Digital Game-Based Learning we have to consider *both* dimensions all the time. Not enough emphasis on learning and we risk falling into being just a game. Not enough emphasis on engagement and we risk sliding into CBT.

It is much better to think about keeping both dimensions high than to think about trading them off, as some suggest we need to do.

So our process is the following: we need to select or create a game style that will engage and a learning style that will teach what is required (each with the other in mind), and then somehow blend the two. We also need to take into account the political context, the technology, and the resources available.

SELECTING A GAME STYLE

Several people studying games have come up with lists of game "elements" to put into a learning game to make it successful. In his landmark and oft-cited 1981 paper, "What Makes Computer Games Fun?,"[4] Tom Malone, just out of Stanford and then at Xerox PARC, provided a checklist of elements for designing enjoyable educational experiences which includes:

- *Challenge*: Does the activity have a clear goal? Are the goals personally meaningful? Does the program have a variable difficulty level? (Determined either by the student, automatically, depending on the student's skill, or by the opponents' skill). Does the activity have multiple goal levels, such as scorekeeping or speeded responses? Does the program include randomness? Does the program include hidden information selectively revealed?
- *Fantasy*: Does the program include an emotionally appealing fantasy? Is the fantasy intrinsically related to the skill learned in the activity? Does the fantasy provide a useful metaphor?
- *Curiosity*: Are there audio and visual effects to stimulate sensory curiosity such as decoration, fantasy enhancement, rewards, and representation systems? Are there elements to stimulate cognitive curiosity such as surprises and constructive feedback?

Dr. Robert Ahlers and Rosemary Garris, of the Navy's NAWCTSD Submarine School, came up with a list of "critical characteristics for fun learning and game play," including: imaginary situation; rule governed; goals specified; competitive/cooperative; progressive difficulty; sound effects; dynamic graphics; user control; outcome uncertainty; simulated danger; performance feedback; high response rates; and informational complexity. [5]

This is all helpful information. But the trouble with an elements approach is that while these elements are indeed found in good games, just having a list of elements does not *guarantee* you a good game, which is why there are so many boring and ineffective learning games. So, another approach is to look at the games and game genres that are out there that work well and, in addition to elements, to try to capture these games' "style" of putting the elements together successfully. (If you *can* design a completely original game that has all the elements and that works, then more power to you!)

The types of games we have to choose from include all the categories of computer games mentioned in Chapter 5. Selecting a game style from these categories can be done in several ways. There may be a commercial game for children or adults that immediately makes sense in terms of the content. *Myst* and children's games turn out to be, in my experience, the two kinds of computer games that non-game-playing adults know best. However, it is best not to stop with what you know, but to look at a wide variety of options—to speak with a lot of gamers, and especially to go to the store to buy and to try some. The variety of gaming experiences between *The Sims, Alpha Centauri, Baldur's Gate,* and *Roller Coaster Tycoon,* for example, is very wide. As I said, it *is* also possible, if you have a good idea, to create an entirely new game from scratch combining elements from many, but you must be very careful to make it a good game. In Ashley Lipson's words, "To be an entertaining and educational game, it must first be a game, and only then, a teacher."[6]

Do not take this phase of the process lightly; consider many options. The type of game you finally choose, and your skill in integrating it with the learning, will determine the level of engagement. To find the potential game styles that will engage, we need to consult our audience.

Our Audience: The Players

Most audiences will become excited when they hear you are designing a game for them, but they will also be skeptical. So much learning is boring and done *to* workers, that people need to be clear that the game is being made to engage them and that they have a real say in its design. In the end, the audience will quickly determine whether the game is engaging, and if it isn't, they will basically ignore it or throw it away, wasting a lot of your effort, time, and money. So, we begin by considering our particular type of audience, from whom we will select a representative group to work with.

In some fortunate situations, we may have an audience that is reasonably homogeneous. *The Monkey Wrench Conspiracy*, for example, was designed for a relatively homogeneous audience of mechanical engineers, over 95 percent of whom are young (20 to 30 years), male, and experienced gamers. The military's *Joint Force Employment* (see Chapter 10) was designed for a relatively homogenous group (at least in their training) of mid-level military unit commanders. Some games have been designed specifically for people with MBAs and/or strategy backgrounds. Others have been aimed at highly competitive professionals, or at a particular type of factory worker. But some audiences will not be as easy.

In business, as in education, we often need to face the reality of fairly diverse audiences for any given type of training. When this is true, among the most important variables that make a difference to choosing a type of Digital Game-Based Learning are:

- Age
- Gender
- Competitiveness
- Previous experience with games

If the audience is diversified along one or more of these dimensions, then there are several strategies for dealing with creating games for such groups.

- Seek a "lowest common denominator" game format; that is, a game format that appeals to both older and younger employees, to both men and women, or to both competitive and noncompetitive employees. Among game formats that may serve this purpose are detective games, adventure and puzzle games, and strategy games.
- Create more than one game; for example, one game that is more competitive and one game that is more cooperative. The commercial Virtual World game centers began by offering two games—a highly aggressive shooting game and a much less aggressive racing game. games2train has created a shell in which the user can choose from among eight games to learn the same content.
- Provide a nongame alternative for those in the audience who are not engaged by the game you choose. This is valuable in every case.

Of these, the danger in the first is that it may involve too much compromise, resulting in a game that pleases no one. The second strategy may be too expensive. In such cases, the third alternative—building the best game you can for the most people, but allowing those who don't like the game learn another way—may be your best solution. We found this extremely important to the success of Digital Game-Based Learning at Bankers Trust.

One of the most important things that you can do in designing Digital Game-Based Learning is to get representatives of the audience involved very early in the process. This can be done through focus groups, informal interviews, and/or by including audience members on the design team. *More than anything else*, player input and preferences will determine the ultimate acceptance and success of the game.

Here's an example. When we created what eventually became *Straight Shooter!* for the financial derivatives' traders and sales people at Bankers Trust, our team's first idea was to create an auto-racing game. After all, we reasoned, these people make a lot of money, they buy and drive fancy cars (that they could acquire, customize, and upgrade in the game), and they love competition and beating their colleagues. An auto-racing game would be perfect. As it turned out, they hated the idea of a racing game for two principal reasons. First, they had no interest in choosing, customizing, or upgrading vehicles in a game (real life was something else). Second, they questioned whether we had the budget and skill to make a computer racing game on a par with the hottest games on the then current video game consoles that they all owned. If we couldn't, they told us, the game would be bogus. As it turned out, they were right; our racing technology was not the best. What the audience *did* want, it turned out, was a first person chase-and-shoot game in the style of *Doom* and *Quake*. This we knew we could do at a high level, as several software engines were available on the market. Our questions to them then focused on whether the women in the group would enjoy this type of game, which has a reputation for being male-oriented. We brought in several women from the audience to discuss and try similar games. In this particular case, the women in the audience were competitive to the point that *anything* the men could do they wanted to show they could do better. So, our choice became clear.

User Choice: Different Strokes for Different Folks

One man's game may be another man's chore.
— Luyen Chou

We don't all like the same game, so offering the player choices is often a good idea. As we saw, one option is to give users a choice of more than one game and a nongame alternative or path through the same material to the endpoint as well. This addresses the fact that some people may not like the game you have, or prefer not to play games at all. One of the defining characteristics of play is that it is free—you don't *have* to do it, you can opt out. When you do give users a choice of not playing, it is helpful if they can opt in and out of the game whenever they choose. What we found, in at least one case, was that players go both ways. About half of players opt for the game and then at some point decide not to play, and half choose not to play at first, but later, when they get bored or frustrated, opt in. Including a nongame alternative often makes your game easier to sell to management as well.

The option of having more than one game may sound difficult, but in some instances, it is not. There already exist, and it is not that hard to create, parallel interfaces that allow you to create content once and have it flow into a number of game formats, thus offering the player a choice of game styles.

THE SUBJECT MATTERS: TYPES OF INTERACTIVE LEARNING

Second in the process—not because it is less important, but because in learner-centered learning the audience comes first and the steps can also be done in parallel—we need to consider the kind of learning we are trying to make happen, and the interactive processes for doing so. "Learning doesn't happen incidentally," says Dr. Ray Perez, of the Department of Defense. "You have to set out to teach those specific skills."[7] In Chapter 3, we discussed how different types of learning require different methodologies. Now is the time to apply that information. There are many different kinds of "content" to be learned in business (and, of course, in education as well) and the type of content and learning will also have an affect your choice of game.

Let us begin by looking at different kinds of learning content to see what kinds of activities are really going on, setting out a taxonomy of learning types. We can then take the different kinds of games, and line them up against these requirements.

The following are types of things to be learned, and some of the options for learning them (other, of course, than just telling):

TYPES OF LEARNING

"Content"	Examples	Learning activities	Possible Game Styles
Facts	Laws. policies, product specifications	questions memorization association drill	game show competitions flashcard type games mnemonics action, sports games
Skills	Interviewing, teaching selling, running a machine, project management	Imitation. Feedback coaching, continuous practice, increasing challenge	Persistent state games Role-play games Adventure games Detective games
Judgment	Management decisions, timing, ethics, hiring	Reviewing cases asking questions making choices (practice) feedback coaching	Role-play games Detective games Multiplayer interaction Adventure games Strategy games
Behaviors	Supervising, exercising self-control setting examples	Imitation feedback coaching practice	Role playing games
Theories	Marketing rationales, how people learn	Logic Experimentation questioning	Open ended simulation games Building games Construction games Reality testing games
Reasoning	Strategic and tactical thinking, quality analysis	problems examples	Puzzles
Process	Auditing, strategy creation	System analysis and deconstruction Practice	Strategy games Adventure games Simulation games
Procedures	Assembly, bank teller legal procedures	imitation practice	Timed games Reflex games
Creativity	Invention, Product design	play memorization	Puzzles Invention games
Language	Acronyms, foreign languages, business or professional jargon	Imitation Continuous practice immersion	Role playing games Reflex games Flashcard games
Systems	Health care, markets, refineries	Understanding principles Graduated tasks playing in microworlds	Simulation games
Observation	Moods, morale, inefficiencies, problems	Observing Feedback	Concentration games Adventure games
Communication	Appropriate language, timing, involvement	Imitation Practice	Role playing games Reflex games

Types of Interactive Learning

One reason that Digital Game-Based Learning is not impossibly hard to create is that the "learning" portion of Digital Game-Based Learning has employed—up till now, at least—many techniques that have been used in nongame forms of interactive learning. Interestingly, one of the elements that makes Digital Game-Based Learning so effective is that many, if not most of these learning techniques have been used in digital *games* since the very beginning (that's often where the learning designers got them!). Additionally, new interactive learning techniques are often "invented" on the fly by creators of both Digital Game-Based Learning *and* games out of necessity, as they observe how their audiences react to what exists. This invention of new interactive learning techniques and approaches will no doubt increase in the future, as Digital Game-Based Learning gains ground, making Digital Game-Based Learning increasingly effective.

Among the interactive learning techniques that have already been used in Digital Game-Based Learning are:

- Practice and feedback
- Learning by doing
- Learning from mistakes
- Goal-oriented learning
- Discovery learning and "guided discovery"
- Task-based learning
- Question-led learning
- Role playing
- Coaching
- Constructivist learning
- "Accelerated" (multisense) learning
- Selecting from learning objects
- Intelligent tutoring

Practice and Feedback. One of the earliest ways of using the computer for learning was practice and feedback. The computer is very good at presenting a series of problems and keeping track, statistically, of how people answer them. Some refer to this as drill and practice, and some as drill and kill. In a sense, this can be thought of as computer flash cards, and programs with exactly that name have been developed. This type of interactive learning has been a staple of edutainment for kids (especially in edutainment's earlier stages) leading to much criticism from many educators. It is certainly not the most interesting form of learning you can do on a computer.

Yet, in my view, practice and feedback has its place in Digital Game-Based Learning because it can be, in the right contexts, an excellent way of learning things that require lots of repetitive practice. (Anyone who denies there are such things should go out and learn to play a musical instrument.) Examples include facts (e.g., names), physical skills (e.g., typing), and reflex skills (e.g., many aspects of language). Even Luyen Chou, the creator of brilliant discovery-based learning games such as *Qin,* who says that as an educator he ignored computers for a long time because all they did was drill and kill, admits that things like typing do require drill and practice, and he has designed a Digital Game-Based Learning game called *Slam Dunk Typing,* to teach it.

One development that has made practice and feedback a lot more acceptable is the creation over the past several years of adaptive programming techniques that shift the difficulty level of the tasks or problems on the fly, depending on how correct (and/or fast) you are at doing them. Certainly, anyone using this type of interactive learning should consider strongly making it adaptive.

Learning by Doing. Many who reject telling as a methodology would replace it with learning by doing. This is great for Digital Game-Based Learning, because it turns out that doing is something that computer games are especially good at—they allow us to interact with them. (When was the last time that you played a game that spent a lot of time telling you anything.) Of course, there is doing and there is doing. The drill and practice discussed above is one form of doing; exploring, discovery, and problem solving are other forms. What is critical is active participation by the learner. So, we will want lots of learning by doing in our Digital Game-Based Learning.

Learning from Mistakes. Many learning theorists agree on the value of mistakes in learning. Among the most evangelical proselytizers is Roger Schank, who refers to this as "learning by failure" (or, perhaps more precisely, learning by "expectation" failure).[8] In this kind of interactive learning, a user moves toward his or her goal until the user comes to a failure point, where the user gets some feedback. Of course, this is precisely what happens in games. Anyone who has ever tried and repeatedly failed to solve a puzzle in an adventure game, or to beat a boss in an action game, or to get somewhere in a flying simulation, knows that doing and failing—or trial and error—is a primary way to learn. Games are good at this because they give players the motivation to keep trying.

One difference between learning applications and games is the way the feedback comes. In most learning applications, it is through some form of telling, be it video-based war stories, coaching, or written feedback. You listen or you read. In most games, feedback comes via action— something happens. You die. You lose. Your company fails. You go back to the beginning (*Doom*). You are mocked (*You Don't Know Jack*). In the learning that Sharon Sansfield designs for disaster recovery at Sandia Labs in New Mexico, "the feedback comes in terms of dead bodies and big bangs."[9] Occasionally in games you do go back to "school" and are told something (*Life and Death*), but that is usually only a small amount that enables you to move on in the game, rather than a lot of lessons to be learned.

Designing feedback to be less learninglike and more gamelike is often a big paradigm shift and challenge for Digital Game-Based Learning designers. The best way to learn to do this is to play a lot of games.

Another point about mistakes and failure in games versus learning applications is that in games players often want to—or are even encouraged by the game to—fail and make mistakes because the consequences of doing so are worth the trip. Game designers usually make the failure consequences interesting, which can help enhance learning. Christopher Horseman, president of Xebec Interactive Learning, says, "There's no value in learning unless they are willing to choose some of the wrong answers, answers they wouldn't normally choose."[10]

Goal-Oriented Learning. Some interactive learning designers distinguish learning that is fact oriented (learning about something) from leaning that is goal oriented (learning to do something). "It's not what you know that's important, it's what you know how to do," says Roger Schank, director of Northwestern University's Institute for the Learning

Sciences.[11] Those who use the term *goal-oriented learning or goal-based learning* may have coined that particular phrase, but the concept has been in games since the beginning. As we saw, a goal is a key element of games—it's what turns play *into* a game. The goals in a game, which are usually considered by users worth reaching (unlike the goals in many learning apps) are what give the player the incentive to push on through repeated failure.

Discovery Learning and "Guided Discovery." Discovery learning is based on the idea that you learn something better if you find it out for yourself, rather than have it told to you. In learning applications, discovery leaning usually implies some sort of problem to solve, which is usually done by searching through data or structures for pieces or clues. This is yet another kind of learning that has a long history in games—discovery learning is what many games, and certainly all adventure games— are all about. You come to a place, or a thing, or an enemy, and you don't know what it does or how to get past it, so you experiment, until you find the solution.

While discovery learning is great in games and many learning theorists support it, it can be frustrating to some learners, particularly those who are linear in their approach and thinking. When Paula Young was creating her *In$ider* program at PricewaterhouseCoopers, she and her team found in focus groups that *too* much pure discovery learning left many users floundering. So, they invented an interactive learning process that they called *structured discovery*. Their goal was to retain the need for the player to discover the solutions for themselves, but to give the players a very clear idea at any time of what the problem is they need to solve, rather than let them work even that out for themselves, as many games require.

Of course, structured or not, discovery learning is better for some things than others.

Task-Based Learning. Much traditional learning of systems and procedures ("how to do something") starts with conceptual explanations and demonstrations, and only then moves on to problems or tasks to actually do. In interactive learning software, this approach is sometimes structured into "tell me," "show me," and "let me do it" buttons, or a variation thereof. Task-based learning is a different approach, a variation of learning by doing. The task-based learning approach is to skip (or greatly truncate) the generalized explanations and go straight to a series of tasks or problems, that build on each other and that gradually increase in difficulty. By completing the tasks, with strong specific guidance and modeling, the user gradually learns the skills. A potential issue with this methodology is that users may learn less of the theory behind the skills, so it is important to think of creative ways to make this available.

When putting together *The Monkey Wrench Conspiracy*, the Digital Game-Based Learning for think3's *thinkdesign* software, the team found the task-based approach to work far better with the audience of engineers than did more traditional training approaches for software.

Question-Based Learning. While in interactive learning applications questions are most often used as some form of test, they can also be a form of primary learning. Answering a question whose answer you don't know forces you to think about the information and reason among the answers, rather than just being told. Question-based learning is is traditionally associated with a particular type of game—the quiz or trivia game. That these games are so popular and so easily grab people's time and attention makes them obvious vehicles for Digital Game-Based Learning.

Situated Learning. Situated learning is an approach in which the learning is set in an environment that is similar or identical to where the learning material will be applied in the future. According to its proponents, when students learn in such an environment, they benefit not only from the learning material that is taught but also from the culture that is in that environment, the vocabulary used, and the behavior associated with that environment. Creating highly realistic and immersive environments is something that games do particularly well.

Role Playing. Role playing is often used as a learning strategy in interactive training, particularly for "soft skills" such as interviewing, communication coaching, sales, and the like. Role playing is, of course, so much a part of games that it has its own genre—role-playing games, or RPGs. One difference between role playing in interactive training and role playing in games is that training role plays tend to be much shorter and more structured than in games, which are usually multihour, multiday, or open-ended. Extending the duration of role plays through games is likely to increase learning.

Coaching. Coaching is a growing element of interactive learning applications. Initially, this was a role left almost entirely to the live instructor or facilitator, but people are finding better ways to build coaches into learning programs. For a particularly good example of coaching in Digital Game-Based Learning, see Imparta's *Strategy Co-Pilot* in Chapter 9. Coaching has been part of games for a long time, often coming from various characters in the game that you happen across as you are exploring. Game designers work hard to make the coaching feel like and integral part of the game rather than a learning session, often designing "practice missions" to coach players through complicated skills.

Constructivist Learning. The researchers led by Seymour Papert at the MIT Media Lab's Epistemology and Learning Group, building on the work of Jean Piaget, have long championed a kind of learning that they call *constructivist*, which takes discovery learning even farther. Constructivists believe that a person learns best when he or she actively "constructs" ideas and relationships in their own minds based on experiments that they do, rather than being told. Constructivists also believe that people learn with particular effectiveness when they are engaged in constructing personally meaningful physical artifacts. Constructivist theory underlies the pioneering Lego/LOGO work that has culminated in the Lego *Mindstorms* kits and other products that are a form of Digital Game-Based Learning. It is the type of learning employed in games such as *Sim City* and *Roller Coaster Tycoon*.

"Accelerated" (Multisensory) Learning. Colin Rose leads a group in England that has appropriated the term *accelerated learning* and specifically applied it to a type of learning involving multisensory experiences. Their original work was in language learning, where, for example, they have beginners learn the numbers in a new language by acting out a kind of "physical rebus" to remember them. (To remember the Japanese words for 1-6—*ichi ni san shi go roku*—you might say "itchy knee, sun she go rock" while scratching your knee, pointing to the sky, pointing to a girl, walking, and doing rock and roll.)[12] Most of their work takes place in work-shops, but it would certainly be easy to incorporate some of their ideas into a Digital Game-Based Learning product. Their attachment of the term *accelerated* to their own process is, I think, unfortunate, because accelerating learning is the goal of many other approaches as well, including Digital Game-Based Learning.

Learning Objects. The idea of learning objects grew out of object-oriented programming, where pieces of a program are built as stand-alone units with input and output "hooks" to link them together in whatever order is needed for the particular task at hand. The concept is that if one can design pieces of content and perhaps certain interactions that are independent, then they can be hooked up on demand in any order by either an instructor or the learner. A number of people are working hard on this idea, including Joe Miller at Knowledge Planet (a part of Milken's Knowledge Universe) and the military's Advanced Distributed Learning (ADL) group. Learning objects is an approach that fits nicely with games, which are becoming much more object-oriented themselves. The military's ADL project includes a deliberate attempt to combine the objects of learning and games.

Intelligent Tutors. An intelligent tutor looks at a learner's responses and tries to decide why he or she made the error and give specific feedback, based on a computer model derived from observing expert problem solvers. Intelligent tutor programs understand many common misconceptions and try to disabuse the learner of those misconceptions early on, as well as giving problems and hints. Second-generation intelligent tutors add the capability to go out and find information needed, and to filter and present it in ways that are most helpful to the learner. The United States military is very bullish on intelligent tutors. Many games already work hard to understand the player's thinking from his or her responses and provide appropriate game playing options and strategies.. "I think that what we need to do," says Dr. Ray Perez, "is to tie the intelligence of an intelligent tutor with a game."

PUTTING THE GAME AND LEARNING TOGETHER

It's a matter of integration.
— Michael Allen, Allen Communications

The "art" of creating Digital Game-Based Learning is integrating the game and learning portions so that the result feels like a fun game and gets the learning accomplished. It is worth reemphasizing that there is no "cookbook" solution as to how to best do this. Rather, this is the place where the highest amount of creative thinking is needed.

Categories of Digital Learning Games: Different Means for Different Ends

Learning games can be categorized in a number of different ways. All of these categorizations are worth considering when deciding how to integrate your proposed game or game style with your content. They include:

- Intrinsic vs. extrinsic games
- Hard-wired games vs. "engines" and "templates" or "shells"
- Tightly linked games vs. loosely linked games
- Reflective games vs. action games
- Synchronous (real-time) games vs. asynchronous (turn-based) games
- Single-player vs. two-player vs. multiplayer vs. massively multiplayer games
- Session-based games vs. "persistent-state" games
- Video-based games vs. animation-based games.

Intrinsic vs. Extrinsic Games. In 1970, Tom Malone, just out of Stanford and working at Xerox PARC, published a landmark paper entitled "Towards a Theory of Intrinsic Motivation." [13] In it, Malone made the argument that there are two main categories of learning games: intrinsic and extrinsic. In an intrinsic game, Malone argued, the content is an integral part of the game structure. His example is a math game, where things go up as you get to higher quantities and down as you get to lower quantities. A more contemporary example is a flight simulation game, in which the game itself is about flying a plane, or *Sim City*, where you learn the rules of urban development by trying and succeeding or failing. Most simulation-type games fall into this category.

Extrinsic games, on the other hand, are games where the content and the game structure are less tightly linked, or not linked at all. The paradigm here is the question or trivia game in which the questions can be about any subject, but the game remains essentially the same. *Bingo, Jeopardy!*, and other often-used training games fit into the extrinsic model.

Which model, intrinsic or extrinsic, is better? Proponents of each will give you reasons why theirs is superior, and this is actually a highly controversial topic among Digital Game-Based Learning designers. "Intrinsic games," says Michael Allen of Allen Communications, "may provide the most powerful learning experiences technology can support. These are perhaps the most noble and worthwhile applications of technology in the learning field."[14] Clark Aldrich argues that "the real power is when you capture the rules at an algorithm level and have people understand them through constant exposure to different circumstances."[15] On the other hand, anyone who's ever used a typing game knows it can be fun *and* can help you to learn. I believe that *both* intrinsic and extrinsic games have their value in different situations. The tradeoff you need to think about is that while intrinsic games enhance certain kinds of learning and add to the engagement, they are typically created on a custom basis and are therefore more costly and often difficult to change or update. Extrinsic games, while lacking the learning power that may come from tightly integrating the content into the game, lend themselves well to templatization and to rapid changes of content, often at lower cost. Remember that intrinsic/extrinsic is not an either/or proposition; it is a continuum. There are a number of states between the two, one of which I refer to as *loosely linked*.

Tightly Linked Games vs. Loosely Linked Games. This catigorization of learning games is somewhat similar to the intrinsic/extrinsic classification, but is actually a different perspective. A tightly linked game is one that is constructed specifically around a fixed set of content. The content is built into the game; knowing the content is vital to succeeding in and winning the game. A tightly linked game can still be extrinsic, and the entire game might be able, with a fair amount of effort, to be repurposed for other content. A detective game in which the clues are pieces of information about the product is an example of a tightly linked game.

A loosely linked game, on the other hand, is one in which the content is essentially separate from the game, but there are "hooks" in the game which bring the two together, and send the player from the game to the content, and back again. In repurposing the game to new content, only the hooks must be changed, not the whole game. *The Monkey Wrench Conspiracy* is an example of a loosely linked game. It is a task-based learning game in which the tasks—which are done outside the game in the software to be learned—are initiated by encountering flashing objects, which, although part of the story line, are easily changed to add, eliminate, or alter a task.

Like extrinsic games, loosely linked games often allow content to be changed much more easily than tightly linked games. That means you would use them in situations where, say, the content was still in development, or changing rapidly. A tightly linked game is better for incorporating unchanging content; for example, the fixed model in the game *Situational Leadership*.

Hard-Wired Games vs. "Engines" and "Templates" or "Shells."
The ultimate tightly linked game is the so-called hard-wired game. Here, the designers and programmers sit down with the goal of building only this particular game. Reusability is not a consideration. *Everything* in the game is designed and optimized around the game, the content, and the player experience. In many ways, if done well, this will produce the best game of all, just as a custom-tailored suit is likely to look and fit better. But it is a very expensive way to do things.

The opposite of the hard-wired game is the template, or shell. In this approach, the content, be it text, graphics, video clips, or whatever, sits somewhere external to the game, is "read-in" or "called" by the program at the appropriate time, and is displayed onscreen. This allows the construction of content-editor software, in which a trainer or teacher can just type in various pieces of the content and have the content automatically displayed in the correct place in the game.

An approach in between hard-wiring and pure templates to use is what is referred to by programmers as an "engine." An engine can be, for example the software that lets you run around a three-dimensional world realistically, not walking through walls and encountering objects and things that move and have various properties. Such an engine can underlie or "drive" equally well a shoot-em-up game such as *Doom*, *Quake*, or *Unreal*, or a nonviolent, more politically correct game such as *Straight Shooter!* A number of game engines are available commercially; game companies often amortize the large expense of developing them by licensing them to other companies for other games. The *Doom*, *Quake*, and *Unreal* engines are all on the market (typically at high prices for commercial use), as are many individually developed versions.

Training vendors often take the trouble to turn what were originally custom-developed, hard-wired games into engines, so that they can resell them in a number of different contexts (this is also referred to as *templatizing* a game.) In this case, the *interactions* in the game make up the engine, and all the graphics and words change according to the new context. Examples of this are *Time Out!*, which was converted from being about a manufacturing company to being about a financial company, and *Running a Hotel* where the same engine was used for games about running a phone company branch office and running an elevator company.

The least happy result of all comes when a game is hard-wired because the designers or programmers are inexperienced with games and just plunge ahead building it as they go without considering reusability. This can happen either because they don't think they have to make things reusable, or because they don't know how to, or both. Hard-wiring a game should be avoided as much as possible in a final product. Prototypes, however, are often built hard-wired because doing so is faster and cheaper.

Reflective Games vs. Action Games. As we saw in the last chapter, there are a number of genres of games, ranging from action to role playing to strategy. A differentiating characteristic between these types of games that has an important bearing on Digital Game-Based Learning design is the degree of reflection they allow, because this is an important part of the learning process that is often under-included. Nonstop action games (also known as *twitch games*), offer the least opportunity for reflection in themselves, while role-playing, adventure, simulation, strategy, and puzzle games often proceed at a slower pace and offer more built-in reflective "space." (There are, nevertheless, twitch puzzles, such as *Tetris* and *Devil Dice*, as well as less reflective real-time strategy games.)

Role-playing games typically let you make choices in various types of dialogs, which provide reflection points. Adventure games, where you go around and find objects that allow you to solve puzzles, also give time for reflection around "how do I solve this—what do I need?" Simulations games, such as running-a-company sims, often allow you to make decisions at your leisure, although some provide real-time time constraints; strategy and so-called "god" games often give you all the time in the world to make up and change your mind.

Does this mean that we can or should never use a twitch game as part of Digital Game-Based Learning? No, it does not. The important thing is that there be a good balance of action and reflection in the final product, just as there should be a good balance of *edu* and *tainment*. Too much action and there's no time to reflect. Too much reflection and it can become boring. Again, we need to find the "flow path" between the two. This is part of the principle of *pacing*, which is so important to novels, movies, games, and other devices meant to hold our attention.

Synchronous (Real-Time) Games vs. Asynchronous (Turn-Based) Games. The distinction between real-time (also known as *synchronous*) and turn-based (also known as *asynchronous*) games is quite important to Digital Game-Based Learning, in at least two ways. In single-player mode, a real-time game must be "paused" or put into a pause state to interrupt it, either for reflection or to do something else. This usually involves saving the "game state" (everything that is happening) at that point. Some real-time games—for example virtual pets—do not allow this. The game continues whether or not you are playing; stop playing long enough and you lose. In a turn-based game, on the other hand—chess for example, but also many strategy games—the machine will wait forever for you to figure out your next move, unless you're "playing by the clock."

The distinction between synchronous and asynchronous is even more important in multiplayer games. While a game in which everyone is playing with or against each other at the same time—for example, a real-time battle or a competitive business simulation—can be very interesting, in training it can usually only work when trainees are in the same situation at the same time, such as in a training class. But this is often not the case in online training, at which point turn-based games, which allow each player to play whenever he or she has the time, may be a better solution. A turn-based game, though, may lack some of the immediate excitement of a real-time game, so the engagement has to be produced in other ways, such as a real interest in the outcome as in *President 96*.[16]

Single-Player vs. Two-Player vs. Multiplayer vs. Massively Multiplayer Games. Games can be either single player, multiplayer on the same computer (some *You Don't Know Jack* games), two or multiplayer over a network or the Internet, or massively multiplayer, which means that hundreds, thousands or potentially even millions (although not today) can play either at once, or on an "in and out" basis.

Most Digital Game-Based Learning to date has been single player, except in the military, where the goal has always been to link people because that's how war is fought. As discussed earlier, an issue for multiplayer games in business is getting the people together. In consumer games, this is often done via a virtual lobby where you first go when you want to play. When enough people are there for a game, the game starts. Some games allow people to join while the game is in progress. Another option for large multiplayer games is the persistent state game.

Session-Based Games vs. Persistent-State Games. Session-based games exist only for as long as the initial players are playing. Although the game may be able to be paused and resumed, it pauses for all players at the same time. When somebody wins, the game is over, and must be played again. In persistent-state games, on the other hand, the world of the game never goes away—each player moves in and out of it as they wish, but like the real world, the game world continues. In persistent-state games, such as *Ultima Online* or *EverQuest* (persistent-state games are often role-playing games), you can build up skill and experience over time, which has obvious implications for learning. Because the world is always continuing, and opportunities may come and go, there can also be penalties for not playing, and this, too, has clear connections to real business life. An example of a massively multiplayer, persistent-state business game is *Star Peace* from Monte Cristo.[17]

Video-Based Games vs. Animation-Based Games. Another interesting choice that designers of Digital Game-Based Learning need to make is whether whatever representations of characters and places they include will be video or animation based. These are two very different schools, often reflecting whether the designers have a video background. The advantage of video is absolute realism. Its disadvantages include the size of the assets (they are large and may limit what can be put on a CD or sent over the Internet) and limits on interactivity (because the scenes need to be prerecorded so they can play out when they are required by the player's choices.) Both of these disadvantages have been overcome to some extent by proponents; the first by better compression and streaming methods, and the second by techniques for cutting videos into pieces as short as 1 or 2 seconds, and assembling video sequences on the fly. A good example of this is *Angel Five* (see Chapter 9). An additional issue to consider with video is that if any changes need to be made, the video many need to be reshot, necessitating reassembling the same cast, sets, lighting conditions, and so on. This may lead to difficulties, as Video Arts found out when they wanted to shoot additional scenes for their older titles only to find the actors, such as John Cleese, had aged considerably![18]

Animated characters and graphics, on the other hand, allow designers a great deal of freedom. They can be made to look and sound any way you want. Unlike live actors, they never age or become unavailable. Their behaviors and actions can be preprogrammed and reprogrammed as necessary. "If I want a character to storm out," says Richard Berkey, creator of *Strategy Co-Pilot*, "I can just hit the 'storm out' key."[19] Animated characters and graphics are less expensive and, of course are totally lacking in ego (although that's not necessarily true of their creators).

Which to use in a Digital Game-Based Learning project depends on several factors. First, a need for absolute realism might suggest using video, although animated characters are fast approaching video actors in the details of what they can do (their voices, which are recorded actors, have always been real; computer-generated voices are currently only good for robots.) On today's advanced gaming consoles, the players in sports games appear almost as real as live TV. Second, in thinking about how much realism you really do need, there is an interesting tradeoff between specificity and universality that is explained very well in Scott McCloud's useful book *Understanding Comics.*[20] As McCloud shows, the more abstract a character is (the most abstract face being a circle) the more easily we can identify ourselves with that character. As they get more and more photorealistic, characters take on identities that are increasingly specific and become more difficult for us to project ourselves onto. So, in some cases video, which is *totally* photorealistic may actually *hinder* player identification with a character. This may or may not be important in a specific instance. If a game's perspective is first-person (through your eyes) and you never see yourself, then it may not matter. If it is "over the shoulder" like *Tomb Raider*, where you do see yourself continually as you play, it may be worth considering.

Richard Berkey of Imparta says that he is planning to move his future Digital Game-Based Learning games quickly from video to animation. In addition to speeding up game creation, he finds that video improves game play, because so many more possibilities can fit on the same CD.[21] Ashley Lipson, creator of *Objection!*, makes a similar argument: "My product is animation based," he says. "My competitor's product is video-based. My game has thousands of potential paths, theirs has one."[22] But Ed Heinbockel of Visual Purple (creators of *Angel Five*) feels that his company's technique of cutting the video into very small chunks and "late-binding" them produces similar results that are more lifelike. [23]

Narrative-Based Games vs. Reflex-Based Games. Another interesting question is how much story to include in the game. Should it be like a movie with an "inciting incident" at the start that makes you want to see the conclusion and complex character development along the way? Or should it be a series of unconnected scenarios or interactions in a gamelike context? The answer depends highly on what you are trying to accomplish. The more you want to create something that is long-term and that builds, the more story is a useful motivator. An alternative, of course, is to have lots of ever-increasing levels of puzzle difficulty, as in *Tetris*.

Although narrative and characters can add emotional impact to a game, which may aid in the recall of certain content, there are also categories of content where not recall but *reflex*—that is, the ability to react very quickly to a stimulus—is what is important. Language learning is one example (How are you? Fine.). Legal objection is another. Acronyms are a third. For such content, reflex-based games, in which stimuli are presented rapidly by the computer (with or without a story-based context) and responses are judged and timed, can often provide an effective, fun, Digital Game-Based Learning solution.

Game Interfaces. I have three things to say about game interfaces for Digital Game-Based Learning. The first, which goes against much conventional wisdom, is that game interfaces do not have to be, nor in many cases should they be, simple and intuitive. This is a myth that is often perpetuated by learning designers who are desperately afraid their audiences will run away. The problem with the simple interface, as Bran Ferren of Disney explains, [24] is that its usefulness quickly levels off and leads to an inability to get better and more sophisticated about using it. "The F16 cockpit is not a simple, intuitive interface," Ferren points out, "and neither is the piano." Nor for that matter are the interfaces to most games. They are full of special buttons, options, access to maps and other tools, which are extremely useful to advanced players, although often quite confusing to beginners. The key, therefore, is to have an interface that, while complex in its full capabilities, is easy to learn as you go along, letting you control only the basic things at the beginning, and assume more and more control as you go on. *Alpha Centauri* and *Battle Zone II* are good examples of this kind of interface.

My second point about interface and Digital Game-Based Learning is that there are a large number of less-than-exciting learning programs already available that could become really fun Digital Game-Based Learning with the addition of a good interface. Many of these programs are numerical spreadsheet simulations that have already been built for teaching purposes. The addition of a game interface often brings these games to life for the players. Two examples where I have seen this work quite successfully are a case study created by Roger Bohn at Harvard Business School called *Kristen's Cookies*,[25] and the derivatives trading games *HedgeManager* and *HedgeFund* created by Jerry DelMissier at Bankers Trust.[26] *Kristen's Cookies* began as a dry, numerical process control spreadsheet simulation, with a cute "story" in the written case. With the addition of a gamelike visual interface complete with ovens opening, cookies baking and calling out their degree of doneness, it became so much fun that the participants in the Harvard PMD (Program for Management Development) called it one of their favorite cases. The second example turned a brilliant but almost unusable spreadsheet-based game into a big winner, used hundreds of times around the globe and in the leading business schools (see Chapter 9). It is worth looking around your organization to see if any of these opportunities exist.

My final point about interface is that merely grafting supposedly gamelike interface elements onto an underlying model does not in itself make it a game. In *TeleSim*, a strategy simulation created for Pacific Bell,[27] the visual indicator for the players' performance was an animated graphic of a ship in a storm—the better you were doing the calmer the seas were, the worse you did the more the ship tossed and turned. This was not, however, an integrated game element, but simply a pasted on visual metaphor that felt strangely out of place. Which leads me to my next point.

Designed with Game Principles vs. Digital Game-Based Learning

A number of interactive learning designers say that they use "game principles" in their designs. What does this mean? And how does it relate to Digital Game-Based Learning? In my mind the two—learning applications with game principles and Digital Game-Based Learning—are very different. While it is certainly true that many learning products do make use of game elements such as interface, user control, interaction, pacing, and scoring to good effect, that by no means makes them games. In some cases, "game-based principles" is the designer's way of saying "I couldn't get them to let me use a game, but I snuck some ideas in anyway." A example of this is what happened to Bryan Carter, a designer who loves games, when he was at NCR. He tried to put as many game elements as he could into such programs as "Digital Communications Fault Analysis," but they would never allow him to call them games or to go as far as he wanted.[28] Their loss.

BUSINESS AND POLITICAL CONTEXT—"BEING PC"

It's now time to return to our original list of things to consider when creating Digital Game-Based Learning. The first three were selecting a game based on the audience, evaluating the subject matter and how to best interactively teach it, and putting the two together. The fourth is fitting the game into the business and political context of your organization.

No matter how much some of your audience may be asking for it, it just won't fly to create a shooting game when the political context is antiviolence, or a sexist game in an organization that is, as most hopefully are, fully committed to equal opportunity, or a local-style game if your audience is international. The business and political context must be considered carefully in all aspects of the game, including its title. In some ways this is a big pain in the butt, and many of the designers or programmers on your team—especially if they have no experience in corporations—may not understand the reason why this context must be considered. But surprisingly, I have found that many unexpected people can and will help you be context-correct if you ask them and make them part of the process.

As an example, in creating a derivatives policy learning game at Bankers Trust, our audience told us they wanted a *Doom*-style shooter, and we had access to a good software engine to do this. But guns and shooting bullets, a *sine qua non* of the genre, were out of the question, particularly because some of the bullets could hit clients (imagine the press!). It was, surprisingly, the bank's corporate council who came up with the idea of using a cell phone that shot out "ideas" (which graphically turned out to be light bulbs). The game's name was also sensitive and went through many changes. Finally, we held a contest. A senior-level executive came up with *Straight Shooter!*, of which he was so proud that he called my boss on vacation to lobby for it. It was a great name, and it stuck.

Another aspect that is quite sensitive to context is humor and tone. Many training folks tend to be humorphobes because they are afraid of offending someone, somewhere. But particularly for the Games Generations, humor—especially sarcastic humor or, "attitude," as it is often called—is a big part of what they like. A classic example is *You Don't Know Jack*, which is nothing *but* "attitude." It *is* possible to get attitude past the corporate censors. Paula Young of PricewaterhouseCoopers is very proud of the tone in *In$ider*; "It's got attitude—lots of it!" she says. Jellyvision, creator of *You Don't Know Jack* has been besieged by requests for Digital Game-Based Learning and is considering branching out in that direction in the future.[29]

Of course gender and racial diversity must also be taken into account in the game's characters, situations, and language, and another important aspect of being politically correct (PC) is increasingly international sensitivity. Games such as *In$ider*, *Straight Shooter!*, and *Build the Band* (see

Chapter 9) were designed to be used by employees—and sometimes customers—around the globe. By now almost everyone has heard the true stories of GM actually marketing a car in Latin America called "no va" (doesn't go), or the Japanese company Pocari marketing its sports drink in the United States as "sweat." But international sensitivity goes beyond just the name. When IBM licensed *The Battle of the Brains*, the game included a choice of three different sports—football, hockey, and tennis. IBM insisted on adding soccer and golf because they were much more widely played internationally. (We also added chess, just for PC good measure.) Stay sensitive, but don't let the PC police ruin your game!

TYPES OF TECHNOLOGY AVAILABLE (OR REQUIRED) FOR IT TO RUN ON

Corporations have a lot of technology—some of it pretty cool—but it is *very* heterogeneous. And very, *very* little of it, if any, is (at least deliberately) devoted to or optimized for games. When you are thinking about creating Digital Game-Based Learning for business it is *crucial* that you keep these facts clearly in mind, because you need to design a game that works for everyone in your audience. What technology is available to that audience (or what will be by the time your game launches) will be a big factor in deciding how you will combine your game and learning.

This is why, and I will reemphasize this in Chapter 11, *your best friend in this endeavor should be IT*. In these days of Internet and viruses, IT runs the corporate world. If they are *not* your friends, they will tell you *nothing* can be done. (Or worse, tell you when you are done that they won't allow it on their systems.) If they *are* your friends, and they get excited about your project—which is usually not hard given what else they work on—they will tell you early on what *really* can't be done, and help you do what can.

As we will see in the examples in Chapter 9, Digital Game-Based Learning has been designed for a wide variety of technologies, from simple email to complex combinations of PC, UNIX, Macintosh, LAN and the Internet and intranets, with wireless and handhelds on the way.

One of the first comments that you may hear, either from IT or HR, is that *everything* must be done over the Web. If you take this too literally, you may never get to do an interesting game, at least not in your lifetime.

With the technology available in most companies, *pure* browser-based games are very limited in scope. But if you combine the Internet game application with some locally supplied material, such as a CD-ROM or download, your possibilities are as great as anything in the commercial market. On the other hand, if you need to be absolutely sure that you reach everyone, your best bet may be an email game or a simple browser-based shell. As we will see, most of the high-end Digital Game-Based Learning applications are currently delivered on CD-ROM, although most have an intranet or Internet component. This is true for commercial games as well, and will be until broadband is ubiquitous. (Some of you may think, as I once did, that because many corporations have relatively fast connections, this is sufficient for a high-bandwidth game. In most cases, it is not. Those corporate "big pipes" are full with data that IT considers very important and certainly a higher priority than your game.) To do really good games totally over the Internet without a CD or download, we need fiber to the desktop.

Two of the most potentially promising yet largely unexplored areas for Digital Game-Based Learning, in my opinion, are handhelds, such as the Palm Pilot, and wireless, such as mobile phones. Both already have a complement of games available—you can play chess visually on many phones. [30] The advantage to using these types of devices for learning is that they are always with us, making it possible to squeeze in some learning in all those in-between moments when we are actually *not* calling someone. The combination of games and handhelds needs no explanation—Nintendo's GameBoy is one of the biggest selling objects in the electronic world, with over 100 million units sold around the globe. [31]

RESOURCES AND EXPERIENCE AVAILABLE TO BUILD IT

The sixth major factor in answering the question "How do I combine games and learning?" is the availability of resources and experience. Obviously, the more sophisticated the resources and experience you have at your disposal, the more complex projects that you can do. Resources include not only money, but designers, project leaders, programmers, subject-matter expertise, graphic artists, testers, as well as others. Paula Young almost gave up on her ultimately highly successful *In$ider* project because the expertise she needed on derivatives was not available within her firm. She ultimately got the firm to hire an outside expert.

Most corporations do not have in-house game designers or programmers, but a surprising and growing number do. I, for example was at Bankers Trust, a joint hire and resource of the HR and IT departments; PricewaterhouseCoopers has Paula Young; McKinsey had Richard Barkey; and Shell had Pjotr van Schothorst. Other creative and capable people have found homes in other corporations, and will increasingly continue to do so as the demand for Digital Game-Based Learning increases. It is important, though, to realize and admit when in-house resources aren't sufficiently capable of designing Digital Game-Based Learning. "Many trainers think they can write game scripts," says Paula Young. "It takes at least 5 years to learn to be a decent scriptwriter."[32] Digital Game-Based Learning created by people who have no experience with games and creative endeavors is likely to reflect this in the end product. A good role for a person who believes in and wants to do Digital Game-Based Learning but doesn't really have the expertise or experience is to become a producer, in the movie sense. The producer is the person who raises the money and pays all the bills, but hires a director to have the artistic vision and create the product.

If in-house expertise is lacking, you can always hire it. The way that you combine the learning and the game will in large measure depend on the creativity and experience of the people you hire. It is possible to hire entire firms or Digital Game-Based Learning vendors, who have a lot of experience in the field and will give you a highly original, turnkey solution. It is also possible to hire game experience piecemeal, such as design expertise from freelance game designers, game creation from programmers moonlighting from other jobs, and graphics expertise from moonlighters, freelancers, or games graphics houses. What about hiring a learning or a training company, or an instructional designer to create your Digital Game-Based Learning? I'd be pretty careful, as—in the name of a lot of self-proclaimed learning principles—you may get something a lot less gamelike than you expected. On the other hand, hiring a pure advertising or Web-creation firm, or even a pure games company, if you can find one, may produce less-than-ideal results on the learning side.

One thing people often assume, to their disappointment, is that they can get assistance from commercial games companies. This was certainly my idea when I first got started. I was convinced that when I told the big game companies that I was making learning games for a large corporation they would rush onboard to help me with my projects. That was not the case. The games companies are focused on the consumer market and particularly on getting their products out the door by Christmas. They do not have time for you. They generally find working with corporations onerous (it is). They may at most be willing to license you some of their characters or some technology, such as an engine. But even if you can't work directly with these companies, the examples of their games are out there for all Digital Game-Based Learning creators to see and learn from.

IMPLEMENTATION—GETTING IT OUT THERE

"Build and they will come" simply doesn't work.
— Paula Young, PricewaterhouseCoopers

Paula Young has her own personal 80/20 rule about Digital Game-Based Learning: It takes 20 percent of your effort to create the game and 80 percent to get it out in the field. And it took her 18 months of effort to create *In$ider!* "Implementation is the biggest challenge facing anyone embarking on the e-learning journey in the corporate world," Young says. [33] If you aren't thinking implementation from day one, then you are doomed to failure, especially if you are serving a large, diversified, and geographically spread out population. It is unbelievable the issues that come up. Many are technology based, such as people not having the Internet, or having older browsers or older computers. But others are attitudinal. This is why implementation affects not only your distribution, but also your game's design. Although Sony, Sega and Nintendo have made many games ubiquitous, you still need to be sensitive to what games are acceptable in the places where you will distribute. For example betting may be unacceptable in some places, and in Japan, they don't play much *Solitaire!*

DIGITAL GAME-BASED LEARNING PRINCIPLES

Based on everything we've discussed so far, is it possible to establish a set of Digital Game-Based Learning Principles? If it were, they would be things that *any* effective Digital Game-Based Learning would have to include. Establishing a set of principles to guide practitioners and users is, of course, not an original idea, even in this emerging field.

What follows is my attempt to create a short list of such principles. Following these concepts will allow you to take any subject matter and create a successful game-based learning experience on the computer. I could have phrased them as prescriptions ("Users should..."), but I think they work better as questions for you to keep asking yourself throughout the entire process. You can put them on your wall and reflect on them as you are considering, designing, building, testing, and rolling out Digital Game-Based Learning.

DIGITAL GAME-BASED LEARNING PRINCIPLES

To create effective Digital Game-Based Learning, continually ask yourself the following:

1. Is this game fun enough that someone who is not in its target audience would want to play it (and would learn from it)?

2. Do people using it think of themselves as "players" rather than "students" or "trainees"?

3. Is the experience addictive? Does it produce great "word of mouth" among users? That is, do users rush out after they try it and tell their colleagues or classmates "You've got to try this—it's "way cool." Do users want to play again and again until they win, and possibly after?

4. Are the players' skills in the subject matter and learning content of the game—be it knowledge, process, procedure, ability, etc. —significantly improving at a rapid rate and getting better the longer he or she plays?

5. Does the game encourage reflection about what has been learned?

Notice, if you will, the *order* of the principles. Fun first, learning second. Other experts have placed fun on their lists, but it's generally much further down. The result is that many of the programs that purport to be game-based learning really aren't—they are just someone's theories of learning or some dry simulation dressed up with game-like graphics. Believe me, users do know the difference.

7

Digital Game-Based Learning for Kids and Students
Edutainment

In a playful context kids seem to have an almost infinite capacity for learning. It's very easy it's effortless, it's exciting. If you put them in some kind of game situation—a computer game or a video game—they'll pick up skills very quickly, learn how to do things, at an amazing rate.
— Danny Hillis

We may be in a society with far fewer learning-disabled children and far more teaching-disabled environments than currently perceived.
— Nicolas Negroponte, in *Being Digital*

What is best about the best games is that they draw kids into some very hard learning.
— Seymour Papert

GROWING UP WITH LEARNING GAMES

Let early education be a sort of amusement.
— Plato

Jim and Lillian Phelan have two boys, Tyler and Russell, ages 6 and 9 years. Their home inventory of video and computer games includes a Nintendo 64, and the following "learning" games on CD-ROM for the computer:

- *Night Safari and the Open Zoo*
- *Flight Unlimited*
- *Mind Storms Droid Developer Kit*

- *Magic School Bus Explores the Age of the Dinosaur*
- *Math Blaster Jr.*
- *Lego Chess*
- *Reading Blaster Jr.*
- *Beethoven Lives Upstairs*
- *X Wing*
- *Tonka Raceway*
- *The Lion King Animated Story Book*
- *Reader Rabbit 2*
- *The Director's Lab*
- *Land Before Time Math Adventure*
- *Science Blaster Jr.*
- *Top Gun Hornet's Nest*
- *Busytown Best Math Program Ever*
- *The Even More Incredible Machine*
- *The Logical Journey of the Zoombinis*
- *Freddie Fish*
- *Sim Town*
- *Roller Coaster Tycoon*
- *Age of Empires*

The Phelans are musicians, not computer jocks, although the father has a degree in engineering and both parents use computers in their work. Lillian struggles hard to give her kids a well-rounded upbringing, including sports, time outside, and many types of play and social activities. Yet, she is fighting what often feels to her like a losing battle against the computer. "Even on a beautiful day like today," she recently complained, "they'd rather be in front of the computer or the Nintendo. I have to tear them away."

Fortunately, they are both well-rounded children, playing soccer, chess, and doing OK in school; but the lure of the computer game is always there. Tyler has been playing with the mouse and using software since he was 2 years old. By the time he hits the first grade, he will have conquered a dozen video games (in some cases beating his older brother); piloted a variety of virtual planes, cars, and tanks; built and run a simulated town and a simulated theme park; played many hours of computer chess (in addition to real chess); plus spent hundreds of hours with language and math "enrichment" programs that he has chosen to play on his own initiative. Russell, entering fourth grade, is already totally adept at all of the above plus mechanical CAD, much of which he learned from a computer game. Other than a little swordplay by Link in *Zelda*, and some shooting among the space ships, there is little here in the way of violence.

These children are by no means atypical. Parents who want to "give their kids the best start possible" have been sopping up billions of dollars worth of computer programs a year, hoping to improve their kids reading, math, and reasoning skills. Computer penetration in households with children is over 65 percent.[1] The main reason cited by adults for buying a home computer is to help their children to learn. Does it work?

There are 53 million children in the K–12 age group.[2] The idea of educating them via computer goes back quite a ways. In his 1969 book *Run, Computer, Run*, Anthony Oettinger laid out a vision of how computers would reform education through their ability to "relieve the schools of the abstract and verbal," and because "children who fumble miserably can be sent back for further study at the machine," with its tireless ability to practice.[3] Of course, it didn't happen quite that way; unadorned drill and practice alone on a computer can be deadly. The earliest computer-based learning applications—long before the PC—were computer-assisted instruction (CAI) "programmed learning" affairs that almost no one *wanted* to do. Computer games, on the other hand, were fascinating and captivating users almost as long as there were computers, but in the early days were mostly made up of typed x's, o's, and other symbols, or else they were purely text-based "adventure" games. While these early games were already attracting a crowd of devotees, they weren't much played by kids or used for learning.

The first computer to change this, and to bring kids, learning, and computers together was the Apple II, which appeared in 1977. One of the early segments that Apple set out to penetrate was the education market, and it put a lot of horsepower into the field. Apple hired experts from many different areas, including computer visionary Alan Kay, and created projects such as the "Apple Classroom of Tomorrow."[4]

In many ways Apple succeeded, and the Apple II eventually became very much identified as an "education" computer. However, it is worth noting that the Apple II was conceived from the very beginning by Steve Wozniak as primarily a games machine. According to Wozniak, "A lot of features of the Apple II went in because I had designed *Breakout* for Atari. I had designed it in hardware. I wanted to write it in software now.…So a lot of these features that really made the Apple II stand out in its day came from a game, and the fun features that were built in were only to do one pet project, which was to program a BASIC version of Breakout and show it off at the club." [5]

Even today there are Apple II's still in use in classrooms. Early learning software released for the Apple II included dozens of games, such as *Gertrude's Secrets; Apple Logo; Snooper Troops; Facemaker; Elementary My Dear; Rocky's Boots; Stickybear ABC and Numbers; In Search of the Most Amazing Thing; Delta Drawing; WizType;* and *Fat City.* [6]

Some of this software was marketed by a company called Spinnaker Software, which was founded in Boston in the early 1980s after the Apple II had been out a few years and the new IBM PC had been launched with great fanfare. The firm was started by two guys who left— to everyone's great surprise at the time—a consulting firm to strike it rich as entrepreneurs. The owners believed they had identified a big strategic opportunity: there would soon be a huge market for children's learning software. And so, as I remember it, when someone came along and offered them $10 million for their budding company, they flatly turned him down. [7] Unfortunately 6 months later the children's software market totally crashed, and the company was practically bankrupt. The market wasn't ready yet, or, as Oettinger says, it wasn't "ripe." One reason why the market had yet to materialize was that the software was still pretty boring—kids weren't interested.

It turns out, however, that my two friends hadn't guessed wrong on the size of the opportunity, only on its timing, which was related to the hardware. When the Macintosh came along in 1984, it opened a whole new world. Suddenly a computer could talk and show pictures. You could do pretty interesting things on it, and even create many of them yourself, though a magical program called *HyperCard.*

The Macintosh unleashed a huge wave of creativity in the programming area, and education was no exception. By 1985, *Sesame Street* had been around for 15 years and the idea of combining fun and children's education was beginning to be accepted by parents. As computer technology improved, a number of pioneers figured out new ways of combining educational content and computer games:

- Jan Davidson came up with the idea of combining an arcade shooting game with practice in reading and math. She created *Math Blaster* and *Reading Blaster*, and started Davidson & Associates.[8]
- Ann McCormick combined reading and writing practice with a cartoon character, starting her company in 1979 with only a grant of a computer and $1,000 from the Apple Education Foundation. In 1983, her company raised venture capital and changed its name to The Learning Company, whose products included *Reader Rabbit* and *Rocky's Boots*.[9]
- Gary Carleston, brother of CEO Doug at the fledgling family firm Brøderbund Software, was interested in geography, and hit upon the idea of a thief who would go around the world, with the player in pursuit, creating the now legendary Carmen Sandiego. In trying to catch her, they thought, you could learn the names of the places she went. Their first software game, *Where in the World is Carmen Sandiego?* shipped in 1985.[10]

If we could look at all of these early programs today (which is hard to do, because it's not easy to find the hardware, as software archivists have found to their dismay) they would look enormously primitive. But even with tiny screens and black and white images, these programs began capturing the imagination of children. From these humble beginnings, the kids' software market literally exploded over the last 15 years as computers penetrated the homes, kids flocked to the computers, and parents tried to give their kids something "educational" to do with them. Kids' commercial software (called variously edutainment, education, or just kids software) is, in the year 2000, a $1.6 billion annual market.[11]

$1.6 billion per year! That's a lot of children's software! What are the kids, and their parents getting for all these dollars spent? And from our perspective, what are the lessons here, positive and negative, for Digital Game-Based Learning? In the remainder of this chapter, I examine some of the categories of kids' and student Digital Game-Based Learning in more detail. However, I think we can draw these conclusions:

- Learning software has strongly influenced kids growing up over the last 15 years.
- There is a huge variety in the design, content, and quality of what is offered in the marketplace.

- The best designs and characters have had a lot of "sticking power" and "legs."
- The good designs and brand names continuously upgrade as the technology improves and continue to attract audiences.
- There are relatively few truly original designs, and a lot of me-too.
- Much of what is out there is "extrinsic" drill and practice games. However, some of these drill and practice games, used consistently, have been shown to improve standardized scores by quite a bit.
- There have been some exciting and successful moves away from drill and practice to construction, discovery, logic, and original-thinking software for kids.
- There is continued room and reward for innovation—the field is still wide open to truly original thinkers.
- Schools have lagged behind the consumer market, except at the university level.

DIGITAL GAME-BASED LEARNING FOR PRESCHOOLERS: JUMPSTART, BABY!

When my kid was born I went out and bought her a Macintosh.
— Don Johnson

As more and more parents are observing to their amazement, small children take to the computer like the proverbial fish to water. Jaron Lanier, the brilliant virtual reality designer (he designed the "virtual glove" for Atari) and musician, has an interesting psychological explanation of why this is so. Small children growing up are typically caught between two forces, he says, that are difficult for them to reconcile. On the one hand, little kids think they are omnipotent; in their imagination they can create anything at all. Want a big green giant in the corner? There he is! On the other hand, they also must live with the reality that they are little kids and no one really takes these fantasies seriously. It's hard for them to share their fantasy creations, especially with most adults. But the computer, Lanier argues, allows them to remain omnipotent creators in many ways, and yet they can finally share their creations with others, and that is why they take to it so naturally.[12] Kids *love* that they can control what happens on the screen. They quickly learn to turn on the computer by themselves, point the mouse, and use the programs.

And it doesn't just start with "preschoolers." There's a fast-growing software category known as "baby programming," targeted at the 3-and-under set. Educational software for children as young as 6 months, called "lapware" because the children are so small they must be held in a parent's lap at the computer, is now the fastest growing segment of the software industry, with titles such as *Jumpstart Baby*.[13] America Online (AOL) is developing a new content area to serve children aged 2 to 5 years, encouraged by an online poll of 10,000 parents in which 25 percent of the respondents said that their children had begun using a computer by age 2.[14]

**DON JOHNSON'S 2-YEAR-OLD DAUGHTER RACHEL
WITH HER MAC IN 1986.**

Some psychologists are not surprised. "Before they have the ability to use language, infants can think, draw conclusions, make predictions, look for explanations, and even do mini-experiments," says Andrew Meltzoff, head of developmental psychology at the University of Washington and coauthor of *The Scientist in the Crib*.[15]

Some, such as former school principal Jane Healy and astronomer Clifford Stoll, find this alarming.[16] They see no "need" for computers at that age and long for the childhoods of the past. But increasingly, for better or for worse, this is the way twenty-first century kids are growing up.

DIGITAL GAME-BASED LEARNING IN GRADES K–12

Putting a computer in a classroom is like strapping a jet engine on a stagecoach.
— Seymour Papert

Despite the fact that the 53 million U.S. children in grades K–12 probably play more combined digital game hours than any other group on
earth, Digital Game-Based Learning is only very slowly making its way
into our schools. While K–12 children can potentially experience Digital Game-Based Learning either at home or in school, the ratio between
the two is probably currently something like 95 to 5. [17]

Many argue that this is how it should be. Learning games, they say,
don't belong in schools. They have, in the words of Professor David
Merrill of Utah State, "gobs of frosting and precious little cake."[18]
Schools are places to learn to read and write, to do math, and to be
socialized. Others, including some in government, argue that because
the future is about computers, they are an important part of what the
schools should be teaching; but they say little about games. Only a few,
like Joe Costello,[19] have argued—as I am in this book—that computer
games are such a powerful motivator for kids that we are crazy *not* to be
using them in schools.

One notable exception, however, is John Kernan of The Lightspan
Partnership.[20] In the mid-1990s John Kernan, formerly with Jostens
Learning, and known as one of the most successful salesmen in the education business, raised $50 million dollars from Sony, Microsoft, and sev-
eral well-known venture capitalists for a massive project—to put the
entire K–6 curriculum on a series of fifty or so Digital Game-Based Learning CDs that would run on the Sony PlayStation video game console.
Later, they expanded to the PC as well, and to grades K–8. Kernan's team
began with the following logic:

- Among the biggest problems with technology education in schools is
  that there is no time to use it. Therefore, the best way to make a difference for technology in schools is not in schools, but at home.
- If the kids are going to use their programs at home, they have to be able
  to beat the other things that interest children—television and video
  games—because at home the kids can *choose* to do it, whereas in
  school you can *make* them do it.

- To get the learning time at home, it has to be fun, which led them to the notion of making it look like a video game, and having stories and characters that interested children.

So Lightspan hired Hollywood writers, graphic artists, and game designers (lots of them), and borrowed ideas from many of the most popular games on the market. They created characters that kids can relate to (in one case, a rock band of dogs). The goal of Lightspan's games was never to teach the material—they leave that to the teachers—but to give kids a chance to practice it: the old review and reinforcement concept. Proponents of purely intrinsic learning often express disappointment at their games. They are, as Kernan will be the first to admit, drill and practice—but in very engaging settings for kids. The average kid uses the games 45 minutes a day. And the evidence is that it works. Lightspan can show rising standardized test scores versus control groups in over 400 district studies (see Chapter 14).

"One thing we learned," says Kernan, "is that the harder you made it, the more kids wanted to do it. They kept wanting more and more game levels, which basically meant harder and harder stuff. It gave the kids real power if they knew the win-state code, which meant that they were the one who was somehow able to master the game at the highest level." Lightspan also found that even though the kids were doing harder work, they felt like *they* were in control: "I'm doing this harder stuff because I *chose* to do it, not because the teacher told me to do it." For all these reasons, the Lightspan games appear to have strong holding power with kids.

From the very beginning, Lightspan made a huge effort to work closely with school systems, integrating its programs closely with the school curricula in each state. They have teacher guides and do a great deal of teacher training as part of their offering. "We think of ourselves as doing education, not edutainment," says Winnie Wechsler, who came to Lightspan from Disney. "The purpose of Disney's stuff is to entertain, with education as a by-product in the edutainment. There's a huge difference between a Disney or any other game developer and Lightspan because nobody at Disney is marketing to people in schools or toward usage in schools."[21]

"We do the serious, heavy duty, industrial-strength, teach-everything-that-the-textbook-teaches with games," says Kernan. "You'll find umpteen games sites on net, but they're not complex games that take 20 hours to play like Lightspan. You go home and you raid some tombs [as in the popular consumer game series *Tomb Raider*] for 20 hours and you learn fractions."

The reason Lightspan chose to deliver its product on Sony PlayStations was that they wanted it to be available to *all* children. If a child doesn't have a computer at home the school buys the kid a PlayStation—at the taxpayers' expense—and gives it to them to keep for a year. The PlayStation sells these days for under $100 at retail, so this is not like buying the kids computers. Of course, the fact that they are PlayStations carries another message as well.

Lightspan's flagship product, called *Achieve Now,* was completed in 2000 (after a second infusion of $50 million) and the process of selling the curriculum to school districts has begun. While they have achieved some notable success (Kernan cites their $50 million in revenue), their market's reaction has not exactly been a tidal wave. *Achieve Now* according to Kernan, has been sold to about 3,000 school districts. Impressive in itself, perhaps, but not when compared to the 70,000 school districts in the United States—that's a penetration of less than 5 percent. Lightspan is also caught up in the transition from CD-ROM to the Internet that is affecting (and confusing) all forms of education and training. They have moved very heavily to the Internet, offering both free and subscription offerings. (You can visit their free site at www.lightspan.com.) They are clearly Digital Game-Based Learning believers. "I would say that we probably have the biggest, broadest sample of Digital Game-Based Learning than almost anybody," says Kernan. "And it's amazing how well it works."

If The Lightspan Partnership represents one end of the Digital Game-Based Learning spectrum for kids—drill and practice—the other end is well represented by Learn Technologies Interactive, Inc. (LTI).[22] Also a pioneer in using Digital Game-Based Learning in schools, LTI is run by Luyen Chou, a bright, personable, and extremely committed educator in his early thirties. LTI is also combining successful elements from games and education, but its products are focused predominantly in the area of critical thinking.

Chou's background is the well-heeled private high school system—the prestigious Dalton School on New York City's Upper East Side. An alumnus of the school, Chou returned there to teach after earning his

Harvard philosophy degree. "I was extremely interested in education and teaching, and extremely interested in technology, but for me they were two worlds where 'never the twain shall meet,'" he says. What changed his mind was a project called *Archaeotype*, one of the first multimedia projects to benefit from a grant of $1 million a year by a former Dalton board member to "build the school of the future with networked multimedia technology." *Archaeotype*, which Chou created with Robert McClintock and Frank Moretti, is a networked, computer-simulated archeological excavation of a fifth century B.C. Greek ruin. Its inspiration was a small, physical, simulated archeological dig that one of the teachers had created in the backyard for the second and third graders. (He would buy replicas from the Metropolitan Museum gift store, and bury them with a certain logic, putting older stuff at the bottom.) What Chou and his team learned from the physical dig was that the level of excitement was incredibly high because the kids were presented with a mystery: What does this pit represent? What can we find out about the culture that left this stuff behind? "Kids love detective work," Chou says. Chou also observed that because there was a mystery orientation to this—in the sense of mission and purpose and a puzzle they were trying to solve— kids were learning everything they needed to learn in order to solve the puzzle, whether or not that stuff was part of the curriculum. "We had kids reading Greek in the third grade because they wanted to be able to read things that were on an object they was buried in the sandpit. Kids learned weights and measures, how to categorize stuff, how to do research in a library. And they weren't learning these things just as skills to be drilled into them, they were learning them as a way to solve the fundamental mystery of the site." When the school wanted to do something similar with the sixth grade kids around a much more expanded curriculum of Greek and ancient history, the physical sandpit was just too small. So Chou and his colleagues built a computerized version of it, working with a couple of teachers who "really drove the vision of the project."

They made a fictitious site a couple of miles square and divided it into four quadrants, "burying" each quadrant into one computer in a classroom. There were four computers, each with a quarter of the entire site. And they put four or five children at each computer and had them spend half of a semester exploring the site and figuring out what was in there— there were hundreds of objects buried.

A key learning feature was that each quadrant told a story that was slightly deceptive with respect to the whole. For example, the creators imagined that one quadrant was next to a hill, and there had been a wash-down of earlier Mycenaean objects from the hill due to storms and floods. So the children who excavated that part of the site thought that the site was Mycenaean. Another team found a lot of Persian artifacts that the designers had hypothesized were spoils of war. They thought it was a Persian outpost. As the children excavated each object from the "virtual dirt," they would try to figure out what it was—a shard of a pot, a sword or a piece of armor, an architectural detail such as a frieze or a fresco—and they would have to do whatever research they could to figure out its origin. They could go to the library or they could search online through images of similar artifacts. And when they figured out what they thought it was, they would send their finding to "the museum," on the file server. Once an object was published in the museum, the children excavating the other three quadrants could get access to it.

"And that's where it got very interesting," says Chou. The guys from the other quadrant might say, "Oh, you're finding Mycenaean artifacts here, but we're finding Persian stuff. So your hypotheses that this is a Mycenaean site doesn't square with what we're finding."

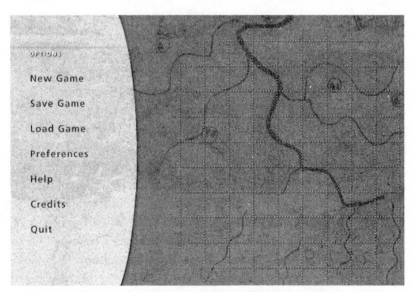

OPTIONS SCREEN FROM *QIN*, BY LEARN TECHNOLOGIES INTERACTIVE (USED BY PERMISSION)

"Not only were the kids highly motivated," according to Chou, "and not only were they imbued with a sense of quest and mission, and learning things that they weren't supposed to learn or that weren't part of their curriculum to solve the puzzle, but they were also interacting. They were working individually but also in small groups, facilitated by the technology and around this process of excavation." That powerful learning mechanism became the model for everything the Dalton group did. Chou began to realize that what was happening is that "kids weren't just being given the story by the teacher, but they were constructing their own narrative explanation of what Greek history was."

Chou points out the irony that what's exciting about scholarship is that it's mystery work. You're given clues, such as phenomena, and you're trying to create a story that explains why that data is there. But teaching is typically the opposite. The teacher tells a story and maybe provides some phenomena as a way of saying "see the story must be true." And that, says Chou, is basically like hearing a joke and being given the punch line ahead of time. It's not funny. *Archaeotype* reversed that whole pedagogy.

Chou and his team ended up developing a dozen applications similar to *Archaeotype*, based on subjects ranging from astronomy, to paleontology, to French language and literature, to Shakespeare. But despite their best efforts, they did not change education at Dalton very much. The board got increasingly conservative and frightened by what they correctly realized wasn't a technological transformation of the school but a pedagogical transformation of the school. And their attitude was "if the school isn't broken why are we fixing it—our kids are getting into Yale and Princeton and Stanford"; so, instead, the project was killed and there was a "huge purge."

To pursue his innovative ideas further, Chou and his partners formed a private company, Learn Technologies Interactive. LTI's biggest and most exciting project from the point of view of Digital Game-Based Learning is *Qin* (pronounced Ching), a beautiful, *Myst*like adventure game about ancient Chinese history and culture, that is set in the tomb of the first emperor of China. *Qin* is a classic consumer adventure game, a quest through a beautiful and strange environment filled with atmosphere, problems, and puzzles, but full of deliberately designed learning. "There are many different ways to solve the problems," says Chou. "The knowledge you need is in the encyclopedia but you have to do things with it in order to succeed through the game. It's puzzle solving and you learn in the context of solving these puzzles, and you don't even realize you're learning something specific." *Qin* has sold about 100,000 copies worldwide. It is used in some high school and junior high school courses, but most sales, according to Chou, have been to individuals.

So while Digital Game-Based Learning probably holds more opportunity for school-age kids than for any other group, it is going to take it a while—as Kernan and Chou have discovered—to get there. Schools change slowly, especially in the United States, where everything must be done on the local level. Although by some estimates almost 100 percent of America's schools are wired to the Internet,[23] still among the widely discussed problems are the continued low ratio of computers to kids, except in the richest or most fortunate schools, which is one reason why Lightspan went to PlayStations. Time, acceptance, and understanding by teachers are factors as well.

Yet, there is cause for optimism. Chess, for example, has made a huge resurgence in schools based largely on the availability of computer chess programs for instruction and practice.[24] The teaching of typing—now known as keyboarding—is now pretty much considered a task that computer games do best.[25] Social studies classes use gamelike simulations such as *The Oregon Trail* and others to help students get a feeling of what historical people faced. A large political simulation of the presidential electoral process on AOL is included in many high school curricula.[26] Progress has been especially great in the area of helping kids who have problems. A number of companies offering Digital Game-Based Learning solutions have recently addressed kids' learning problems and medical problems through games.

Scientific Learning, founded in 1996, is one of the first commercial attempts to bring many of the most current findings in brain research to children's (K-12) learning.[27] With a number of well-known neuroscientists on its management team, the company targets students with language and reading problems. Starting from the premise that many reading difficulties stem from problems in "signal reception," such as the inability to differentiate, remember, and use phonemes, the company's products, such as *Fast ForWord* and *4wd*, attempt to "retrain" children's' brains about phonological awareness and language comprehension through a program of computer-based exercises. Programs for older students address grammar, syntax, vocabulary, and sentence-structure skills as well.

Because the training involves a great deal of practice, involving repetition, and intensity (100 minutes per day, 5 days a week), keeping users motivated is absolutely key. That is why Scientific Learning's student interfaces are *all* computer games. They range from board games, matching games, and capture games for the younger kids to sports, card, and story games for the older students. According to their literature, the elements of games that provide motivation include "engaging graphics, onscreen rewards, and progress feedback."

Scientific Learning, as its name implies, has done quite a bit of research on the effectiveness of its approach, which is discussed in Chapter 14.

Click Health's[28] products were another deliberate attempt to enlist video games' holding power with children to influence their thinking and behavior, in this case, about the self-management of their own health problems, including asthma, diabetes, and smoking. The company, started in 1998 by members of the health care community, was cofounded by Alan Miller, who had previously created two highly successful interactive entertainment companies, Activision and Accolade. Click Health believes that interactive video games "offer unique advantages over conventional methods of health education," according to Debra A. Lieberman, vice president of research.[29] She finds games' biggest advantage over the traditional didactic content presentation of pamphlets, videos, and health education classes is repetition of the message. The engaging power of video games leads children to play a game they like for several months, repeatedly trying to complete the same game levels so that they can progress further in the sequence. Other benefits cited by Lieberman include that games allow players to rehearse new skills and to see the consequences of choices they have made. "No other form of mediated or face-to-face health education offers this combination of interactivity, entertainment, challenge, decision-making, feedback, repetition, duration, and privacy," she concludes.

Click Health's games included *Bronkie the Bronchiasaurus* for asthma self-management, *Packy & Marlon* for diabetes self-management, and *Rex Ronan* for smoking prevention. Like Scientific Learning, a notable feature of Click Health is the extensive clinical testing that it has done. The results of this testing is discussed further in Chapter 14.

Home Is Where the Digital Game-Based Learning Is

As Lightspan and Click Health have already realized, the best answers for the K-12 group may lie in the home. Lightspan estimated that by playing their disks an average of 45 minutes a day and several hours each weekend, children effectively get an extra day of schooling a week, or almost 2 months extra a year.[30] While Lightspan sells primarily to school districts, a wide variety of K-12-targeted Digital Game-Based Learning programs are available for individual purchase on the commercial market. Parents can buy these programs and encourage their children to use them.

The availability of good Digital Game-Based Learning software for kids in the home should increase dramatically as broadband to the home becomes a reality through cable modems, fiber-optic cable, and other high-speed connections. Fueling the growth from the demand side is likely to be the dramatic increase in home schooled children. The increase in good Digital Game-Based Learning for children might be particularly important in view of the fact that the size of the newest baby boom—generation Y—is causing concerns about finding classroom space.[31]

Math and science are particular areas in which many K-12 educators are working, trying to go beyond the "drill and practice" orientation of many of the consumer edutainment tiles. "Popular culture offers little outside-of-school support for children's mathematical learning. Computer games are a potential exception," according to one website.[32] Seymour Papert's work at the MIT Media Lab has led to LEGO's *Mindstorms* products, which help teach kids programming. A math game called *Green Globs and Graphing Equations* is the one game that has been shown to be effective, according to Dr. Susan Chapman, a math education specialist.[33] Other Digital Game-Based Learning projects related to science and math include *Wyndhaven*,[34] a virtual environment for teaching science and math to fifth graders, and *TERC*,[35] which creates children's mathematical games and has focused particularly on girls. Other projects of note include *Whoola!* (Wholesome Online Learning Adventures),[36] and MIT's *Education Arcade* at www.educationarcade.org.

Although I have highlighted a few innovative companies in the area of Digital Game-Based Learning for children, it is not my intention to recommend or criticize specific products. There are many sources, both on the Web and in newspapers and magazines, that perform that function. What I *do* recommend is buying things *with* rather than just *for* your kids, trying out as many different kinds of games—drill, puzzle, exploration, logic, etc.—as possible, trading with friends, and working with your kids and listening carefully to their reactions. While you can and should be a guide to them, let them be a guide for you as well. If you buy them what they enjoy, what *they* find fun, you will be unlikely to go wrong.

DIGITAL GAME-BASED LEARNING IN COLLEGES AND UNIVERSITIES

I skipped my exam to beat the game.
 — A student

College students, free at last from parental supervision, spend an extraordinary amount of time playing video games. This is, of course, abetted by the fact that most college and university students have high-speed Internet access. And, as the quote above shows, it is often to the distraction of their studies. Yet, college is one place where certain aspects of Digital Game-Based Learning are making great headway as more and more instructors realize the power of games and simulations to engage and instruct. Unfortunately, much college-level Digital Game-Based Learning consists of localized and isolated efforts by individual professors rather than widespread commercial products.

Our colleges and universities are going through a great crisis. They have traditionally been conservative bastions of slow changing knowledge, but knowledge has begun to move quite fast. They have traditionally been the knowers, but they are increasingly unable to provide the new skills that students demand. They have traditionally removed themselves from the world of commerce, but they increasingly have to show a profit to survive. Their bricks and mortar "ivory towers" are being assaulted by the need to teach across the Web. And, as the true fortresses of tell-test, they are facing a new, Games Generation of students.

Of course, not all college courses are lectures, but the college lecture is not only a cliché but a pretty accurate picture of the way things are still done. It's certainly the way professors are "trained," if training is imitating your peers. Beginning teachers are even *called* lecturers. Later, if successful, they get to not only lecture but to "profess."

Yet a growing number of college and university faculty—some of whom are from the Games Generations themselves—have, by themselves or in concert with other professionals, taken the initiative to create Digital Game-Based Learning in their own particular domain or subject area. These are not always the most polished commercial games, but they are often quite effective at getting points across to students.

Many of these, in fact, are "diamonds in the rough," just waiting to be given a good game treatment. An excellent example of this is the previously mentioned *Kristen's Cookies*,[37] named for the daughter of then Harvard Business School assistant professor Roger Bohn. *Kristen's Cookies* is a Harvard Business School Case about Process Simulation—part of the Production and Operations management curriculum. Its premise is that you've just started a bake-to-order cookie business in your apartment, and you have many orders to be delivered the next day at different levels of "doneness." However the three secondhand stoves you bought are a little off between what the dials said and what the temperature actually is. Your goal is to figure out how to calibrate the ovens by the morning. The answer involves zeroing in on the behavior through a process of experimentation that it is your job to determine.

When I first experienced Kristen's Cookies as a student, it was a spreadsheet, distributed along with the paper case. You had three ovens (Columns A, B, and C) where you entered numbers for the time and temperature for each batch of cookies in cells, and you saw the results (Doneness: 1 to 9; Burned: Yes or No) in other cells. The point of the case was that the cookies took time to bake, so you couldn't just try everything but needed a strategy. The underlying "engine" of the game contained everything needed mathematically to solve the problem, but 3 hours staring at a spreadsheet—ugh! So, my team at the firm I was with, working with Bohn, came up with a Digital Game-Based Learning redesign. We made Kristen's apartment come to life before your eyes, with stoves, dials to set for time and temperature, cookies on sheets that went into the ovens which "dinged" when the time was up, and cookies that came out looking their various levels of doneness from "raw" to "burned." You could even click on a cookie and hear how good it was ("yum!" to "yech!"). As in the spreadsheet, the data from the trials was collected and displayed (but this time on the virtual blackboard) for you to analyze.

The results were dramatic—suddenly it felt like a game, and people loved it. I remember a study group of middle managers all putting on their chef hats and sitting down to bake cookies. The original black-and-white HyperCard version was later upgraded to a better color version.

In another example, Professor David Merrill of Utah State created a simulation for anthropology students that operates along the lines of the game *Myst*.[38] Instead of pushing levers and collecting clues, students go into a simulated African village to determine how a tribe would be affected by a corporation's plan to establish a diamond mining operation nearby. In this program, based on a real case, students have simulated discussions with villagers, collect other data, and finally generate an ethnographic report with their recommendations.

Medical students have benefited from Digital Game-Based Learning as well. In the 1980s there was a widely-used videodisk-based medical simulation game called *Dexter*.[39] There are also games for training MASH-type surgeons.[40] "Talk about heart pumping," says Don Johnson of the Pentagon. "A guy comes in on a stretcher and he has a sucking chest wound. And it's very realistic. They guy is crying 'am I going to die?' and you have to make a decision, and based on what you do, the guy either dies or he recovers." Many law schools are using Ashley Lipson's training game *Objection!* in their programs as well (see Chapter 9).

Contest 5: What is the best learning game you know of for children or students of any age? Email your entries to *Contest5@twitchspeed.com*.

CONCLUSIONS

From very humble beginnings, Digital Game-Based Learning has quickly inserted itself at *all levels* of childhood and student-hood, from lap kids to grad students. Sure, it is possible to criticize the designs, methods, means, and even the motivation of its creators, as many do (see Chapter 14). The point is, though, that this is how twenty-first century kids grow up. Even if we want to, we are not going to be able to turn back the clock, or stop it or prevent it from happening. The issue is not to pull our kids away from the computer—if that's really where they want to be, they'll find a way to get there behind our backs—but to make it worth their being there. This is a very different situation from television, where the means of production were so expensive and control was in the hands of so few. As I will show in Chapter 15, we can *all*—including and especially teachers and kids—create examples of Digital Game-Based Learning that will make learning what we need to know much more enjoyable. When Nolan Bushnell, creator of Atari and Pong, told me of his vision of computer-infused schools,[41] I said to myself, "yes, and the kids can design the software." They, along with teachers, are already starting in many schools and programs to do this. It is our job as adults not to stop them, but to encourage, join and help them mix their new style with what we have learned about learning and life.

8

Digital Game-Based
Learning for Adults

We don't stop playing because we grow old—we grow old because we sto..
playing.
  —Oliver Wendell Holmes

Adults, Not Kids, Now Dominate Computer-Game Market.
  —*The Wall Street Journal*

It's not just the kids who are playing. Mom and Dad are too.
  —Lawrence Schick, AOL

GAMES ADULTS PLAY

It is one thing to say that Digital Game-Based Learning works for children, and even college graduate and professional students. Most people, educators or not, can accept that. But what about grownups? Don't we mature and get more serious? Do adults *want* to learn from games?

Of course, adults play *recreational* games in a big way. Many of those games are sports such as tennis or golf, but a great many are not. Gambling and casino gaming—both games of chance and games of skill—has been growing phenomenally over the last few decades. There are more than 700 unregulated wagering sites on the Web, generating over $1.2 billion annually in bets, with more sites appearing every day and the amount wagered doubling yearly.[1] Bridge is a huge phenomenon, with over 35 million players nationwide.[2] Ride on any commuter train or subway and you'll see adults of both sexes playing puzzle games from computer solitaire to crosswords to hidden word jumbles. And if you broaden your definition of games to include lotteries, over half of America is involved.[3] It is probably safe to say that there are almost no American adults who do *not* play some kind of recreational game or games on a regular basis. And many, if not all, of these games have become computerized as well, most playable over the Internet.

According to the Interactive Digital Software Association, some 70 percent of computer and video game players are older than 18. Computer games of all kinds are now reaching adults, big time.[4]

Returning home in a plane the other night, I looked over to see a tired executive using what I first thought was his Palm Pilot. It turned out on closer examination to be a Nintendo GameBoy. "I borrowed it from my son," he said. "It's really addictive."

My wife, who is from Japan, used a computer only for work before she came to this country five years ago. Now she plays *Solitaire* and *Hearts* regularly, searches the Web for interesting games, and recently decided to remove *The Sims* from her laptop because she was spending too much time playing it. "It's addictive" were her words as well.

Interestingly enough, the exact same words were used again when I first showed the *Straight Shooter!* Digital Game-Based Learning application to Harvey Slater, a 40ish operations technology manager at Bankers Trust, who had heard about the program's use for Derivatives Policy training, and was interested in it for his own Operations Policy training. I expected our meeting to last 10 minutes, but Slater played for well over half an hour, calling other executives in to try their skill as well. "It's addictive," he said.

John Smedly, president of Verant, the maker of *EverQuest*, says that while the average player, who is 22 years old, plays 20 hours a week, he has seen logs of up to 126 hours in a week. "That's really scary," he says. "That's why some people call it *EverCrack*."[5]

Of course, it's only in rare cases that adults get *truly* addicted to computer games. But what they do get is *really engaged*. It is clear that a great number of adults of all ages can find computer games highly engaging. But how about games and adult learning? Can adults learn by playing games? Do they want to? Can games-as-entertainment and games-as-learning mix for grownups as well as kids? Can we have *entertraining* as well as *edutainment*? What will bosses think? What do *users* think? Why, where, and how is Digital Game-Based Learning an effective learning tool for adults?

We all know adults have a work side and a play side—"work hard, play hard" has been around for ages. What we've discovered, relatively recently, is that the two can be combined, as more and more adults are finding to their surprise and satisfaction. And Digital Game-Based Learning is just one of the ways this is happening.

We saw in Chapter 5 that work is becoming more playful, that the concept of fun at work is catching on. Games, toys, and sports equipment (even miniature golf courses) are found in our workplaces.[6] Workplace culture has become—along with life in America in general—much less formal. People see less and less need for putting on a suit and tie to get work accomplished. More than half of U.S. workers dress informally for work every day,[7] and a large percentage of the rest do so part time, even at former bastions of conservatism such as law firms, consulting firms, and investment banks, and even IBM. Fun is moving through all parts and levels of the business culture. "At Burger King one of the pieces of the culture that we're trying to create is 'work is fun,'" says Annette Wellinghoff, director of Worldwide Training.[8] As we will see in the next chapter, Burger King uses Digital Game-Based Learning to train workers of all ages.

Lightspan, the children's learning company that we discussed in the last chapter, came across the very interesting fact that that in many cases parents use it too—for themselves. Lightspan's help line gets lots of calls from parents in the middle of the school day asking for help to the next step of the game. "There's no kid there," says John Kernan, "the kid's at school."[9]

COMPUTER GAMES AT WORK

One of the earliest ways that computer games were used for training was to build familiarity and skill with newly arrived computer hardware. In the mid-1980s, Jim Freund's job was to teach people at Citibank in New York to use computers—at the time suspicious, unfamiliar objects, that often inspired considerable fear on the part of potential users. The fears took many forms: fear that they would look stupid, fear that they would fail, fear that they would break something. Freund hit on the idea of using off-the-shelf computer games to help them relax as they learned to master the controls. (This may not have been an entirely original idea. Microsoft is said to have included *Solitaire* with Windows to help people learn to use a Mouse.) In any case, one day a big shot at the bank, a former Army chief of staff, came walking through Freund's classroom. "What are these people doing?" he boomed, and Freund explained, thinking about his place on the unemployment line. He later found out—to his great relief—that the executive had not only been impressed, but he had recommended that the technique be used to speed up the teaching of basic computer skills throughout the organization. "The military mind was no stranger to using videogames for training," says Freund.[10]

Ron Zemke, an editor at *Training* magazine, wrote in that magazine in 1997: "I would like to say a word on behalf of computer game playing on company time. Playing games on a regular basis is not only very low cost stress and boredom relief, it has cognitive skill enhancement value as well. I am totally serious here." Zemke feels that experiences gained from video games can be cheaper, more comfortable and "just as valuable" as expensive experiential outdoor offsites (i.e. rock climbing). Games like *Minesweeper*, *Solitaire*, and *Myst* hone attention to detail, logical thinking, deductive reasoning, and color identification, he believes. *Tetris* and *Doom* help hand-eye coordination "not to mention office politics," and network *Hearts* promotes "wonderful lessons in team effort and forming temporary alliances."[11]

But times have changed and today productivity is king. Most big corporations tend to see themselves as serious places, with IT often removing the *Solitaire* and *Minesweeper* games that come with Windows from employees' computers before delivering them, so that the workers won't waste time playing the games. This has sometimes been referred to as the corporate "games police."

Still, as classroom teachers have known forever, you may be able to keep people from having fun in front of your face, but you can't control what happens behind your back. Business people *will* play. When I first joined Bankers Trust Company in 1994, I was amazed at how many times I would walk into vice presidents' and managing directors' offices and surprise them in the middle of a game of *Solitaire*. And as soon as work ended on the trading floor, I discovered, the computer games began. Today, you can walk the aisles of any airplane and find a large percentage of people using expensive-company-paid-for-laptops to play games. Many early games had "boss keys" that instantly turned whatever you were playing into a spreadsheet, but today the boss is likely to be playing, too. I heard one senior executive justify his computer golf playing by complaining that his company was not letting him take a vacation. In technology companies with superfast networks the playing of *Quake* and *Unreal* "death matches" and tournaments on company networks is legendary, to the point where they have seriously slowed down some company systems, and in some cases, the games have been banned, at least during working hours. Many companies have moved on from removing games to restricting Web sites that workers can access, with games sites—along with porn—often among the first to go. Of course, workers retaliate by putting games on their Palm Pilots—hundreds are available, including the *Doom* clone *DREADling*.

But can they *play and work at the same time?* Can we make games with business content that are as compelling and relaxing as the others, while helping employees learn what they need to know? *That's* what Digital Game-Based Learning is all about. Can Digital Game-Based Learning ever be made to work in a business setting? Surprisingly, yes. Business is slowly but surely adopting Digital Game-Based Learning as a corporate learning methodology.

The gradual but steady acceptance and adoption of Digital Game-Based Learning by businesses is based on a number of forces that, fortunately for us, are both inexorable and irreversible. They start, of course, with demographics. Do what we may, the Games Generation is growing up, and will continue to grow up. It now comprises almost half of our workforce. Its members have, as we saw, a very hard time with traditional corporate classroom learning. They want to prolong and continue in their business life the same behaviors that they have used their whole pre-business lives, including email, instant messaging, online gaming, Internet browsing, and *learning through games* (remember all that *Sesame Street* and edutainment?). Legislating against this is an approach unlikely to work, particularly at a time of full employment and expansion. Workers tend to flow towards environments in which they feel comfortable, and businesses are forced more and more to cater to these people, rather than being able to push them down the old corporate path. When corporate workers put out their next "list of demands," as they did recently at Salomon Smith Barney, "fun training" is likely to be on it. So business' moving to Digital Game-Based Learning is, in many ways, a case of "if you can't beat 'em, join 'em."

A second, related reason is the growing inability for trainers to "get over" to people material that is extremely "dry and technical" (the corporate euphemism for boring). That kind of material, unfortunately but truthfully, comprises much that has to be learned in business training. Games help ease this material down. "While the 50-year-old partner may take a workbook and pencil to learn derivatives," says Joanne Veech of PricewaterhouseCoopers, "this isn't going to work for today's learners."[12]

But the third and most important reason that Digital Game-Based Learning is moving into business is the bottom line. It is increasingly clear to managers that (1) training impacts that line and (2) that "traditional" training isn't working very well. (Everyone has a pet exception, but in general this is true—ask any manager.) John Chambers, CEO of Cisco, says, "the thing that's slowing down our momentum in any market right now is our inability to educate our employees quickly."[13] So, the more practical-minded of managers and executives—increasing numbers of whom are *from* the Games Generations themselves—are becoming more and more open to whatever works. "They have to learn this," said one CEO, "and if it takes a game, so be it." And Digital Game-Based Learning works. As a relatively young managing director at Goldman Sachs put it, "This is an idea whose time has come."

So because of building pressure that is both bottom-up and top-down, Digital Game-Based Learning is gradually making its way into businesses.

But, interestingly, another important influence comes neither from the top nor the bottom, but right from the middle. The fact is that Digital Game-Based Learning is *already working successfully in almost all our corporations, for adult workers of all ages.* It's called *Jeopardy!*

JEOPARDY!: THE HIDDEN TRAINING TOOL (SHHHH!)

The television game show *Jeopardy!* is a truly amazing phenomenon. It is on television daily around the world. Eighteen million people tune in to watch it each day, and 32 million watch per week.[14] On the Net, at www.thestation.sony.com there are several online versions, with over

375,000 games played each week.[15] There are *Jeopardy!* CD-ROMs. There are box games. Although they won't disclose the numbers, I would guess that *Jeopardy!* generates hundreds of millions of dollars a year in profit for its copyright owner, the Sony Corporation.

Jeopardy! is essentially a Baby Boomer phenomenon. One story goes that Merv Griffin invented the now-famous reverse question-and-answer format in reaction to the television quiz show scandals of the 1950s—if some producers were giving out the answers anyway, why not just give the contestants the answers and let them come up with the questions? It began in 1964, caught on after a few separate starts, and stuck like glue.[16]

Alex Trebek, the show's genial host, has been earning his living this way for more than 16 years. Who between the ages of 35 and 55 in America would not know where the words "I'll take [category name] for 300, Alex" come from? Or would not know that an answer, to be acceptable, must be phrased as a question?

Sony knows it has a gold mine here, and it jealously guards its precious intellectual property. The name, the logo, the answer-question structure, are all copyright-protected elements, and have been the subject of numerous lawsuits and litigations.[16]

Except in training.

There is possibly not a Fortune 1000 corporation in America in which some trainer, somewhere, has not used some form of *Jeopardy!* as a training tool. *Jeopardy!* exists in companies as an oral game, a board game, and in many different digital incarnations, all more or less faithful to the original.

Jeopardy!-style templates can be bought from LearningWare, games2train, and, until recently, Stillwater Media (Game Mill).[17] These templates let you put in your own questions, and run a game that is more or less faithful to the original, to the point, in some cases, of having real buzzers to bang on as you "buzz in." Or, given how simple it is, almost any custom training house or Web development shop will be glad to make you a *Jeopardy!*-style game (which will probably mean just pulling one out of its archives and customizing it for you).

While templates and custom development are the more sophisticated ways to do *Jeopardy!*, many trainers have used other development and authoring tools in-house, or have gone the far less expensive (i.e., free) PowerPoint route, creating slide-show *Jeopardy!* games. Sony encourages the use of its games in schools and the academic sector. It applauds the use of the game by educators, saying that teachers often create their own versions of *Jeopardy!* to encourage student participation in the classroom and quotes one college professor as saying *Jeopardy!* is "the SAT of game shows." Because Sony does not license the game or logo to corporations for training, corporate *Jeopardy!* users are not enlarging Sony's coffers either. Like music from Napster, *Jeopardy!* for training is something many feel entitled to "just use." Sony, as you might expect, has a somewhat different position and, as we shall see in a minute, plans to do something about it.

So who uses *Jeopardy!*-style training? The easier question is probably "who doesn't?" LearningWare's roster of companies on their Web site includes:

COMPANIES USING LEARNINGWARE'S GAME SHOW PRO.
(USED BY PERMISSION)

3M	Eli Lili	Northwestern Mutual Life Ins.
Abbot Laboratories	Enron	Norwest Corp
Aetna	Foster Wheeler Corp.	PECO Energy
Allmerica Financial	General Electric	Pfizer
Allstate	General Motors	Philip Morris
American Express	Goodyear Tire & Rubber	PPG Industries
American Family Insurance	Harris	Procter & Gamble
Amoco	Hartford Financial Services	ProSource
Anheuser-Busch	Hilton Hotels Corporation	Prudential Insurance
AT&T	Honeywell	Reebok International Ltd.
Automatic Data Processing	Humana	RJ Reynolds
Baker Hughes	IMC Global	Rohm and Haas
Bell Atlantic	International Paper	Sara Lee
Bestfoods	Johnson & Johnson	Sears Roebuck
Boeing	Liberty Mutual Insurance Group	Sherwin Williams
Chevron	Lucent Technologies	Sprint
CIGNA	Marriott International	State Farm Insurance
Circuit City	McDonald's	Sun Microsystems
Cisco Systems, Inc.	MCI Communications	Sun Trust Bank
ConAgra	Merck	Texaco
Continental Airlines	MicroAge Integration	Union Camp Corp.
CSC	Micron Electronics	Unocal
Daimler/Chrysler	Microsoft	UpJohn
Dana	Mobil	UPS
Dayton Hudson/Target	NationsBank Corp.	US West
Delta Airlines	Navistar	Wells Fargo & Co
Digital Equipment	Nike	Whirlpool
Eaton	Northwest Airlines	Xerox

In most cases, this represents individual trainers and not necessarily the whole company. Companies not on their list use it too, of course: Paul Ventimiglia, a trainer at Ford, is reported as using a *Jeopardy!*-style game "every Friday." [18]

What have they used it for? You name it. The list ranges from such universal favorites as: *Don't Take Chances With Electricity Jeopardy!* to *Diversity Jeopardy!* to *Balance Sheet Jeopardy!* to *Cargo and Baggage Handling Jeopardy!* to *Forklift Safety Jeopardy!* to *Name That Congenital Abnormality Jeopardy!* (really!). One of its greatest attractions is its capability to be used for any material at all, and especially dull stuff.

Is *Jeopardy!* Digital Game-Based Learning? Sure, although it's certainly far from being state-of-the-art. *Jeopardy!* is an excellent example of simple question and answer (on the learning side), extrinsic (on the game side) Digital Game-Based Learning. Many academics would scoff at it. Yet, it combines relevant business content with a game format in a way that excites, engages, and adds to learning. The content is highly customized to the learners. The elements of emotional involvement (which often run quite high) increase retention. Of course, in terms of a *type* of learning (question and answer) it is certainly not the most sophisticated there is—it is basically a "review and reinforcement" mechanism and not the primary learning that Digital Game-Based Learning can sometimes be. But it's a big step up from the standard tell-test classroom, even if, in many cases, it *is* essentially the test. Trainers and students almost universally give it high marks. LearningWare quotes one off-the-chart-enthusiastic participant as saying, "I can recall every question and answer in the game we won." Great! Now if only we could make the tell part equally exciting. (We can—keep reading.)

How strong is trainers' fixation with *Jeopardy!*? I have been with potential customers (both Boomers and younger) demonstrating new, innovative question-and-answer games with interfaces ranging from *Solitaire* to *Tetris* to *PacMan*, and all they asked was, "Do you have *Jeopardy!*?" And people want it to be as much like the real thing as possible. One group using a shell called *The Battle of the Brains*, a sports-based question-and-answer game whose design was a deliberate attempt to stay as far away from the look and feel of *Jeopardy!* as possible, insisted on entering their multiple choice questions *only* in the form "The answer is ..." and having the players' answers entered by the emcee as "right" or "wrong" only *after* the answer was received "in question form." People love what they are familiar with. LearningWare cites as one of the great advantages of its *Jeopardy!*-style game that "you don't have to teach people the rules."

By the way, are all these training incarnations of the famous game legal? "You can't copyright a grid," says Baila Celedonia of the legal firm of Cowan, Liebowitz, and Laitman who has done some copyright work for Sony.[19] But if you add things like the name, the logo, the "reverse-answer" questions, and *especially* Alex, you're on a lot shakier ground. "We haven't licensed or authorized the use of the trademark to any corporations," says a *Jeopardy!* spokesperson. "If we found out a corporation was using our trademarked name and format we'd probably tell them they couldn't continue to do so."[20]

Don't despair, however. Sony, which knows a profit opportunity when it sees one (although it says it's motivation is to have people "do it in the right way") is creating an "official" shell version of *Jeopardy!*, to sell to both educators and trainers. And for trainers who can't afford even that—or can't go without a fix till it appears—another Sony spokesperson opined, "Have you ever seen a school or company prosecuted for this? There's your answer."[21] So you can always take your chances.

Contest 6: What is the strangest use of *Jeopardy!* for training that you know of (don't make it up) and where was it used? Email your entries to *Contest6@.twitchspeed.com*.

Of course, the *next* great opportunity in this Digital Game-Based Learning direction is ABC's—i.e., Disney's—*Who Wants to Be a Millionaire?* Not only is it, as I write, the most popular show on television, but the computer game, which sells for $19, is also the top-selling game on the market. LearningWare has been quick to capitalize on this with a look-alike corporate template, called *Is That Your Final Answer?* that they are already marketing. It will be interesting to see as time goes on (1) if *Who Wants to Be a Millionaire?* has the same "legs," or staying power, as *Jeopardy!*, and can last another 35 years. No matter how much they pay him, there may be only a finite number of times Regis can say, "Is that your final answer?"; (2) whether Disney will be more or less aggressive than Sony in protecting its copyrights; and (3) if the show will have the same holding power over today's generation that *Jeopardy!* had on the Boomers.

So at least one form of Digital Game-Based Learning, albeit a very simple one, has totally succeeded in incorporating itself into America's business training. But what about others? How widespread is Digital Game-Based Learning? In the next two chapters, I examine more than forty examples of Digital Game-Based Learning used in a business and military context. The examples range from incredibly simple—simpler than *Jeopardy!*—to amazingly finely detailed primary learning games for very complex and difficult subject matter. But before we get to those examples, let us consider two other important factors in Digital Game-Based Learning: simulations and the Internet.

SIMULATIONS: ARE THEY GAMES?

You can have a game that's not a simulation and a simulation that's not a game, but when you get one that does both, it's a real kick-ass situation.
— Elliott Masie

As I write, the best selling PC game of all time is *The Sims*, from Maxis, a division of Electronic Arts.[22] *The Sims* is the latest joy to spring from the fertile mind of game genius Will Wright, who brought us *Sim City* and a whole host of other economic and systems simulations. Maxis was one of the first companies to make simulation games really popular, in large part because they added a highly intuitive, fun interface to what had previously been presented mainly as numbers. In many, if not most, previous simulations, in fact, *all* you saw were numbers—in reports, in charts—all very abstract representations of what was going on. (This is still, today, the case with many training simulations.) With *Sim City*, you could actually see each element of city grow—or decay—depending on what you did. Buildings, roads, utilities, and other objects were built by dragging icons, and those icons or "tiles" changed dynamically depending on the variables in the underlying model. Roads filled up with traffic or decayed, factories grew or died, disaster struck when services, such as fire or police, were insufficient.

Not only that, but *Sim City* and its successors incorporated a *variety* of ways of modeling dynamic systems, including linear equations (like a spreadsheet), differential equations (the province of system dynamic-based simulations like *Stella*) and cellular automata, where the behaviors of certain objects came from their own properties and rules for how those properties interacted with neighbors rather than from overall controlling equations. This gives them a much more "realistic" feel than pure spreadsheet or system dynamic-based simulations.

A whole host of other consumer simulation games have adopted many of their techniques (as well as their top down "2D" isometric point of view) to other situations, such as history (*Age of Empires*) and outer space (*Command and Conquer*), and, as we shall see, many training simulations have now taken this route as well. Creating a world piece by piece and watching each piece grow or decay has become part of the language of games, which makes it part of the vocabulary of the Games Generations. Today, if you were to say, "I want this to be like a 'sim' game," most people would know what you mean. *The Sims* takes the whole concept a step further by letting you create and control the inhabitants of *Sim City*, right down to their going to the toilet (and don't forget to do it!).

As was noted in Chapter 5, simulations are a genre of computer games. And lately "simulation," long confined to gamers, scientists, and the military, has emerged as a huge buzzword in training. Elliot Masie, founder of the Masie Center and an influential consultant in the technical training arena, has declared it a key area of interest, and organizes entire conferences around it. So, what *is* simulation? Is it the same as Digital Game-Based Learning? How do the two relate?

There are a host of definitions of "simulation," ranging from:

- *Any* synthetic or counterfeit creation.
- The creation of an artificial world that approximates the real one.
- Something that creates the reality of the workplace (or whatever place).
- A mathematical or algorithmic model, combined with a set of initial conditions, that allows prediction and visualization as time unfolds.

All of these are useful. But the most interesting point of view to me is that of J. C. Herz, who contends that simulation is not a noun, but a verb. (Or, in her terms, a predicate rather than a subject.) So, if an object (real or virtual) "simulates" something, it is a simulation. If a "toy" simulates something, it is a simulation. If a "story" "simulates" something, it is also a simulation, and if a game "simulates" something, it is a simulation as well. In this definition, "tools" can also be simulations and often are. [23]

So simulations are *not*, in and of themselves, games. They need all the additional structural elements that we have discussed—fun, play, rules, a goal, winning, competition, etc.—to make them into what Masie calls "kick-ass situations."[24] There are lots of good reasons to simulate things or processes in training—the ability to "practice in safety" and to do "what if" experimentation being two of them. But if attention is not paid, simulations can easily, once the initial novelty wears off, become almost as boring as tell-test training, even though you many be actually doing something. Examples might include virtual reality (VR) simulations of going through a building or getting to a place—interesting the first time, perhaps, but not more. They might also include numbers-based simulations with no visual interface—*boring*. Another example might be highly technical, complex, noncompetitive "what-if" models (these are, technically, "toys," but no one except the creators might want to play with them). Or physics simulations—here's how gravity, or friction, or the solar system works. Interesting, but so what? Even simulated tasks, which many praise as learning by doing, can easily lack any motivating factors and turn into merely a succession of boring things to do. As one participant put it, "the simulation was more fun than the rest of the course, but not much more."

Alfred Hitchcock's formula for a successful movie is to *remove* the boring bits.[25] To get something interesting and engaging in simulations, the boring bits must be removed as well, and fun added. Making them into games is a great way of doing this.

Elliott Masie calls the difference between a game and a simulation "the extent of mindset of the learner." "In a game, what we're triggering is the competitive/cooperative spirit, we're triggering a playfulness, and we're triggering the achievement, greed, and victory element. All of which I think have not only a psychological impact but an actual physiological impact on folks."[26]

Take, for example, the flight simulator. Often thought of as a brainstorm of the military, the flight simulator was originally conceived as an entertainment device for fairs.[27] Nevertheless, the flight simulator is acknowledged, rightfully so, as a revolution in learning and training. Pilots and prospective pilots can spend hours and hours doing something remarkably close to actual flying, experiencing all sorts of scenarios and "what-ifs" in terms of weather, location, flying conditions, time of day, and, of course, mechanical difficulties without risking either expensive planes or peoples' lives. (This is what I mean by "practice in safety.") Not only has flight simulation become *de rigueur* for pilots, but it has spawned a whole generation of virtual flyers, who virtually pilot incredibly realistic versions of everything from 747s to the latest military jets and attack helicopters.

I maintain that, although there are people who just "love to fly" in simulators, simulated flight can become boring, in the same sense that driving your car to work is boring or doing any move over and over is boring. What is *not* boring in a flight sim is two things—learning and competing. Both happen when goals, rules, challenges such as emergencies, and sometimes narrative ("you are deep in enemy territory") are added to the "toy"; that is, when the simulation *also* becomes a game. The goal can be to "learn to take off"; or to "land successfully ten times"; or to "deal with wind shear"; or to "land safely even though your two starboard engines just flamed out"; or to "shoot down as many enemies as you can and come back safely"; or to "figure out the best way to attack the target"; or whatever. Goals can be either be built-in to the game, or self- or instructor imposed, but as soon as you add them, suddenly there is more engagement, whether or not there is actually a "score." Masie adds that making a simulation into a game changes our inhibitions. "There is a permission to move out of our sort of staidness," he says.[28] We try things in play that we might not try in life.

Another example of this "engagement" issue is found in military simulations. Military simulations traditionally have very different objectives from entertainment simulations. Entertainment sims are driven by excitement and fun. Players must want to pay and use them repeatedly, so to increase excitement dangerous and unrealistic situations, exaggeration of hazards, multiple lives, and heroics are acceptable, and even desirable. Defense simulations, on the other hand, "overwhelmingly stress realistic environments and engagement situations. The interactions are serious in nature, can crucially depend on terrain features or other environmental phenomena, and generally rely on the user's ability to coordinate actions with other players."[29]

Put another way, creators of military simulations work hard to be as "physically" correct as possible, at whatever level of detail is appropriate.

If it takes a full 2 minutes for a tank's main cannon to cool down after a shot before you can reload and shoot again, that's what it takes in the simulation. It's important for trainees to know this, or they might have unrealistic expectations in battle, with highly negative consequences. But in a tank *game* you want to just click that mouse and cream the hell out of your opponents.

That's often a big problem with using simulations as learning tools. Reality (as anyone who's ever attended a business meeting can attest) can lead to boredom, which then actually *reduces* learning. As we shall see in Chapter 10, Navy trainees in a submarine simulation found their task boring, and didn't do well—until the Navy made it into a game that was totally unrealistic from the point of view of reality, but highly effective from the engagement and learning perspective.[30]

This raises the issue of what is known as a simulation's "fidelity." Many trainers differentiate between "low-fidelity" and "high-fidelity" simulations. Low-fidelity simulations are situations in which one or a few elements are abstracted from reality to be emphasized. For example, you are baking, but all you have to do is set the time and temperature for the altitude you are at—you don't have to put things in the refrigerator, the ingredients are not messy, and so on. They can also be metaphorical or hypothetical cases with only a few factors, such as, "Imagine that you and the other five people at your table are in an leaky lifeboat on a shark infested ocean, and your lifeboat can only hold four people. You must decide how to cope with this situation." Thiagi suggests that low-fidelity simulations result in the learning of general principles and insights that can be used in a variety of situations.[31] They are also very useful for beginners who would be confused by too many details.

High-fidelity simulations, on the other hand, are attempts to model reality as closely as possible. They include models that use a large number of factors and complex relationships among these factors, and physical objects that are the same as their real-world counterparts. For example, a high-fidelity flight simulator combines the actual cockpit from an airplane containing all the exact instruments and controls with a computer-driven rear screen projector that shows what the pilot would see in real life. The virtual reality program responds to the pilot trainee's every action and dynamically changes the outside view and the readings on the cockpit controls. In business, high-fidelity simulation includes highly realistic modeling of on-the-job challenges, such as an authentic sales-call role-play. High-fidelity simulation, says Thiagi, results in very reliable transfer of training. Users learn exact procedures that they can apply to their work situations. It's great for practicing concrete, consistent steps in a standardized procedure.[32]

The reality is that there is always a continuum between the two extremes. "It is impossible," says Will Wright, "to tell where a high-fidelity simulation begins."[33] And it is often hard to tell without testing precisely how much fidelity is necessary to get across the required learning—it is often different for beginners than for those who are more advanced. The degree of fidelity required is very important from a cost perspective as well as a learning perspective. As the military has learned, extreme high fidelity simulations are not cheap. They are now using commercial simulations, in some cases to "off-load" certain tasks from higher-cost assets.[34] But low-fidelity or high-fidelity, *all* simulations can be made into games.

Making a Simulation into a Game

How do we make simulations into games? First, we need to begin by adding some or all of the formal structural elements of games—fun, play, rules, a goal, winning, competition, and so on. As Eric Goldberg explains, "As a business person I want to screw up and learn from my mistakes. As a gamer, I want to win."[35] Boring simulations assume that the former is enough motivation. It isn't. Not for a kick-ass situation, anyway. The *worst* simulation games are merely a set of learning points with the simulation part designed only as a sneaky way to get the player to each of them. The best keep pulling you to continue to the end in spite of yourself.

One of my favorite games of all time, the one that got me into this field, is called *Life and Death*.[36] The first version that came out on the Macintosh in the mid-1980s was about performing an appendectomy. (A later version graduated you to brain surgery.) In *Life and Death* you don't get to operate right away—first you have to find a patient who actually has appendicitis, as there are other reasons as well for pain in the gut. So you begin by conducting examinations—you are paged into various rooms and find patients lying there whom you can question, examine, and perform tests on. You discover that you must palpitate to see what side the pain is on. You need to do x-rays to distinguish between certain things. When you finally get a correct diagnosis of appendicitis, you go to the operating room, pick up your scalpel, and begin cutting—only to have the patient die because you forgot to scrub. Next thing you know you're in the morgue staring at a toe-tagged body. If you make a less-fatal mistake you are sent temporarily to "medical school" where you are given a quick hint on what not to do next time. There's a lot to learn along the way—cutting through muscles, dealing with bleeders, administering lidocaine and other drugs at the proper times—a lot of which I still remember 15 years later. But my goal, dammit, was *never* to learn this stuff; it was just to save at least one patient.

So, you don't have to hit people over the head with learning points or "failure points," just make them want to win. The people I know who say they learned important things from simulation games—whether budgeting tradeoffs from *Sim City,* or survival skills from *Oregon Trail,* or how to do manage a business from *Roller Coaster Tycoon*—generally learned these things surreptitiously and stealthily, not directly. Too many so-called simulation "games" are just a series of mini-role plays in which you are being openly directed to a "right" answer.

Simulation can be a fabulous way to learn, but to keep most learners' engagement you have to keep making it fun—fun from the *player's,* not the creator's, perspective. Perhaps counterintuitively, having an extremely high-fidelity simulation that exactly imitates life can sometimes take the fun out of it. So can not giving the player enough choices, or enough humorous or even outrageous possibilities—one of the great things about consumer-oriented simulations is the sheer number of options they give you. "They said we could be a toy company," said one e-commerce simulation player, "but we wanted to be a *sex toy* company."[37] Sorry. Forget it. Not part of our design. Of course, adding fun can be tricky, because different audiences have different ideas of what "fun" is. Speaking of his FBI simulation *Angel Five,* Ed Heinbockel of Visual Purple said the users *loved* the surveillance part, even though to the creators it was "like watching paint dry."[38] But one thing to always be wary of is pleasing yourself as the designer, or even the clients paying the bills, at the expense of the players. Makers of consumer games are generally in a situation in which the developers and the players are the same people—"We just make games we would like to play," says one.[39] Makers of training games often are not.

Take, for example, a customer service simulation, of which there are, by now, hundreds. Typically a customer (animated or in video) walks into the hotel, or the auto dealership, or the bank, and needs help, and you, the employee, get to have a simulated conversation with that customer based on a "tree" structure with branching choices. The results are different because of your decisions. Nongame-based simulation creators will often design this with a fixed mix of customers who are as real as possible (in video, no doubt), in a number of different types and situations, each designed to play out one of the points you are teaching about. There is feedback along the way, certainly, including the customers' having negative reactions to things that you do wrong. When you fail, you typically get a lot of feedback, often in text, but sometimes even an "expert's" explanation of why you were wrong, possibly through a so-called "war story" of someone telling you what once happened, either in text or video. This *may* work—assuming you care enough about your job and the program to want to actually practice it and get the right answers. But it typically still feels like *training*. If not forced by trainers or other pressure to complete the exercise, many users would just go for the obvious and outrageous wrong answers, get whatever fun there was from the customers' negative reactions, and leave it at that.

Here's another way to design this type of simulation as more of a game. You, the player, get to *design* your customers, from millions of possibilities. You decide what they look like, what their personality is, what mood they are in that day. You also decide what mood *you* are in that day—happy, depressed, wanting to be somewhere else, hung over, and so on. Then you set the game on play and it randomly generates customers. The customers are computer animations—not realistic, but exaggerations. If you piss them off, they trash the place. If you do the right thing they kiss you, or give you good stuff, or money, and so on—outrageous, memorable stuff. You have a goal—accumulate as much "success" as possible, become the top salesperson, or the bartender with the most "regulars," or keep your "cool meter" at a certain level no matter what they customer does. But you don't have to get there right away; in fact it's *hard* to get there. You can explore the whole range of bad scenarios, which you do immediately because you've already heard, by word of mouth, that they are so much fun. In each situation, there is not just a list of three choices but a gallery of the most creative (and outrageous) things to say in that situation that you can even add to, and they will show up (after being vetted) in other's games later. Prizes are offered for the cleverest phrases and approaches that work. Unexpected diversions occur, such as holdups or amorous interludes. There is also a multiplayer mode, where live players run the customers, and their role is to make you lose your cool as they continually interrupt you. You *do* learn the right things to do and say, because there's something personally fun in it for you—the whole list we saw about what makes games engaging, including winning on the game's terms or on your own. It's fun—not like learning a lesson is fun, but like having the best city, or theme park, or sim family is fun. This is the design approach that led to the creation of a game called *Where in the World is Carmen Sandiego's Luggage?* rather than a simulation called *Customer Service at SAS Airlines.* (See Chapter 9.)

Other designers, with a more cinematic/narrative bent, might design their simulation game somewhat differently, setting up, for example an inciting incident at the beginning that makes you, the player, *really care* about the end result.

My point is that just because something is a simulation does *not* mean it's engaging, and that a simulation game, to be effective does *not* necessarily have to be a totally realistic portrayal of the situation or job. Real *elements* need to be combined in an interesting, entertaining, and addictive way, to make the player have fun and care. In fact, the content and messages of a "simulation" and a "simulation game" can be exactly the same—the difference comes from the game's engagement and challenges.

The Role of Processing in Simulation

While much can be learned from just "playing" the simulation game, to be most effective in terms of learning, the game must be "processed," or reflected upon. "I think we've got to be really careful," says Masie, "because there's an assumption in the game that people will learn from their experiences. But part of what happens, and I think this is true in athletics as well, is that the endorphin rush of the game in many ways makes us very nonanalytical about our own success and failures."[40] So, simulation games are often followed by "debriefings" where the players sit down and discuss what happened, usually led by an instructor or coach. In the military, this is known as the "after action review," when the players climb out of their simulated tanks or cockpits or command tents and discuss the battle. Some of the feedback comes player-to-player—"You know when you went over that hill, and the red tank was over there? I was trying to get your attention because I would have hit that guy for you." However a good debriefer or processor will help players highlight and generalize the various lessons learned so that they can later apply them to other situations.

An advantage of *digital* simulation games is that much of this processing can be built-in. As you're playing, the game itself can tell you that you could be doing better and ask you if you want to know why, with the you setting the level of processing that you want. There is generally a mode in a digital simulation to "replay" what happened for one or all players to see—and artificial intelligence-based "critiques" can be added to this. Networked game players often use chat and messaging to debrief each other, both during and after a game, and a nonplaying coach can be watching and messaging as well. One particularly good reason for making a simulation into a game—something that someone is motivated to play over and over—is that after the debrief players can often learn a lot by doing it again.

Fun Digital Game-Based Learning Simulations: Monte Cristo

Monte Cristo, a French company, specializes in management simulations. It's founders come out of top business schools, consulting companies, and investment banks. With titles like *Wall Street Trader, Start-up, Airport Tycoon, Economic Wars,* and *Business Strategy,* you would think that their target market is training. Right? Wrong! Monte Cristo is a consumer games company.[42]

It did grow out of business training. The first engagement they had was from the European Commission who wanted to show the members of the Commission and the members of the European Parliament the advantages of going to the euro. But once they had built the market engine, the founders realized it could be used for a wider purpose, such as simulating the whole stock exchange itself. Hence, the first game that they produced, called *Trader 97.*

Monte Cristo chose the consumer market rather than the training market because they wanted to take a more mass-market approach with more multimedia. "Training tools tend to be more sober, a lot of Excel graphics and spreadsheets," says Marc Robert, head of marketing for Monte Cristo. "We wanted a more entertaining approach to it, hence the idea of going mass market." The founders were also influenced by a French TV show called *Capital*, whose objective is to bring economic and business issues to the general public.

Underneath, the Monte Cristo products are well-modeled economic simulations, but on the screen they are as graphically exciting as any other commercial game. The offices, trading floor, and pub (where you get gossip) in *Wall Street Trader* are state-of-the-art 3D, as are your digs in *Start-up* (you have a lot of capital). In *Start-up*, you have little employees walking around (like in *The Sims*) and you can see how busy they are, and even what their mood is. You get to recruit and motivate your staff, design, develop, manufacture, and sell a variety of real-looking products from video game consoles to mobile phones to cyber-TV, and manage the entire company over 5 years, hopefully to success.

All of Monte Cristo's various games can be networked and played online (if you have the CD), and several are massively multiplayer, including *Star Peace*, in which teams of 500 to 1,000 players build *Sim City*-type worlds that are huge and ultimately interconnected; *Economic Wars*, where you play the head of a country; and *Business Strategy*, where you play the head of a multinational corporation. Monte Cristo's goal is to eventually link *Wall Street Trader, Start-up, Economic War,* and *Business Strategy* into one huge online management simulation at many different levels.

Management training outside of work! Doesn't it just feel like *more work*? No, and that's the point. Although big selling games like *Sim City* and *Roller Coaster Tycoon* have a lot of management detail, people have a lot fun playing them. "When *Sim City* first came out, people said 'a game where you manage your own city? That sounds like work,'" says Robert. "When we talk about *Start-up 2000*, a game where you start your own company, we sometimes get the same reaction. Well it is in a way, but it is also an occasion for people to know what it feels like to be in the shoes of a Jeff Bezos or a Bill Gates." The trick is not making it look or sound too serious. "You want a graphical interface that's going to be amusing and fun for the eyes," says Robert. "But at the same time it has to be based on a very realistic model. You want players to think that if they're succeeding in the game, somehow there's a parallel to reality."

Monte Cristo, which bills itself as the Management Games Company, has two main target markets. The first is university and college students, especially in business schools. The second is young executives, people in their thirties or forties, "some of whom were the first people born with the computer," says Robert. "They played *Pong*, they played *PacMan*, they had an Atari, and maybe an Apple II. They've played it all."

In the future, the company plans to do a wide variety of management games, from managing a space station, to managing a zoo and aquarium, to managing a holiday resort, to managing a sports team. So, you might find yourself playing a team owner such as Ted Turner or George Steinbrenner, rather than a Bezos or Gates.

Given the combination of underlying veracity and visual appeal of their management games, it's not surprising that corporations have approached Monte Cristo looking for training versions. But they have turned all these requests down to stick with their consumer focus. I will talk more about their reasoning for this in Chapter 15.

DIGITAL GAME-BASED LEARNING AND THE INTERNET

When you play against people, all bets are off.
— An Internet Gamer

Along with simulation, the biggest training buzz is around the Internet. Internet-based learning companies are everywhere, many of which went public to large multiples in the initial dot-com boom. Intranets—the same technology inside the security "firewall"—are also big for learning, as are extranets (external secure access to intranets). Many companies now flatly declare that they want all technology-based training to be delivered over the Web—internally, externally, or both.

What is the relationship between Digital Game-Based Learning and the Internet? Gamers—the recreational kind—are, of course, rushing to the Internet and embracing it in huge numbers, finding it an enormous advantage and a natural home. The Internet is opening up a whole new dimension of game playing—multiplayer gaming "24/7/365" around the globe. The Internet arcade never closes.

Playing games online is one of the "hottest new forms of entertainment," according to Lawrence Schick, the executive director of interactive entertainment for America Online.[43] The attraction is not only the ease of finding games and partners, anywhere, anytime, but also the challenge of playing against a human mind instead of computer AI (artificial intelligence). There are dozens of online sites for finding partners and playing online games, ranging from shoot-em-up "death matches," to massively multiplayer role-playing and strategy games, to simple bridge and chess games. There are hundreds of game sites in total, including sites *with* games, sites *about* games, and sites for individual games. Chat and discussions of how to play, how to win, and how to solve problems are one of the biggest and most widely used features of all these sites.

What we actually have in the online games world, as Clark Aldrich points out, is a self-generated, well-served, highly active, thriving community of learners.[44] And the game skills that they learn apply to life. J. C. Herz points out that online stock trading is the largest and most successful massively multiplayer game ever invented.[45]

But when people log on to the web for learning, rather than gaming, what do they find? Lots of courses to sign up for, certainly. There is much on the Web (and on their company's intranet) under the title of training and learning. But despite the hype of the providers, "embracing" the Internet for training is hardly the term I would use. Mostly their employers send them. Outside of employer-paid courses there is technical certification, which many do on their own to get a job, and college degrees, which more and more colleges and universities are now offering online.

Business-oriented computer-based training providers, who previously distributed their wares on CD-ROMs, have all moved to Internet distribution. Yet, for the most part online games and online learning couldn't be further apart. Digital Game-Based Learning for business training is still very new on the Internet. Why is this so? It's not that people don't want to play games over the new medium, as the growth of online gaming attests. So what's up?

One reason is technology. We're in a strange intermediate period in the history of computer development. We've hooked everybody together, but only with thin little wires or "pipes." Where the pipes are slightly fatter (e.g., the T1 and 10-megabit connections in most corporations), we quickly fill them up with "traffic," making them no more useful for sending large quantities of graphics and other data. The games companies, including Monte Cristo, have found a workable solution in the form of hybrids. Gamers buy a CD (or download a large file) that contains the graphics and the speedy local engine for playing the game. As little information is sent over the Net as possible.

The reason for this is time. Although it's typically measured in milliseconds, sending information from one computer to another takes a finite amount of time and the more information, the more time it takes. Time is the enemy of fast online gaming because of something called "latency." If you shoot somebody, you'd like the information (and therefore the bullet) to arrive before that person has sauntered away unaware. If you are making a trade at a certain price, you'd like that trade to happen before the market moves again. Much of what online game designers do is to figure out ways to reduce latency, especially when connection speeds vary widely from player to player. A key piece is putting as much as possible on the user's machine where it can be accessed quickly, and sending only small amounts of information relative to each players actions over the Internet, rather than, say, sending a whole new graphic of your representation or "avatar" every time you move.

This hybrid model is not necessarily a good one for training, at least from the perspective of IT management. Many companies would like to avoid CD-ROMs and have everything run from the server to the browser. But this makes the combination of high-speed gaming and high graphic values very hard to do. Thus, until now purely Web-based Digital Game-Based Learning has, in most cases, been limited to relatively simple games—either classic one or two screen games such as *Jeopardy!*, *Tetris*, *Asteroids*, or *PacMan*, or very simple adventure games, or to games with a very low-graphics interface.

But all this is bound to change as bandwidth gradually increases. It may take a while, but once most connections are optical fiber (or something even faster), large graphics will have fewer problems arriving when you want them to, and the Internet and Digital Game-Based Learning will come together very quickly.

DIGITAL GAME-BASED LEARNING ON HANDHELDS
AND ON DIGITAL PHONES

Gadgets do well in business; people like to have them, often buying them on their own. The day a friend showed me his original Palm Pilot I ran out and bought one, and when I showed it to my boss so did he and everyone reporting to him. Two months later so many people at Bankers Trust had them that the IT department had to start supporting them, and Palm Pilots became a company-authorized purchase. Handhelds like the Palm and its competitors, and communications devices like cell phones have become ubiquitous in much of business—a platform that is in place and just waiting for Digital Game-Based Learning to happen.

Games and handhelds are, of course no strangers. The GameBoy is what generates a major percentage of Nintendo's profit. [46] The ability to play games anywhere (except in class, if you're caught) is a major advantage. Games started showing up on the Pilot from the very beginning. Palm even bundled some Digital Game-Based Learning—*Giraffe*—that helped you practice and learn the "graffiti" data-entry language (see Chapter 9). Today, you can go to a variety of sites and download hundreds of games into your Palm Pilot, including *Doom*-style 3D shooters.

As these tiny computers drop in price, they are becoming ubiquitous, almost commodities. The Navy now gives one out to each Annapolis graduate. Handhelds are connected to the Internet and interconnected between themselves through wireless, infrared, and other technologies. Soon handhelds will reach a price at which companies will just give one to each employee, painted with its own corporate logo, complete, hopefully, with the company's latest Digital Game-Based Learning.

Even more exciting in many ways are the Internet-linked phones, already widely popular in Europe and Japan. The phones have screens, albeit small ones, on which you can play chess and other games. In the Unites States, they are being manufactured by Motorola and others. At some point soon, handhelds and phones will clearly merge, as they have already begun to do.

Will Digital Game-Based Learning appear on these devices? It's already there. In Japan, you can take English lessons on your phone.[47] Click Health is producing handheld-based learning games for management of diabetes, asthma, and other medical conditions.[48] People at MIT in the US, as well as several Europeans and Asians, have designed learning games for handhelds, often incorporating the devices' geolocation and camera functions. One great advantage of these devices is that they make the "anytime, anywhere" slogan of the e-learning marketers—which too often turns into "no time, nowhere" even with the Web—into a reality. Learn about your company's new strategy on the train or the bus; take an English lesson outside the restaurant while waiting for your colleagues. You'll do it—not just because it's learning, but because it's fun.

CONCLUSION

We've now seen that:

- Adults like and play games in a big way and are highly engaged by them.
- Digital Game-Based Learning is already being used widely in business in at least one form.
- Simulations are most engaging when made into games.
- The Internet is the gaming place of the future, but it is the gaming place of the present only with small games or when combined with local assets.
- Handhelds will be important platforms for Digital Game-Based Learning.

Let us look now at the variety of ways that Digital Game-Based Learning has been used in business, on the Internet and off, with adults of all ages. It's high time for some case studies and examples.

Part Three
WHAT LEADING ORGANIZATIONS ARE DOING

This is an idea whose time has come.
— A Goldman Sachs Managing Director

9

Digital Game-Based Learning in Business

41 Examples and Case Studies from the Incredibly Simple to the Amazingly Complex

Putting up a bunch of information on a Web site was just as boring as being handed a binder ... so we decided to incorporate a game.
— Amy George, PepsiCo

It's much faster, and also more fun —you get to shoot ideas and kill the monsters.
— Gene Kim, financial trader

The same thing that drives us to be casual five days a week also allows us, culturally and attitudinally, to learn through a game.
— John Parker, Dean, Leadership College, First Union Bank

Why do so many managers complain about the quality of the workforce despite the fact that U.S. companies spend well over $60 *billion* annually on training?[1] Our employees are certainly *working* harder. Could it possibly be that they are not *playing* enough?

A growing number of companies have embraced Digital Game-Based Learning in one form or another. Digital Game-Based Learning now shows up in a variety of industries, organizations, and styles, for an extremely wide variety of content and uses, ranging from procedures and policies to products and skills. Although they might not *all* be games yet, the *McKinsey Quarterly* estimates that more than 60 percent of all United States corporations have used some kind of learning simulation.[2] We are certainly on the way.

In the following pages, I present both short examples and more extended case studies of specific examples of Digital Game-Based Learning, and show to what ends they are used. I demonstrate how Digital Game-Based Learning is used in the fast food chains, where games and simulations train the young, high-turnover workforces. I show how it has made strong headway into financial services companies, which have an extremely competitive population with easy access to computers. I also look at the health care industries, which have successfully employed Digital Game-Based Learning, especially with doctors. The detailed case studies presented include Ameritrade, Bankers Trust, The Boston Consulting Group, Burger King, McKinsey, Nortel Networks, PricewaterhouseCoopers, and think3.

While I have included 41 examples here, the list is, in reality, much, much longer. There is an additional list on the book's companion Web sites *www.socialimpactgames.com* and *www.twitchspeed.com* with the examples that there was not room to include here. You can help this list grow by reporting other instances you know of to the site. After considering several different ways, I have presented the examples by *type of use*, in alphabetical order (see next page).

I will now look at specific examples of Digital Game-Based Learning. Let me be clear, though, that these examples are neither all-inclusive nor intended in any way as a "top 40" list of the best Digital Game-Based Learning available, or even as any particular endorsement by me. It is intended solely to highlight the *great variety* of Digital Game-Based Learning that exists. For those who care what *I* consider to be "state-of-the-art" in Digital Game-Based Learning, I provide that list at the end of the chapter.

The examples begin with external training, because this is a growing area for Digital Game-Based Learning. I then move to internal training.

EXTERNAL TRAINING

Using Digital Game-Based Learning to Educate Customers

In addition to training their internal employees, a number of companies have turned to Digital Game-Based Learning to educate their customers. Obviously, this is a form of marketing as well. Customers, or potential customers, may be even less motivated than employees to learn about a com-

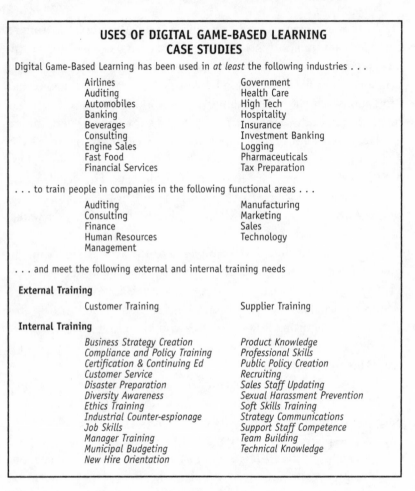

USES OF DIGITAL GAME-BASED LEARNING
CASE STUDIES

Digital Game-Based Learning has been used in *at least* the following industries . . .

Airlines	Government
Auditing	Health Care
Automobiles	High Tech
Banking	Hospitality
Beverages	Insurance
Consulting	Investment Banking
Engine Sales	Logging
Fast Food	Pharmaceuticals
Financial Services	Tax Preparation

. . . to train people in companies in the following functional areas . . .

Auditing	Manufacturing
Consulting	Marketing
Finance	Sales
Human Resources	Technology
Management	

. . . and meet the following external and internal training needs

External Training

Customer Training	Supplier Training

Internal Training

Business Strategy Creation	*Product Knowledge*
Compliance and Policy Training	*Professional Skills*
Certification & Continuing Ed	*Public Policy Creation*
Customer Service	*Recruiting*
Disaster Preparation	*Sales Staff Updating*
Diversity Awareness	*Sexual Harassment Prevention*
Ethics Training	*Soft Skills Training*
Industrial Counter-espionage	*Strategy Communications*
Job Skills	*Support Staff Competence*
Manager Training	*Team Building*
Municipal Budgeting	*Technical Knowledge*
New Hire Orientation	

pany and its products—the engagement of the game format can be used to draw in people who have no other "compulsion" to learn the material. I look at eight examples here—a very low-tech Web-based trivia game; a relatively low-tech email game; a much more sophisticated Macintosh-based game created by a consulting company to explain its engagements; two highly complex trading games used to explain financial products, one used in a classroom setting, the other distributed via CD-ROM; a game used with physicians; and two games to help use and sell hardware and software.

1. The Aspirin Trivia Game. Probably the very simplest form of Digital Game-Based Learning imaginable is represented by Bayer's Aspirin

Trivia Game, which was formerly online at Bayer's US site. It has just five questions, one graphic (unnecessary for the game) and is entirely written in HTML. It is so simple that any HTML programmer could probably create a similar game on your Web site in under an hour.

Yes, it is simple, but it is also engaging. The five questions have been chosen so that they are neither easy nor obvious, and will almost certainly teach you something you don't know. They are (with the answer choices):

1. Each year, how many aspirin tablets are taken worldwide? (50 million/50 billion)
2. What is the most popular use of aspirin today? (prevention of heart disease/relieving headaches)
3. When was aspirin first marketed in tablet form? (1900/1933)
4. Aspirin is consumed in a variety of ways around the world. What form do the British prefer? (aspirin powder/caplets)
5. Which tree contributed to the development of aspirin? (White willow tree/birch tree)

Players are then *invited* to find out more by clicking on a link. While four of the five questions are true trivia, there is one highly useful piece of information: that aspirin is a drug used more for heart disease prevention than for headaches. This might actually drive some people to buy the product!

There is no subject, I would venture to say, that could not benefit from a simple game like this. Skeptics will of course ask, "Why is this a game, and not just a quiz or test?" The answers are several. One is context. Another is that trivia has become one of the most popular forms of game. A third is lack of compulsion, and a fourth is the content of the questions, which are designed to engage and to educate, not to test. However, as I said, this is Digital Game-Based Learning at its most basic.

2. The "We'll Pay Your Taxes" Game. Would you play a game if the prize were having your taxes paid by someone else? H&R Block used an email game from Yoyodine (now part of Yahoo!) to build interest in and knowledge of a new Premium Tax service they were offering. Why a game? "Learning about a new tax service," says Seth Godin in his book

Permission Marketing,[3] "isn't high on anyone's list of ways to spend a Saturday." What's more, they were looking to reach an upper-income group unlikely to think of H&R Block when it came time to do their taxes.

The game was promoted in banners on the Internet that said "Play the H&R Block We'll Pay Your Taxes Game." According to Godin, about 60,000 people clicked on the banner. After clicking, they saw a registration page that explained that in order to have their taxes paid next year (up to $25,000), they had to answer a bunch of trivia questions about Block and taxes over the next 10 weeks. More than 50,000 people (over 80 percent!) enrolled. Twice a week, for 10 weeks those people were sent an email about the game and Premium Tax. The game drove people to Block's Web site to look up the answers to tax trivia questions and created a curriculum that taught people about the benefits of H&R Block and Premium Tax.

Each email sent averaged a 36 percent response rate, very high compared with direct mail. The mail was opened because it contained their score. H&R Block saw a noticeable improvement in traffic to their Web site, and, more importantly, saw traffic increase to all parts of their site.

Did people learn? After the campaign a follow-up campaign sent a multiple choice question about Premium Tax to three groups: Internet users who didn't enroll, people who enrolled but never responded, people who were regular responders. Of the first group, 20 percent (the amount expected by random chance) got the question right. Among the second group, 34 percent got it right; and among the third group, 54 percent knew the right answer. Not perfect, but more than twice the random number, in a group with no particular incentive to remember.

What is interesting is that these results are with a random, self-selected group. Think of what you might be able to achieve with a group that really *needed* to know something, like, for example, a new corporate strategy. "Suppose Lou Gerstner (CEO of IBM) offered a Porsche for the best score," speculated one IBM Learning executive. "Who wouldn't play?"[4] As we shall see later in this chapter, companies like Nortel Networks have already begun to use Digital Game-Based Learning in this way.

3. Time Out! In the late 1980s, the Boston Consulting Group (BCG) began advocating a new approach to business improvement—Time-Based Competition. Based on work done initially by George Stalk and

Tom Hout, and popularized in their best-selling business book *Competing Against Time*,[5] BCG realized that various cycles and systems within any business, from product development, to service and repairs, to manufacturing, could be shortened dramatically, sometimes from months to days, cutting major costs and making the company dramatically more competitive. However, a time-based competition analysis was a major undertaking in a company, involving numerous interviews at all levels of the organization, examination of many documents, plant and office visits, interviews with suppliers and customers, and more. Despite the success of the book and the thoroughness of their methodology, the officers at BCG found some competitors to be better at communicating the nature and power of the procedure to clients. "If only," they thought, "we could let our clients experience for themselves what we are about to do, they would be able to be so much more involved and engaged in the process."

The result was a Digital Game-Based Learning project that eventually came to be called *Time Out!* It is both a game and a simulation, but in a different sense than many other simulations. For *Time Out!* is a dysfunctional company, Cellular, Inc., presented *only* as it appears, with no built-in "if you do this then this happens" relationships *at all*. It is really just a graphic database of the information a consultant or other observer would find if he or she came to analyze the company—reports, executives to interview, factory tours to take, workers to buttonhole—presented exactly as an observer would find it. To accurately construct this was not trivial. The BCG team analyzed a large number of the firm's past Time-Based Competition cases to see what the consultants actually found when they went in for the first time. They went looking "not with the consultant's eye of what's the solution, but what might you have learned in a conversation, what might you have seen in a plant tour, what might you have seen in documents distributed around the company," said the BCG project manager Bob Wolf.

Time Out! is typically played by several teams of four to six players in a facilitated environment, a design intended to create a sense of competition. Each team is given two computers. All the teams are given the same assignment to analyze one of four potential problem areas. Their job is to explore the company and come up with recommendations that will be shared in presentations to the other teams. "It compresses the case team process down from 4 months down to 3 hours," says Wolf.

Teams can choose to interview a variety of people on the computers, examine all available reports and factory data, visit the factory and other parts of the organization, and observe and ask questions. As in real life, few issues are obvious on the surface; one has to dig to find out what is really going on, and there is never enough time to do everything. Interviews are structured as decision trees, so that what you learn depends on the questions you ask. Data is distributed in various reports and often not available until specifically requested. The effectiveness of your onsite visits depends on what you choose to look at and what questions you ask. In 3 hours, each team needs to do the field work, go through diagnostic steps, analyze the data that they pull out, come up with elements of analysis—process maps, cycle diagrams, "fishbone" diagrams, etc.—and come up with their logic and recommendations. "We embedded the ability to do a dozen different analyses, but we will only ask a team in some reasonable period of time to only do four to six," says Wolf.

As in many simulation games, teams get extremely involved. "There was enough competition introduced that it made everybody engage and care about it and they would lose the idea that this was actually a game on a computer," says Wolf. "There was passion about Cellular, Inc., as though it were real—much better than I ever anticipated. There was always a time when teams thought there was no way that they could get it done in another hour and a half, and they'd come and ask for 'personal dispensations.' Everyone understood that they weren't really on the hook, but everyone was driving themselves. It was exciting to watch."

A couple of things about *Time Out!* are worth noting. As mentioned, in contrast to most simulation games, there is no "black box." This means that no set of relationships and no dependent assumptions have been built in (such as "do this and this and later that happens.") There are no decisions to be made inside the simulation. There is only data, as close as possible to what is found in the real world. The relationships and decisions must be created in the players' heads and within the team. From BCG's perspective, this approach increased conversation and interaction among the players, which was a prime goal of the exercise.

A second of note is that the *Time Out!* was constructed as a relatively simple set of templates, making it very easily updateable and adaptable to other industries. The initial manufacturing version was later supplemented with a financial services version. The types of interactions in the product are really only a few: interviews, reports, emails, and site visits. Yet filled with appropriate data, these interactions both model the real world well and give a very rich picture of the company. A key to the effectiveness of the game was the BCG consultants' ability to create the content of the interactions in a way that was at the same time true to what they had experienced, comprehensive, and fun to use. "There's a big distinction between doing this in a half-assed dry fashion and doing it so it's engaging, so it's funny, so that people can get lost in the experience," comments Wolf. Client executives commented that they had "lots of MBAs who could deal with polished data and can present fancy reports, but they didn't have people who could walk into a dysfunctional plant floor and start moving machines around, look upstream and downstream, and be a good detective about what the problems are and where the opportunities are. This game us that intimate look into what's necessary."

Time Out! was used by BCG at more than 200 different clients, according to Wolf, and often multiple times. "It started as an awareness seminar to position ourselves relative to some competitors and it did that very effectively, but it basically became a core training tool for client case teams. And also for five or six years it was used in our own orientation of our first-year consultants who would be coming in because it was not 'dumbed down' but reflected state-of-the-art understanding at the time. So, it turned out to be a very versatile tool. It was highly successful from our point of view. I don't know of a failed client application."

4. Darwin. Options trading is not for the faint of heart—or the uneducated. Options trading is extraordinarily complex even for options traders, says Cindy Klein,[6] former director of Educational Product Development at Ameritrade. "That's why so many go belly up." Ninety percent of options, it turns out, expire unexercised.

Klein joined Ameritrade, a 25-year-old brokerage house in 1994, just as the online trading market was getting started. Her background includes a master's of arts in film and multimedia writing and producing in San Francisco's "Silicon Gulch." She spent her first year and a half at Ameritrade helping to design the firm's online trading experience. "We and a couple of other competitors launched online trading to the world," she says. "We essentially democratized personal investment in a way that had never been seen. The Securities and Exchange Commission and Arthur Levitt were issuing dispatches that were threatening us about how irresponsible it was of us to put these powerful trading tools in the hand of the uninitiated. And it became obvious really quickly that we had a responsibility as well to teach people how to use them."

Talk about need!

Ameritrade decided to develop training to help customers who were trading options but who were losing money because they really didn't know *how* to do it. They also had a marketing goal—to reach and teach MBA students who could eventually become their customers. A simulation enabled them to dramatically illustrate the risk, and show clients how they could make money or lose money "in a way you really can't in a handbook." But they also decided to make their product, which eventually came to be named *Darwin, Survival of the Fittest,* a real game.

"Part of what we were trying to simulate in *Darwin* is the mania of trading in the pit," says Klein. "It's one thing to teach people how to trade options and basic put-call principles. That's all fine and dandy, but 'Hello? that's boring.' *Darwin* is fun, and it's gamey, because we throw them in an options pit and make them race against the clock." In part, the game was the vision of the CEO, J. Joe Ricketts, the sixtyish entrepreneur who runs Ameritrade. "He had this insane idea that people would want to learn how to trade options in this bizarre gaming environment—and he was right," says Klein. "It's easier to get people engaged in a game than a simulation," she continues, "because we can provide them an experience that will keep them coming back and frankly that will make them think 'wow, this is really cool, its fun, and Ameritrade gave it to me.' It's a compelling way to bring people in. It keeps them coming back; it's something with which we could engage students in the demographic we were after, which was people coming out of business school and coming out of college. How do you appeal to those people? Well, frankly, they're gamers. There's a lot of crossover there between the typical 25-year-old MBA student and a gamer, and it was a great way to appeal to those people and to introduce them to Ameritrade for when they were ready to open an account."

Klein's team developed a game in which they created twenty bogus companies. As a player, you go in and trade in a pit that includes five companies. Each company has a variety of news articles that come out on it. The newsfeeds are built in a tree formation and the game takes a circuitous route through the tree each time, so every game is different.

There is also a randomization of how each piece of news affects the price of the underlying stock. So there are approximately 176,000 scenario possibilities that you can have playing *Darwin*—a player will never play the same game twice. They use a Black-Scholes pricing model, and the market responds differently in each game. *Darwin* can be played single- or multiplayer, and over the Internet or a local area network (LAN). You meet other players in a virtual "lobby," and compete. You don't actually trade with them, but you compete for the fattest portfolio. The whole game takes approximately 50 minutes, the idea being that you could play in the span of a classroom period. You trade in and out of your positions, and you can do double and triple option combinations as well as single calls and puts, and you can also trade equity.

Did *Darwin* serve its purpose? "Joe had the idea that people would like this," says Klein. "Fortunately, he was right." People did like it and it still is a very valuable training tool for Ameritrade. They found that people really did understand options better after they played this game (see Chapter 14). People liked this kind of learning and wanted more of it.

Like many of today's high-end Digital Game-Based Learning applications, *Darwin* is a hybrid of old and new. Its single CD contains, in addition to the game, a very traditional click and page-turn computer-based training (CBT)-type tutorial with a quiz at the end of each section—very tell-test. "A very big question for us," says Klein, "was can you thread the game and the tutorial together, and how do you do that?" Although it would have been ideal to thread the two together to make an on-demand tutorial, they decided that threading the tutorial through the game would make the tutorial complicated and hard to follow, and would slow the game down. So they separated the two—you never have to go into the game and you never have to go into the tutorial if you don't want to. "We poured our heart out in making the game real groovy," says Klein.

The team that put Darwin together was a large one in total—more than 40 people, including all testers and focus groups. The core group consisted of Klein, as producer, chief game designer, and chief script writer; an options trader with 15 years of experience as the chief content expert; an art team from Mondo Media; a couple of programmers who called themselves PDG (for Pretty Darn Good) and who brought in other programmers as needed; and a comedy writer from Los Angeles. "When you get into the game there are several characters in the pit with you and they give you rumors and sometimes you have to trade on these rumors—those characters were developed, in terms of their dialog, by our comedy writer." The characters bring reality and "attitude" to the game. Klein also had people creating the tutorial and glossary, and a team of professional focus-testers from San Francisco. Name Lab in San Francisco provided the name for the product. The game took 15 months to create and in the end 300,000 CDs were pressed.

If she had to do it over, Klein would make the product Internet based. But she realizes that to do that she would have to give up a lot of the bells and whistles. "The part when it gets fun and gamey is what you can't simulate on the Internet because you can never depend on the connection speed," she says. Klein also regrets not having made the product compatible with NT. "At that time, 89 percent of our user base was on Windows 95. We didn't know that so much of our user base would move to NT and would want to play in the office."

Klein would also have focus-tested the concept earlier, relying less on instinct and more on actual, solid market information. She thinks that while their instincts were "basically correct," they were not in every instance, and if they had done research sooner they could have had a slam dunk and a game with more staying power.

A copy of *Darwin, Survival of the Fittest* can be obtained directly from Ameritrade at *www.ameritrade.com.*

5. HEDGEManager and HEDGEFund. It is interesting that the content area of financial derivatives has been the subject of a number of different Digital Game-Based Learning initiatives. This is likely a combination of the fact that the subject is extraordinarily complex and that the audience is relatively young and game-oriented. When derivatives marketers at Bankers Trust perceived that corporate treasurers were having trouble understanding how the bank's new derivatives-based products could be used to hedge their corporate risks, the derivatives "rocket scientists" at Bankers, led by Jerry DelMissier in London,[7] created two complex spreadsheet-based games to explain them. The massive spreadsheets let people manage either a company with a lot of potential risk, or run a risky hedge fund. In the cleverly designed competitive games, each player or team tried to manage the company or fund through a series of rounds of changing economic news and conditions to see who could produce the highest return while taking the least risk.

There was only one problem. The spreadsheets were *so* complex—hundreds of columns by hundreds of rows, at times referencing proprietary bank pricing algorithms written in other code—that no one except the traders could understand them. It was almost impossible for the target users to get a handle on what was going on. In this case, the "guts" of the game were all there—what was needed was a better interface.

My team at Bankers Trust, known as "Corporate Gameware," was called on to help out. Because none of the three experts who had created the game could leave their trading desks, we flew to London. During a hectic August during which I saw almost nothing of London except my hotel room, Bankers Trust's Trading Floor, and the inside of a lot of London taxicabs, a programmer and I created a easy-to-use interface for the games, using only VBX, the programming language built into Excel.

What emerged, with the help of Ruth Gregory, a British graphic designer we hired, was a deceptively simple-looking interface, which we first prototyped in Authorware. Users had a choice of only a few screens—you could see your portfolio, view your balance sheet, P&L and cash flows, and enter trades. The trades were set up as simple input output forms, with everything required for a particular type of trade entered on the left, and the prices calculated on the right, based on Bankers Trust (BT)'s proprietary pricing models. The whole thing was very clean and easy to use, and at the same time extremely powerful. The lone programmer, Allen Brian, did a yeoman's job of pulling it all together in a month, particularly given that the inputs from the content experts could only come sporadically between trades or at the end of long days.

To play the game, the players are divided into as many teams as there are computers, with typically two or three people to a team. (For client offsites there are typically eight to ten teams; for BT's new hires, twenty to thirty.) Each round begins with a news brief, which gives some clues as to the coming environment, and each team evaluates its cash flows and risks and makes its trades to hedge the risks. Typically, there are derivatives traders walking around the room to help. When all teams have made their trades (by a given time), a password is given that unlocks the results, and shows the news for the next round (each round represents a month.) Each team's results are posted to a central board, and after five rounds, the team with the greatest return at the lowest risk is declared the winner, often with prizes.

The game was used at scores of Bankers Trust client offsites around the world and was played regularly at Harvard and other top business schools as a recruiting tool for the Bankers Trust derivatives business. It was also used as a training tool for all new hires at the firm. Among the things that made the game an effective teaching tool was that it was used in a class-roomlike situation where the emcee, always an experienced derivatives trader, could debrief and interpret results, and the other facilitating experts (typically actual traders) could immediately handle problems that arose. A feature of the game was that new scenarios could be entered by the emcee or his staff before each game, making the game both current and tailorable to real historical scenarios, such as the crash of 1987.

The HEDGE*Manager* and HEDGE*Fund* games were big hits, with one of them eventually ported to the Web, and Harvard Business School offering to purchase them. But as with many Digital Game-Based Learning efforts, changes in Bankers Trust's fortunes and executives led to a loss of focus on the games. That, along with the fact that Bankers Trust's exec-utives were very concerned about the proprietary pricing algorithms built into the games, meant that the games were never sold and quietly disappeared as Bankers Trust was acquired by Deutsche Bank.

6. Dobutrex Dosage Game. Moving out of finance to medicine, here's a great story about the power of good Digital Game-Based Learn-ing to create memorable experiences. When I happened to tell VP Mike Junior of McGraw-Hill that I was looking for Digital Game-Based Learn-ing examples, he said, "Hey I know of one. My wife works for Eli Lilly and they have a game for doctors."

Getting doctors' to focus their attention on new medications is something that pharmaceutical companies constantly struggle with. They have armies of "detail men" who call regularly on doctors looking for a minute of their time, compressing their presentations as much as possible, and trying to find leave-behinds that will get physicians' atten-tion. For a cardiac drug called Dobutrex, Eli Lilly created a digital game for the doctors in which they had a patient that needed attention and they had to prescribe Dobutrex in the right dosage. As a result of their pre-scription, the patient either died, recovered, or was somewhere in between. "It was a great game," said Junior, "I played it a lot, even though it wasn't meant for me."

I assumed this was some time last year. But it turned out to be 15 years ago! Not only does Junior vividly remember the game, but he still remembers the name of the drug! Why? "I remember my behavior as being determined to save this life," he says.

7. Giraffe. Some readers may remember the Apple's Newton being touted as being able to read anyone's handwriting. It really couldn't decipher much of it, and led to such strange interpretations that Gary Trudeau did a whole series of Doonesberry cartoons mocking it. Although in many ways ahead of its time and a fabulous machine, the inability of people to use it for writing led directly to its failure and ended the career of John Scully at Apple. So the Palm Pilot, which first appeared in 1996, decided to take a more limited approach, reading not your own handwriting, but a more standardized style of writing called Graffiti. The only trouble with Graffiti was that users had to learn it.

"No problem," Palm thought, "these are consumers. And consumers love games." So, bundled with all Palm Pilots comes this cute little game called *Giraffe*. In *Giraffe*, letters begin falling from the top of the screen, and your job as a player is to write them in Graffiti with the stylus on the computer before they hit the bottom. They then disappear. But if too many hit the bottom, you lose and have to start the level over. Simple, huh?

Not really. They start out with the easy letters, and then add the harder ones. Then things go faster, and then capitals are mixed in. Then symbols. It is not only a challenging game, but it is a lot of fun. And most of all, it does the job. While there's probably no way to measure how many have actually played it, even if only 15 percent of the more than 7 million[8] Pilot buyers used it, over a million people learned Graffiti this way.

Giraffe is a great example of a "reflex game," that is, Digital Game-Based Learning designed to train you to respond quickly. It is neither particularly fancy in its graphics nor expensive, but it is addictive, and it works. How many other things could, and should, be taught this way?

8. The Monkey Wrench Conspiracy (continued). We began our discussion of *The Monkey Wrench Conspiracy* in Chapter 1. Here are some additional details.

DOCTOR MONKEY WRENCH HIMSELF!—CREATED BY DUBMEDIA (FROM THE COVER OF THINK3'S DEMO CD)

The Monkey Wrench Conspiracy, programmed by Jon Fabris and Rob Posniak in C++, consists of a three-level *Quake*-style game (based on an independently written 3D engine we licensed) combined with thirty "tasks" that are done directly in the thinkdesign software. The user is motivated by the game to complete all the tasks. Examples of motivators include: You can't fire the weapon you need till you design a new trigger. You can't open the gate until you fix the switch. You can't get through the wall until you've cut a hole through its various layers. You can't transport to the next level until you repair the transporter. Each of these tasks requires more sophisticated uses of the software than the last, but CADA, your "Computer-Aided Design Assistant," is always there to push you through as quickly as possible. In the final task in each level, the assistant breaks down somehow and you are "on your own" self-testing how much you have learned. (You are also free to do the tasks without the game or out of order if you prefer.)

The game part is designed with three degrees of difficulty, chosen by the player, so that it is challenging, but not too much so, for beginners at this type of game, and yet can be *extremely* challenging to advanced players—our testers, all experienced gamers, had trouble getting through it. There are lots of monsters to overcome (all robots), space walks, mazes, puzzles. Even without the learning, it's a really good game.

The game is constructed as a "shell" to which the tasks, all defined in terms of a structured set of files (models, asxs, and avis), are loosely linked via flashing objects in the game that you "run over," launching a task in the think3 software. One goal was to make the tasks not only interchangeable, but to define a standard task "module" that anyone—think3 employee or product user—could create. This aspect worked extremely well. Says Joe Costello, "the whole concept behind *Monkey Wrench* is that it was a very modular approach. And I think one of the great things about the games-based learning approach that you guys helped us with is, yeah it's a game, but it also has to have a good pedagogical underpinning and a sound thought process about what you're going to teach people and how you're going to teach people. *Monkey Wrench* was a very modular orientation and little bite-size chunks of significant content. And one of the things that we've done since then is that people get used to that bite-size content view or module view of learning, so we continue to produce modules that we allow people to do over the Web, or download over the Web, however they like to do it, and so we've extended all the original courseware from *The Monkey Wrench Conspiracy* for future releases of the product after the original 3.0 and also just for special topics. That's what we contemplated originally and that's worked out very well, and people really like that."

In fact, think3 is already at work on their next piece of Digital Game-Based Learning. "We are looking at doing another generation of *Monkey Wrench*," says Costello. "That's just become the generic term for 'cool educational stuff,' for us. So, whenever we talk about some cool educational thing we talk about *Monkey Wrench*. And we've got a new idea for a more fun approach to these online seminars when they're recorded. And we're really inspired by *Monkey Wrench* trying to do something that's more engaging, more interesting, more exciting. The other thing we've thought of doing is trying to appeal to a potentially different group in terms of engaging people. The game resonates really strongly with a certain group of people and so we're looking to come up with a theme that will engage another segment. It's an entertainment theme, it is edutainment, but I'd say it was much more in the class of a *Riven*-type game or a *Myst*-type game. Our internal people are doing a lot of it."

Customers, place your orders now!

Using Digital Game-Based Learning
to Educate Suppliers

Along with customers, Digital Game-Based Learning should also be very effective at educating suppliers. However, to date I have not found any instances of this. If you know of one, please report it to the Web site *www.twitchspeed.com*. Even better, create one!

INTERNAL TRAINING

Using Digital Game-Based Learning for
Business Strategy Creation

Business strategy is an area in which various forms of gaming have been used for some time. However, until not too long ago (and still today in many cases), the "games" were quite dissimilar from those that the Games Generations play. The games were just large numerical simulations that took data and decision inputs and spit out financial statements and comparative results. This is changing dramatically, however, as individuals and companies struggle to make the sometimes arcane concepts and practice of strategy creation accessible to more and more people. What follows are three examples

9. Strategy Co-Pilot. McKinsey and Company, the well-known consulting firm, has been creating business strategies for clients for generations. In the mid-1990s, consultants in their London office began using live role-playing exercises to help clients create strategy in a fictional company. They found, somewhat to their surprise, that the clients were able to come up with the same strategies as the consultants, and have a lot more ownership in the process. But they also found that while the process was effective, it was enormously inefficient because you needed fifteen or twenty people in a room. One of the McKinsey consultants, Richard Barkey, who is also a hardware engineer and an avid gamer who speaks proudly of programming his PDP11 to play chess when he was 13 and playing all of the Infocomm games, began to explore digital alternatives as a way of "scaling " the solution. "I thought 'the hardest thing possible to teach with a computer would be something qualitative like strategy, so let's have a go,'" he says. Before starting, he looked around to see what was out there and was "amazed" by just how awful things were. "I thought if you just took the quality of design and production values of computer games and applied it to business training you'd come up with something quite cool," he says.

A first product, *Strategy Mentor*, was created by Barkey and his team inside McKinsey, and was used throughout the firm for internal training of consultants. In 1997, with McKinsey's support and blessing, Barkey spun out of the consulting firm to form his own company, Imparta.

Imparta's first product, a refinement of *Strategy Mentor*, is called *Strategy Co-Pilot*. It is now used by McKinsey as well as IBM, Prudential, Nortel Networks, EDS, and other companies for training consultants and employees on the process of creating business strategy. Like *Darwin*, the product has two parts. The first is the tutorial—a series of short animations, intended to impart the theoretical concepts. These are "tell" voiceovers, with cartoon visuals that are intended, Barkey says, to make the messages more memorable. They are definitely not Digital Game-Based Learning. But what *is* Digital Game-Based Learning, and of great interest, is the part they call the "simulation," whose purpose is to let you practice the theory you've heard about.

The simulation begins, as do many of these games (and this *is* a game), with you at your desk receiving a mission. Your assignment is to help the CEO decide whether to accept an offer made for one of the company's divisions, and of course you have only a few hours to prepare your recommmendations. You have a task and a toolkit of analyses and data that you can research, and you have to think your way through. You need to get information by calling the people who manage the company and looking at reports, fill in a set of "slides" (of course there are slides—you're a consultant!), and present a logical argument and recommendations to the CEO. Calling the wrong people at the wrong times, or asking the wrong questions and gets you a face full of sharp and sarcastic retorts. Fun? Sure, but so far this is not unlike many other Digital Game-Based Learning examples.

What makes *Strategy Co-pilot* unique and interesting, however, is its built-in coaching, which they call the "intelligent coach." He is a cute little animated guy with an English accent. His intelligence is, of course, of the artificial variety, but it works quite well. He can be there either a lot or a little—because you the player, set, via a slider, the amount of coaching you think you need. He can either lead you all the way through the process ("I really think it's time that you got the annual report"), provide you with helpful hints ("Maybe you should try calling X"), or, if you haven't done anything for a while, ask if you are stuck ("What are you trying to do here?"). Unless you *are* really stuck, most of his coaching comes in the form of questions rather than direction. "The AI [artificial intelligence] coaching intrinsic to the program is extremely hard to get right," says Barkey, "and is something we've spent a lot of time refining and under-standing what works and what doesn't work. It adapts itself, so as you start to do better it backs off, but if you're struggling it kind of increases itself automatically, so that we keep people in their 'learning sweet spot.'" In other words, in the "flow" state.

Barkey likens *Strategy Co-Pilot* to an adventure game and a role-play-ing game. "If you took *Monkey Island* and crossed it with *Baldur's Gate*, you'd have something that wasn't a million miles away from this, in terms of the intent, at any rate. I would say there's an awful lot of crossover [between our products and consumer games], including the fact that things are not always obvious—clues scattered around that you have to piece together in order come up with an insight. For example, the obvi-ous objective of the company may be to maximize profit, but there are some hidden objectives that are scattered around in various pieces of information that you have to piece together. It's kind of like finding the keys to open the Grand Poobah's cave."

The program's connection to games also includes the way the pro-gram introduces the player to the interface. It is similar to *Alpha Centauri* and *Battle Zone II* in that it leads you through the process as you use the program. Because people are only going to play *Strategy Co-Pilot* for a day and not a year, they need a rapid learning curve, so they try to optimize that aspect. They also face the issue that consumer games have been struggling with—the balance between telling a story and allowing people freedom of movement. There is a story line in *Strategy Co-Pilot*. "If you make a game that has no story at all it's usually a pretty crap game," Barkey says. "People are looking for a variety of pace, and what happens all the way through."

On the learning side, Barkey says that the closest academic to his beliefs is David Kolb with his Experiential Learning Cycle. "What's inter-esting about Kolb's stuff is that it says that you learn a skill through prac-

tice, which is kind of self-evident, although it's sadly lacking in most computer-based training. But the critical part of that is the reflection process,
and that's a lot of what the coach does in *Strategy Co-Pilot*. He's there to
help the people reflect on what's happened so that they can generalize
into a new situation. It's kind of experiment, conceptualize what's happened and create a mental model of what's happened and then reflect on
that to understand how it would replay. A combination of common sense
and academic stuff as well."

McKinsey spent roughly $500,000 to develop the original *Strategy
Mentor* version, and Barkey has spent another $1 million since then. "It
started because I wanted to do it. The office manager in London brought
in the head of global training and development who then became the
sponsor or the project." It was created entirely internally, with Barkey
developing the first version by himself in Visual Basic. "I knew how to do
a bit of programming," says Barkey, "plus being a games player and a having a business background." He also did the 3D artwork for the first version, which took one and a half years plus half a year of testing and
tweaking. Then he brought in a couple of guys, and the next version was
in C++. "The team was two people and me. It was kind of a skunk works,
really, but I think you had to, because there was so much iteration
because we were really trying to push the envelope, and with a small
team it was a lot more effective."

The current version of *Strategy Co-Pilot* uses a lot of interactive
video. However, Barkey plans to move to real-time rendered characters
very soon. As we discussed, the reasons are bandwidth, and a lot more
freedom to do things. "The best computer games don't use video,"
Barkey says, "they use rendered characters, because you've got so much
more freedom to be a director inside the game environment. The proto-
typing cycle time is much shorter. You've got a lot more flexibility both
in terms of how quickly you can do stuff and what you can do. To put it
bluntly, you can get a lot more different options on the CD in a given
bandwidth. Video is a useful interim measure until the rendering technology gets to the point where it's good enough, and it's pretty much
there."

In addition to McKinsey, Imparta is supported by a consortium of
companies including Smiths Industries, Abbey National, and BAE Systems (formerly British Aerospace).

Using Digital Game-Based Learning for
Compliance and Policy Training

Compliance and policy training is about as dull as it gets. A book several inches thick of material to learn, and they sometimes even ask for your John Hancock at the end to prove you've read it. Many, if not most, people don't actually read it—at least not thoroughly—as more than a few companies have learned to their dismay. Compliance directors and trainers are always looking for more engaging ways to do their training. Here is one Digital Game-Based Learning example.

10. Straight Shooter! *Straight Shooter!*, the world's first (and possibly only) *Doom-style* training game for policy training, grew out of a major business crisis at Bankers Trust. When the markets turned against the bank in the mid-1990s, several clients sued, saying the bank had engaged in bad sales practices. As result of the discovery process, they found that, indeed, in a minority of cases, things had happened on the trading floor that they were unhappy with in terms of the behavior of some traders. The company paid out several hundred million dollars in make-good payments, was censured by the regulators at the Federal Reserve, and signed a consent decree that suggested a series of actions on their part that they would agree to in light of the difficulties that they had.[9]

An important piece of this was training these young, very aggressive traders to learn what they needed to know about derivatives policies and practices, and the bank's being able to demonstrate that it had not just gone through the motions, but had in good faith had made every effort to ensure that these people had really absorbed and understood all of it.

"Looking back on this you almost couldn't have written a better prescription for Digital Game-Based Learning as far as taking this population of young workers—a particularly computer-literate group of people who would require much more constant stimulation in order to be effective learners and needed something beyond 'please read this manual'—to get them to master these materials," says Mark Bieler, former HR director of the bank. That was the beginning of this game alternative to teach these materials to this particular population.

A few years earlier, in happier circumstances, I had been hired by Bieler to help reform learning at Bankers Trust by creating online learning that the "very young, extremely-bright-but-generally-disinterestedin-forms-and-procedures-and-things-like-that people" at the bank (Bieler's description) might actually want to do. I and my team were tapped by Bieler to help him in this current crisis.

We began not with the game, but on the learning side, asking ourselves, "What would satisfy the Fed that we had 'effectively accomplished peoples understanding and mastering of that body of material?'" Our thinking was the following: Seminars given by lawyers and compliance people—the usual method of teaching policies—tended to stay at a high level and not get into the many details of the 2-inch-thick policy manual, such as "How many times do I need to call the client" or "What approvals do I need for this type of transaction." We reasoned that were we to go though all the policies and circle the 200 or 300 points that people had to know, we could make up a question about each one. By presenting these questions to the traders we would force them to actively confront the question and make a set of choices (most questions were of the "choose all that apply" variety). If they got a question correct, we had a record that they said they knew this. If they got it wrong, we showed them the part of the policy in question to see why their response was incorrect. Later the question they missed would return, with the answers in a different order (a feature added after user feedback), until all of the questions were answered correctly. So, this was not a "test" with a grade, but a certification that each user knew all the answers. ("Who wants our people to be trained at 85 percent? We need 100 percent," was the way one compliance person put it.) Completion of each of nine topics of approximately twenty questions each was recorded on the server, so the company had a record of each person's being fully trained.

All agreed that this would be a good way to comply with the Fed's training requirement. But 300 questions? Come on, that's *really* boring. It was clear the traders would never do it. So we embedded the 300 questions into the most exciting game we could think of and, according to the focus groups we held, the game the traders most wanted, *Doom!* We didn't use the actual *Doom* engine from Id Software, which would have been far too expensive, but rather a competitor's version which we were able to license for only $10,000. (I don't recommend doing this unless you *really* know what you are doing; our programmers had to do an awful lot of debugging without much guidance.) We were fortunate to have a top-notch programmer, Jon Fabris, who was able to seamlessly integrate the game engine and the question engine. The game's design, we decided, would be about searching for clients, who, when found, would ask you a question and, if you got it right, join your client roster (if you got it wrong, they would tell you to "Go back to B-School" or some such). Players would get to "run" through a series of places where clients are typically found—cities such as New York, London, and Hong Kong; airports; hotels; an "emerging" nation's old castle; and even outer space! We were really excited. Bieler, an executive vice president of the company, was behind it. The budget was agreed at $500,000. Ready to roll, right? Wrong!

In the 2 months between the time the design was finalized and the Investment Proposal (IP) was finally approved (see Chapter 13)—which meant we could actually begin work and pay people—I learned quite a few corporate lessons. The most important was that the bigger and more visible your project, the more constituencies there are that need to have their own particular (and legitimate) needs satisfied in order to get it approved. Technically, for example, the budget for the project did not come from my boss but from the Derivatives Steering Committee, a large group that had to be consulted, demoed to, and satisfied. The IP also required sign-offs from a number of different people, some in HR, some in technology, some in finance and control, and some in purchasing, all of whom had their particular concerns. I spent two tough months as a salesman, pacifier, and adjuster, at times despairing of ever getting the thing done, but it finally reached the bank's Executive Committee (top of the house) for approval. Mark Bieler reports what happened:

> The reactions were all positive with one exception—and it was a tough call. When we thought about the firms' reputation in the press and elsewhere, and the possibility of their painting us, for lack of better expression, as being "irresponsible cowboys," the public relations side of having a shooting game came under some scrutiny from our lawyer and PR people. They were worried that some fuddy-duddy bureaucrat at the Fed looking at that would say "here they go again" rather than say "gee, isn't it great that they spent all this time and spent all this money and creativity to really make sure that their people are really aware

of all the policies and procedures in the derivatives area." And so that was a tough call. And I don't think that the people who were raising the issues were being irresponsible—it was a fair point. Because of the hole we had put ourselves into it was a fair point that we could no longer raise that kind of sensitivity. [10]

So, back to the drawing board. Rock, hard place. If we have shooting we might be branded as "cowboys." If we don't have shooting, the game just isn't fun. What to do? Our solution, amazingly enough, came from the very lawyer who had voiced the concern—the Bank's Chief Corporate Council. "How about if they hold a cell phone instead of a gun," he suggested, "and it doesn't shoot bullets but 'ideas' that can overcome problems. Nobody could fault us for that." "Quick," I said to the graphic artist, "draw me a cell phone. We're on again!"

Fortunately, other than that little piece of required reengineering, the response of the Management Committee was "uniformly favorable." "There are in a management group like that a lot of people who are my age (53)," says Bieler. "I would say that half the people were kind of diffident about it and weren't particularly excited but still thought it was a good thing, but half the people were not just approving of it but were *really excited* about what we had done."

So the game evolved through alpha and beta versions, and people liked how it came out, but we still didn't know what to call it. Again, the answer came from an unexpected quarter. A senior compliance executive decided "Straight Shooter" captured both the essence of the game and the fact that BT wanted it's people to be "straight shooters." (How can anyone argue with John Wayne?) He got so excited that he called my boss who was on his vacation to lobby for it. It won hands down. *Straight Shooter!* it was.

Preparing the "content" also raised some issues. Creating the questions and answers and links to the policies was not hard; we hired a former derivatives marketer who was familiar with both the material and the audience, and she created the questions relatively quickly. *Vetting* those questions, however, was another matter, especially in the tiptoe climate at that time. A committee of three—a derivatives person, a policies person, and a lawyer—was formed to review every question for absolute accuracy. Case studies about "gray areas," originally envisioned in the design, were abandoned in favor of black and white letter-of-the-policy accuracy. Vetting took four times as long as creating the questions (although it should be taken into account that these were special circumstances.)

The final issue, not a small one, was distribution—the game had to go to 5,000 people in 23 countries. Each user got a little squeezable "brain" imprinted with *Straight Shooter!* along with a miniature plastic joystick. Because this was pre-Web, our distribution alternatives were LAN and CD-ROM, both of which were used. Fortunately we had built our bridges to IT early (see Chapter 11) and they had appointed an able manager, Neil Berkowitz, to oversee the rollout. But still it was not easy—again, many conflicting needs and constituencies. We rewrote the install program several times to accommodate different configurations in different offices. Fortunately, the game had a real strategic mandate, and mentioning "the Fed" had an effect. The rollout was completed.

Straight Shooter! was widely covered in the financial press, with headlines such as "Derivatives Policy: The Game," "Training the Twitch Generation," "BT Trains MTV Generation," and "Just Don't Shoot the Client."[11] One of BT's traders said in an interview: "*Straight Shooter!* is very similar to 3D games that you see on the market, such as *Doom* and *Duke Nukem*, but it incorporates questions and you get to bet based on your risk profile. It gives you a better chance of retaining the information longer. Its much faster, and also more fun—you get to shoot ideas and kill the monsters."[12]

A key factor in the game's acceptance was that no one *had* to play the game to complete their certification. Users could opt initially for either "Game Mode" or "Question-only Mode," and could switch back and forth between the two at any point while using the application. We found that about half the people started with the game and at some point wanted to go faster and switched to the questions. The other half started with the questions only and at some point got frustrated and said, "let me check out this game." People switched a lot, which was fine with us; our real goal was to get them to complete the questions.

Once it was fully rolled out *Straight Shooter!* became the *only* training for the policies—the seminars were canceled. New derivatives employees were given 6 months to complete all the questions on all the topics, or they could not keep their jobs. Corporate Compliance monitored this through an administrative module and sent out the appropriate notifications.

Of course, the end of the story is that Bankers Trust couldn't survive independently and was acquired by Deutsche Bank, with its own policies. And although *Straight Shooter!* was designed as a shell into which new policies could be entered easily, this was, unfortunately, never done.

Using Digital Game-Based Learning for Certification and Continuing Education

Certification and continuing education are those pesky little requirements for which it would be great to have a game-based solution. Long required in certain fields such as accounting, continuing education is now moving into other fields, such as finance and IT. Professionals in the fields are required to complete a certain number of certificates, courses, or "credits" in a given time period, often each year. One issue though, is that in order to bring some standards to the field, certain requirements have been set up, such as "listing the course objectives," which may not immediately fit into the "style" of Digital Game-Based Learning. Nevertheless, some forms of Digital Game-Based Learning are currently approved and in-use for continuing education. Here's a great example.

11. Objection! *Objection!* has the distinction of being the first computer game ever to be professionally certified for continuing education credit. The California Bar Association accredited the game, in 1992, for its Mandatory Continuing Legal Education Program. The game is accredited in nineteen states—nearly every state that permits self-study.

Objection! is perhaps my favorite example of Digital Game-Based Learning, because it illustrates the enormous power that an individual with a good game idea can have, even in a field where you might not expect it.

Ashley Lipson, Esq., would qualify as prolific by almost anyone's definition. He practices law, teaches law at UCLA, Pepperdine, and Laverne Universities in California, has written four books on evidence, and has earned additional degrees in mathematics and computer science and studied physics post-Ph.D. But what he is most excited about is none of these, but rather the highly successful series of legal computer games he created, used by lawyers, paralegals, law schools, high schools, the United

States Justice Department, and attorneys general throughout the United States.

"If a person is going to design a game, they should be like me," says Lipson, "kids who were arcade junkies. We grew up in the arcades, we know what a game is, and that's where the design really has to come from—people who play the games. Chronologically I am 55, but mentally and emotionally I'm about 12. You gotta be the kid, or you're not going to be able to design this stuff."

Lipson originally designed his game "just as fun." He had no idea that when the agents grabbed hold of it and started to play it "within 30 minutes they were arguing about complex hearsay objections and knew more than my partners." Lipson thought: "I've accidentally got a great teaching device here." And a great teaching device it is. The game has sold tens of thousands of copies.

There are actually four games in the *Objection!* series. In *Objection!*, a Beverly Hills heiress has been murdered. Acting as defense attorney, it's your job to keep your client out of the gas chamber. In *Civil Objection! AutoNeg*, your client has been injured in a nasty auto accident. As her attorney, you must use your trial skills to get her the best possible settlement. In *Civil Objection! SlipFall*, your clumsy client can't seem to step out of her house without injuring herself. Your accuracy and quick response are put to the test to get her the highest possible jury verdict. And in *Expert Witness!*, the focus is on the issues and procedures of expert testimony most critical to successful direct and cross-examinations of expert witnesses.

The player always takes the role of an attorney, watching as questions are presented to witnesses. After each question the player presses a key that indicates whether the question is proper, or a basis for an objection. There are a dozen objection bases to choose from: argumentative; best evidence; conclusion; facts assumed; hearsay; irrelevant; leading; multiple; privileged; repetitive; speculative; and vague, so the game is no cakewalk. The judge sustains or overrules, and points are awarded for both speed and accuracy.

The game goes deep into the nitty-gritty. It is different for the rules of each state as well as the federal, Washington, DC, and military codes. Each odd-numbered level involves direct examination of a witness, while each even-numbered level entails cross-examination of the same witness. Subtle differences between direct and cross-examination are covered, as are the differences between lay and expert witnesses. Strategic comments specific to the question at hand are offered. The player has access to substantive discussions of why some objections are better than others. State and federal rules and citations are outlined. There are 10,000 questions built into each game. And each game has over 32 *trillion* different ways it can play out.

Good content? You bet! But at its heart, *Objection!* is really a twitch game. "In a trial, you have only a few seconds to object," says Lipson. "You have to be prepared."

Legal experts agree. Not only is the game accepted for Continuing Education Credit in nineteen states, but many law firms and law groups endorse it and recommend it to their partners and members, and the legal press sings its praises. "Challenging and fun. . .teaches the player to make objections quickly," says the *Harvard Law Record*.[13] "It is rare that one gets to study the rules of evidence and enjoy oneself at the same time," writes *Washington Lawyer Magazine*.[14] "*Objection!* scores high in both the fun and learning categories," says the *Detroit Legal News*.[15] Lipson provided me with more than thirty pages of glowing reviews. A large number of them cite the value of combining a game and learning in the way Lipson has done it.

Lipson's "way" is to be very creative and engaging in the gameplay, but not necessarily high-end in terms of graphics. In fact, compared with today's games, the graphics in *Objection!* are pretty *low* end. But the game still grabs people and holds them. "I have a very specific theory of what separates the perfect learning game from all the other bullshit and the tutorials that are dressed up and made to look like games, that don't fool anybody," Lipson says. "People don't quite get the subtle distinction between a tutorial that's dressed up and given some buzzers and bells and meant to look like a game as distinguished from a true addictive game—and that's the key, it's got to be addictive—that causes you to learn. With the perfect scenario, you will get a game, play a game, and not pay any attention to the fact that you coincidentally happen to be learning. You're addicted to the game, you're having fun, and then when you walk away from the game—lo and behold you have all these skills you didn't have."[16] Unfortunately, says Lipson, there are very few games like that.

But there *can* be more games like that. Lipson's recipe for an addic-tive game includes approaching the game from the "fun" not the "educa-tion" side of the spectrum, making it "a game that delivers a lesson" rather than "a lesson dressed up as a game," and including variety, levels, ran-domness, the perfect balance between frustration and reward ('flow'), score balance, and entertainment versus tutorial content."[17] He cites Microsoft's *Flight Simulator* as one good example: "As you play it you really do develop pilot skills."

Needless to say, Lipson already has his next game planned. "One of my pet peeves is the horrendous quality of mathematics teachers in this country. I sat down and I said, 'I wonder if I could create a game like the one that we were just talking about—as opposed to a tutorial wrapped up in a game, which doesn't fool any kids. Could I create a game that would really teach kids algebra accidentally—in other words they'd be playing an arcade game.' And I came up with the design. And I regret that we've been so bogged down with the success of *Objection!* series that I haven't had time to fool with it. But I've got a scenario of a real game that I think would teach algebra." Lipson also plans to introduce more Digital Game-Based Learning for lawyers into the curriculum of the Laverne College of Law Institute for Legal Technology, including giving symposia and semi-nars on how to create games for lawyers.

Note: The *In$ider* game, discussed in Chapter 1, also provides con-tinuing education to accountants. Four credits are earned on completion of each of its four modules for a possible total of 16 credits.

Using Digital Game-Based Learning for Customer Service Training

Customer Service Training, which often involves face-to-face or tele-phone interactions, is an ideal place for Digital Game-Based Learning, and was one of the first areas in which it was successfully used.

12. Where in the World Is Carmen Sandiego's Luggage? In the early 1980s, Jan Carlson, then head of Scandinavian Airlines Systems (SAS), created a Customer Service Institute with the goal of helping both his company and others provide world-class customer service. One of its projects was to help customer service agents learn to take advantage of all the partnerships SAS had established with other airlines. Carlson wanted to bring home to the agents the fact that calling on the partners for assistance when appropriate would allow them to give better service to SAS's customers.

This happened right around the time that the Macintosh first hit the market, and there was much excitement over a computer that could show pictures and "talk." One of the hottest pieces of software for the new Macintosh was a very engaging game called *Where in the World Is Carmen Sandiego?* The training company I was with had been engaged by the Institute, and I thought, "Wouldn't it be fun to use *Carmen* for training?" The idea of traveling around the world by plane obviously had some relationship to SAS, but how could we adopt the game to the customer service concept? We came up with the idea that Carmen had lost her wallet somewhere along her current international trip, had called SAS Customer Service, and got you. You, the customer service agent at the desk, would need to help her find it. On the computer at your station you could look up her itinerary and make calls to your partner airlines in various cities. As you did, clues were provided along the way, as in the real game ("She was here—she took off on a flight with a big star on its tail.") or some such, which meant that you had to identify the airline and place, and try calling there.

We contacted Doug Carlston of Brøderbund, who graciously gave his permission to use his game in this context. We hired a HyperCard programmer (they were in great demand at the time) and got to work, designing paths in the game by sticking Post-it notes on a larger paper covering an entire wall.

The game, finally called *Where in the World is Carmen Sandiego's Luggage?*, was delivered as part of an SAS classroom-based Customer Service Training course. People sat two at a computer, and played the game together, encouraging interaction and increasing the fun. When all had found the missing wallet (a 15- to 30-minute task) all got together for coffee and a discussion about how and why.

The game was so successful that the company commissioned a sequel about a stranded traveler going around the world, which was to be called *Will Jørge Jørgenson Ever See Sweden Again?* (a sort of "Charlie on the MTA" kind of theme). But personnel changes and financial crunches at the Customer Service Institute intervened, and the second game was never completed.

Using Digital Game-Based Learning for Disaster Preparation

An important part of the mission of the FBI and other government organizations is to protect our citizens from terrorist attacks in our own country. This typically involves the coordination of many government agencies—FBI, police, fire, national guard, and so on—which are not in the habit of working together. Because it is difficult to train for this in the field, these agencies (as well as the military) have increasingly turned to simulations. Of course, these very sorts of "disaster" scenarios have been dished out to us for years by the games companies. So, why not put games and reality together? As it turns out that's exactly what's happening. Here's an example.

13. Angel Five. Visual Purple, run by Ed Heinbockel, is one of the few true examples of the games and training worlds coming together, and is in many ways a harbinger of things to come. Heinbockel comes out of the hard-core games industry, having spent 15 years at Sierra Online. His previous games company, Tsunami Media, created the submarine game *Silent Steel*, which sold 4 million copies. At Tsunami, his mission was to "create interactive entertainment that would be enjoyed by the masses— you didn't have to be a 'geek' to enjoy it—and that would not be of a 'twitch' nature, shying away from the more classic puzzle-driven story line of animated adventures for a more cerebral, more strategy, more interactive movie kind of approach, pioneering the use of video in an interactive environment."

So, how did Heinbockel ever get into training? It seems that a few years ago, a very senior individual in the FBI bought a copy of *Silent Steel*, took it home, and played it over the weekend. He came to work on Monday morning, literally threw it on the senior agent's desk at the bureau and said, "this is how we have to train our agents—look into it."[18] That prompted a call to Heinbockel at Tsunami. An employee intercepted the call and handed him a message that the FBI had called. He thought it was a joke, and called back to see if there really was a special agent there. Indeed, there was. The special agent said, "Well, Mr. Heinbockel, would you consider throwing your hat in the ring for DAA?" "What's DAA?" asked Heinbockel. It turned out the FBI was requesting applications from companies—he found out later there were 15 companies bidding, and it was a year-long process—for a $5.2 million contract to do several simulations for the FBI.

Having won the contract, Heinbockel sold Tsunami and, along with some partners—a Hollywood script writer (Chuck Farr: *The Jackel*), an investment banker, and a "technical genius," started Visual Purple to do the projects. Their goal was to take what they had accomplished at Tsunami to a much higher level of sophistication. The company's first project for the FBI is a counterterrorism training game known as *Angel Five* (the name of the terrorist cell, taken from Revelations.) Although Visual Purple has now completed several projects, *Angel Five* was the only one Heinbockel could show me without killing me, because his work has since become increasingly classified. ("Can you tell me anything about it?" "No." Can you point me to anyone who can?" "No.")

So, what is *Angel Five* like? There are many kinds of digital games that play at very different speeds and rhythms. *Myst* and *Riven*, beautifully illustrated imaginary travelogues with puzzles play at an infinitely slower pace than twitch games such as *Doom* and *Quake*. In between are realistic "detective" games such as the *X-Files* that combine searching, conversation, and decision making with action consequences. *Angel Five* is one of these.

In *Angel Five*, you play the role of the FBI Special Agent in Charge dealing with the terrorist group. The incident unfolds in real time over 5 to 12 days, depending on how it plays out. Your goal is *not* to learn how to do investigative work (FBI agents are good at this), but to learn to work and coordinate effectively with other agencies. If you just turn the program on and do nothing, most of the time it will sit there counting the seconds with nothing interesting taking place in your world. However the "bad guys" are continually working hard behind the scenes, and every so often an incident occurs, played out in video, at the end of which you must make a decision (or not make one and learn that not deciding has consequences, too—usually bad). You can compress time by clicking ahead to the next decision point.

In some ways *Angel Five* is a classic "in-box" simulation, where you receive calls, faxes and other information you must react to. The thing that makes it very different is the way the technology is used to simulate the "bad guys." At the beginning of the sim the computer randomly sets hundreds of parameters, and those parameters probabilistically set into motion 12 days in the life of some terrorists. The simulation unfolds completely differently in each situation, with everything, including messages and video montages, generated "on the fly." (Visual Purple calls it "late-binding.") You as the player are reacting to what's going on behind the scenes. As you prosecute the case and do your investigative work, more and more information comes in, and, as in real life, you gradually learn more tidbits about the bad guys. The goal is to gain expertise in dealing with the multiagency teams that are typically found in a domestic weapons of mass destruction (WMD) incident— who all the players are; who should you call; what should you expect; what happens if you don't call; what happens if you do "stupid investigative things." You're playing against the bad guys all the time, and there are windows of opportunity to make changes in their lives, and the game is watching all kinds of things you do. For example, there are operational security (OPSEC) decisions that you might make that would raise your profile and let the bad guys know that you're on to them. If you make bad OPSEC decisions at some point the terrorists will catch wind and they'll change their plans. "It's a very dynamic, very reactive simulation," says Heinbockel. "No two sim runs are the same—the chances of that happening are millions to one."

And it all happens in full-motion video. The product is delivered on six CDs with more than 5 hours of video, yielding more than 30 hours of training time, according to Heinbockel. When they shoot, they shoot a big script, often running to 500 to 1,000 pages. They then take the video and splice it into little pieces "so it's like a deck of cards that they are continually reshuffling." This gives them a lot of replayability because instead of a 5- or 10-second clip, they might have five or six clips that are 1, 2, 3, or 4 seconds each that the simulation assembles on the fly and presents to the player seamlessly. This allows, for example, one central scene conveying the "guts of some information" to be introduced and exited in many different ways depending on how the situation unfolds.

Although at first all Visual Purple's products were stand-alone on CDs, the company is now application service provider (ASP) based as well, and can either stream the video or distribute the asset disk with the video. The sim itself is client-server based and Java enabled. It sends a very small player applet (145KB) and streams the rest. Using encrypted disks and security levels in ASP deployment, Visual Purple has a "very secure environment," which is important when your work is superclassified.

Although their goal is to make the game feel more "Hollywood"—"it feels like a Tom Clancy movie at times," says Heinbockel—one thing even they still haven't gotten around is telling. "We need to be faithful to the doctrine and policy and teaching points," Heinbockel says. "It's not unusual to have a number of briefs [read lectures]. You have to get across some real mouthfuls of doctrine; there's just no way around it. So you try to deliver it with the best actors you can get and try to parse it out so that people can get their arms around it. But you need to have these 'kibbles' (i.e., action sequences) so you get payoffs along the way, visually, like taking the bad guys down. Just one run through the sim could go 8 to 10 hours, and your payoff for all that hard work, and sitting through all the briefs, and making the decisions is to have the opportunity to bring the bad guys down, and, hopefully, get all of them and not have one of them get away from you. Because if they do, they're going to set the bomb off or a smaller yield device. And that makes it engaging because it really puts pressure on you." Unfortunately bringing the bad guys down is a "kibble" that Heinbockel wouldn't show me. But then, I didn't put in my 8 hours.

One feature in Visual Purple's work that I found especially interesting in terms of its Digital Game-Based Learning possibilities is a mode they call "i-squared." Using this feature they can make the simulation play *against* a player's needs and style. By tracking the player's actions, the game—in real time—gets a "very firm" understanding of the player's decision-making process. And it can start using that information against the player to make it more frustrating for him or her. For instance, if you typically need a lot of information before you can make a decision, they can ascertain that in the first 5 or 10 minutes (after they normalize for reading speed, etc.), and start giving you *less* information—the options that come up are truncated, for example, giving you fewer options with less information with each option, and playing *against* your need for more information. So much for accommodating people's "learning styles"—let's make 'em sweat!

Using Digital Game-Based Learning for Diversity Awareness

Diversity awareness is one of those sensitive and tricky subjects that is often difficult to teach. Not only does the training involve numerous examples and case studies, but there are often mind-numbing statistics involved that can be hard to remember. Several board games exist in the area of diversity training, but one company, at least, turned to Digital Game-Based Learning.

14. The Battle of the Brains. One of the hardest things to get across in an engaging manner in a classroom is statistical information and facts. When Bankers Trust's Human Resources department wanted to include the statistics of the Hudson Institute's "Workforce 2000"[19] report as part of their classroom-based diversity awareness training, they turned to games2train's *The Battle of the Brains* Digital Game-Based Learning shell to do it. The question-based game, designed for projection on a screen at the front of the room, is based on a sports competition theme. Each round can have an individual sport—soccer, tennis, football, golf, hockey, or chess—complete with crowd sounds and announcers. Each team has a mascot who does an animated "victory dance" each time they win a round.

The Bank's Diversity Team created it's own questions from the heavily statistical materials, such as "What percentage of the 2000 workforce is Hispanic?" (15 percent), and "What percentage of working age women are in the labor force?" (85 percent). The process of competing for the answers rather than just reading them off a slide helped make them more memorable to the participants, and provoked lively competition and interaction around the facts in the seminars.

Using Digital Game-Based Learning for Ethics Training

Ethics is a serious subject, right? Yes, but Scott Adams, creator of the Dilbert comic strip can still make us laugh about it. Lockheed once used Dilbert and Dogbert in an ethics training board game.[20] But has Digital Game-Based Learning been used for ethics training? You bet. Here's an example.

15. Quandaries. If you go to *www.usdoj.gov / jmd / ethics / quandary.htm*, you will find, as I did, an interesting surprise. You can download what the Department of Justice calls its Quandaries Ethics Training Program, a simple, but informative graphics-based romp through your career at the department focusing on ethic issues. The game's purpose is to "teach the Standard of Conduct to federal employees," according to the site, but anyone is welcome to try the program. There are fifteen jobs in the game, and performance-based promotions to five levels of increasing responsibility. You get to deal with questions such as who picks up the tab at lunch (you or your boss), whether you can do favors for people, and whether you should do nongovernment work that your boss requests, along with the usual bribes and other temptations. As the web site says, "Good luck!"

The Quandaries game can be downloaded from *www.usdoj.gov / jmd / ethics / quandary.htm* .

Using Digital Game-Based Learning for Industrial Counterespionage

Who would have thought? The following article appeared in the *Wall Street Journal*.[21] I'm not sure whether or not this example of Digital Game-Based Learning—which was in German—came from the training department. Can "situational learning" games be created? Reality says it better than I can.

16. Catch the Spy. "Frankfort—Super Mario, meet Super Lopez. A game called "Catch the Spy" on a General Motors Web site lets contestants chase an industrial spy through GM's Adam Opel unit and try to catch him before he escapes with company secrets. 'A spy has sneaked into the Opel factory and is attempting to flee with important documents he has stolen,' the directions say. 'You could stop him.'

"It seems highly reminiscent of the charges of industrial espionage leveled against former GM executive Jose Ignacio Lopes de Arriortua. 'I can't believe it,' groans a VW spokesperson when told of the game.

"In 1996, GM and Volkswagen AG reached a settlement over allegations that Mr. Lopez, dubbed 'Super Lopez,' had taken confidential GM documents with him when VW hired him away. Just this week a six-count indictment was unsealed in which the U.S. Justice Department received those allegations. Mr. Lopez's lawyers have denied the charges.

"Mr. Lopez, who no longer works for VW, isn't mentioned in the German-language game. An Opel spokesman insists the game has nothing to do with Mr. Lopez or VW. 'It's just a gag,' he adds."[22]

Using Digital Game-Based Learning for Job Skills

One of the most fertile areas for Digital Game-Based Learning is in teaching job skills. Sure you can simulate the skills, but that's often not enough to get people's attention. A game offers excitement, challenge, and an incentive to do it right (and fast!), because you want to win. Here are a few examples.

17. The Whopper Challenge. Burger King serves over 1.4 *billion* Whopper sandwiches a year in its 11,000+ restaurants around the globe.[23] That's more than 4 million every day. The Whopper is the chain's "flagship sandwich" and they want it built right. In fact, they have a "gold standard" for exactly what building it right means, both in terms of order and quantity of ingredients. Doing it right is made more complex, of course, by the fact that a key part of the Burger King message is that you can "have it your way."

So, how fast could *you* build a "gold standard" whopper? If you are about to work that station at one of their restaurants you're likely to find out—to the second—and you won't even get covered in ketchup as you try. As part of a DVD-delivered training program that Burger King has produced centrally and is offering to its franchisees throughout the world, they have created the *Whopper Challenge*, an action game that does just that.

How were these workers trained before? Live practice with real food and a supervisor standing over them: ready, set, build. Oh darn, I forgot to hold the ketchup!—throw that one away—kaCHING! Food waste and supervisor time are big costs for the restaurants.

What could be more natural for the Games Generations than building Whoppers on the screen? An ingredient added out of sequence? BZZZZ! Too much ketchup?—game over! Forgot to hold the pickle? You lose!—Back to Whopper school. Took you 60 seconds? Forget it, the champs do it in 10. There are even levels. In the first level, ingredients disappear as you use them, but Level 2 is more lifelike—the ingredient just sits there to see if you were daydreaming when you used it the first time.

What led Burger King to Digital Game-Based Learning, at least for this part of the training (the rest is more standard)? Annette Wellinghoff, director of Worldwide Training at Burger King in Miami, explains: "At Burger King, one of the precepts of the culture we're trying to create is 'work is fun.' If the *training* isn't fun, we'd have a hard time making that case. Plus our new members are mostly young."

Another advantage of the game is that it's not very wordy. That makes it "the easiest part of the training to internationalize," says Wellinghoff. Burger King is delivering this training program initially in seven languages: American English, British English, Spanish, German, French, Turkish, and Korean. It is also very easy to change the game to reflect different geographical variations in the gold standard (e.g., different sauces or amounts in different places). The game tested extremely well with focus groups in the United States and Germany. They found no differences in preference for the game between males and females, although people who have built whoppers before tend to do better. Unfortunately, Wellinghoff would not release her own best time.

For the next DVD in her "Right Track" training series, Wellinghoff is working with a university on networked computer games simulations for multirestaurant management training. "With just numbers," I asked? "Oh no, there'll be people!" she said. Stay tuned for *The Whoppers*.

18. The Bagging Game. And it's not just *making* the food correctly. It also has to be bagged correctly, so that it doesn't spill, and so on, and workers have to be trained to do this. (Hey, these kids are young!)

At the El Pollo Loco fast food chain there is a proscribed way to pack the orders. You don't put the coke on top of the hamburger, for example, because it's not going to be stable. The workers who do this task are typically "very low-level 15- and 16-year-olds who don't even necessarily speak English," according to interactive designer Cindy Steinberg. So, as one of their digital training games they get a virtual bag, and somebody's yelling out an order and there are different foods and drinks all over the screen, and they have to pack it in the right way in a given amount of time with click and drag to get points. If they put things in the wrong order the stuff spills or something else happens. "It's a gas," says Steinberg. Send your kids.

19. Visiting Heidi's Grandmother. And since we're talking about food, let's visit the National Food Service Management Institute, centered at the University of Mississippi, which trains cafeteria workers. As part of a training program created for them by Allen Interactions—run by Michael Allen, the well-known learning designer and creator of the

Authorware authoring language—there is a game to teach cafeteria workers who are not trained cooks one of the basic rules of food preparation: recipes are generally set for sea level, and must be adjusted as you go up in altitude.

According to Ethan Edwards, Allen's partner, the game works as follows: You are Heidi and are going to visit your grandmother on top of the mountain. Of course, you want to bring her some goodies, so on your way you stop at the houses of several of her neighbors to help them bake cakes and bread. Conveniently, one neighbor lives at 2,500 feet above sea level, one at 5,000 feet and one at 7,500 feet. Each time you bake, you either get the recipe right and continue up the mountain, or a goat comes along and knocks you back to the bottom to start over. The purpose of the game, says Edwards, is to give the workers some motivation to practice what are otherwise just rote facts. At the same time, because most people get booted down the hill a lot and have to start over, it also reinforces the most basic part, which is baking correctly at sea level.

In addition to the fact that the game puts rules that one might read and forget into a more motivating context and allows practice, there is also value, says Edwards, in abstracting the particular thing you want to reinforce from everything else. In other words, a low-fidelity simulation. It's clearly a fake kitchen, there are no ingredients, nothing spills, it has nothing to do with the actual act of baking—all you have to do is set the appropriate dials correctly. But the combination of the isolation of the task and the motivational context of the game allows people to focus, explains Edwards. "Pulling it out of content is a stronger instructional strategy for a single goal."

20. Train Dispatcher. Moving on from food itself to how food (and other goods) get distributed, we come to a training game for railroad workers. Tom Levine first created the game *Train Dispatcher* on his Commodore 64 computer in his spare time. He was working for a company where he programmed the "real" systems, and he was promoted to management. "Once you move into management, you kind of lose your technical abilities," says Levine, "so I did this at night to try to keep up to date." He later migrated the $44.95 consumer game to the PC and then to Windows. While his first version let a player dispatch trains on a single territory only (and had a scoring mechanism to tell him how well he did),

Levine later introduced *Train Dispatcher 2*, that allowed any number of territories.

"The game is mostly bought by retired people," explains Levine. "Most of the people we talk to create territories and they're usually ex-railroaders or dyed-in-the-wool railroad fans." An important feature of *Train Dispatcher* is its companion program, *Track Builder*, which allows people to design their own territories. "Most commercial systems don't have that capability," Levine says. "This is a little unusual. What it's allowed us to do is to use our customers to generate libraries of track territories. You go to our Web page and there are 335 track territories all over the world. So you can dispatch trains in Sydney, or you can dispatch trains in Japan, or you can dispatch trains throughout the United States, or you can dispatch trains on tracks that no longer exist."

It turns out that many of the territories people build for the game are quite accurate, because a lot of the people that create particular territories in the game are actually retired railroad employees who worked those territories, and have fairly accurate information. A couple of those highly accurate territories were spotted by a vice president at Burlington Northern, who thought, "Were having capacity problems here. Maybe if I ran this I could learn something." So Levine is now converting his commercial game into an industrial training product, adding such features as crew dispatching, better at-grade crossings, a larger number of blocks, signals and switches, and helpers.

"It's moving from being a game to a simulation," says Levine. "It's becoming more accurate." Originally, Levine put more emphasis on scoring, which is actually difficult to do in this context. Now there's less emphasis on scoring, and the game is becoming a much more precise simulation—more like a flight simulator you buy for your PC. "Not only does it teach you about the basic dispatching things, but it helps dispatchers learn their territories quicker," says Levine.

Challenge, however, still remains a big part of the game. In the consumer game, as you learn one territory and get better and better at it, you go on to another territory. "Some of the territories we have in Germany can get extremely challenging," Levine says. "I'm not sure how you can really control them." You also have the option of how fast vs. real time you want to run your simulator. You can run it at one-time regular speed—24 hours takes 24 hours. But you can also run it up to

40 times speed, in which you are simulating 24 hours in 34 minutes. "On some systems that's fine," says Levine, "because there's not a lot of traffic. But on areas where there's a lot of traffic you wish you were running at half speed."

One thing that's attractive to a real railroad is that a person can simulate an 8-hour shift in an hour and run 8 simulations in the same day. "Each time he learns a little more," says Levine. 'I should have held this train, I should have let this train go.' 'If I had done this two hours earlier I wouldn't be in this mess here.' There are a lot of issues there that you can learn very quickly by speeding it up."

An issue that Levine himself struggles with is how much "eye candy" to put in to the game, which is not especially graphical: it mostly simulates what a normal railroad dispatcher would see. "We've improved the graphics to some extent, although the real hard-core fans and hard-core railroad people don't like that—they'd rather see the more traditional lines and things of that nature," says Levine. "The problem with our program for most people is that they are expecting a lot of graphics. But when we've gone in that direction people complain because that's not truth."

An interesting direction that Levine is taking with his next version, *Train Dispatcher 3*, is to allow the game to actually control things—to make it into a "tool." It will be set up so that you can control either a real railroad or a model railroad with it, so it's more versatile than a game or a simulation.

What a great model for Digital Game-Based Learning. Create a game that captures the knowledge and expertise of people from all over the world as they build a database of fun, useful modules (like *Doom* WADs or *Unreal* MODs [24]) for other players to use. Then use that expertise to train new workers in a more robust setting and feed those improvements back into the game. Finally, make it into something functional so that people can actually use the game to do their jobs!

Levine is typically modest about his accomplishments. "I can't play my own games. I'm always looking for problems, for how can I make it better. I can't concentrate on moving trains. People ask me 'How well do you do?' I don't do well at all."

21. The Loggers' Game: The Importance of Peripherals.

Sometimes in Digital Game-Based Learning the key to success lies not in the game itself, but in the things that help put it in context. One big piece of context is the controller—the direct physical interface between you and the game. Controllers—the mouse, joystick, or control unit that the player uses—are a part of digital games and game play that have received less attention than I think they merit in the PC and home video game world. Although we are now seeing interesting developments in the area of "force feedback"—you feel the rumble in the joystick—controllers have traditionally been limited in their design. This is, to a large extent, because game manufacturers do not want the expense of creating, and shipping, a separate controller for each type of game, so they try to fit all games into one "all purpose" set of controls.

This works for many games, but often with a loss of reality—driving a plane using a mouse is less realistic than a joystick; driving a car with a mouse is less realistic than a steering wheel. The place where controllers have been most developed and differentiated is in arcade games and simulators—driving games have steering wheels, pedals and shifters as controllers; shooting games have realistic feeling guns; sports games have skis, snowboards, and surfboards; and some games even let you use kayak paddles and horses to maneuver (in Japan, of course!).

Training loggers—big, burly he-men—via games was not a problem, a designer at Weyerhauser found—they are people who like plenty of competition. The problem came when testing—they were not particularly enamored with the little mouse. The solution? Create a controller with "heft." They created a floor-based unit with a big stick that took "he-man" effort to manipulate. The loggers loved it.

Finding the "right" controller does not always have to be an expensive, custom solution. When introducing *Straight Shooter!* at Bankers Trust, I came across little plastic joysticks that fit over the arrow keys on a standard keyboard, turning the arrow pad into a joystick.[25] At a few dollars a piece, they were distributed along with the game, helping everyone get in the mood. Another example of a specialized controller is the stethoscope used in the medical example coming up.

Of course, as we move on in technology, it is highly likely that voice will become one of the most important game control mechanisms as well. And Digital Game-Based Learning designers should be considering how this can work to their advantage.

Using Digital Game-Based Learning
for Manager Training

Manager training is an excellent subject for Digital Game-Based Learning in that it is possible to create virtual companies, both functional and dysfunctional, for learners to manage. In addition to the games listed here, there exist numerous numbers- and graphs-based management simulations and management flight simulators. However, the two games described below go much further than those in their gamelike interfaces and structures. In this regard, check out as well the consumer-targeted management games from Monte Cristo.

22. Branch Manager Training Game. When Holiday Inn was looking for a new way to train its hotel managers to make their units more profitable, Cindy Steinberg, award-winning interactive designer (she has won several "Cindys," although there is no family connection) came up with the idea of making the entire training a game. She designed a complete virtual hotel environment that a manger could walk through, searching for problems.

Players in the game "walk" around the virtual hotel and look for things that they're doing wrong, according to Steinberg. When they find something they go to a list of problems. On the list might be fifty potential problems but only twenty that really exist. The problems are targeted to how players run the business, such as not marketing themselves properly, having an out-of-date business plan, improper rate and inventory management, customer service issues. Players have to find the correct ones and check them off. When they check off a problem, they get five different solutions for every problem, which are weighted. Players get negative points for picking a solution that actually makes things worse. The game records what players do, and there is a maximum amount of time allowed. At the end of the time the system looks at what you've done, adds up your score, and translates that to how well you've done versus your goals (e.g., increasing revenue by x percent or decreasing costs). The player also gets a "prescription" that they can use in their own hotel. To encourage replay, the prescription covers only the problems that the player finds, so they can go back and play again to find problems they missed.

This same approach—environment, problems, and solution list— was later turned by the creator into an "engine" that was resold to several other businesses such as AT&T and Otis elevator, where the player took the role of a branch manager of a regional business office. "It works well whenever you have a company with branch locations to manage," said Steinberg.

23. Virtual U. Speaking of management, do you think a college president has an easy job? You can give it a whirl at *Virtual U.*

For more than 30 years, William Massey was a professor of business administration, vice provost for research, and vice president for business and finance at Stanford. Now he has put that experience into a Digital Game-Based Learning product.[26]

Using a *Sim City*-like interface, *Virtual U* players take on the role of a university president. Players must deal with angry professors, try to prevent students from dropping out, and fight with government officials who control the budget. Players of *Virtual U* can choose to manage many types of institutions—public or private, large or small, prestigious or not. Tuition needs to be set, budgets drawn up with limited resources, and investments made with an eye toward increasing the endowment in a volatile stock market. The game includes issues such as juggling research and teaching and deciding what gets priority in admissions and financial aid. Faculty morale drops if classes get too large or too much is spent on athletics. The school's academic ranking falls if students cannot get the classes they need to graduate. Alumni gifts decline if the football team loses. "If you push in at one place, it pushes out someplace else. You have so many different constituencies," says Massey. "Everybody has their particular agenda."[27]

Virtual U was funded by a $1 million grant from the Alfred P. Sloane Foundation, and developed by Massey and Jesse Ausubel of the foundation to train university administrators and graduate students. The game is available commercially from Enlight Software, and sells for $60 to $130, depending on the version.

Using Digital Game-Based Learning for Municipal Budgeting

"I learned budgeting from playing *Sim City*," says Cathy Clark, formerly of the Markle Foundation and currently a venture capitalist with Flatiron partners. Many others have as well.

24. Sim City. Will Wright originally conceived *Sim City* as a city planning game. Who better to do city planning than mayors? So in the mid-1990s the *Sim City* folks showed up at the United States Conference of Mayors convention in Miami to run a little friendly competition. It's highly likely that every mayor, in moments of frustration with the status quo, dreams of razing it all and starting over with a clean slate—but what would they do? To find out, Maxis had them play individually, and then tabulated and announced the results—*x* percent of you did this, *y* percent did that. A fun learning time was apparently had by all.[28] This is an excellent example of using an existing, off-the-shelf commercial game for training.

Using Digital Game-Based Learning for Orientation

Orientation is a great use for Digital Game-Based Learning—why not start workers out on a job with a fun experience? Here's how two companies have done it.

25. The Pepsi Challenge. I'd never heard the term "onboarding" until I met Amy George, director of organizational capability at PepsiCo headquarters in Purchase, NY. She'd graciously invited me up to see the Web-based orientation system for all new hires at Pepsi Cola North America. The online training system is a complex one, involving Shockwave, QuickTime, and a half-hour download inside PepsiCo (they give people in the field a CD).

Much of the orientation is standard, module-by-module multimedia computer-based training. But George and her group realized early on that this wasn't going to be enough to motivate people to learn things such as Frito-Lay's share of the United States' snack chip market. "We decided that putting up a bunch of information on a Web site was just as boring as being handed a binder—it's just a different way of looking at it. So we decided to incorporate a game into the Web site," says George. The key words they kept in mind, she says, as they were developing the games were "compelling" and "fun," so that people would be drawn to the site, encouraged to go through all the material, and tested on their learning, all while they were having fun with it.

Throughout the Web site there are "click here for the Pepsi Challenge Bonus" questions, part of an ongoing game that's embedded throughout the whole experience. There are additional games at the end of each module—three different games, with two used twice: a *Jeopardy!* game; a "Soda Jerk" game in which a right answer gets you a full cup of Pepsi; and a "Shoot the Can" game where you get to knock Pepsi cans down with a slingshot. All are multiple choice, and "require only changing the graphics," says George. Xpedior, the site developers, presented Pepsi with a number of gaming concepts, only some of which were accepted. Pepsi selected the games that they thought were "fun and fit with the associated modules." They rejected game concepts such as a little truck that was going around to customers and dropping off product, because "it was too complicated to get all of the different customers represented, and it wouldn't add anything to the learners' experience."

As further motivation to new hires to complete the orientation, Pepsi offers as game prizes gift certificates for Pepsi merchandise. If you get 100 percent on all the internal questions plus all the questions at the end, you get a $100 gift certificate; 95 to 99 percent gets you $75; 85 to 94 percent $50; 60 to 84 percent gets you $25; and 50 to 69 percent gets you $10. Anyone can access the site, but you have to be at Pepsi for under 6 months to be eligible to get a prize. Certificates are redeemable for Pepsi shirts, umbrellas, watches, and so on. There's also an arcadelike "top ten" list of high game scorers.

To allow Pepsi to update and change the content easily on its own, the developers created a word-processing type of editor applet. Although the games "doubled the price of the project," George thinks adding the games "was definitely worth it. The site wouldn't be anything without the games," she says.

George won't reveal the dollar cost of the site—Coke and all that. And while she asserts that age didn't play any role in her decision to include the games, she does offer that "as a gross generalization new hires would probably be younger rather than older." One can't help wondering what group she is talking about when she explains the games' immediate feedback on each question by saying: "We thought that it was important for adult learners that they get instant satisfaction."

26. Oil Platform Orientation Game. Of course, there's another kind of "onboarding" that is much more literal—the physical orientation one gets when one first comes onboard a complex, and unfamiliar location such as a ship, factory, or offshore oil platform. How do you get around? Where's the workspace? Where's the bathroom, for goodness sake? It is particularly useful for an employee to know about an oil platform before getting there—especially from the company's perspective—because people are being highly paid for this and need to become fully productive as soon as possible.

Pjotr van Schothorst, a training developer at Royal Dutch Shell in Holland, used a commercial first-person 3D (*Quake*-style) game engine to create a special module mimicking the interior of an oil platform. The player moves around using the arrow keys or mouse looking for the appropriate facilities and stations.

One interesting thing about "walk-through" games such as these is that they can often be created relatively inexpensively. In most instances, it does not require licensing the game's engine—often an extremely expensive proposition—but only creating what are known as modules. Modules, or "places to go through" in this type of game—known as WADs in *Doom* and MODs in other software—can be created, often without any charge from the game maker, using tools provided by the game makers themselves.[29] You may not know how to do this (or even have any idea what I'm talking about), but the chances are good that your kid or your 20-year-old worker does, and would love the opportunity to do it. You then buy and install the required number of copies of original game (at $40 or so) and run your own module inside it.

Because just running around looking for the bathroom soon gets old—that's one place where the virtual is definitely less satisfying than the real—to make his orientation game more interesting van Schothorst gives players a fire extinguisher as their "weapon" and has them learn to fight emergencies at the same time.

Fun, efficiency, and safety, all at a reasonable cost—how can you beat that for training?

Using Digital Game-Based Learning for Product Knowledge

Training on product knowledge is often filled with loads of boring facts that need to be learned, yet, at the same time, products are often best learned by using them. That is a combination tailor-made for Digital Game-Based Learning solutions.

27. The Farmer Game. Hydro Agri, a division of the giant Norsk Hydro of Norway, is a global player in the agriculture industry, with involvement throughout the value chain—from the raw materials in fertilizer production to guidance in the supply of nutrients. Hydro Agri Academy's job is to continuously improve employee knowledge of its products and services, ensuring that they meet the needs of the customers. To help employees better understand the company's fertilizer products, Hydro Agri worked with vendor Powersim to create *The Farmer Game*. The employee plays the role of a farmer managing a crop from planting until harvest, with the aim of growing the most profitable crop with minimal environmental impact. Changes in soil type, weather, and water availability affect how well the crop grows. The employee influences crop growth by applying fertilizers at various times throughout the simulation. At the end of the game, the program shows the employee how profitable the farm was, and what impact his or her decisions had on the environment. *The Farmer Game* is made available to all of the company's 6,000 employees on an individual and business unit basis. It has proved most useful for training employees with little or no knowledge of the company's products.[30]

28. The Glue Game. 3M makes a variety of glues all with different properties. To help its workers learn about and make sense of these, 3M turned part of the learning into a game.[31] Instead of just memorizing the properties of each glue, learners get to virtually try out the different glues and see how they work on different materials. The game, built by ICONOS Interactive, is a fun fantasy, using paper phone books, plastic milk bottles, aluminum mailboxes, and wooden tree trunks as building materials. The player's goal is to glue these materials together as they appear, in order to build a bridge across a gully strong enough to hold an elephant. If you use the appropriate glues for the different combinations of materials, the bridge holds. If not, there's one less elephant in St. Paul!

Using Digital Game-Based Learning for Professional Skills

Doctors, lawyers, nurses, accountants, you name the profession—Digital Game-Based Learning has been used extensively for professional skills training. This is no doubt to some extent because so many of our professionals are now young people—the average age of an auditor, for example, is 24. As the Baby Boom generation retires and the even bigger Games Generations grow up, this trend will only increase. We've seen a lawyer game example. Here are doctor, nurse, and auditor examples. If you know of any Digital Game-Based Learning for Indian Chiefs (or other professions), please email me at *www.twitchspeed.com*.

29. The Auscultation Challenge. Games have long been used in the training of doctors. To help physicians better diagnose heart murmurs, the medical publisher C. V. Mosby created an auscultation game. Auscultation means listening to sounds that arise in body organs (such as the lungs) as an aid to diagnosis and treatment. To make the game realistic they used an electronic stethoscope as one of the game controllers. Designer Cindy Steinberg recalls going down to heart surgeon Dr. Denton Cooley's lab at the Texas Heart Institute in Houston with her Nagra tape recorder to "collect" literally thousands of murmurs. In the game, "you have these chests," Steinberg says, "all male, and you have a stethoscope headset that you plug in and you listen to the murmur. You have to place the stethoscope on the chest in different positions and you hear different parts of the murmur." Then you have to match the murmur with the diagnosis in a limited amount of time. Auscultate. Can you say it ten times?

30. Incredibly Easy! Professionals such as doctors and nurses have lots of standard-type exams to prepare for, and the classic way to do it is to review as many questions as possible that are similar to those on the test. To make doing this a bit more palatable for nurses preparing for their certification exams, Springhouse Corporation (now Lippincott-Williams & Wilkins) created its highly popular series of "Incredibly Easy" books, with titles such as *Neo-natal Care Made Incredibly Easy* (you mean you haven't read it yet?) The book series stars Nurse Joy, the smart, competent, personable nurse that we'd all like to have should we ever find ourselves a patient in the intensive care unit.

In making the Incredibly Easy book series into a computer review program, Springhouse turned to games to relieve some of the study tedium. They designed three games for each subject. The first, called *Endless Lecture*, requires that you answer enough questions to get out of a horrible classroom lecture. Right answers get you praise, while wrong answers get you insults and erasers from the teacher. In the second game,

Tedious Textbook, the text *itself* ("Tessie the Textbook") abuses you if you don't get the answers right. And in the third game, *Problem Patient*, wrong answers make the patient scream at you, while correct ones win you compliments.

Games are how these people learned as kids, that's how they want to do it as adults. Edutainment is growing up along with its users.

31. In$ider (continued). When I introduced Pricewaterhouse-Coopers' *In$ider* game for training auditors and accountants on derivatives in Chapter 1, I asked that you stay tuned. Now, as we continue, I ask you to recall that understanding derivatives is so difficult that one investment bank paid an instructor $10,000 a day (no kidding!) to teach about them. Clearly being able to teach this arcane subject with clarity and without your audience falling asleep is worth a lot, and is definitely not easy. Many have tried and failed.

Into this cauldron boldly stepped Paula Young. She almost didn't make it. Here's the rest of the story.

In 1997, realizing the upcoming need to train the auditors in derivatives, Young came up with the idea that because this was a really complex, dry subject, trainees needed to be able to experience what it's like to use it and why you'd use it. So she drew up her plan for a game and an accompanying live academy, and took it to the partners. "Nobody had a clue of what I was going on about at all," she says. "I had this idea in my head." But on the strength of her track record and arguments, she was able to get 30,000 pounds—about $50,000—to build a prototype. She completed her prototype within a month. "As soon as I had done that, the idea became tangible and exciting, and the response was 'we've got to do it,'" she says.

The next step was her investment proposal, which is described in Chapter 13. That was approved in March of the following year, and her team began design work. The engagement side and story line came relatively easily given Young's cinema and TV background—she had earned a communications degree, and then worked at a TV station and a film company. "You've been assigned to the finance team at Gyronortex, an intergalactic mining company in the central zone, circa 2030. There's a war going on, and your job is to help your boss, Jan Goldstein, deal with risks." The initial challenge came rather on the learning side—how to present the complex materials on Forward Rate Agreements (FRA's), futures, swaps, and options inside of the story line she had established. The approach they "invented" was what they call "structured discovery" in which your tasks are clear, but you need to figure out (with more or less guidance depending on your preference) how to accomplish them. As in many programs, you can consult various people for help. In *In$ider* they gave all the characters distinct personalities—they really are characters—in order to increase the identification and fun. The characters' fortunes progress and change over the course of the four CDs that make up the game, in something of a soap opera approach. "We build in a 'hook' at the end of each disk to make you want to move to the next one," Young says.

JAN GOLDSTEIN, FINANCE DIRECTOR, GYRONORTEX, FROM *IN$IDER*
(USED BY PERMISSION)

Sounds exciting, right? But 6 months later, in September, Young was ready to walk away from the whole project—and threatened to. "We couldn't get the subject matter expertise we needed," Young explains. "It turned out that the few people in the firm who had really deep knowledge of derivatives were high in demand with clients." Young's team couldn't get enough of their attention. "I believe that the value of what you get out of a product depends on what you put in," she says, "so we stopped. We virtually did nothing. I kept saying 'we're going to waste our money. We need the experience. In order make something simple you need to be an expert in it.' So, finally, we got the line to pay for an expert. We got a dealer from the City under contract to sit with us."

From that point on it became smoother sailing, but there was still the challenge of cultural diversity to address—the program was designed for the whole firm, which meant over 150,000 people in virtually every country in the world. The product had to work in St. Petersburg, Seoul, and Manila, as well as in Paris and Madrid. (It is currently in use in more than fifty countries.)

Young used a "rapid development" process that she says "really worked." By May, the first CD was finished and ready for focus testing, and others followed month by month. In October, they began systems testing, which, given the size of their firm "takes forever," says Young. But by November, they were already beginning their phased implementation. As Young discusses later, implementation is 80 percent of the job. "You can't just frisbee the disks out there, or even just put the content on the intranet," Young says, "you have to be proactive."

The game has been enormously successful. Over 10,000 copies have been distributed within the firm. People are not only using it, but requesting it for their clients.

Young would love to do it all again (she loves being a producer!) but would change a few things next time, especially the relationship to the subject matter experts. She would also have a closer alliance with IT and a quicker adoption of standards in the development process.

For players of *In$ider,* the biggest shock comes in Disk 1, when the bank you recommend putting a lot of money in fails and you get sacked! (It doesn't matter which bank you picked.) But players get their revenge in Disk 3 when Bash, the pompous trader, gets demoted to janitor.

Using Digital Game-Based Learning for Project Management

Project management is often a pain, but it's a pain that more and more people are having to deal with. IBM is reshaping its whole organization around project management, as are the big consulting firms. Rumor has it that some people actually do enjoy it. But for the rest of us, wouldn't it be nicer if project management were a game?

32. Project Challenge. Thinking Tools was the name of the business simulation spin-off of Maxis, *Sim City's* creator. It was started by John Hiles and run by him until 1998, when the company changed its business focus. Among the simulation games that Hiles and his team created was *Project Challenge,* for the Canadian consulting company Systems House. "Essentially," says Hiles, "it is a flight simulator for a project manager. We put you into the project manager's office and you run the project. A feedback system in the office gives you a partial picture of your project. You can also complement your knowledge of the project by getting informal and tacit types of knowledge about the status of your project in the field." Others have used project management as the basis for Digital Game-Based Learning as well.[32]

Using Digital Game-Based Learning for Public Policy Creation

Remember when Bill and Hillary Clinton were going to lead us happily into the promised land of better, cheaper health care? We all learned that you don't get something for nothing, there's always a tradeoff. In fact, public policy is a whole series of tradeoffs. Helping people understand tradeoffs in public policy decisions was a key goal of the Markle Foundation when it pumped $1.2 million into Digital Game-Based Learning.

33. Sim Health. The Markle foundation, a not-for-profit philanthropy with an endowment of over $200 million, was at the time pursuing two principal themes. One was trying to help media develop in ways that encouraged public participation in decision making, and the other was using interactive technology to motivate people to get involved with, and learn about intricate subjects. Under the leadership of Lloyd Morrisette and Edith Bjornson, and the project leadership of Cathy Clark, the two themes came together nicely in the *Sim Health* project, designed and built by Thinking Tools.

In *Sim Health*, you play a newly-elected politician trying to improve the health care system of the town and make the policy decisions. At the start of the game you make explicit what you value, trading off various components of "liberty versus equality" and "community versus efficiency." For example, should competition take precedence over regulation? As you play, failing to make choices that reflect your values gets you booted out of office. The game's interface is reminiscent of *Sim City*. Pour too much money into health care at the expense of education, and the hospital grows immense while the school deteriorates before your eyes. Bankrupt the government and the capitol dome cracks.

"A *Sim City*-style game was a good choice for what we were trying to do," says Clark, because "it allows you to manipulate a complex system, get feedback, and adjust your assumptions. In the case of health care the underlying assumptions were so important that we created a 'value grid' to make them explicit and allow them to be adjusted by the player."

The *Sim Health* game was published commercially at a subsidized price of $29.95, and was used at the White House, and by politicians, insurers, academics, and consultants, as well as by some people in the general public. In the end, the health care reform issue died down, and *Sim Health* faded away. "Although it was educationally responsible," says Clark, "it was not really a compelling, motivating game. It was more educational than gamelike." Let that be a lesson to Markle and to you.

Using Digital Game-Based Learning for Quality Training

Deming, Juran, Crosby. These are the giants of Total Quality Management (TQM), a management tool of the 1980s and 1990s that is still around in the form of *Six Sigma* and other programs. Lots of charts, lots of statistics, not always lots of fun. Here's one way it was.

34. The TQM Challenge. How would you like to pit your knowledge of quality against the experts? In *The TQM Challenge*, you get to do that at five difficulty levels, each level giving you less time to answer, with Dr. Deming himself being the hardest opponent. The game's TV quiz show format, complete with host, gives you the chance to answer first, but if you miss you can count on the expert's getting it right. Racking up a perfect score against the experts is not easy.

This simple but effective Digital Game-Based Learning shell was adopted for many other uses as well. At Bankers Trust, for example, the experts became the Bank's top management, with Deming replaced by Charles Sanford, the bank's chairman at the time (BT's management, unlike some, was open to self-caricature.) I even used the game once as my résumé!

Using Digital Game-Based Learning for Recruiting

Because recruiting is typically aimed at young people starting out in business, it is an ideal place for Digital Game-Based Learning, and one that I'm sure we will see increasingly in the future. Many companies are using creative quizzes and tests as part of the recruiting process, and noncontent games are used as traffic builders for Web sites. Slowly but surely, the two are coming together.

35. Learning Solitaire. Until its demise in 1999, Bankers Trust was making a concerted effort to hire top-end technology people. No longer a first-tier name like Morgan Stanley or Goldman Sachs, it needed to do something extra. One part of its strategy was to imply "we are cool," via a very high tech, state-of-the-art recruiting Web site. One attraction of that Web site was to be a game called *Learning Solitaire*, which my team designed.

Having long watched executives and others wile away their time in the office and on planes playing *Solitaire*, it seemed to us that the popular game could be put to learning use as well. So, we designed a version of *Solitaire* with "content." The content comes in two forms: interchangeable sets of "concepts or facts" about a topic that appear on the playing cards, and interchangeable sets of questions about the same topic that appear in a window whenever you bring a card up to the top row. Each question and fact is linked directly to any reference document anywhere on the Web. The game, written in Java, is a simple shell, that can be seen at *www.games2train.com*.

Unfortunately, Bankers Trust was sold before the recruiting site made it to the Web.

Using Digital Game-Based Learning for Sales Force Training

Games are a great way to motivate a sales force that needs to be trained or updated—is there an audience that is more competitive than salespeople? Digital Game-Based Learning is a natural here, and has been used with great effectiveness by a number of companies.

36. Cummins Secret Agent. At one point Cummins, the international Fortune 500 industrial equipment company, was experiencing difficulty in communicating with the sales force of its dealer network and, in turn, with customers. The industrial equipment company was preparing to launch a new product that was revolutionary for the material-handling business.

The training for the sales force was provided through an interactive detective game that assigned the salesperson a position as a "special investigator." The salesperson was required to complete a series of interviews with suspects in order to successfully answer the questions of a "committee." The sales training program was delivered on CD-ROM directly to the sales force in advance of the introduction of the new product. The salesperson had to successfully complete the game in order to be allowed to print a customized certificate of completion, which was required to be presented to the sales manager of their dealership. "The verdict?," asks the vendor on its Web site. "The most successful and effective launch of a new product in the history of the company."[33]

Using Digital Game-Based Learning for Sexual Harassment Prevention

Who would use a game for something as serious as sexual harassment prevention? Lots of people, it turns out. Outside of a few firms with "brutal" corporate cultures (you know who you are), most firms have realized that fun and humor go a long way to getting even serious material retained. "Lighten up," says Nicolas Negroponte of the MIT Media Lab. "Your customer will appropriate the knowledge much more quickly if playing is at the root of what you are doing."[34]

37. The Sexual Harassment Prevention Certifier. games2train, at Bankers Trust and a number of other companies, takes the concept of learning through playing to the extreme with its *Sexual Harassment Prevention Certifier*, whose motto is, "Sexual harassment is not a game, but learning about it can be fun and exciting." The "serious" content is provided by the top-tier labor law firm of Seyfarth, Shaw, Fairweather, and Geraldson, who vets it for completeness and accuracy of information. The purchaser gets to add its own policies and tweak the generic content. The "game" helps companies create a good "prevent defense" in case of lawsuits, because it keeps records that employees have answered all sixty questions correctly about the company's sexual harassment policies and procedures.

The *Sexual Harassment Prevention Certifier* is actually *seven* classic games in the styles of *PacMan, Tetris, Asteroids, Solitaire, Monopoly, Jeopardy!*, and *Who Wants to Be a Millionaire?* Any of the games can be selected by the player at any time as they to complete their certification. A special feature of these Web-based games is that the same content, created and entered only once, appears in whichever game the player chooses. The user can also opt for no game at all. And any subject matter can replace or be added to sexual harassment in the game shells. So come on down to the old arcade, folks, where your favorite classic games are up and running in a new way!

Using Digital Game-Based Learning for "Soft Skills" Coaching

Management training in what are called "soft skills" is often done face-to-face, but a number of companies have begun to offer this type of training online. In the forefront of these companies, both in terms of design and thinking, is Ninth House Networks. From the beginning, its aim has been to engage learners. But is what it does Digital Game-Based Learning?

38. Situational Leadership. When I asked Tom Fischmann, one of the founders of Ninth House Networks, whether he calls what they do "games," he replied: "We would tend to call them activities or modalities.... I think that we would definitely say that there are gaming principles involved but we wouldn't refer to them as games.... We see the real hook not being so much the game element as much as the story element."

But that isn't necessarily how their clients see it. John Parker, dean of the Leadership College at First Union Bank, Ninth House Networks' biggest client, does think of them as games. "Culturally and attitudinally, the same thing that drives us to be casual five days a week allows us to learn through a game," he says.

Parker describes how, when people in his company first saw Ninth House's online version of *Situational Leadership*, a training program originated by the Ken Blanchard Companies, "everybody in the room just dropped their jaws. We thought 'this is unbelievable.'" Parker's team, which does leadership training for all levels of the bank—from the top of the house to the front-line employee—grasped it's value quickly. "The methodology they're using is absolutely blowing people away," he says.

With a lot of venture capital money—over $70 million—and a big influx of talent from Hollywood, including the assistant director of *Seinfeld*, the lead writer from *Home Improvement*, the executive producer of *Party of Five*, and an executive producer from Pixar, according to Jeff Snipes, the other founder, Ninth House created a product that is in many ways far beyond anything else in the online market. They did this by focusing on two particular aspects of engagement—story and personalization—as well as on what they call "three-dimensional content" and very high production values, much more like the movies and TV than what is usually seen in training. From the very beginning, their goal has been to engage people. "If people are at work a great chunk of their lives and they've got other media—sophisticated media—that are targeting them all day long, how are you going to get through all that stuff, and all the other stuff that's going on in their day and get them to pay attention?" asks Fischmann.

People *are* paying attention to Ninth House's product. Parker reports that one of his chief financial officers, "a general in the army type, very financially driven, starched white shirt, traditional banker" went through it and reported that he didn't remember being so engaged in learning in a long time. "I learned the model, I had fun, and I am exhausted," he said. First Union uses the *Situational Leadership* course, along with other Ninth House offerings, in conjunction with classroom learning in its Leadership Discovery program. They target three groups in particular: capital markets, capital management, and e-commerce. "I guess their workforces are more of Gen X'" says Parker. "But I don't know that I can say definitively that those who are more on the cusp or even into the Baby Boomer generation have been turned off—no one's been turned off by it. What they may have said is 'I got it, it was engaging, it was competitive, but I need to have some follow up relational kind of discussions.' So, we do some other things to support or supplement it. But to my knowledge—and we've had hundreds go through it—I haven't seen on evaluations or heard of anybody who's said, 'That's not going to work for me and I'm not going to support it for my people.' Which has been nice."

Some of Ninth House's efforts have gone in a sitcom direction—not surprising given the team that they hired—where periodic episodes with the same cast allow identification and ongoing learning and practice. I suspect Ninth House will eventually move in a more fully gamelike direction as well. While their heavily movie and TV-based offerings are successful at engaging a wide band of today's learners, eventually just watching parable-like movies, playing true-false quiz games—however much "attitude" they many have—and doing "interactive adventures," which by the nature of their cost and planning can't change very much, may not cut it with the Games Generations' style of learning. What if a user would rather have his or her adventure in space rather than in the Old West? Or in ancient Rome? Or in medieval France? These are the kinds of adjustments that games can more easily make than film. "Stories have been with us as long as there were people," says Fischmann. True, but now the people have changed. And story, even interactive story, is only one aspect in a larger, more engaging digital gaming paradigm.

This is not a new point of view for Ninth House; they have already heard this from other sources, such as Clark Aldrich of the Gartner Group. "I keep telling them to get more gamelike," Aldrich says. And Jeff Snipes has expressed interest in upping the game component of the product. Wouldn't it be great if Ninth House could move their already exciting offering from just incorporating "game elements and principles" to being the high-end of full-fledged, exciting, multidimensional, engaging, and behavior-changing Digital Game-Based Learning? Says First Union's Parker, "I think frankly our employees see it as a lot of stress relief from a crazy work environment where everybody walks around with cricks in their neck and yelling at each other and short time pressures and goals and conflicting agendas and politics." The Games Generations' version of stress relief is, of course—games! So let's see what happens.

Using Digital Game-Based Learning for Strategy Communication

Communicating new strategies to a huge, global workforce is never easy and requires a variety of methodologies. One company, Nortel Networks, found Digital Game-Based Learning to be a useful part of the process. But inserting Digital Game-Based Learning into an old tradition-bound corporate culture that is at the same time extremely high-tech is by no means an easy task.

39. Build the Band. Sylvia Kowal, of the corporate communications department of Nortel Networks, first got involved with Digital Game-

Based Learning while doing a children's project that that was part of her company's social responsibility portfolio. They wanted to teach children about a network—what it is and how it works. "Because we knew that children would not sit still through a long explanation, we thought the best way to reach them was by virtue of a game. And by watching my own children, it came to me that this would be the best way to learn—in the medium where they're the most excited and comfortable." While that project was eventually shifted out of the company, Kowal had been bitten by the game bug.

"Fast forward," she says, " to a big marketing campaign." Nortel was launching a brand new marketing campaign for the entire company that was a big departure from its image as a staid, old company that sold to the telephone companies. They were becoming a dot-com company, a new, energized, young company in cyberspace. There was big change in their marketing message and they wanted to tie all these things together. It was both internal and external, and it had to launch very quickly. Nortel had an image problem not only externally but internally as well. Its employees were changing because Nortel was hiring new types of people—more entrepreneurial, definitely younger, and who had been weaned on the Internet and the digital world.

Nortel had appointed a chief marketing officer and he challenged Kowal's group to come up with some novel way of addressing and launching this message. Kowal started developing an Internet Web site, thinking, "if this is what we're going to be, let's speak in that language." Her site had a whole lot more attitude than they were used to internally. "But there was something still not compelling about the site," she says, "so I came back to 'why don't we play a game?'" From her earlier research Kowal realized that there were huge game networks that adults joined for a fee, and that these adults spent hours and hours online playing games.

The group Kowal developed this with was very small. They didn't even look for a huge group to get approval from. It was done almost like skunk works. Kowal's boss was very supportive because he could see that this was something new needed to really appeal to the audience and shake them up. The company had a new advertising campaign and the Chief Marketing Officer decided they should link the new message and the messages of the advertising message all together and make it fun. The advertising used the Beatles' "Come Together" song and the marketing message was "Unified Networks." So, Kowal created a game called *Build the Band* that incorporated the theme song, the marketing message and "just fun." It had sixteen questions, and the challenge was to build the band by getting them right. Each time a player got a correct answer a new band member or an instrument would come on the screen along with some music. "It was pretty basic," says Kowal. "We didn't have a whole lot of money for it." Players would get the first part of the song if they got the first answer, and would progress in terms of song and image. The band players—they couldn't use the actual Beatles—were very kooky looking characters that were very appropriate for what was out there.

When they finally launched the game, it was extremely successful, but getting to that point was not easy, according to Kowal. Because of Nortel's huge network she had to get cooperation from the IS (Nortel's term for IT) people. "When you have anything that's on the network you need support, and they have a support line," she says. So the first thing was that the support people would have to know what it is, and if the people were having problems, how to fix it, because she didn't want to field the calls. Nortel's help desk is worldwide and available 24 hours a day, so it was a massive job to teach just these people about the game.

Another issue was that Kowal insisted on using Shockwave, because she wanted to do something that was very current and that allowed animations. "I felt we should walk the talk that I should keep pushing the envelope and force people to look at what could be done on the Internet," she says. Nortel did not support Shockwave. So Kowal found in the IS organization collaborators, people who understood the concept and would help her out. "I just kept trying until I found somebody to help me." Did she follow corporate policy and structure? No, and that's the lesson. To get Digital Game-Based Learning implemented you sometimes have to take risks. Kowal kept calling people until she found the people that would help her. When she got pushback from people in IS saying "this is not a standard. We've got to check what Shockwave will do to our network," Kowal found people to test it. "I went out and found IS people who were interested in doing something different and in pushing the envelope. They would test it and we would go back to the team and say, "we've tested it and it doesn't take any load on the network and there's no issues on loading," she says. They went through all kinds of scenarios in which they had to decide whether you would download the whole game, or whether you would go back and forth to the server. "What I had to do," says Kowal, "was find my support in the IS organization and then use it. I felt my job was to take a risk and push the envelope within reason."

A key to Kowal's success was a very supportive vice president, and the risk-taking attitude of the chief marketing officer, who was a long-term Nortel employee and very respected, and who was "willing to go for it." "Whatever people didn't understand they tried to put a stop to," says Kowal. "But I had a very supportive boss who let me do my thing."

There were other technical issues and Kowal, a nontechnical person, had to find all of those out. For example, they had to design to a minimum common denominator. In a network with 70,000 users all over the world, some users would have very small laptops and some wouldn't have a lot of bandwidth. Kowal had to make sure she could reach all of them. So, she had to decide what characteristics of the common denominator she would accept and which would affect the project negatively. She made a decision to use sound after she checked with the IS people and found their purchasing recommendations did include sound—it was up to each department. So, Kowal saw this as a way of pushing new technology at people. "If you want to play this game go get sound. It's not a big deal; they would learn that they could just go get speakers."

Kowal's team were careful about gender and language issues in the game as well. Their designer was initially "having some fun" with the female singer in the band, but they "curved her down." They used only global language. To increase participation, they turned the game into a competition. If you got all of the answers right on the first try, then your name was entered into a drawing for a *Come Together* CD. If you got the right answer on *both* games the first time you played, then you were eligible for a portable CD player. Winners names were posted on the Web. The budget was $40,000 Canadian (about US$30,000). Kowal got an external company to build the game and got her internal people to build the back-end that tracked it and gave her scores.

Kowal went through "tons of conference calls" trying to explain what she was doing. "I did feel like an evangelist. I had to every night make sure that I believed in what I was doing to go on with it. I really had to persevere, because there were a lot of days when it was clear that this was really not a mainstream activity for a company like Nortel. But I know it makes a difference to people."

"Some people within my organization think that this is trivial. But when I get the positive results that I got—we reached 28 countries and in 6 months got 2,618,000 hits, 29,425 unique visitors—it was just great, phenomenal news. It was really quite astounding that we reached so many people and so many people played the game. And we got great comments saying 'what an easy way to learn and I didn't know this.'"

Kowal regrets that there is not a greater acceptance in her company that creating Digital Game-Based Learning is "real work." "It's sort of light," they say. What's *not* light, says Kowal, is the putting together of it and making it work. "We had a UNIX environment and a PC environment, so I had to make sure we had an HTML version with sound and movement and a Shockwave version. I had to give people instructions on how to play the game and what to do. There were an awful lot of pieces to it that you didn't think of at the very beginning. And there were a lot of technical issues I had to solve."

Kowal feels the concept of Digital Game-Based Learning is slowly catching on at Nortel Networks. She is going ahead with a new game for her next marketing plan, and people have approached her from training. Kowal thinks it's going to be slow to evolve—"we're in a very serious business." "For me, in terms of my career, it was a bit of a risk" says Kowal, "but I've had so much fun doing it I don't want to quit right now. We'll see after the next game what happens. At this point I'm not formally marketing it but it's in every one of my presentations."

Using Digital Game-Based Learning for Team Building

What do business and the Army have in common? Both need their people to work well in teams and team situations. At least one company has invented a unique way of doing this using Digital Game-Based Learning.

40. Saving Sergeant Pabletti. Molding people who are not naturally team players into a well-functioning team involves changing their behavior. The firm of Will Interactive has gone so far as to patent its Digital Game-Based Learning approach to doing this. One game that they sell to both the Army and to business is called *Saving Sergeant Pabletti.* It is a video-based game in which a pretty realistic and scary incident occurs right up front—an Army platoon is on a routine patrol deep in the woods when the drill sergeant is accidentally shot by a hunter. They need to work together to build a stretcher and get him to help, but on the way, the teamwork breaks down completely, and in the end, the sergeant dies in front of their (and your) eyes.

But wait—he doesn't *have* to die. You can go back in time to save him *if* you learn the right values, which lead to the right behaviors. And so the game involves playing the role of each of six team members before the incident and making values-based choices in their lives that will impact their behavior in the shooting incident. Each character (you or the group play them all) has four decisions to make. Based on a complex tree, their decisions impact the other's videos and decisions and the combination of all the decisions alter the final video. Choices are built around values—for one character it's integrity, for another it's personal courage, and for another it's sexual harassment. If a player makes three of four decisions correctly, then their part of the mission to save the sergeant is successful. "It's really a cross between a movie and a video game," says Sharon Sloane, president of Will.

Not only has Will's approach been used for changing behavior related to teamwork, it has been used for changing individuals' behavior as well in the area of preventing binge drinking, AIDS, and sexually transmitted diseases.

Sloane created her programs by looking at what would appeal to young people. "We decided to figure out specifically what would engage kids. And the answers that we started to get were video games, and movies. And we said if we could invent something that would do this that would meet the MTV-video game generation on its own turf, then we would have a chance of making a difference." She believes her programs work in large part because most people don't want to be losers. "This applies to kids certainly, but even to adults. If they lose, and they end up with a negative outcome, they will invariably go back and try to figure out where they messed up and pick it up and try to fix it. We very rarely see people walk away with a losing outcome. And the positive reinforcement of a good ending is retained on an emotional level."

There is a version of *Saving Sergeant Pabletti* that is specifically geared to corporations. The text screens reflect corporate policies, but the footage is exactly the same. Corporate people like it because people can identify with it, but it's not so close that they become defensive. Often, in other training of this kind, says Sloane, "there may be a fictional scenario, but everyone looks at George."

Using Digital Game-Based Learning for Technical Skills

Technical Skills often lend themselves to technical solutions, and Digital Game-Based Learning can often provide the solution needed. From mechanical design software to learning keyboard commands, here is our final example.

41. Monster Command and Key Commando. Companies in the newspaper design industry that produce newspaper ads need to produce them very quickly in order to be profitable and to make deadlines. To help, they use a software packages such as Quark Xpress, Multi-Ad Creator, and Adobe's InDesign. However the speed of their use depends very much on the skill of the user, and can be considerably enhanced by using keyboard shortcut commands instead of the mouse to do many frequently used functions.

To speed up training of employees in this area, who tend to be young part-timers, Jeff Turner and Steve Zehngut decided to build a game. In fact, they built two games: *Monster Command* and *Key Commando*. Zehngut's company, Zeek Interactive (Turner owns the ad company) specializes in creating games for marketing, so game design was not a problem. They made a database of all the shortcuts in the three programs. As you play the game various things (monsters in one game, soldiers in another) attack you, and the name of a command flashes on the screen. By hitting the correct shortcut key combination you "kill" the attacker— if not, you lose one of your lives. Speed counts. The game has a score, so at the end supervisors can see how a player has done.

The games, built in Macromedia Director, are a good example of "reflex" games, designed to speed up the speed and accuracy of physical or verbal reactions. They are also a kind of "shell," in which the content is the commands of a particular program. The company's current model is to give the games away, and sell databases of shortcuts for various other programs, such as additional Quark products and Adobe Illustrator.

THE DIGITAL GAME-BASED LEARNING:
THE STATE OF THE ART

I am often asked what is the "state of the art" in Digital Game-Based Learning? Although this is a moving target, and will hopefully always be so, I would say that the following represent the "state of the art" as this book is written. I have chosen several because, as of yet, no one program has everything. One thing that a number of these programs (though not all) have in common is that the "game" part, which is quite good, is linked in some way to a much more tell-test, much less engaging tutorial, in which the concepts, facts, rules, or doctrine are presented. I expect that this will be one of the things that will improve in the future, as Digital Game-Based Learning designers learn from game designers how to embed this kind of information into the game. But for now, these are my nominations:

- For state of the art in game play: *Objection!*
- For state of the art in coaching and reflection: *Strategy Co-Pilot*
- For state of the art in teaching a highly complex subject: *In$ider*
- For state of the art in software learning: *The Monkey Wrench Conspiracy*
- For state of the art in action scenarios: *Full Spectrum Warrior*
- For state of the art in interactive video: *Angel Five*
- For state of the art in graphics: *Start-up* and *Wall Street Trader*
- For state of the art in Web-based interactive TV: Ninth House's *I-series*

Most of these can be obtained to look at, either through off-the-shelf purchase or demos. See the book's companion Web site at *www.twitchspeed.com* for how to do this.

> **Contest 7:** What is your nominee for a state-of-the-art Digital Game-Based Learning project and why? Email your entries to *Contest7@.twitchspeed.com*.

CONCLUSION

"Not bad," you might say. "An impressive list. I didn't know there were that many examples." And you would be right—it is impressive. Or, you might be saying, "Yeah, but relatively few great ones," and you would be right as well. Remember that we are still in the infancy of this phenomenon. But whichever point of view you take, as we are about to see, very little that has been done in business in the area of Digital Game-Based Learning even comes close to what has been done and is being constantly created in the forum that *really* needs to train people well—the United States military.

10

True Believers
Digital Game-Based Learning
in the Military

We know the technology works, we've proven it over and over again, and we just want to get on with using it.
— Don Johnson, the Pentagon

Adopt the role of Joint Force Commander and tackle ten realistic scenarios to hone your knowledge of doctrine. Adjust friendly and enemy forces in four selectable scenarios to test varying military possibilities.
— JFE Training Game Box

Boy, can't you see I'm flying here? Go away.
— An Air Force General in a simulator to a Trainer (Quoted in *Training* Magazine)

Business people are slowly "getting it." Schools "get it" here and there. But the U.S. military "gets it" big time. The military has embraced Digital Game-Based Learning with all the fervor of true believers. Why? Because it *works* for them. And trust me, the guys in charge of training at the Pentagon are a very sharp group. They have seen and evaluated *everything*.

"We're a few standard deviations ahead of most, including those in industry, yet most people don't know who we are," says Michael Parmentier, head of the Readiness and Training unit of the Department of Defense at the Pentagon.[1]

The military's training mission is a daunting one. It has to train 2.4 million men and women in the four services (Army, Navy, Air Force, and Marines), plus almost another million civilian employees,[2] to work as individuals, as teams, as units, and in combination to meet all sorts of unforeseen and difficult objectives around the world under very high-pressure conditions. It has to train its officers to lead, manage, and command. It has to educate military dependants. Turnover is huge enough to make any corporate executive shudder and among those who stay, job change rapid, particularly at the officer level. Strategy, tactics, and equipment are all continually evolving at a rapid pace. Extremely sophisticated technology is playing a greater and greater role. And the training has to be fast. No time for lollygagging around—this the Army! (Or the Navy! Or the Air Force! Or the Marines!) We've got missions to perform and they'd better be done correctly!

Not only are the branches extremely complex organizations themselves, they need to be coordinated to work together in most mission situations. The services have a combined incoming cohort of a quarter of a million enlistees[3] to train each year in military training basics and then in over 150 military occupational areas, and in literally thousands of specialties and subspecialties. They need to train for war, yet increasingly they need to train for peacekeeping missions, as America's role in the world changes. Finally, their incoming recruits are not seasoned adults, with work experience and habits on their résumés. Typically, they are high school graduates and nongraduates, most of who have never worked before. Molding these people into a well-trained force is a staggering job, and the military approaches it with the purpose and budget of a major mission. The combined training budget of the armed services is about $18 billion, excluding trainees' salaries, including $6 billion institutional training and $12 billion operational (unit) training.[4]

It is precisely because of this mission that the U.S. military is the world's largest spender on and user of Digital Game-Based Learning. The military uses games to train soldiers, sailors, pilots, and tank drivers to master their expensive and sensitive equipment. It uses games to train command teams to communicate effectively in battle. It uses games to teach mid-level officers [local commanders-in-chief (CINCs) and their staffs] how to employ joint force military doctrine in battle and other situations. It uses games to teach senior officers the art of strategy. It uses games for teamwork and team training of squads, fire teams, crews, and other units; games for simulating responses to weapons of mass destruction, terrorist incidents, and threats; games for mastering the complex process of military logistics; and it even uses games for teaching how *not to* fight when helping maintain peace. In fact, there seems precious little that the military doesn't use some form of game to train. (Many of these are listed on the site *www.dodgame community.com.)* Let's start with an example.

JOINT FORCE EMPLOYMENT

The day I arrived at the Pentagon for a meeting with the Training and Readiness Unit of the Assistant Secretary of Defense, the guys in the shop were eager to show me the first copies of a brand new game prepared by the Joint Chiefs of Staff for mid-level officers—Captains, Majors, Lt. Commanders, and such—that had just been completed 2 weeks ago. The game has the rather prosaic, but highly descriptive, title *Joint Force Employment (JFE),* but it is anything but prosaic. Its purpose is to ensure that officers from each of the military services have the opportunity to prepare themselves for Joint Task Force operations, which is the integration of military personnel from different services— Army, Navy, Air Force, and Marines—into a cohesive interoperable military organization. The Joint Staff has established Joint Doctrine, ("doctrine" is the military's term for "the way it should be done") a set of standard guidelines and rules of engagement associates with specific joint operational tasks and functions. *JFE* is, essentially a "how to" field training exercise for these officers. According to its official description, it is designed exclusively for today's U.S. military to convey the concept that joint warfare is team warfare and to enhance knowledge of Joint Doctrine within the U.S. military.[5]

How much of a real game is *JFE?* Well, for starters it comes in a game-sized shrink-wrapped box printed with fancy graphics and screen shots, looking for the entire world like it should sit on the store shelf right next to *Quake III, Age of Empires II,* or *EverQuest.* Even the (real) official Joint Chiefs of Staff logo on the front of box looks—to those of us unfamiliar with it—like an artist's conception right from a commercial game. In fact the *only* thing on the box that gives away that this *isn't* a commercial game are the words "This product is the property of the United States Government," in the lower right-hand corner.

So, right from the beginning, rather than *hide* the fact that is a game behind the corporate-speak of "training challenge" or "competition," the military instead *flaunts* the product's "gameness." Just listen to the box copy:

- Select from computer-assisted walkthrough mode or player-controlled mode to create and control large combinations of forces and compete against state-of-the-art computer artificial intelligence (AI).
- Adopt the role of Joint Force Commander and tackle ten realistic scenarios to hone your knowledge of doctrine. Adjust friendly and enemy forces in four selectable scenarios to test varying military possibilities.
- Spectacular photorealistic terrain maps that range from the frigid arctic to the vast desert.
- 3D military units pulled directly from the U.S. military arsenal.
- Dazzling high-resolution and high-detailed graphics.
- Dynamic 3D battle effects including flying debris and smoking buildings.

So, *JFE* definitely *looks* like a game. But, much more importantly, *JFE* also *feels* and *plays* like a game. In fact, it's two games. The first is a traditional quiz game played after a fairly computer-based training tell-test introduction to Joint Doctrine, but the quiz is spiced up with high-powered graphics and sounds. It's the second game, however, that's the "real" game, the meat of the program. That game is a heart-pounding war simulation in which you set your forces rolling and shooting, take out bridges and enemy planes, have air cover flying overhead (if you request it), all in the same dynamic 2 1/2 D top-down view as up-to-the-minute games such as *Warcraft II, Command and Conquer,* and *Tiberian Sun.* In fact, the subcontractor of the JFE game, Semi-Logic Entertainments, is the maker of the games *Real War, Stunt Track Driver,* and *Legacy of Kain: Blood Omen.* We're talking state-of-the-art gaming here; the U.S. military trains its commanders-in-chief staffs with a high-end video game version of Digital Game-Based Learning. This kind of gaming technology fills a particular niche—training the top of the war-fighting command structure. Although the number of personnel in a Joint Task Force (JTF)'s staff is relatively limited, the ability to rapidly integrate military personnel into a JTF and prepare for unanticipated missions "on the fly" justifies the use of online digital games.[6]

A BIT OF MILITARY HISTORY

The relationship between computer games and the U.S. military is a relatively long and complex one. The flight simulator, which some think of as coming from the military, was originally designed by Edwin Link in 1930 as an entertainment device. His "Blue Box" was sold to amusement parks until 1934, when Link, a pilot himself, met with the Army Air Corps to sell the Corps on the concept of pilot training with his device.[7] But eventually, as the military devoted more and more money to research, things began to go the other way. By the 1980s and early 1990s the military spent billions of dollars a year on research and on training, creating very complex, sophisticated types of simulations. Through the early 1990s, the military was the technology leader, inventor, and financier, and the games companies were the beneficiaries. To a surprising extent the technology in today's commercial games was invented and created in these military-sponsored projects, paid for by DARPA (Defense Advanced Research and Production Agency), STRICOM, the Army's Simulation Training and Instrumentation Command, and others.

The entertainment industry now rests on a technological foundation laid by large amounts of government-funded research and infrastructure, including advanced computing systems, computer graphics, and the Internet. In the area of computer graphics, for example, Department of Defense (DOD) funding resulted in development of the geometry engine in 1979. This technology has since been incorporated into a number of game devices, such as the Nintendo 64 console. Similarly, early advances in networking in the late 1950s and 1960s laid the groundwork for the ARPANET, which grew into today's Internet and has become the foundation of today's growing networked games industry.

In the 1970s, the DOD developed aircraft, tank, and submarine simulators, and in the mid 1980s SIMNET pods, networked tank simulators that trained the troops up through and including the Gulf War. The DOD has invested more than $1 billion in JSIM, its current high-end simulation technology. The military-sponsored and funded display, simulation, and networking technologies in these projects have made their way into most commercial computer and games, and, of course, into military sim games such as *Apache* and *Harpoon*. By the time of the Gulf War, commercial computer games were so close to military reality that—as J. C. Herz wryly points out in her computer games history *Joystick Nation*—General Schwartzkopf felt the need to explicitly state in a war briefing that "this is not a computer game."[8]

But toward the end of the decade, as the military's budget got crunched, and as cheaper, smaller, more powerful computing power became available commercially, the tide began to turn again. Today, the computer games industry has eclipsed the Department of Defense in terms of what it can do and how fast it can do it, and industry is again leading the technology. Today's military often borrows or buys its game technology from the best commercial games. In fact, today's commercial military games have gotten so sophisticated—having used a battalion of ex-majors, colonels, and generals to create superrealistic versions of everything from submarine to tank to the latest fighter and attack helicopter simulations—that they are now being used for training *inside* the military. (This actually began around 1978, when Atari adapted it's *Battlezone* game for ARPA, DARPA's predecessor.) Today, the Air National Guard is working with Spectrum HoloByte Inc. to modify the *Falcon 4.0* flight-simulator game for military training to compensate for decreased flight training time.[9] The Navy and Air Force are negotiating with the makers of consumer flight-simulation games to create military versions. The U.S. Marine Corps continuously evaluates commercial war games software for use in training, and the Marine Corps commandant has authorized commanders to permit certain games—including (in 1996) *Harpoon2*, *Tigers on the Prowl*, *Operation Crusader*, *Patriot*, and *DOOM*—to be loaded onto government computers and to allow Marines to play them during duty hours.[10]

And it's not just *equipment* simulators. Other kinds of commercial games and interactive movies, created by companies that create consumer games, are being adapted for military team training, antiterrorism, and weapons of mass destruction training, as well as other projects too secret for them to tell me about. Today, when the military has an idea for a training game like *Joint Force Employment*, it farms it out to commercial game houses such as Semi-logic, Visual Purple, and others, rather than building it in-house.

All this, and, yes, the military uses *Jeopardy!* for training as well![11]

Why has the military embraced Digital Game-Based Learning so completely? The first reason, says Don Johnson,[12] is cost. "We did it because the other forms of training are so expensive. Even virtual simulation can cost millions to build and millions to maintain. This doesn't cost you anything to operate once you've built it."

The second reason is motivation. Johnson's group is part of the office of the Secretary of Defense for Personnel and for Readiness, whose job it is to worry about things such as recruiting and retention, quality of life, and quality of education and training. They are very mindful that the people that they're trying to bring into the military—the 18-year-olds—are probably the first generation that grew up with computers, who "get bored real easy" with traditional classroom instruction. They keep this in mind when designing all their recruiting strategies and training programs, as do the individual military services, who turn the young people into soldiers, sailors, airmen, and marines. The military is now using the Web and developing games as a way of recruiting and retaining kids. "I do think the point about being motivational is really a very, very relevant one," says Johnson.

In addition to cost and motivation, add relevance. Because modern warfare increasingly takes place on airplane, tank, or submarine computer screens without the operator ever seeing the enemy except as a symbol or avatar, simulations can be surprisingly close to the real thing. In addition, because war is a highly competitive situation, with rules (or at least constraints), goals, winners, and losers, competitive games are a great way to train. In the words of one former officer: "You play these games as a kid, you grow up understanding the risks and rewards of making decisions in real life."[13] Chess has grown up. War gaming has become a business term.

KINDS OF MILITARY TRAINING

All but war is simulation.
— Military Trainers

The military divides its combat simulation training (as opposed to skills training) into three categories: live, virtual, and constructive.

Live training is just that, but over a big range, from very large exercises with from 5,000 to 10,000 people going to Korea or Hawaii or other places to simulate landings or battles, to just a dozen guys in a room, being fed information from the outside to test communications and decision-making capabilities under field conditions.

Virtual training includes the SIMNET (simulation network) pods and other simulators. Since 1997, all equipment simulators have been designed—by decree—according to a High Level Architecture (HLA) that lets the simulators communicate with each other and the trainees work as a team. Virtual training can happen at the individual level, unit level, collective service level, JTF level, or the coalition level. At the lowest organization levels, today's fledgling pilots, submarine crews, and tank drivers climb into SIMNET pods that teach participants to do everything from learning to drive their vehicle to reenacting entire virtual battles, such as those from the Gulf War. The modern version of SIMNET is JSIMS, which involves literally thousands of pilots, tank commanders, ships, submarines, and various levels of officers linked by T1 and T3 lines all playing out the war "at 1-foot levels of granularity."

At the mid-level of virtual training are the Joint War Fighting Centers to which come units of commanders and subcommanders and their enlisted support. They play against ex-military officers known as OPFOR (opposing forces). The military units are shown on computer screens in the same symbolic shorthand that the commanders draw on their battle maps. The commanders are "blind," with the communications from the field as close to the reality as possible. The idea again is to see how the communications really flow and what the problems are.

And at the highest level of virtual training (in terms of command structure, not number of people) are Joint Coalition simulations. For example as a part of NATO's fiftieth anniversary celebrations, a virtual joint war-training simulation was set up linking Washington, the Netherlands, Sweden, and England, with each of the "component commanders"—air, land, and sea—based in a different country. They had to confront issues of time difference, languages, and so on. They used a non-combat scenario: Two countries were battling each other with the conflict threatening to spill into a third, and the mission was to evacuate a city in the third country, so there was no actual combat in the sim. "The reason to do that," says Johnson, "is that some of our 'Partners for Peace' allies are not really interested in participating directly in war fighting as part of NATO, but they still need to be able to synchronize their military operations with other countries around the globe. A significant first step is the development of interoperable simulations and learning environments."

Constructive games are the strategic war games that used to be played on sand tables. Tabletop war games for officers go back to the Romans, and probably even earlier, with the formalization of it dating from the training of the Prussian Army in the nineteenth century. Now a lot of this has been rolled on to the computer.

JFE is a new hybrid between the virtual and constructive, first tried because the other methods are so expensive. It teaches decision making, critical thinking, and some level of performance. "In terms of motivation, in terms of getting them to spend time and becoming deeply absorbed in it, and in terms of the competition, it's really amazing how effective this is," says Johnson.

Let me now leave the Joint Staff for a minute (I will come back) and look at some Digital Game-Based Learning in the individual services.

THE ARMY

The Army has a variety of Digital Game-Based Learning projects in use and under construction.

One of the Army's (and all the services') biggest needs is to quickly take individuals and mold them into well-functioning teams. How can they be sure people will work together well when a crisis occurs? The simulation game *Saving Sergeant Pabletti* (described in Chapter 9) is used with over 80,000 soldiers each year for training on some of these team skills from a values perspective. Following basic training, drill sergeants use the interactive video game with large groups of trainees, sometimes up to 300, typically with 1 or 2 soldiers designated as the "mouth."

The game got its start when the former chief of staff of the Army, General Reimer, saw products that Will Interactive had done for kids. According to Sharon Sloane, Will's president, "He called us to the Pentagon and said 'Could you build me something on prevention of sexual harassment, army values, equal opportunity, cross-cultural communication?'" The Army contracted directly with Will to create a customized program, at a cost of $600,000 for the application and accompanying instructor guide. Sloane says the Army is getting "much better results" from the students because they're engaged and having fun. Because the one program covered so many topics, the Army was able to get 15 hours of training down to 4.[14]

PEO-STRI, the Army's Strategy, Training, and Instrumentation Organization, sponsors several Digital Game-Based Learning projects, including *Taskforce 2010*, a PC game for brigade and battalion staff wargaming over the Web; *Spearhead II,* a tank game; and, like the Navy and Air Force, modification of Microsoft's *Flight Simulator* for Army aviation.[15]

At the University of Southern California's Institute for Creative Technology, a PEO-STRI-sponsored project involves bringing in creative artists from Hollywood's special effects studios to work with scientists and Army researchers to create huge "Holodeck"-like environments for mission rehearsal. The idea is to give Army personnel going off to a new part of the world a realistic preview of the environment they can expect, including 360-degree visuals, sounds, language, and so on. To do this (and other projects), the institute will receive $45 million in funding over 5 years.[16] ICT has created the state-of-the-art training games *Full Spectrum Command* (for company commanders), *Full Spectrum Leader* (for platoon leaders), and *Full Spectrum Warrior* (for squad leaders).

Recruiting is also a key need for the Army. In 2001 John P. McLaurin III, the Assistant Secretary of the Army for Manpower and Reserve Affairs, sponsored a project proposed by Colonel Casey Wardynski of West Point and Michael Zyda of the Naval Postgraduate School to create a computer game that would raise young Americans' awareness of the Army and what it means to be a soldier. "From the outset we set a high bar," wrote McLauren. "The game had to provide an engaging and cutting-edge channel for strategic communications with young Americans and those who may influence them about the Army and soldiering."

The project resulted in *America's Army,* a networked, multiplayer, realistic action game based on the "Unreal" first-person 3D "engine," used in many commercial games. *America's Army,* an extremely detailed and accurate game, was developed by a team at the Naval Postgraduate School's MOVES institute led by Zyda, using Army personnel as subject matter experts. Beginning with "Operations," the game added modules for several Special Forces tasks, for Combat Medics, and for other specialties. The goal, in Zyda's words, "was not just to produce video games for the Army, but to connect the new power of the Internet and video games with the Army's mission."

America's Army is distributed free on CD's and the Army-sponsored website. Players must first complete virtual "basic training," which includes the same marksmanship and physical tests as "real" basic training, before being allowed to undertake missions, which involves joining a team playing against other teams. Every team playing the game, however, sees itself as the U.S. Army, and sees the team it is playing as "the enemy."

One feature particularly important to the Army, according to Colonel Wardynski, is the ability to demonstrate the interplay between soldiering and the Army's core values of duty, integrity, honor, loyalty, self-less service, courage and respect for others. The game does this by "rewarding soldierly behavior and penalizing rotten eggs" in a variety of situations and ways. Players who consistently violate the rules wind up in the brig.

America's Army has been tremendously successful, with, at this writing, nearly 4 million registered users, of whom over 2 million have completed "basic training" and gone on to play missions. The game is estimated to have been played for more than 50 million hours around the world and has, according to Wardynski, "engendered positive awareness of Soldiering among twenty-nine percent of young Americans ages 16–24."

All these benefits did not come cheap, however. The game cost roughly $7 million to develop and costs around $3 million per year to maintain, including upgrades, servers, high speed lines, support, publicity, etc. The good news for the Army, though, is that this represents only one-third of one percent of the Army's total marketing budget.[17]

What does the Army get for its money? Attractiveness to its recruits on the one hand, and tons of potentially useful data on the other.

"Games hold their audience," explains the original proposal for *America's Army*, "because they are attractive on the outside (what the player sees and hears while playing) and gripping on the inside (what the player thinks and feels while playing). Sound, music, image, and animation all play their part in satisfying the ears and eyes. Inside a computer game identifiable characters and a dramatic story both play key roles. In addition, because one PLAYS the computer game, a smooth, uninterrupted sequence (or loop) of actions and decisions must be present. When a game works well, the player may execute this inner loop for hundreds of cycles. If it is smooth enough, the effect is compelling."[18]

The game's many servers collect every move the players make, data that can later be analyzed for patterns of behavior, leadership potential, team focus, and other things. In addition, the game may eventually be linked up with instruments such as the Armed Forces Qualifying Test (AFQT) and the Armed Services Vocational Aptitude Battery (ASVAB.)

America's Army represents the first example of Digital Game-Based Learning's reaching a large, mainstream audience. It has, according to

Colonel Wardynski, "exceeded our expectations, and proven the value of games as a medium …"

THE NAVY

Like all the branches, the U.S. Navy simulates as much as it can. There are high-fidelity simulations of everything from landing on an aircraft carrier to putting out fires on a submarine. One Navy project, the Submarine Skills-Training Network (SubSkillsNet), puts simulations onto laptops that can be used onboard the subs. SubSkillsNet includes simulations of a surfaced bridge view, radar, sonar displays, fire control functions, and a periscope, all linkable together, so that they can train whole teams as well as individuals, and change the training scenarios on the fly.

While these simulations have the necessary degree of fidelity, one issue the Navy experiences is that with this type of instructorless learning, the students have to take the initiative to start and to persist until they have obtained the necessary level of knowledge and skill. So, increasing motivation is a key goal.

"What you want to do is motivate people to spend more time on the training voluntarily," says Rosemary Garris, of the Naval Air Warfare Center Training Systems Division.[19] Using any kind of training product onboard a submarine is largely based on the initiative of the individual student, so you have to entice them. "You're not going to do it by telling them to read the technical publications," says Garris, "and a lot of CBT [computer-based training] is very, very dry."

The more Garris and the group of psychologists, computer scientists, and engineers in the Science and Technology Division thought about who these learners actually were—19-year-old males, not well known for lightness of touch or finesse, according to Commander Adrian McElwee, director of the Navy's Submarine Onboard Training System (SOBT) at the Naval Submarine base in New London CT—the more they began to think seriously about using games for motivation—as many of their users had already suggested. "We wanted to hook submariners. They're all young guys, and they're jazzed by *Quake* and a variety of other games," says Garris. Not rushing in lightly, the Submarine Team, led by psychologist Dr. Robert Ahlers, began a 3-year project on training games that ended in 2000.[20] "We did a thorough literature review of the educational and psychological literature on games to find the defining characteristics of games and to find out where everyone who has done research in this were coming from and where they ended up," Garris says. (See Chapter 6.)

The team decided, based on their research, to turn one of their own simulations into a game and evaluate its training effectiveness. The task they chose was Periscope Observation for Surface Contact Management. What submariners are supposed to do after identifying a contact is call its angle on the bow—which is how much it's aiming at or away from your ship—and also count divisions, which are tick marks in the reticle of the periscope that help determine range. Calling the angle is one of the most difficult periscope skills. In the standard simulation, trainees looked, counted, entered estimates of angle and divisions, got corrective feedback, and looked, counted, and entered again—not very interesting. What was missing in terms of the engagement that would get this stuff learned quickly? Ask any gamer: *If the target gets too close, you want to blow it out of the water!*

And so, using what they had learned about game characteristics, Garris' group built the game they call *Bottom Gun*. As in the conventional trainer, the player makes estimates of angle and counts the divisions. What makes the game different and fun is that any ship determined to be a threat to ownership safety—defined as any contact that will have its closest point of approach within 4,000 yards—can be destroyed by firing a missile at it. The missile's firing solution is determined by the angle and division calls the trainee made, so that a hit is dependent on the player's accuracy. "It's totally unrealistic," says Garris. "In real life—or with a conventional simulation—you don't shoot collision threats out of the water, you don't get a score, and you don't get credit for maintaining weapons stores until the end of the game. There is a lot of fantasy and drama built in that aren't in the conventional trainer."

Why? Years of video games, which quite likely included commercial sub simulations, have trained these 19-year-olds to expect this kind of real-time, exciting action and feedback. With the game there's a *reason* to know how to tell the range—if the enemy comes too close you can cream the sucker! And you can't fall asleep either. Let them get too close and they start shooting missiles at you!

"Hey, I can do this," say the trainees. And scores go way up, and train-ing time way down. Or, that's what the Navy expects, anyway. They are collecting pilot data at a local university where they are running up to 120 subjects to do this side-by-side comparison. And because they designed and developed both sets of software, it is a very clean compari-son—the graphics are exactly the same, the simulation running the appli-cations is exactly the same—between conventional and game-oriented training approaches. Data from the first sixteen subjects indicates a desir-able learning curve. If the rest of the data does not arrive before publica-tion, stay tuned for the second printing. But where would you like to place your bet?

Who designs and builds these games for the Navy? Not surprisingly, it's kids from the Games Generations—college students who are gamers themselves and contemporaries of the trainees. Garris's group is located near the University of Central Florida and employs most of the programmers on the university's programming team, basically college students who are big-time game players. The developers also participate a lot in the design. The initial design of *Bottom Gun* began with a radar game, which "just seemed boring" to Garris. So she went to the kids and said, "What do you think would be more fun?" Together, they roughed out something that was very consistent with the guidance provided by the academic literature and more appealing to the kids. Garris feels it's very important to include game players on the design team to make sure the "fun" element doesn't get left out.

This is the future in training design—trainee contemporaries redesigning the old training in their own new style, with experienced guidance. Creation by players is the way it has always worked in the games world. It's the way it will have to work in the training world to cre-ate effective learning for the Games Generations.

Garris and Ahlers' 3-year training game study includes not only a review of the literature but also an exploration of game-playing motiva-tion. They are evaluating the value of Victor Vroom's V.I.E. (valence, instrumentality, expectancy) theory[21] to help understand why these games are so popular. Expectancy theory deals with how much control over an activity or its outcome a person feels is possible, how effective they believe they would be in that activity, and the degree to which they find the outcome of the activity attractive. "If we can determine what people find so attractive about playing games, we hope we can create training products that meet these same goals while imparting useful knowledge and skills," says Garris.[22]

The submarine team is pleased enough with their initial results to have begun work on a new game, based on a virtual walkthrough of a submarine, designed to speed up the transition of submariners from training school to functioning onboard. "I know a walkthrough doesn't sound much like a game," says Garris, "but we have lots of exciting gamelike things in mind. People are moving faster and faster towards games," she says.

Another Navy-based Digital Game-Based Learning initiative is the Microsimulator Systems for Immersive Learning Environments project, known as MiSSILE.[23] The goal of the MiSSILE project is to identify consumer PC games and technologies that the Navy can use directly in its training in order to cut costs. The project has determined that while consumer games cannot totally replace higher fidelity simulators, they can support "task shedding" off of those higher cost assets, particularly in the early stages of learning. One of the most interesting observations of the project is that "Student naval aviators will continue to use PC flight simulators whether or not we endorse, use, or provide them as part of the training tool kit." Wake up and smell the coffee, guys!

An older but interesting Navy-based use of Digital Game-Based Learning came in 1991, when the Chief of Navy Technical Training asked Dr. Henry Halff, a research psychologist, to develop a computer game to teach avionics technicians about basic electricity and electronics.[24] "Two well-known limitations of conventional training and education are lack of opportunities to practice the skills being taught and failure to sustain motivation over the long periods needed to achieve competence in the target skills," says Dr. Halff. "Adventure gaming addresses both of these problems."

Because of the combination of their challenging nature, structured concepts, need for quantitative problem solving and qualitative reasoning, technical and scientific subjects such as electronics lend themselves well to Digital Game-Based Learning, according to Halff. "The fantasy aspects of adventure games also offer unique opportunities for instruction," he adds.

The game Halff's team created was called *Electro Adventure*. The scenario is that the *Electro*, a Navy ship from the future, has been transported through a mishap to the present day and must be repaired by the player. The player has to discover technical and safety tricks, combine materials to create things, and solve technical problems in each of the ship's compartments. The program combines some adventure game format with some traditional CBT elements, and uses what were, at the time, high-end game graphics. Like *Bottom Gun*, the Navy tested *Electro Adventure* against its other learning systems (see Chapter 14).

THE AIR FORCE

According to a number of sources, consumer flight sims have become a *de facto* part of Air Force flight training. "It's almost like that's the first phase of training—you come here fully trained up on flight simulator and we'll throw you into an Air Force simulator and see how you handle it," says one source.

The Air Force, for budget reasons, is being forced to cut back on the number live training sorties pilots can fly by up to 25 percent.[25] According to Major Peter Bonanni of the Virginia Air National Guard,[26] pilots are most proficient when they are first deployed, but as the deployment wears on with no additional training, pilot proficiency slips. While most high-fidelity simulators in use today are not deployable to the field, the most important (and perishable) skills, Bonanni thinks, can be honed by very-low-cost simulators. He cites the computer game *Falcon 4.0* as an example of a commercial product that is shattering the fidelity threshold and providing a model for very-low-cost simulation. Key components of *Falcon 4.0* that allow this type of breakthrough include "SIMNET-like" networking protocols that create a large man-in-the-loop environment. They plan to enhance this capability with commercial head-mounted displays and voice-recognition systems.

In a different area—target identification—consultant David Twitchell and instructional design professor David Merrill of Utah State University created a quick recognition game, called *JVID and Finflash* (VI is visual identification and "finflash" is the marking on an aircraft's tail) for the Air Force, after pilots accidentally shot down two "friendly" Army Blackhawk helicopters over Iraq in April 1994.[27] The game, which is a kind of "reflex game" (discussed in Chapter 6), has three levels. In Level 1, the player starts by seeing the plane on the runway from above, not moving, and does basic WEFT (wing engine, fuselage, tail) identification. In Level 2, the player sees the plane from 200 yards in a single view. In Level 3, the player is in the cockpit, the plane is coming at the player, and the player has only 3 or 4 seconds to identify it, just like in real life. Players can choose from many backgrounds, such as sunny sky, cloudy sky, jungle, or desert that may affect identification. (Before the advent of the game, photos were used, and the players often remembered the clouds in the pictures rather than the plane markings.) Names and scores are posted, and, like with any good video game, the pilots come back to improve their scores. One of Twitchell and Merrill's objectives in the game is to push pilots to the point where it is *impossible* to identify the aircraft, and to get them to recognize and admit that sometimes it *can't* be done—an admission that top-gun "jet jockeys" have a hard time making.

THE MARINES

In addition to allowing its officers and men to play certain military-related commercial computer games on base computers,[28] the Marines have also been busy creating some training games of their own. Using a version of the commercial game *Doom* adapted with the help of Lt. Scott Barnett, Marine fire-teams have been training at computer labs in Virginia, Georgia, and North Carolina, learning battlefield tactics and decision making. Interestingly, the skills Barnett was attempting to teach with these action shoot-'em-up games were not shooting and killing, but teamwork, communication, and concepts of command and control. What he certainly got was engagement. "It's funny, because at the end of the day I had to kick my Marines out of there and send them home," he says. "The Marines know they're learning, but they're also having fun. I think that's critically important to get them to want to learn."[29]

Marine Doom was played as a networked game. Four-member fire-teams were given four separate computers in the same room. Their goal was to coordinate their movements to eliminate an enemy bunker. "In the lab, we crank the sound up just to add to the confusion and the chaos. Each Marine can shout to his comrades; the fire-team leader shouts commands and they advance on the enemy using what they know about strategy and tactics," says Barnett.

Marine Doom is no longer in use. It has been replaced by more customized and sophisticated games such as *Marine Air-Ground Task Force* (MAGTAF XXI) from MÄK, and *Close Combat Marines*, an internally created "mod" (game modification) of the Close Combat engine created by Atomic Games. In addition, the Marines officially sanction the use of the commercial games *Medal of Honor* and *Soldier of Fortune* for various aspects of training.

THE NATIONAL GUARD AND RESERVES

According to Lt. General Paul Glazer,[30] the National Guard uses games to do constructive-level (war-gaming) training, leadership training, and battle training. There is a large National Guard "Battle Lab" at Fort Leavenworth, Kansas, and smaller labs in other places. One game General Glazer describes has soldiers engaging computer-generated enemies with air-powered M16s and mortars. Like the games in arcades, the soldiers see the immediate results of their actions—the enemy goes down or doesn't go down. However, unlike the consumer games, the military ones carefully track where each bullet goes, so that soldiers can learn through replays why they missed; for example, the soldier was not "leading" a moving target.

When it ordered a survival training CD-ROM from IBM Learning, the Army Reserves specifically requested that Digital Game-Based Learning be included as part of the design. It wanted an adventure game that trainees could play to dramatically illustrate the value of bringing along all the necessary objects for survival, as well as the problems one could encounter if something was forgotten. Interestingly, the game that the IBM developers started with as their "model" or paradigm of how this should work was the Freddi Fish series of children's adventure games.[31]

Could this mean our preschoolers are learning valuable military skills as they play?

The National Guard also commissioned a special version of *Joint Force Employment*, known as "Guard Force" that focuses on the Guard's combat and non-combat missions, from counterinsurgency to rescue.

Contest 8: Do you know of a cool military Digital Game-Based Learning project? Email your entries to *Contest8@.twitchspeed.com.*

MILITARY TRAINING'S OTHER MISSIONS—
SCHOOLS AND STANDARDS

Despite the enormity of their primary mission—to train and prepare the military—the folks in the joint staff training office think bigger still. They do this in at least two ways, both of which are relevant to Digital Game-Based Learning. The first is extending what they do to other settings outside the military. One instance of this is what they refer to as "interagency" training. In an instance of domestic terrorism, or weapons of mass destruction—referred to in the trade by the much more pleasant-sounding acronym WMD—many groups will have to be coordinated. "If you think a coalition is hard," says Mark Oehlert,[32] "try putting together different units within this country. If something happens in DC, there are 12 different law enforcement agencies that have potential jurisdiction, not to mention the DOD. How can we train the FBI, local fire and police, DOD, National Guard, and Army reserve to all operate in the most effective manner when we're facing a crisis?"

It turns out there is a serious lack of common doctrine and procedures regarding the roles and responsibilities across local, state, and federal organizations. Johnson's group would like to see these tasks better defined, and training implemented in an interagency game similar to JFE, which would train members of the various agencies to work as a team. "We are just beginning to understand the power and necessity of digital team training," says Johnson.

The second "other mission," of military trainers is to create common standards for reuse and interoperability of training technologies, a mission that grew out of the government's need for cost savings. In the past, training platforms would change every few years; for example, from 1-inch tape to 3/4-inch tape to half-inch tape to interactive video disk to CD-ROM to DVD, all of it proprietary. Each time the platform changed the trainers had to adapt the training content to the new media format. Because of this they could never implement learning technology on as large a scale as they would have liked. In the early 1990s, realizing that they weren't able to have one flight simulator talk to another one, they decided to set standards. They created DIS (distributed interactive simulation protocol), which morphed into HLA (high-level architecture), common standards that allowed interoperability between simulators for team training and reuse of simulation "objects," such as tanks, ships, planes, and projectiles. In doing so they saved quite a bit of money by not constantly rebuilding the same objects and reinventing the wheel.

Having solved that problem in the simulation area, they began looking into how such common technology standards might be used across the broader education and training areas. The Quadrennial Defense Review (QDR), led them to conclude that using learning technology on a very large scale could save a billion dollars a year.[33] To be able to use technology without having to reinvent it every 5 years, they realized they needed a common standard so that content could be built once and reused over and over again. If the same standard cut across the public and private sectors and academia, it would allow the development of shared learning objects, which would seriously drive down investment costs. The result was the development of ADL (Advanced Distributed Learning) which provides a framework for a distributed learning environment, allowing distribution of high-quality content to any device, anywhere, at any time.

A new ADL specification, the Sharable Courseware Object Reference Model (SCORM), extends the common standards to digital games. Developed in conjunction with Microsoft, Oracle, IBM, Macromedia, and standards groups, it enables games to be played on any kind of platform and to share and reuse objects. As a result, the development of Digital Game-Based Learning will be made "several orders of magnitude more efficient and effective," says Johnson, who is one of the project's team leaders.[34]

LINKING ENTERTAINMENT AND DEFENSE— THE CONFERENCE

Military training has a complex organizational structure, with responsibilities divided between the Joint Command and the services. The military appears to communicate, to share its experiences, and to create joint approaches and standards among its members reasonably well when compared to industry. This may be because there are only four "companies," and the same parent owns them all. In general, their goals and objectives are roughly the same, and except for any pride of ownership, there is no reason *not* to share.

This does not extend, however, to sharing with industries *outside* the military. The military may have been doing the same things and trying to solve the same problems as many business trainers, but for a host of reasons, until relatively recently, only a handful of business people, if any, knew about it, despite the considerable work that the military has done and the successes it has had.

A similar situation obtained with the entertainment industries. The two groups, military and entertainment, were working on almost exactly the same set of difficult problems—simulation and modeling—but because the two groups differ widely in their motivations, objectives, and cultures, they were not talking to each other and often clueless as to what the other was doing.

In 1996, the Department of Defense's Defense Modeling and Simulation Office (DMSO) asked the National Research Council to convene a multidisciplinary committee to "evaluate the extent to which the entertainment industry and DOD might be able to better leverage each other's capabilities in modeling and simulation technology and to identify potential areas for greater collaboration."[35] A two-day workshop, titled *Modeling and Simulation: Linking Entertainment and Defense*, was held in Irvine, California, in October 1996, for members of the entertainment and defense industries to discuss research interests in modeling and simulation. The workshop was unique in that it brought together two communities that traditionally shared little information and transferred little technology between them.[36]

At the workshop more than fifty representatives of the entertainment and defense research communities discussed technical challenges, obstacles to successful sharing of technology and joint research, and mechanisms for facilitating greater collaboration. Participants came from the film, video game, location-based entertainment, and theme park industries; DOD; defense contractors; and universities. Through presentations on topics such as electronic storytelling, strategy and war gaming, experiential computing and virtual reality, networked simulation, and low-cost simulation hardware, the committee tried to encourage dialogue and stimulate discussion of research areas of interest to both the entertainment and defense industries. Because the workshop represented one of the first formal attempts to bridge the gap between the entertainment and defense communities, the committee also hoped to encourage personal contacts between members of the two communities as a means of facilitating future collaboration.

Eric Haseltine, of Walt Disney's Imagineering Group, remarked at the workshop that "the thing that the entertainment industry can get the most from DOD is just knowing what's been done, so they don't have to reinvent the wheel."[37] This type of military-civilian conference is a really helpful thing to do, and something that the training community might well consider. Given the military's experience and predilections, sharing information between the military and corporate trainers might result in a lot more Digital Game-Based Learning in companies!

CONCLUSION

The real problem for the military, as Danny Hillis observed at the workshop, is not to simulate a tank or airplane, but to train the person's mind so that when they get into a real tank on a battlefield, they do the right thing.[38] This is why military training has relevance to *all* training. But the question is always *how do we do this?* Michael Parmentier is clear that 18-year-old recruits expect to be hooked up electronically to the world "because that's the way they do things. If we don't do things that way, they're not going to want to be in our environment."[39] As Don Johnson says: "We *know* the technology works. We just want to get on with using it."[40]

In the next section, I show you how to do this. I illustrate how *you* can introduce—starting tomorrow—Digital Game-Based Learning into *your* organization, no matter what its size, budget, or learning persuasion.

Part Four
IMPLEMENTATION

You need a lot of elbow grease.
—Sylvia Kowal, Nortel Networks

11

Bringing Digital Game-Based Learning into Your Organization

The art of curriculum design is figuring out what means you want to use at what point and where it becomes effective.
— Luyen Chou

Invention is the mother of necessities.
— Marshall McLuhan

Where do I start?
— A Trainer

GETTING STARTED

When I speak on Digital Game-Based Learning at training and education conferences, the two questions most frequently asked are, "How can I convince my management?" and, "How can I get started introducing Digital Game-Based Learning into my organization?" I deal with the convincing-management issue in Chapter 13. As for how to begin, there are actually a great number of ways to start, many of them relatively simple and inexpensive. They range from a low-end of HTML-based Web trivia games that you can probably create yourself or with a colleague for "free," to small, Digital Game-Based Learning tools that can be purchased for a few hundred dollars with little or no approval, to high-end projects of companywide importance with budgets in the millions—with a variety of steps between.

This chapter describes five categories of Digital Game-Based Learning that are useful to anyone considering using this form of learning for business training. These categories are based on practical considerations rather than the more learning-based—oriented categories described in Chapter 6. I will then help you assess the Digital Game-Based Learning style of your own organization, in order to answer such questions as, "What type or types of games are likely to work in my environment?" and, "Are there environments in which Digital Game-Based Learning is out of the question?" I will also address the question of how Digital Game-Based Learning relates to Learning Management Systems.

Finally, for the budget conscious—and that, hopefully, includes everyone in business at any level—I set out a table of what can be obtained and accomplished at various investment levels that may be available for a particular learning need, starting with no money at all!

CATEGORIES OF AVAILABLE DIGITAL GAME-BASED LEARNING

When assessing what is available by way of Digital Game-Based Learning, it often helps to think of the possibilities in five categories:

- Simple question-and-answer games
- Off-the-shelf games
- Email games
- Game templates
- Custom games

Each of these categories can be created and delivered totally in-house, or in partnership with vendors or developers, or can be brought in and delivered "turnkey" by outside consultants.

Let's look at each one, starting with simple question-and-answer games.

Question-and-Answer Games

Sometimes you just need to call a spade a spade. While I usually describe my cleverly designed question-and-answer games to clients using high-sounding terms such as "question-led learning," I recently overheard an employee answer a friend's question "What does your company do?" with "We make trivia games." I was deflated, but that's the modern term.

So-called trivia, or question-and-answer, computer games come in a variety of complexity and sophistication. At the high end is *You Don't Know Jack*, or complex question-and-feedback-driven adventure games such as *Ultima IV*. But in their simplest, low-end form, these types of games are probably the easiest place to start, at least for creating Digital Game-Based Learning with content that is *customized*.

Remember Bayer's *Aspirin Trivia Game* that we saw in Chapter 9 (www.bayerus.com/aspirin/game/main.htm)? It has just five questions, and is constructed entirely out of HTML text. Here's how to start Digital Game-Based Learning immediately. To create a similar game, make up five (or more) questions and use the HTML code I provide on the book's Web site, *www.twitchspeed.com*. If you know *nothing* about HTML programming ask around among your junior staff, or go to IT to find someone who does understand HTML programming. Assuming that you or they have ever done simple HTML programming before, you should have a game ready in roughly an hour. Your company's Webmaster can help you get it online and to make it available on your company's internal or external site.

The key point is that the content of even these simple trivia games doesn't have to be trivial. In fact, they are actually a lot more fun when the content is *really challenging* to the intended audience. When Ernst & Young created a trivia game about the company and its partners several years ago (*The Professional Development Game*, created by Bob Dean),[1] the partners practically climbed over one another trying to get to the computers to play during breaks from their conference meetings *because the questions were challenging to them*.

There is also, as we have discussed, a lot of potential *primary* learning in the question-and-answer format, not just review and reinforcement. My guess is that I will remember the five answers to *The Aspirin Game* for the rest of my life.

If these types of games turn out to be a hit in your environment—as they have in many (see Nortel Networks' *Create the Band*)—and you want to move to versions of Digital Game-Based Learning that are somewhat more complex and/or sophisticated with customized content, then you can go to the email games and game templates below. But before we get there, let's take a look at what's available off-the-shelf.

Off-the-Shelf Games

Another easy way to start—although not necessarily the least expensive way—is with off-the-shelf games. These are purchased, or licensed, complete Digital Game-Based Learning experiences that have all content included. In certain cases, you can literally turn to the off-the-shelf consumer games marketplace—an under-$50 commercial consumer game might serve your needs right off the video game store rack. The Council of Mayors used *Sim City* right out of the box. Games such as *Start-up* can easily be used "as is" to teach internal entrepreneurship. Other business-oriented consumer games, such as *Wall Street Trader*, *Airline Tycoon*, or *Pizza Syndicate*, may also be useful. *Sim Health, Roller Coaster Tycoon*, or *Virtual U* can be used to practice various aspects of policy formation and management as well.

Another opportunity with off-the-shelf consumer games is to modify them for your purposes. Many consumer games now allow for this by providing "editors" or "mod builders" that allow you to create your own worlds, as well as the characters. An example is Shell's creating a *Quake* mod to represent the interior of an offshore drilling platform for orientation purposes. Often these do not require any more investment than purchasing the needed number of games (at retail or with negotiated volume discounts) and doing the modifications either internally or via a consultant (possibly your 12-year-old).[2]

In addition to consumer-targeted games, ready-made business learning games *with content* exist for a variety of topics and price ranges. They are principally designed for review and reinforcement, but in some cases may serve as primary learning vehicles as well. Some run on CD-ROMs, some over the Web, and some are hybrids. LearningWare, for example, has created a safety *Jeopardy!*-style game that is sold as part of The MARCOM Group's safety-training package. LearningWare also offers basic finance-oriented games as well. games2train has an off-the-shelf package in sexual harassment prevention training developed in conjunction with a major law firm that allows you to tailor the off-the-shelf content to your company's particular policies and language. MBA Games has licensable Internet-based games in the areas of management skills and team leadership. SMG, the Strategic Management Group, has ready-made simulations in e-commerce and other areas. PowerSim will license the *Beer*

Game for understanding operations, as well as other ready-made simulation games. For soft skills such as coaching there are the interactive movies and reinforcement games of Ninth House Network.

There are also a number of nondigital off-the-shelf games that are in the process of "going digital." A well-known board game for teaching basic management is *Zodiak* from Paradigm Learning. Paradigm Learning recently announced an online version of *Zodiak*, created in conjunction with SMG. Don't look for any fancy graphics, though. This is more of a numbers-based simulation than a commercial game.

Some licensable off-the-shelf games have been created by companies looking to teach their clients or to turn their own expensive internally created tools into profitmakers. Increasingly, organizations that have invested big bucks in building a custom game will sell it to others as an off-the-shelf product to help recoup their investment. These organizations include large consulting companies such as PricewaterhouseCoopers and Andersen Consulting, as well as industry-specific companies such as Bankers Trust and Ameritrade. Should you have a need for a financial derivatives training game, for example, you could have your choice of Ameritrade's free *Darwin* options-trading program, created for its clients, or the expensive, but highly sophisticated, *In$sider* from PricewaterhouseCoopers, created for its own internal training (both programs are discussed in Chapter 9). Off-the-shelf Digital Game-Based Learning is often also available from vendors in either stand-alone (i.e., here it is, you do it) or facilitated mode.

Email Games

Although Digital Game-Based Learning comes in a variety of levels of technical sophistication, there is almost always some multimedia capability required. In large, global organizations with a variety of hardware standards and legacy systems, this can often raise issues and problems that can lead to the abortion of otherwise interesting Digital Game-Based Learning projects. In such cases, an interesting alternative to explore is email games. Probably the best thing about email games is the *lack* of new technology that they require; they require an email account and nothing more. These days, just about every businessperson with a computer has an email address, and it is possible to *give* an address to any employee, even if they do not have a personal computer of their own but must log in on a kiosk to get to their email.

What is an email game? Put simply, it is a Digital Game-Based Learning variety where all information received, as well as all information input by users (such as answers to questions, moves, or other) are communicated solely through email messages. Just as with all other categories of Digital Game-Based Learning, email games come in a variety of sophistication levels and costs.

The simplest email games are games anyone with email can set up and run for themselves: a review after a course, or a "stump your colleagues" game among a small group. As the group widens, more sophistication is needed. Let us look at how these work, and what you, as a trainer, can do.

The most basic email games are just data collection. You send out an email asking a question and somehow rate the answers. You could ask, for example:

- What is the most important thing to know about x (product, process, etc.)?
- What is the thing most often missed about y?
- What is the best example of z? (best practices)
- What is the best way to explain a difficult concept to a customer? (marketing)

What makes it a game is that there are rules, competition, and winners. Thiagi's Web site, *www.thiagi.com*, provides a number of free email games of this type, with descriptions and detailed instructions. Many of his games are requests for "tips," or for definitions, or for good examples of an idea or concept, with the participants voting at the end to determine "winners." They are often played in a series of "rounds" of a few days or a week.

A second type of email game is a quiz-type game in which there are right and wrong answers, and players are scored on how many questions they answer correctly (and possibly on how much time they take). This type of email game involves creating questions, rules, and a scoring mechanism. To do this on a large scale, it helps to have question experts and dedicated email game server software. A company called Yoyodine used to provide this, but when Yahoo! purchased it, the product was discontinued.[3] Other vendors can provide on a custom basis, if needed.

Game Templates I: Classroom Templates

Along with email games, another easy way to get started in Digital Game-Based Learning is with game templates. Templates are prebuilt games, usually using a recognizable game format (such as *Jeopardy!* or a board game), into which you, the trainer, put your own content before playing the game with users. Several varieties of these templates exist, both for livening up a classroom course, and for delivery and use online and over the Web.

Examples of templates for classroom use include LearningWare's *Game Show Pro* and *Game Show Pro II*. The former, which has been available since 1994, includes games similar to *Jeopardy!, Family Feud,* and *Tic-Tac-Toe.* "We use games everybody knows to shorten or eliminate the learning curve," says general manager Victor Kluck.[4] To use their games, you enter the content in their editor, and then project the game in front of the class. The trainer acts as emcee. You can purchase buzzer-type pads to have a team leader "buzz in." *Game Show Pro II* adds a new game, similar to ABC's *Who Wants to Be a Millionaire?* It uses the same prize levels and is called *Is That Your Final Answer?* If the popularity of the TV show is any indication, it should be a hit.

One piece of good news for those getting started is that Learning-Ware will sell an individual license for a single computer. Thus, a trainer can use the templates in several classes with many types of content for a license fee of only a few hundred dollars. While the company boasts over a thousand large companies as users, most of these are single licenses or small multiples. The company will sell unlimited use site licenses when requested, typically in the $15,000 range.

Another vendor of classroom game templates is games2train with its *Battle of the Brains*, a sports theme-based game, and *Conversations*. These flexible and easy-to-use templates are sold on a site license basis only. This approach typically appeals to centralized training centers that provide a service of creating games for their internal clients. Templates let them do this extremely quickly. "One client came to us asking if we could have a game for them in 2 weeks," said a corporate trainer at Chase. "We bit our tongues, because we knew we could do it overnight."

Classroom-based templates derive their power from the fact that the content is easy enough to enter that any trainer can do it, and that the content is thereby highly "customized" for the course and audience, making it much more relevant and interesting. Some trainers have their classroom participants each create one or two questions to "stump their colleagues," which questions are then entered by the instructor during a break. Seeing their own question on the big screen is often a big deal for participants.

Classroom game templates have been around for some time, and I, for one, would have thought their popularity would have faded. In fact, just the opposite is true. Many trainers in many companies have still never seen them, and it is one of the easiest training "sells." Prices, unlike other software, have either held steady or gone up. One reason is that technology has changed. Computer projectors for use in classrooms have become smaller, better, and cheaper, and many more classroom instructors now have access to them, facilitating the use of classroom-based game templates.

Although game templates are one of the simplest and most primitive forms of Digital Game-Based Learning, the power that they have to liven up a classroom and get people's juices flowing is truly amazing. "When the questions came up I'd think 'Oh, I remember that,' and BANG! I'd be leaping across the table to get the points," says a flight attendant in a Canada Airlines course, according to the LearningWare Web site.[5] My own experience is similar. This is, of course, both a tribute to the power of games and competition and an indictment of just how dull most classes are. Their basic uses are for keeping people awake, reviewing and reinforcing material, and showing instructors what has and hasn't been absorbed.

If there is an issue about spending even the few hundred dollars required for an individual license or the several thousand dollars required for a site license (which is extremely economical for a large company if it is widely used), then a good way to demonstrate the games' effectiveness and impact is to do a trial. When some IBM trainers wanted to purchase *The Battle of the Brains* for their classroom training, they set up the game at a kiosk at one of their conferences. The kiosk attracted enough attention that they went ahead with the purchase, making the application available to the whole of IBM.

Game Templates II: Web-Based Templates

A second category of game templates are those that work over the Web, which can be used either stand-alone or as part of other Web-based training. games2train has a series of templates based on classic computer games such as *Solitaire, PacMan, Monopoly, Jeopardy!, Millionaire,* and *Space Invaders,* into which any question-based content can be added. These templates can be used with or without tracking. Nortel Networks, for example, has used these templates to communicate to employees worldwide its new strategy.

Custom-Designed Games—How to Create Them

While HTML, off-the-shelf, email, and template-based games are often a good way to start, you and your organization may already be beyond them for a number of reasons. For one, you may require learning beyond what the primitive, extrinsic game shells and email games provide. There may not be an appropriate off-the-shelf product available for your needs. Or, you may have a vision of an original, highly integrated game that will truly get the learners involved with your material. You may have an idea for how to adapt a particular consumer game you have seen to a training use. Or, you may have thought up a particularly clever original way to teach something through a game. In all of these instances, you require a custom-designed game.

There are many strategies for creating custom-designed games, and all of them involve reasonably large expenditures of time and money. Done right, however, the results can be spectacular. Before you start down the custom path, however, you should consider all of the following carefully.

Sine Qua Non's for Completing a Custom or Moderate-to-Large–Scale ($25,000 or more) Digital Game-Based Learning Project. Assume that you are a trainer who has been convinced by the preceding chapters (or, even better, by your own personal experience) that Digital Game-Based Learning would be an important addition to your training program. The following necessary conditions must hold in order for Digital Game-Based Learning to be successfully introduced into your company.

1. *There must be some "content" that management feels is absolutely critical to be learned.* Put differently, there has to be a strategic training need (see Chapter 13). There can be a variety of reasons for this

urgency. According to its former head of HR, Bankers Trust's management was "almost desperate" to convince the Fed that it was doing something to train the traders and salespeople in the details of the policies that had allegedly been violated. In the case of PricewaterhouseCoopers, changes in the law required that its auditors quickly learn the details of very complicated derivatives products to keep the firm competitive. At Nortel Networks, a change in strategic direction needed to be communicated to everyone in the firm as an urgent marketing priority. In the case of IBM, becoming a project-oriented firm was a strategic priority and it needed everyone in the firm to understand its version of project management. Other companies were hit by large lawsuit settlements stemming from not having done as much as they could to train people in certain areas (such as sexual harassment prevention) and top management wanted to avoid any such liabilities in the future. In the case of think3, learning was a barrier to its product's adoption by the marketplace. Today, in many companies, helping workers to quickly understand the basics of e-commerce is of great urgency.

It is very important to note that the impetus that leads to a Digital Game-Based Learning solution generally comes *not* from HR or "training," but from market forces that are important to various arms of the company. Sometimes it is the "line," but just as often it is an internal or external *marketing* need. What this means is that just developing a game to train on subject matter from the HR or corporate university catalog is typically not a good way to go. A specific, urgent learning need has to emerge.

2. *The "content" or subject matter of this urgent learning needs must be "boring," "complex" or "difficult."* That is, it must *not* be something that normally motivated employees would go out and learn by themselves to do their jobs better. (Despite training hype, how many workers really *ever* do this, apart from a few very highly motivated "comers.") A subject is a good candidate for Digital Game-Based Learning either because it is dry, dull, or technical (the politically correct terms for boring), or because it is extremely complex and difficult to learn (like financial derivatives), or because it must be repeatedly practiced to be done correctly on a reflex basis (such as courtroom objection, language, typing, or even what a manager says

in various situations). For example, you probably don't need a game to teach people to use the new handheld-based email system that they've been awaiting eagerly for six months, but a game is very effective for teaching the somewhat arcane, complex, Graffiti writing system that requires some practice to master. That is why *Giraffe*, a game for learning Graffiti, comes bundled with every Palm Pilot.

3. *The population to be trained must be one that is likely to be amenable or susceptible to a game-based approach, or, if the population is diverse, to a variety of game-based approaches.* The target population for *The Monkey Wrench Conspiracy* was engineers and engineering students, 20 to 30 years old, 98 percent of whom were male. These were people known for being heavy video game players, and so using a video game, and even a strongly male-oriented *Quake*-style game, was appropriate. If one were dealing with a population in their forties or fifties, a game-based solution would either have to consist of games they play—*Jeopardy!*, golf, and so on—or no game at all. The target population for Bankers Trust's derivatives policy training was 25- to 35-year-old traders and sales people of both sexes, many of whom actually played commercial computer games on their machines at work to unwind after the markets closed.

4. *There must be a person in the organization (possibly you) who is willing to push a custom Digital Game-Based Learning project through all the difficult stages involved in getting it done.* These include getting approvals at many levels, creating and securing budget, and gathering resources, both human, such as content experts, and physical. Sometimes just finding space to put a team is a big problem. Other difficulties can include setting up focus groups, working with IT, working with one or multiple vendors, finding volunteer testers, and so on. Almost everyone I talked to who took on this project manager or "producer" role described it as "fun" or even "one of the best things I've done at work." Yet, some of those same people would admit that it may not have been the best choice from the point of view of advancing a "normal" career.

5. *There must be at least one highly placed executive sponsor for the project.* This must be an executive who both "gets it," that is, believes that Digital Game-Based Learning is the best way to reach the audience in question, *and* who has the organizational clout to secure the budget,

to overcome objections by other executives, and to make it happen. Although they may have the interest, generally this sponsor will not have the time to follow the project on a close basis, so they will have to be someone who trusts you, the project manager, to do it right. You will need them to intervene on your behalf when particular resources—such as valuable content experts—are needed, and to run interference when other executives threaten to kill the project, or, possibly worse, mutate it in more traditional learning directions that you know are incompatible with effective Digital Game-Based Learning.

If all of these conditions obtain in your situation, then you have a fighting chance of creating something good. What do you do now? At this point, you can go directly to Chapter 13 to learn how to convince management and get the money.

Consultant-Provided Games

Should you be interested in using or experimenting with Digital Game-Based Learning but lack the time and staff to do the research yourself, or should you feel the need for additional handholding, using a consultant may be a good route to take.

More and more consultants (as opposed to vendors of specific products) offer "turnkey" Digital Game-Based Learning solutions as part of their offerings. This runs the entire gamut of possibilities. Consultants can create the questions and answers for simple games and can fill in the templates for template-based reviews and reinforcement games. They can include these games at a live training session or put them on your Web site. Consultants can help you find off-the-shelf games, and sometimes even customize them for your organization. And consultants can help you find and manage the providers who will create custom Digital Game-Based Learning for you.

In most, if not all, of these cases, the consultants act as intermediaries between you and the vendors, evaluating products, knowing what's out there, and in many cases, having their own licenses to the products that they can reuse in your context. Many can begin by showing you a variety of potential game styles, although you may be able to do much of this research on your own.

ASSESSING YOUR ORGANIZATION'S
GAME-BASED LEARNING STYLE

It is important to determine what kind of Digital Game-Based Learning is right for your organization. Obviously, every organization is going to have a variety of individuals, styles, and opinions. Although the love of games is universal, the specific games *an individual* likes are almost certainly tied to his or her culture and age, and other factors, such as gender. The games that appeal to each of us are very dependent on what we grew up with. Playing the games we grew up with comes naturally, but getting good at new ones, such as golf or *Tetris*, may require a major investment of our time and energy. There is also, as we have discussed, a wide variation in people's tolerance for mixing learning with fun, play, and games.

So, is there such a thing as the game-based learning "style" of an organization? Possibly, in the following sense: what will work in any organization is a function of what the users will enjoy, what the management will accept, and what all agree is effective.

We saw earlier that a good audience evaluation is a key to creating any Digital Game-Based Learning, and that this evaluation needs to consider factors such as:

- Homogeneity vs. heterogeneity
- Age mix (although this can be deceptive, e.g., in terms of "digital immigrants")
- Gender, which must also be seen in terms of Competitiveness

  From the point of view of management, factors to consider include:

- Age
- Attitude
- Tolerance for unconventional solutions
- Urgency of need
- Attitudes toward learning
- Corporate culture

And from the point of view of effectiveness, there are a number of measures, which are considered in Chapter 14.

While there is really no formula, it is important to think very carefully about the above factors in the context of your own organization's culture and pick something—either more or less aggressive—which is most likely to "fly." Assuming it is not wildly out of synch with their culture, people tend to like Digital Game-Based Learning when they try it. When they like it, they ask for more of it, so starting small and strategically is often a good idea.

It is also worth remembering that management's perceptions of what will appeal to its employees may be very different from what the employees themselves think. It often helps to use focus groups or other means to "get the voice" of the employees heard.

> **Contest 9:** How would you describe your organization's Digital Game-Based Learning style and why? Email your entries to *Contest9@twitch speed.com.*

FITTING DIGITAL GAME-BASED LEARNING INTO ANY BUDGET

If you are considering introducing Digital Game-Based Learning into an organization, in addition to the type and style appropriate for that organization, a key consideration is the budget that is realistically available. Organizations are structured in a variety of ways, with centralized training organizations having a lot or a little budgetary discretion, and budgets for individual courses or interventions ranging from literally zero (say for an established course that a trainer wants to liven up) to almost unlimited (say for the learning component of a CEO's or senior executive's highly strategic project).

To provide you with a guide, the following section lists what is available in the way of Digital Game-Based Learning at various price points, or, read conversely, what it will cost to get a particular Digital Game-Based Learning project completed.

Budget Range: $0

There are many trainers who would love to do some Digital Game-Based Learning but who have *literally* nothing to spend. If you are one of those, what can you do? A lot, it turns out. Among the learning games available for free are:

- Promotional games, such as Ameritrade's *Darwin*
- PowerPoint-based games that you create such as a *Jeopardy!*-style game
- Demo games that can be used once, or for a limited period on an evaluation basis[6]

Budget Range: $100–$1,000

If you have a real, but very limited amount of budget to spend on a particular training project, don't despair; this amount brings you into the range of some of the learning templates or shells, albeit for single licenses, as well as simple internal projects. You can:

- Buy a single license to LearningWare's *Game Show Pro*
- Create simple Web-based question-and-answer or "trivia" game internally (see the Web site www.twitchspeed.com)
- Buy relevant consumer "boxed games" off the shelf

Budget Range: $1,000–$15,000

In this range, choices begin to expand. You can get

- Multiple and site licenses to templates
- Worldwide licenses to simple template games
- In-house—designed email games
- Simple games included in Web-based learning applications
- Consumer games modified to your needs via custom "mods"

Budget Range: $15,000–$100,000

In this range, choices expand even further. You can get:

- Worldwide licenses to templates from such companies as games2train and LearningWare
- Custom-designed email games
- Licenses to games built by other companies
- Prebuilt games included in other learning projects
- Modest, fully custom games from small custom developers

Budget Range: $100,000–$5,000,000

This is the budget range at which *custom* Digital Game-Based Learning projects are created. You can:

- Have a vendor modify one of its existing custom game to your needs
- Create custom Digital Game-Based Learning from scratch

It is certainly possible, and even desirable, to move up this ladder gradually, building positive feedback and experience as you go. If you are considering any of these, one place you might think of looking for support, budget, or distribution is your organization's "Corporate University." So, let us stop there for a second.

FITTING DIGITAL GAME-BASED LEARNING INTO CORPORATE UNIVERSITIES AND CURRICULA

Most of us prefer to walk backward into the future, a posture that may be uncomfortable but which at least allows us to keep on looking at familiar things as long as we can.
— Charles Handy

Corporate Universities have come into their own. These days nearly every large business organization has its own university, from McDonald's Hamburger University, to Motorola University, to Casket U for undertakers (no kidding).[7] Interestingly, this is happening just at a time when, because of the digital revolution, traditional universities are undergoing a huge rethinking of their missions and delivery mechanisms.

Corporate university approaches range from dedicated brick-and-mortar sites such as GE's Crotonville Executive Center, IBM's Palisades Learning Center, and Chase Manhattan's Executive Learning Center; to instructor-led training located in corporate classrooms; to instructor-led distance learning; to totally Web-based training on intranets and through outside vendors who provide courses on their own Web servers. Generally and increasingly, corporate universities include a smorgasbord of many of the above.

Do today's corporate universities include much Digital Game-Based Learning? Not really. Corporate universities are marching into the future with one foot (or in many cases two feet) firmly rooted in the past. Among the familiar things in a corporate university—online or not—are courses, instructors, course catalogs, classes (real or distance), tutors (in person or online), exams and degrees.

Where does Digital Game-Based Learning fit within corporate universities? At the moment, not very far. Sadly, there is not a lot of Digital Game-Based Learning in use. If any readers are aware of Digital Game-Based Learning projects, instances, or applications within corporate universities, I would appreciate your making me and the members of the community aware of this through the book's Web site, *www.twitch-speed.com*.

So, in the absence of examples to show, what I have decided to do is conduct a classic Einsteinian thought experiment. I will *create and describe* what Digital Game-Based Learning in a corporate university might look like. While much of this will be pure invention on my part, I will fill in the blanks wherever possible with real courses and approaches that already exist, and indicate where they are actually being used.

I originally thought of making up a fictional corporate university, which I was planning to call FunU, the corporate university of YRLWH, Inc., the "You'd Really Like Working Here Corporation" (pronounced YORELWAH). (You can see my brain was already leaping to game design—I may return to this later.) YRLWH, as its awkward name indicates, was to be an old-fashioned, 1980s-style conglomerate, with businesses in the manufacturing, service, financial services, health care, high tech, and consulting industries. It was going to employ a variety of people, but with its ranks increasingly being filled from the younger generations, and each year the average age of its employees skewed downward. And the director of its corporate university, *FunU* was going to be a 20-year-old.

But, as with so many things these days, it turned out that I needed to look no further than my computer screen to find a *real* corporate university curriculum. When I mentioned to Martha Gold, editor of the *Corporate University Newsletter*, what I was looking for, she said, "funny you should ask," and graciously pointed me to ColdwellBankerU, which had just put its entire curriculum online! I will, therefore, use Coldwell-BankerU as my example: first as a "thank you" to Coldwell Banker for putting it up there; second, because it is real; third, because it is online;

and fourth, because it is probably representative of a wide range of corporate universities in that it has courses that are about general skills and about company/industry information.

My goal here is in no way to criticize—I applaud Coldwell Banker for putting its catalog online and providing education to all of its farflung network of brokers. My point is that going forward more and more of Coldwell Banker's new brokers will be coming from the Games Generations. This is just a result of demographics and aging. (Remember that magic age of 39 in 2000—every year it gets one year greater, so that in 6 years, the 45-year-old woman who goes back to work as a broker will be from the Games Generation!)

Here is the original ColdwellBankerU (CBU) catalog, which you can find, updated, at *www.cbu.com*. I have changed the hyperlinks to an outline to make it easier to read in book form. Under each underlined category are the "courses" in italics, and under each of these are the "classes" in each course. At CBU, each class can be purchased individually (some are free).

COURSES FROM THE COLDWELLBANKERU CATALOG

Live classes and events
(I have skipped these, which consist mostly of regional events.)

Agent Track
- *Marketing to Buyers*
  - Buyer and Seller Orientation Seminars
  - Classified Ads
  - Open Houses
- *Marketing to Sellers*
  - Expireds
  - For Sale by Owners
  - Cold Calling
- *Personal Promotion*
  - Farming
  - Referrals
  - Web Sites
- *Strategic Marketing*
  - Elements of Marketing Strategy
  - Competitive Factors in Strategic Marketing
- *Customer Service*
  - Fundamentals of Customer Service
  - Building the Service Foundation
- Writing the *Marketing Plan*
  - Writing a Marketing Plan: Phase I
  - Writing the Marketing Plan: Creative Strategy

- *Marketing Prep*
  - Analyzing the Market
  - Competitive Factors in Strategic Marketing
- *Marketing Management*
  - Marketing Management
  - Creating a Marketing Campaign

Life Skills
- *Achieving a Balance in Your Life*
  - Discovering Balance
  - Keeping Balance

Continuing Education
- *Agency* (rules, laws and ethics— rules and laws are different for each state)
- *Fair Housing* (laws are different for each state)

COLDWELL BANKER Classes
- *Discover the Difference*
- *Fast Start* (Coldwell Banker tools and systems)
  - Module 1   – Module 4
  - Module 2   – Module 5
  - Module 3   – Module 6

(continued)

(continued) COURSES FROM THE COLDWELLBANKERU CATALOG

Technology
- *Top Producer 1* (a software program)
  - Introduction to Top Producer
  - Setting up Top Producer
- *Top Producer 2*
  - Top Producer Basic Data Entry
  - Top Producer Advanced Data Entry
- *Lightning CMA Plus* (a software program)
  - Introduction Lightning CMA Plus
- *Lightning CMA Plus 2*
  - Building a CMA from Scratch
  - Modify an Existing CMA
- *Microsoft Office*
  - Microsoft Office Basics
  - Microsoft Word
  - Microsoft PowerPoint
  - Microsoft Outlook
  - Microsoft Excel

Broker/Manager
- *Management Fundamentals*
  - Competencies for Tomorrow's Managers

- Development Tools for Tomorrow's Managers
- *Managing Diversity*
  - Corporate Culture and Diversity
  - Management Skills for the Diverse Work Force
  - Create a CMA by Dialing
- *Coaching Techniques*
  - Tips for Effective Coaching
  - Implementing the Coaching Model
- *Leadership Fundamentals*
  - The Mark of a Leader
  - Communicating a Shared Vision

Communication
- *Communication Skills for Business*
  - Communicate to Increase Understanding
  - Listening, Influencing and Handling Tough Situations

Free Classes (a mix from the above)

Let me take each of these categories in turn and speculate as to how Digital Game-Based Learning might be used.

The first, *Agent Track*, is an easy one. If it hasn't already been done (and a quick check of the Web suggests it hasn't), it is certainly possible to create an exciting, multiplayer simulation game, with a strong online component, about selling residential real estate. There already exist games for commercial real estate—*Sim Tower* is one such game, and others exist as well. Many, many game models exist for business startups in particular industries: *Airport Tycoon* and *Start-up* from Monte Cristo come immediately to mind, as does, in a different way, *Angel Five. Airport Tycoon* and *Start-up*, which are economic business simulations with game interfaces, you, the player, are starting up and running a business.

A real estate game like this could certainly cover all the marketing courses in the catalog: creating a marketing strategy, writing a marketing plan, and managing the process. (There is always *Strategy Co-Pilot* by Imparta as well, in case you have trouble with the strategic aspects.) You would learn by doing, with plenty of references and guides to help you along the way. You would use the actual tools available, so those courses would be covered as well. Of course, you would be competing with other brokers playing online. This could easily be a persistent world, just like the real one, so if you don't get that listing or sell that house, somebody else will. Predators, mentors, and alliances could be part of the picture.

In the *Angel Five*-like part of the game, you would get down to the nitty-gritty of actually going out and marketing yourself, visiting homes, and conducting open houses. Here you could meet or even create real people, and see how they respond to your efforts. Not just a series of fixed branching scenarios; modern game techniques allow thousands of different customers and conversations with infinite replay value, plus, you would have real people online. As you build customers, you would need to learn to improve and keep up your customer service.

Two questions one might justifiably ask here are: Why would anyone take the trouble and cost to do this? and Would anyone play? A third question is: Would they learn anything? One great reason to build such a game is strategic. Companies are always competing for people; real estate is no exception. People, especially today's young people, go where they think they can make money and where they will have fun. In our competitive job market, companies are increasingly finding games useful as recruiting tools. Telling a prospective employee who is 20-years-old, "you'll learn the job via a great online simulation game" may be a lot more effective than telling him or her, "you'll have to take nine or ten online courses." A second strategic reason is marketing. The game could be constructed in such a way that by playing it prospective customers would learn a lot about buying and selling real estate—what to do, what not do, how a good agent works with them, and so on. So, the simulation could be learning and practice for buyers and sellers, that is, *customers*, as well. "Oh, you're looking for your first home? You should play Coldwell Banker's *SimFirstHouse*," or some such. CDs can be sent out by mail in an AOL-type campaign. (Ameritrade sent out over 300,000 discs to its customers; think3, a small company, has shipped out close to 1 million discs.)

Would people play? Yes, if it's a good game and it gets a good "rep." Word of mouth is key. Following the think3 strategy, the game could be given for free to all teachers of real estate, who could include it in their courses. There can be both intrinsic rewards (you see your own wealth grow, as in *Sim City*) and extrinsic ones, such as prizes.

An issue that one might want to address here is the question of gender—a large percentage of real estate agents, if not the majority, are women. Would they play this type of game? Well these are *not* the macho shoot-'em-up games that women complain about. At business schools, which now have a student body that is roughly 50 percent female, the women do simulations right along with the men. So, it is highly likely that this type of game, done well, would appeal to both sexes.

Life Skills

The life skills courses offered here, *Discovering and Keeping Balance in Your Life*, are exactly what *The Sims*, right off-the-shelf, is about. In fact, each sim has a little meter that measures the balance in that character's life along several dimensions. This game might be able to be used as-is as part of the course, or with some small modifications to fit the life of a real estate broker. Online coaches or interplayer chat could help debrief and clarify the situations in the game.

Continuing Education

Continuing education in the real estate brokerage business means learning the agency rules and laws as well as the fair housing rules and laws for the particular state or states in which you are doing business. Again, a Digital Game-Based Learning solution already exists—nothing new has to be created here other than entering the appropriate content. Online and CD-ROM-based certification games have been specifically designed for this type of learning. One example is the "Classic Game Certifier" series from games2train. The player gets to choose from a variety of games, including *Solitaire*-style, *Jeopardy!*-style, *PacMan*-Style, *Millionaire*-style, board-game-style, and *Tetris*-style, as the method for getting their certification by answering questions about the rules correctly.

Coldwell Banker Classes

The Coldwell Banker classes are about using proprietary Coldwell Banker systems and approaches to selling residential real estate. They consist of several modules, each of which has a number of scenarios. It would not be hard to put these scenarios into a game that would let an agent confront the situations as realistically as possible. One possibility might be a game such as *Saving Sergeant Pobletti*, in which you start out in a terrible situation and then have to go back and remake a series of decisions in order to fix it.

Technology

The Coldwell Banker technology section consists of two parts—learning two real estate-based systems, and the Microsoft Office suite of programs, customized, potentially, in a real estate sense. The learning of computer programs through games has already been demonstrated: *The Monkey Wrench Conspiracy* has engineers learn a very complex piece of software by doing tasks in the actual software that are needed to win the game. It would certainly be possible to create such a game for the real estate software, and for the Microsoft software as well. Such a game would be very helpful in that the tasks involved could be highly customized to the needs of the brokers, and could even vary depending on each broker's competence and experience.

Broker/Manager

This section consists of management skills: management fundamentals, managing diversity, coaching techniques, and leadership fundamentals. In all of these areas, Digital Game-Based Learning solutions exist in one form or another. Coaching, for example, is covered in great detail with the engaging gamelike interactive movie structure of Ninth House Networks' *Situational Leadership* Course.

Communication

The final course, *Communications Skills for Business,* involves classes in listening effectively and in listening, influencing, and handling tough situations. This is tailor-made for a game. Who wouldn't prefer to have tough situation after tough situation thrown at them in a safe environment to see how well they could handle them? There are several games and game styles that do this. One is a game template from games2train called *Conversations,* that lets you create simple models of effective and ineffective conversations over the Web. Many custom games include role-playing sequences in which you must choose the proper responses in a branching "tree" structure, in order to reach a particular goal (e.g., close a sale), or come to a successful resolution with difficult customers. A piece of this process that is less frequently incorporated but that has the potential to be a lot of fun, is to get to play the opposite side—the irate or difficult customer, the unreasonable person who won't listen or budge—and see what it takes to convince you. The ultimate opportunity here is the multiplayer game, in which the players all have different roles and the communication is live, with feedback and coaching either through AI or a live coach.

LEARNING MANAGEMENT SYSTEMS AND DIGITAL GAME-BASED LEARNING

We are now in the stage of putting pieces of the online corporate learning infrastructure together. Important pieces of this infrastructure are Learning Management Systems (LMS) and Content Management Systems (CMS).

It is important to realize that, although some adaptation may have to be done, there is no inherent conflict at all between these systems and Digital Game-Based Learning. Learning games can output data just as any other digital learning application can, and, with the proper attention, they can fit into any system. The requirements of such systems should, however, be understood when undertaking any customized Digital Game-Based Learning project. As standards come into place for these systems, the vendors of Digital Game-Based Learning will surely adopt them.

CONCLUSION

Any trainer, in any organization, can use Digital Game-Based Learning. How quickly you can get started with Digital Game-Based Learning depends mainly on your aspirations. If they are modest, you can begin almost immediately. If you aspire to the state-of-the-art, or to even to push that state even further such as with a Digital Game-Based Learning Corporate University, it will take you—let's be honest—a great deal of effort and up to a year or more of your time. But pretty much all who have gone the route—creators, organizations, and sponsors—feel it was well worth it and would like to do more. In most, if not all, cases, both internal and external rewards have accrued. Both learners and management have been satisfied. Prizes have been won. Other organizations have appreciated—and in some instances even purchased—the end results.

In Chapter 13 I will show you how to convince management and obtain the budget to do a Digital Game-Based Learning project. But before I do, let me address another key element of the process, the role of teachers and trainers.

12

The Roles of Teachers and Trainers in Digital Game-Based Learning
Digital Game-Based Instruction

Teaching itself, as we know it, doesn't fit the world we now inhabit.
— Edward L. Davis III, Designs for Learning

Any teacher who can be replaced by a computer, should be.
— The Aging Sage

I am not a teacher but an awakener.
— Robert Frost

In many ways, this is the most important chapter in this book. If Digital Game-Based Learning is ever to really succeed, trainers and teachers *must* be behind it. Of course, demographic forces are inevitable. "People die," I remember Bill Gates saying in his more arrogant days when asked how Microsoft was going to deal with older computerphobes. Change *will* eventually come as the Games Generations take their turn at running the world. But temporary blocking strategies are certainly possible on the one hand, and, conversely, there is much that can be done to speed Digital Game-Based Learning on its way. A great deal of this depends on the attitude of teachers and trainers.

Teachers and trainers do not have an easy job. I know, having been both. For 4 years I taught math in a New York City public high school.[1] In the late 1980s and early 1990s, I worked at a small training firm in Boston.[2] In both cases, the hard part was never *what* to teach. That was either proscribed, or not too hard to figure out. The real struggle was always *how to do it*—how to *hold the attention* of people who were usually convinced that they had better things to do than to be in your classroom.

Getting inner city kids to focus on math problems was tough. We tried to make the problems relevant, but that didn't help much. What did help was fun. We used as many toys and games as we could (Cuisenaire rods, competitions, etc.) to motivate the learners. We used all the games we could think of, but they had to be invented each time. There was certainly nowhere we could send the kids to practice math in a fun way on their own.

At that time (1968), personal computers hadn't been created yet, and there were no computers of any type in schools. There were, however, computers in universities. I worked with a project at Dartmouth that attempted to teach our kids the rudiments of BASIC programming—line numbering, RUN, GOTO, STOP, and so on. Although interesting to me, this stuff was pretty abstract and irrelevant to my students, especially because they couldn't see the results of their programs. The project was not very successful. We were too early. Today, I could certainly interest those kids in computer programming by using programs such as *LEGO Mindstorms* or LTI's *Robot Club.*

My experience as a trainer came at the time that the microcomputer (principally the IBM PC) was entering businesses, and most senior executives had a need to learn to use spreadsheets on the computer. Here finding relevance was much easier—our approach was to create spreadsheet models of the executives' actual businesses that they could then modify. But even with this, holding participants' attention was still a big issue, and games such as *Spreadsheet BINGO, Find the Microprocessor,* and so on, were a big part of our process. Later, as much of our training moved to networks and then to the Web, the problem remained the same. How to keep people staring at the screen.

Again, we were early. Today, I could and would organize networked competitions, games, or "death matches" around whatever subject matter I wanted them to know.

LEAVING PLEASANTVILLE

But if a few others and I were ahead of our time, many more were, and still are, far behind. Recently, I gave a speech at a number of training conferences entitled "Leaving Pleasantville—Getting Beyond Tell-Test." The 1998 movie *Pleasantville*,[3] turns out to be a great way to highlight some behaviors that prevent trainers from moving to the world of their trainees. The movie is about a 1958 sitcom world where everything is always the same, and, well, *pleasant*. Bud and his sister Jen, teenagers who live in contemporary 1998, are sucked into the TV, and unexpectedly find themselves actually *inside* the 1958 sitcom. Because this is before color TV, everyone and everything in Pleasantville is in black and white, which, of course, seems perfectly normal to them. Not only that, but the people of Pleasantville *enjoy* doing everything in their lives over and over, exactly the way it's always been done.

LOGO FROM THE MOVIE *PLEASANTVILLE*.

Jen finds this horrible and says, "We're stuck in Nerdsville—we're supposed to be in color." And the two begin breaking the rules, encouraging the people they meet to do things in new ways—their own ways. Jen gives her repressed mother a few lessons on self-gratification, and shows the captain of the basketball team what lovers' lane is *really* for. David encourages the guy at the soda shop to do things in a different order. Miraculously, as some of the people of Pleasantville do these new things, colors begin to appear in their lives.

The old timers of Pleasantville hate and fear these appearances of color in their midst, and the changes that they represent. The changes threaten their very way of life and disrupt everything they've been doing everyday for their whole lives. But the people who've experienced the changes *like* them, and don't want to go back. When they start doing new things and asking dangerous questions, such as, "What's outside of Pleasantville?," the townspeople rise up and try to stop the invasion. "It's a question of values," says the mayor. "It's a question of whether we want to hold on to those values that made this place great." They try establishing a code of conduct ("The only colors allowed will be black, white, and gray..."), but to no avail—the future has arrived. By the end of the movie, Technicolor has come to Pleasantville, and people are learning to live with uncertainty. George: "Do you know what's going to happen now?" Betty: "No, I don't. Do you?" George: "I don't either...."

Despite our best intentions, the fact is that a huge percentage of our teaching and training is still happening "in Pleasantville," and many of our teachers and trainers are very much like the people of Pleasantville before David and Jen showed up. The comparison is an easy and humorous one to make:

- You can generally tell a Pleasantville trainer by the way he or she speaks. If you meet one, in introducing themself they'll probably use phrases such as, "In this conversation, you will learn three things about me." And as you leave, they'll tell you again exactly what you've learned about them.

- Pleasantville trainers go pretty slowly—you'll never see them moving at the twitch speed of, for example, a video game or MTV. They tend to go step by step; doing things in a logical order is very important to them. And, of course, they *never* leave anything out, because they never want to be accused of not covering all the material.

- Pleasantville trainers are very text-oriented. One of their greatest loves is *PowerPoint* slides with lots of words on them, especially if they are arranged into lots of logical bullet points. In fact, given half a chance, a Pleasantville trainer will insist on reading to you *every* word on *every* slide.

- Pleasantville trainers like to see everything arranged neatly: into courses, lessons, and modules. They *love* outlines. They have heard of random access, but think it means going anywhere in an outline.

- The greatest love of Pleasantville trainers is video, which is not surprising as so many of them are from the 1950s. They will use video wherever they possibly can. Being from Pleasantville, they don't have much experience with MTV, so *their* video is mostly talking heads.

- Pleasantville trainers generally classify their trainees according to an old system invented by two other Pleasantvillers, Mr. Meyers and Mr. Briggs.[4] Many of them think that is the *only* way to classify people and that *all* people fit into these classifications. They certainly don't think that people might possibly change radically from generation to generation, because in their world, people never do.

- Most of all, Pleasantville trainers love to tell. They thrive on "laying out material," and then reading it to you. "If there something to be learned, let me tell you about it" is their motto. Of course, to check whether you were listening, Pleasantville trainers follow up with a test. And curiously enough, they think you can almost always equate a grade on that test with learning and job performance. Pleasantville is the true home of tell-test learning.

- Pleasantville trainers are not *totally* cut off from the outside world; in the last few years, the World Wide Web has even made it to Pleasantville training. And on the Web the Pleasantville trainers have put their 1950s-style tell-test learning just as fast as they possibly can. That text, graphics, and video can come down telephone wire just gives them another way to do the same old Pleasantville stuff.

- Frowned upon—even banned—in Pleasantville is learning totally randomly, with no logic at all. Pleasantville trainers haven't a clue how their kids learned so much about computers without ever taking a logical course!

- Also not very well thought of in Pleasantville are fantasy and play. If you are a trainee in Pleasantville, no matter how many hours you may have spent in front of your video games, you will find yourself constantly accused of having "the attention span of a gnat." The Pleasantville trainers find little use in their training for the skills you have so painstakingly acquired. So, trainees shouldn't expect to have a lot of fun at Pleasantville training. The sarcasm and "attitude" trainees love and share with their friends is best left home unpacked.

- Trainees might be thrown an occasional fun bone in Pleasantville training—possibly a *Jeopardy!*-style game—in sessions labeled "review and reinforcement." In general, however, the learning process in Pleasantville is pretty dull and serious.

My point is not just to poke fun. While the comparison is true for many trainers and not true for many others, *this kind of training once worked—when the Pleasantville trainers were trainees*. But as in the movie, change has come to the Pleasantville trainers in the form of new people to train. David and Jen, sucked in from the Technicolor future, see Pleasantville as "nerdsville" and they break the rules, inserting elements of their own "real-world" existence into the Pleasantville life: random access, desire, sexuality, danger, modern art, and new kinds of fun.

Remember, as the people of Pleasantville accept these new things into their lives, their life begins to take on color. In the end, the whole world moves into Technicolor, despite all its newness and uncertainty, partly because it's better, but mainly *because it's reality*.

NEW ROLES FOR TRAINERS AND TEACHERS

I was initially a skeptic [about Digital Game-Based Learning]. But I changed 180 degrees.
— Katheryn Komsa, Corporate Training Manager

Any trainer or teacher who has their eyes open knows that their world is rapidly changing, and few, if any, know what's going to happen next. While many trainers and teachers eagerly embrace, and even seek out, new approaches such as Digital Game-Based Learning as something their students need, many others express skepticism. This is reflected in such frequently asked questions as, "How do I know it works?" and "Don't we need face-to-face time?" Behind many of these questions lies a deeper concern and fear that is much less often vocalized: "If Digital Game-Based Learning comes, will I know how to use it?"

Most trainers are not "gamers," although this is gradually changing. Remember, the principal role of many (though not all) trainers until now has been filling three-ring binders with *PowerPoint* slides and being "sages on the stage." With Digital Game-Based Learning (and probably even without it) these particular roles will eventually disappear—it *is* a new world and there are different functions that trainers and teachers will have to perform. But the really *good news* for trainers and teachers is that the roles required of trainers and teachers using Digital Game-Based Learning are really not new for them at all—most of them have been playing all of these roles already, in one way or another, for some time. Let's look at these "new" roles one by one.

"New" Role #1: Motivator

We spoke about motivation earlier in terms of games—not people. But the ability to get students engaged in learning, as opposed to just throwing content at them, has always been a big part—if not the only part—of what makes a teacher or trainer great, rather than just ordinary.

Part of this is *style*. A great teacher will do practically anything to motivate. Elliot Masie describes his Shakespeare professor up on the desk (see below). Arthur Miller, the distinguished Harvard Law Professor, has been known to come to class in a dress. My favorite college history teacher told jokes that were typically a little bit naughty. The great teacher keeps students on the edge of their seats, off balance, waiting for the next thing to happen.

Another piece is *passion*. Great teachers communicate their passion by painting vivid pictures of new vistas and possibilities. They don't teach you, they *will you to learn*. The movies are rich with stories of great passionate teachers, with exciting roles played by actors such as Anne Bancroft, Sidney Poitier, Robin Williams, and Richard Dreyfuss. The source of this passion is often the content itself; seeing what is already there through the teacher's eyes motivates students. Teachers who show us this are often, as Robert Frost describes himself, "awakeners."

Training could certainly use some more awakeners other than coffee. But, unfortunately, company policy is not *King Lear*. Michael Allen says "there is no such thing as boring content, only boring presenters," and that instructional designers "have to see the fascinating element."[5] He's right in reminding us that a big part of motivation has always been *presentation*. And a lot of corporate training content, let's face it, is tough to present. Yet, no matter *what* the content, one method of presentation has always been particularly effective and useful to teachers and trainers—people naturally gravitate towards fun and games. In a pre-Digital Game-Based Learning world, trainers often turned to the humor of John Cleese's training films as motivators.[6] If you've ever seen one, compare its motivating power to a standard talking-head corporate video. Lockheed put Dilbert and Dogbert into its ethics training videos for just this reason.[7] This works great for the TV generation.

But now we are facing the need to train *interactive* generations of learners—the Games Generations. What kinds of presentations motivate *them*? We have already seen how and why games do. At least one form of motivational presentation appealing directly to the Games Generations is available to trainers and teachers—Digital Game-Based Learning.

But it's one thing to say that, and another to figure out exactly *what* useful games are out there and *how* to actually use them to teach the necessary content and curriculum. So, while a big role of the future trainer and teacher is still that of *motivator*, what that means in a world of Digital Game-Based Learning will change somewhat. The part that involves understanding students and steering them in the most engaging direction will still be there. However, *what they get steered toward* will be different. It will increasingly be learning games, and choosing the right ones for the mix of the content and the students' level, age, sex, and personality will always be a challenge, even as there are more to choose from and computer-based tools arise to make this easier.

"New" Role #2: Content Structurer (Integrator/Reformulator)

One of the things that many creators of Digital Game-Based Learning have repeatedly found is that the way content must be presented to be effective in Digital Game-Based Learning is very different than the way is has been presented traditionally. I'm not just talking about "chunking" content, or turning content into "learning objects." In many instances, completely new forms of organization and direction often need to be created. Doing this is exciting work, one that trainers are often well suited for, once they get their minds around it. In my and others' experience, getting content providers and designers to get their minds around these new learning structures is often one of the hardest tasks in Digital Game-Based Learning—and the most time-consuming. But once they do get it, they are on a roll and enjoying the process, which is an intellectual challenge.

Examples of what I am taking about include:

- For *In$ider*, they had to invent a new learning process that they later dubbed "structured discovery."

- For *Darwin*, they had to invent a system of simulation markets, a process for which they later applied for a patent.
- For *The Monkey Wrench Conspiracy*, the traditional learning process for software based on features needed restructuring in terms of tasks. Conceptual explanations had to be reduced from several minutes to less than 30 seconds.
- For *Angel Five*, potential paths had to be analyzed so that plausible scenarios could be created on the fly.
- For *Straight Shooter!*, content traditionally presented as "policy" had to be reformulated in terms of questions and scenarios.

Again, some of this is already what trainers do when creating content for various types of online training. However, in the case of Digital Game-Based Learning, this often goes much further, often going against traditional methods and turning traditional concepts of instructional design on their heads. Trainers who are open to reconsidering the best ways to present content have a big role to play in Digital Game-Based Learning.

"New" Role #3: Debriefer

Elliott Masie tells a wonderful story about his first Shakespeare class at Stuyvesant High School in New York City.[8] The school is one of a number of specialized (public) high schools for the very gifted that draw top students from all over New York City based on a rigorous competitive entrance exam. Stuyvesant specializes in science and math. Many of its students could probably, without much objection, be classified as "geeks." Elliott, at least, freely admits he was one, and not particularly inclined to the arts or literature.

When Elliott walked into his Shakespeare class on the first day, the teacher was standing on top of the desk wrapped in a long black cape. As the bell rang the teacher threw some exploding firecrackers to the floor, making a big noise, and proceeded to recite the ghost scene from *Hamlet*. Dramatic? Absolutely. He had their attention. But then, as the class continued, he began to explain *why* he was doing what he did. In Masie's terms, he "debriefed" his performance. And this, says Masie, made it much stronger from a learning perspective.

This is the third "new" role of teachers with Digital Game-Based Learning: *Debriefer—helping students reflect on what is being learned*. For even if we are able to use Digital Game-Based Learning to motivate students to go through material, it's not always clear that they will leave with exactly the conclusions, mental models, and ideas that we want them to, or that they will be able to apply what they have learned to future situations. To do this they need to reflect, and the reflection part of Kolb's "Learning Loop"[9] is, and will remain an important role for teachers and trainers in Digital Game-Based Learning. Many are already combining Digital Game-Based Learning with live, instructor-led debriefings. The military holds debriefings after each of its simulated "missions," whether for groups of 8 or 8,000. After trainees at PricewaterhouseCoopers complete the *In$ider* game, they attend the "Academy" which is a live discussion and debriefing session.

Suppose that every student who showed up for training in entrepreneurship had already completed the game *Start-up*. Or, that every medical student beginning surgery had completed the brain surgery game *Life or Death*. This is already easily possible, because these are consumer games. Suppose, as will no doubt be the case in the future, every student came to the debriefing session—there *are* no more "telling" sessions—having completed, on his or her own own, *because it was fun*, Digital Game-Based Learning games in whatever the subject.

Why, you may ask, is this different from students doing *any* pre-work—reading, multimedia, or simulation? The answer is because they will actually do it. Did I do the required reading before my first year of Harvard Business School? Heck, no! I read a few pages of *My Years at General Motors* by Alfred P. Sloane and gave up; I had better ways to spend my summer. Ditto for the programmed accounting text they gave us. But suppose the prework had been to play *Roller Coaster Tycoon* and the assignment was to beat the game? Or, even better, a game just as much fun as *Roller Coaster Tycoon*, but geared toward particular principles they wanted to teach?

The role of the instructor is to ask the following kinds of questions, which every facilitator knows:

- What did you take away? What factors were important in winning?
- What assumptions were built into the game?
- What was realistic? What was not?

Even as more and more "reflection" opportunities get built into Digital Game-Based Learning—as they undoubtedly will—the live debrief will remain an integral part of the learning process. This can only make the trainer's job better—it is certainly a lot more interesting than "telling."

"New" Role #4: Tutor (Individualizer, Steerer, Selector, Adjuster, Guide, Facilitator)

One of the great opportunities that both technology-based learning in general and Digital Game-Based Learning, its "fun" instantiation, provides us, is the opportunity to customize and individualize learning to each learner. As we progress, increasing amounts of this control will be built in to the games to be set by the player. Just as today's games have difficulty levels that players can set, there will be user-settable controls for a variety of things—pace, language, style—and even, as I have hypothesized, for the mix of *edu* and *tainment*. However, this does not remove the fact that there are always things that an outside observer of a learner can customize best. In his description of the Apple Classroom of the Future, James Lengel wrote that even though technology is ubiquitous, "teachers guide and facilitate learning. They organize and direct the entire learning experience of their students. They actively coach them through their work. They set objectives and accept responsibility for their student's progress. Teachers are the center of the learning process and the life of the school."[10]

The most effective model for learning is the tutor. Researchers have found that even average tutors could increase the learning speed and retention of students by two standard deviations and that they would learn better than 98 percent of the students in the classroom environment.[11] While "adaptive" learning games will become more "tutorlike" in the future, sensing more and more of the player's situation from his or her responses and adjusting accordingly, a human is still best at seeing exactly why a learner may be having difficulty.

"New" Role #5: Producer/Designer

Which brings us to the final, and perhaps the most crucial, role of the trainer in Digital Game-Based Learning—that of producer/designer.

Almost all trainers and teachers, I think, have a strong sense of what their students enjoy and what they would enjoy if they could get it, even though their ideals may rarely get realized. I know from talking and working with many trainers and teachers that among their ideas to engage their students are many types of games—sometimes based on the games they see their own children playing—and sometimes on games they play themselves. "If only I could make them this" is a thought that many trainers and teachers, I'm sure, have often had. Well, today, in more and more cases, they can. As the many examples in this book show, trainers in all industries and types of companies have created—on their own or with teams—the Digital Game-Based Learning of today. This will only increase in the future.

WHY TEACHERS AND TRAINERS WILL MAKE LEARNING GAMES

OK, you say, that's great. I can see how some really creative great thinkers could do that. But I'm not one. I'm a trainer or teacher who just wants to do the best job I can—what can I contribute to making learning games? The answer is *everything you know*. What you have to contribute is *all that you have learned in however long you have been doing your job.*

I am convinced that we will get to a learner-centered training and schooling world, and that many, many trainers and teachers will create learning games. Why? Because the knowledge is there already, and, increasingly, the *tools* to make games will be there as well. Given such tools, will trainers and teachers make learning games? After all, authoring systems are out there to make training modules, yet most trainers don't use them.

I believe many will, for the following reason. Suppose you are a good (or even a great) committed trainer or teacher. You are not just a writer of bullet slides or repetitive lesson plans; you have something to say and a special way to get it across and share your knowledge and passion. If you teach, you get to communicate that to thirty kids in a year. If you train, maybe you get to a couple of thousand people, tops.

If you make a game, however—and that game is *really* engaging—you can share it with every kid, or every trainee in your field, in the United States and possibly the entire world! Why is this different from making a videotape or creating an online course, you might ask? The answer lies in the *engagement* factor. Most videotapes and online courses are just more boring tell-test, and do not generate wide demand, if they generate any, outside of their initial audience. This is because it's not just the content that motivates people—in fact, in most cases it's hardly the content at all. It's the presentation. If you are a great comedy actor, like John Cleese, you can make hilariously funny training movies. If you are a great motivational speaker like Zig Ziglar, or an inspiring lecturer like John Kenneth Galbraith, you can make motivational audio and video-tapes. If you are a big name, like Peter Drucker, you can create almost anything and people will listen to you. And if you are a great writer, like Gore Vidal, you can tell stories that will pull people in. But most of us can't do any of the above.

However, if you are a great—or even a good—trainer or teacher, it is not *at all* out of the question that you can think up a *game* as a way of sharing your thinking and approach in a fun, engaging way. In fact, you may have already done so! Most trainers and teachers can leap immediately to seeing their material in *Jeopardy!, Family Feud,* or *You Don't Know Jack*-type formats. The jump to learning-oriented simulation-type games such as *JFE (Joint Force Employment)* or role-playing games such as *In$ider,* is often not much of a leap. Or to a "reflex" speed/practice game, such as *Objection!* Or even to a simple "learn these ten points" or "learn these acronym" games such as *Scout Law.*[12] You've probably already seen some consumer game and said to yourself: "That would be great for my training."

Could most teachers or trainers make a game about their particular way of presenting things? If we give them the tools, you bet! Many already have (see Chapter 15). Most of the work—Paula Young would say 80 percent—is in the *design,* not the execution, anyway. Create a great design for a learning game and you'll almost certainly get it built. So start thinking!

The most interesting thing to me about the five "new" roles of the Digital Game-Based Learning trainer is that the roles are *not very different from what trainers do today.* The differences lie mainly in means and in priorities.

In today's training world, trainers who are given a specific training void to fill will typically first look inside the organization, scour the Web, and talk to vendors to see whether the *content* they need exists, and evaluate any competitive offerings along multiple criteria of usefulness, cost, and so on. If nothing exists, they will move to create the training they need, using whatever means are at their disposal—from slides to custom courses to online courseware development—that fit the budget and time frame. They will then make plans to for delivering that course or courseware and for tracking who has taken it. If the course includes a simulation in a live situation, there will likely be a debriefing, or reflection phase, as part of the process.

In the world I am describing—the Digital Game-Based Learning world—*motivation* comes first. Whatever the topic, the first questions asked are: How will I get my audience to focus on this? What motivation can I use? Do any games exist in this area? Do they fit my audience? Is this topic important enough to create one? Can I put the content into a game template? Can something existing be modified? Are there alternatives and other nongame ways of motivating those who many choose not to play?

The second priority is *reflection*: Is there a way, along with the engagement, for the learner to *think critically* about whatever it is that they do in the learning process. In some games, this will be built in. In others, live sessions, threaded discussions, individual voice or email coaching conversations, or even written assignments might be added to the process.

The third priority is *individualization*. How can I help steer this training in the best ways for each participant? Is there a choice of games for different styles? Are there alternatives for those who many choose not to play? Are there ways to have people move more quickly or slowly and adapt the training to their skill level? These types of parameters will soon be built into the various game alternatives that are available.

The fourth priority—to the extent that there is no way to do the above that meets the needs of the topic at hand—is *creation*. Here the model in Chapter 15 can be used to make a Digital Game-Based Learning solution that will serve both the immediate need and the probable needs of the future.

The *final* priority, after all the others have been considered, is the content (which has not, by the way, lost any of its importance, only its place in line). How can I obtain what I need and structure it in the ways that motivation, reflection, and individualization demand?

GETTING PRACTICAL

"Sure, all the great things you described may happen in the future," you retort, "and I actually support many of them. But I'm a trainer *today*. My department has shrunk and I'm feeling a lot of pressure to do more in less time. Yes, I'd like to do some Digital Game-Based Learning, but, hey, I'm just one person under a mountain of work, and my job, frankly, is to crank stuff out. What are you offering me to make my life *easier*—not to do more work?"

That's what *I* would ask as well. Here's the answer. Start gradually. Go back to Chapter 11. Figure out a *really simple way* to start that makes sense in your organization. Take one step—try it in one thing that you are teaching. Observe the reaction among your students, which is likely to be highly positive, making your job, in fact, easier. Make adjustments based on their feedback and try other things. Share the results with your colleagues and enlist allies (there may be others doing this already). Also, go to the book's companion Website (*www.twitchspeed.com*) and obtain copies of the high-end examples that are available. Study them and the examples provided here carefully for ideas. Buy and try some commercial games off-the-shelf. Then, when you are ready, find a project you want to do, that (1) you are really excited about; (2) that is important to the business you are in; and (3) that you think will really work and make a difference in your organization. Then read (and reread) the next chapter on how to get the bucks to do it!

13

Convincing Management and Getting the Bucks

Making the Business Case for Digital Game-Based Learning

If companies were smart enough to understand that training would have some life and death issues for them, perhaps they would think more about more creative directions.
— Mark Bieler, former head of HR, Bankers Trust Company

Not everything that counts can be counted, and not everything that can be counted counts.
— Sign hanging in Albert Einstein's office at Princeton

The difficulty lies not in the new ideas, but in escaping the old ones.
— John Maynard Keynes

WHAT'S THE PRICE TAG?

Before we can begin to make a business case, we need to know how much we are talking about. How much does Digital Game-Based Learning cost? The answer is an easy one—between $300 and $3 million. The lower figure is the cost of a one-user license for *Game Show Pro*. The latter is the cost to develop a military-scale project such as *Joint Force Employment* or *Fifth Angel*. That is, not surprisingly, also the cost to develop an average consumer game.

Let's get more specific:

- Classroom game shells cost hundreds of dollars for single licenses, $10 to $20,000 for corporatewide licenses.
- Web-based shells typically cost more, often up to $100,000 depending on sophistication, tracking, games chosen, and so on.

- Sophisticated email games from vendors can cost $75,000 and up.
- Custom-developed, relatively simple Web games typically cost between $50,000 and $100,000.
- Custom-developed consumer-style CD-ROM, Web, and/or massively multiplayer games cost between $1 and $3 million (or even more), although frequently up to half of this can be in-house resources rather than actual cash.

GETTING THE BUCKS

I will not claim that getting a budget to do Digital Game-Based Learning is easy; we are talking about an approach that is still struggling to be taken seriously both as a learning and a business proposition. But it *is* possible, as the large number of instances in this book and elsewhere have shown. In fact, budget for Digital Game-Based Learning is probably being approved somewhere, on average, just about every business day. (I say this because there are roughly 250 business days in a year, and I would guess, if Digital Game-Based Learning projects of all sizes and shapes are taken into account, far more than 250 are done each year.)

So let's say you're convinced that Digital Game-Based Learning has a place somewhere in your organization's training; now, how do you get the budget to get started? What does it take to convince management, skeptical or otherwise (and most are highly skeptical), to release *actual dollars* for a new way of doing things? A business case, of course. So let's talk about how to make one.

While a business case will usually contain some numbers, it is *not*—as many think—a quantitative document or argument. Most business decisions are made on *qualitative* judgments such as "given our objectives, is this the best course of action." Financial analysis is only one piece of that answer, and generally not the biggest one.

I suggest eight steps to building a business case for Digital Game-Based Learning:

1. Find a strategic use
2. Consider your audience
3. Find a champion
4. Pick a range
5. Do a preliminary design and build a prototype

6. Involve IT
7. Write an investment proposal
8. Overcome objections

Let's look at each of these.

1. Think Strategically!

In the end, there is only one good *strategic* argument for doing *any* training, and that is that doing it will *improve the business' market value*. This can happen by enabling the company to do something it currently cannot do that is important to the business' existence, profitability, or competitive position. Or, conversely, *not* doing it will erode the same and cause the market value to fall. If one cannot make the case that training will affect the company's market value, why do it?

When it becomes clear that this is the case—that particular training will affect the company's market value—suddenly finding money is never a problem. "How much will it take?" and "When can we get it?" are the only questions management asks. Here are some examples.

When Bankers Trust Company got into trouble with regulators over some of its employees' alleged misbehavior around derivatives policies, "We [i.e., the management committee of the corporation] were almost *desperate* to find a way to show the Fed we were doing a good job of training our people on the policies," according to Mark Bieler, former executive vice president and head of HR of the bank.[1] "We would have done almost anything to certify that these very smart, short-attention-span traders knew and understood the policies." What Bankers Trust did was create *Straight Shooter!*, a game for derivatives policies certification. The cost—which turned out to be roughly $500,000 in cash and $1 million overall—was never an issue.

When PricewaterhouseCoopers knew that its auditors would have to be able to handle derivatives better than its competitors or the company would lose business, money was made available for *In$ider*.[2] When the Polaroid Corporation thought that having its people perform along the principles of Total Quality Management would improve its strategic position, there were suddenly several millions of dollars available to spend on training.[3] The same occurred when Lexus decided better-trained dealers would produce more sales (or lose fewer to the competition);[4]

when FedEx realized its service had to be practically flawless to compete;[5] when Ford lost a sexual harassment case and needed to train all its plant workers;[6] when Lou Gerstner decided that IBM needed to become a project management organization;[7] and when the Joint Chiefs decided that military commanders had to follow joint force doctrine precisely to win battles.[8] Suddenly there were millions, or even tens of millions of dollars to be spent on training.

So, the first lesson in "getting the bucks" is this: Forget return on investment (ROI). Forget the four levels of training evaluation. Start from the strategic perspective of senior management. Find a training need that is strategic, and make your business case a strategic one.

Believe it or not, saving money is not necessarily a strategic reason. Most trainers and training vendors have at some point done the calculations that show that quite a lot of money can be saved by not sending people around the world to attend training sessions (trainees eat a lot, too, particularly at nice places). The savings are typically quite large and easily cover the cost of developing or buying technology-based training, with money to spare. But if management concludes that *strategically* the value of the people's getting together and communicating face-to-face is worth more than these savings, *it doesn't matter*.

The reason that—as trainers often bemoan—training is one of the first things to be cut in hard times for the company or economy is precisely this—most of it isn't strategic. It's nice to do in the same way that bonuses are nice to give, when you have the money.

This is why ROI, while not useless, is *not* the best business case to make when looking for money. ROI is a useful tool to help management *choose between* alternatives, but it has no bearing whatsoever on the strategic necessity of the alternatives.

Most of the traditional arguments used for training—our people will like it (Level 1), do better on tests (Level 2), behave differently (Level 3), or even improve the bottom line (Level 4)—along with ROI, the current champion, are not strategic arguments; instead they are *middle management* arguments. Of course, any training head, head of a corporate university, or other middle manager with a fixed budget, would like to see that budget go further and do more. But one of the facts that every vendor of training knows is that *middle management does not spend big bucks!* Five thousand dollars, $10,000, $50,000, and even $100,000, yes, but not numbers in the millions. Not without approval from upstairs.

So, we are looking for strategic reasons. A strategic reason is almost certainly not going to come from trainers or human resources, unless they are keen observers of the business (such as Paula Young foreseeing the changes in the accounting rules that necessitated *In$ider*). Strategic reasons for training will come only from the circumstances that the company finds itself in, and trainers need to be poised to take advantage of them. Strategic reasons for training include:

- Outside threats (the government is currently spending big bucks on training for dealing with potential terrorist attacks)
- New technologies (business is currently spending a lot on e-commerce training)
- Competitive moves
- Refocus on new businesses or new ways of doing business.

2. Consider the Audience

So in your quest to introduce Digital Game-Based Learning, you have been on the lookout for a highly strategic training initiative. And perhaps you have spotted one. Your next trick is to convince senior management that a Digital Game-Based Learning solution is the right way to spend those millions.

Here is where everything we have discussed in the previous chapters comes into play. If you propose a Digital Game-Based Learning solution to a strategic training need, you will have to address, repeatedly, clearly, and succinctly, a number of key questions that management will rightly ask, including:

- Why a game?
- Will it work?
- Will it trivialize the material or process?

You need to show why audiences have changed and why a game is now the best way to reach them. You will need to explain the structure of the game, compare it to others and to nongame alternatives, and explain why it will work. You will need to show how the content will be presented in a way that is not trivial.

**"Our business depends on your knowing this
and you want it to be *A GAME?*"
"That's how our generation learns, sir."**

It is helpful to have potential users involved at this point, possibly through focus groups. They can often provide valuable input for the investment proposal. Also be sure at least one person from the audience sits on your design committee. (You do have a design committee, don't you?) Showing examples of Digital Game-Based Learning to the focus groups and committees is a good way to get their interest up.

Of course, even if your audience is solidly behind you, you should still be aware that if your corporation is typical, it will take *months* of writing and rewriting investment proposals, convincing ever larger groups of people, getting higher and higher approvals, and navigating politics before you can stop biting your nails and get to work.

In Chapters 9 and 11 and in this chapter so far I have described in some detail the things that others and I have gone through to get Digital Game-Based Learning projects funded and off the ground. Now, let us consider the other six steps in the process.

3. Find a Champion

With the exception of the purchase of single-user licenses to small game shells or other small-budget projects, there is really no point in thinking seriously about a Digital Game-Based Learning solution of any magnitude until you have found a champion. (If you are an executive reading this, this is your cue to step forward!) There are typically so many nonbelievers to convince and so many corporate hurdles to jump that you need someone on your side with major organizational clout. At Ameritrade the champion was the CEO. At Bankers Trust the champion was the head of HR, an executive vice president in the corporation. At consulting firms it is at least a partner or, better yet, a senior partner. At investment banks, it is typically a managing director. Just having your boss on board (unless he or she is one of the above) does not typically cut it. Remember that we are talking about big bucks here. The role of the champion is to convince the skeptics at his or her level in the organization. Don't try to convince them yourself; let your champion do the work for you. You, however, must convince the champion. And then, after you have convinced your champion, you must arm that champion with the best arsenal you can—typically a great prototype, a set of information, and, if possible, some stories on where it has worked.

4. Pick a Range

It is very helpful to "ballpark" the amount of money you will need. You will need to include this information in your investment proposal. The breakdown does not have to be very detailed at the early stage. However one thing is *very* important. *Never* ask for less than you think you might need; in fact, ask for *double* whatever you think it will take. It *always* takes more than you think, and it's very hard to go back to the well a second time. If you have chosen your topic strategically, the amount will be less important to the funders than your ability to deliver what you promise on time. Having enough budget is crucial to doing this.

Some advocate picking a high-profile (i.e., strategic) topic but starting small, perhaps with a game as only a part of what you are doing. I recommend trying to realize your vision—whatever it is—rather than compromising, but not biting off a lot more than you can chew. Deliver small, and you'll get to do more. Fail big....

5. Create a Prototype

Because a great many people won't immediately "get it" based on your description—i.e., they won't immediately jump to the conclusion that putting training and video games together is the greatest thing since sliced bread—it really helps to show them how this can be done. (You can give them this book, but their reading time is typically limited, and they *still* might not get the idea.) It is very important to create some sort of demonstration or prototype that will get them to an "Aha, I see what you mean" experience. There are many ways to do this. Some people, familiar enough with authoring tools, can build a prototype themselves. Others have staff who can do this. Others have used storyboards. Others have taken time from a team already in place doing other things (such as online training) that would like nothing more than to give a game a go. Another way is to put some of your content into an existing shell or template that you license. And even if you can't do any of those, you can just *find* another game—either a Digital Game-Based Learning application or a consumer game that comes close to the idea that you have in mind—and tell a convincing story about how it would work in your case.

6. Link with IT

Listen carefully. Because Digital Game-Based Learning is, by definition, digital, at some point it will use the networks that are run by your company's Information Technology (IT) department. One of the biggest mistakes made in implementing Digital Game-Based Learning—one that I hear repeatedly—is not involving IT early enough. If you happen to be part of IT, so much the better. But Digital Game-Based Learning initiatives often come from other departments within an organization such as training, human resources, corporate communications, or even a line department. In such cases, *it is crucial to work to get IT on your side from the earliest possible moment.* One good way to initiate this is to get your champion to talk to the head of IT or someone close to that level to explain what you are doing.

The reason it is so crucial to involve IT is that they want, and need, to maintain strict control over what passes through their networks. Put yourself in their place. If the network slows down, they are blamed. If a virus should enter the company's network, it is their fault. If a system should crash, they are responsible. So, any prudent IT person is careful about what goes on the network. After having experienced some loss of control with the spread of personal computers, IT is regaining it with a vengeance with the Internet and intranets. Most IT departments have strict rules about what can go on computers and on networks, and what can come through the corporate firewall. Some don't allow plug-ins. Some don't allow Java. Some don't allow new DLLs (dynamic link libraries, which are packets of code used by programs but that frequently interfere with each other).

In addition to the natural fear that IT has of *all* unknown software, what you are proposing are games. Games—as in commercial consumer games— have a terrible reputation for messing up computers. Often this is because, in an effort to have the latest and best features, they use the very latest code, DLLs, and approaches, staying perilously close to the "bleeding edge."

To make matters worse, games are known as resource hogs—a commercial game can take hundreds of megabytes for even a minimal install. Web-based games may often send large graphics files over the network.

I have seen many noncorporate game designers and first-time vendors approach corporate games with glee. Unlike the home market, corporate computers tend to be connected by relatively fast networks, T1 and T3 lines to the outside, and at least 10 megabit Ethernet to the desktop. In the vernacular, corporations have "big pipes." Broadband is here! Games should be no problem in this environment! Wrong! The pipes may be big, but they are big for a reason. They are generally filled with important corporate data, often from mission-critical systems that can't be allowed to slow down or be displaced.

All this is to say that when you do come to IT to talk about games, even though many of them may be gamers themselves, they will have an instinctive fear and bias against you. It is your job to overcome this bias and win them over.

An excellent way to do this is—as early in your process as possible— to have the most technical people on your team meet with a group that IT picks (the IT rep for your department or the corporate Webmaster are good places to start to organize this). Explain to them what you are trying to do and get their sense as to what the concerns and constraints will be. For example, are you planning to serve the whole global firm out of one server in, say, New York? IT may not want your traffic crossing oceans and may prefer three servers around the world. Are you planning an implementation in Java? They may have restrictions. Are you planning to run through a browser? They may have an upgrade plan, or not have an upgrade plan, or have several different browsers on different platforms (did you remember UNIX?). Are you planning a CD-ROM game? How will you distribute the discs? Will there be enough room on hard disks for the install? What if they or some of their offices prefer a network implementation? What if they are phasing out CD-ROMs in favor of Web-only solutions?

One thing to remember is that while IT can at times appear to be a "bully" (other game implementers' words, not mine), they are in business to serve legitimate business needs. If you (or possibly your champion) can make the case high enough up the IT organization that what you are doing is important for the business, you will get their cooperation. This will often happen in the form of one or more IT person's being assigned to your team. This is a great help, because they speak the language that you may not, and can get great things accomplished for you. "I saw it as my job to facilitate and make sure the project worked," says Neil Berkowitz, the IT executive who managed the rollout of *Straight Shooter!* at Bankers Trust. "I had to grapple constantly with questions like 'What's the best way to roll this out to the desktop? How do you manage different versions of the game? How do you put the game onto an enterprise network?' As a computer manager I knew the answers from my experience, and others trusted me enough to follow." But even then, it was a struggle at times. During the implementation, Berkowitz would often say to his IT colleagues in frustration, "This is the most interesting and fun application in the *whole company* and you guys won't pay attention."

Do not forget this—from the simplest template to the biggest corporatewide game, you *always* want IT on your side.

7. Write the Proposal

Companies typically have very specific, formal criteria, and even forms, for investment proposals, and you should begin looking at yours as soon as possible. This will help you to understand what is required—what sponsors, what approvals, and so on. Many times costs must be split into expensed and capital components. Many levels of justification are required. Here are a couple of examples to guide you generally. But bear in mind that every company is different in this area.

Investment Proposals: Two Examples.

Example 1: Straight Shooter! The investment proposal (IP) process at Bankers Trust was very clear: fill in the blanks in the Lotus Notes-based form, and send it around for approvals, which executives could provide with a click. The following is the actual form submitted and approved. (Note that Bankers Trust no longer exists as a firm, having been purchased by Deutsche Bank in 1999.)

STRAIGHT SHOOTER! INVESTMENT PROPOSAL

Overview

Project Number: xxxxxxx

Project Start Date: 12/96
Length of Project: 0.9 (years)
Title: Training System for Policies
Project Type: Research & Development
Project Location: North and South America
Description: Creation of an advanced, network-based training system shell for generic policy training that is available to all BT employees, reusable for different types of policy training within BT, motivating for our users, and marketable outside the bank through Corporate Gameware

Capital Amount: $0
Expensed Amount: $500,000

Expense Code:	Division:	Business Line:
xxxxxxx	xxxxxxxx	xxxxxxxx
APPLICAT DEVELOP	HUMAN RESOURCES	CORPORATE STAFF

Is the Capital expenditures portion of this project included in your Capital Plan? (Y/N) N
        If Yes, enter Capital Plan Number:
Is the Expense portion of this project included in your expense budget? (Y/N) Y

Preparer:	Marc Prensky	Sponsor:	Mark Bieler
Title:	VP	Title:	MD
Location:	BTP 12	Location:	BTP 12
Telephone:	xxx-xxxx	Telephone:	xxx-xxxx

Approving Division Manager: Mark Bieler   Additional Approver: xxxxxxxxx
Other Contacts :_____

Impact on Other Business Areas: System can be used by any BT business area with policy training needs that is willing to invest in the development of content.

Justification

Business Justification:
BT needs to show the regulators that we are doing something clear and consistent for policy training, and it is clear that we need to better train our employees on our policies, such as Derivatives Focus Policies, Technology Policies and other Control Policies. These are typically lengthy, dense and difficult to read, but have to be understood in detail. The current method, classroom sessions with experts, can only focus on the summary of key points and not cover all the material, and taxes the time of the subject matter experts. This investment will enable us to create the architecture for a computer based training system that can (1) provide training in any type of policies at varying levels of detail, (2) verify training and track completion of various segments including updates (3) motivate our population to learn the material, and (4) recoup our investment and generate income through sale of the system (minus proprietary content) to other institutions.

No ROI. The only other form required was a one-page justification of the vendors selected, and a spreadsheet showing how the $500,000 was arrived at. The sponsors believed in, and needed, the project.

Example 2: In$ider. The business case for *In$ider* was presented by Paula Young via a snazzy, animated presentation prepared in Macromedia's *Director.* (The same thing, more or less, could probably be accomplished in today's versions of *PowerPoint*, with animations used to their max.)

The proposal consists of eight sections:

- Drivers
- The Gap
- Potential Solutions
- Training Interventions
- The Integrated Solution
- Implementation Issues
- Business Benefits
- Investment Decision Required

Clicking on a section leads to three or four bullets, each of which has an illustration, chart, or additional text. Under Drivers, for example, are Changing Business Environment, Increasing Audit Risk, and Accounting Standards React. The Gap discusses the research her team did and "frames" the problem (yes, in a gilt frame). Potential Solutions discusses changes in working practices, training interventions, and leadership commitment, concluding that all three are necessary. Training Interventions discusses alternatives, from doing nothing, to expanding current offerings, to outsourcing, to purchasing an off-the-shelf solution, to creating an in-house solution, which she recommends for both competitive advantage and as the best use of in-house and external skill sets. Young then presents her "Integrated Solution," which consists of the game, the "live Academy" followup, and various support elements. Her "Implementation Issues" are divided into Strategic, Operational, and Values and Attitudes.

It is not until all of these are thoroughly discussed that Young turns to the "Business Benefits," which include cash and time and cost savings, but in a very *qualitative* way: "reduce learner time, more effective use of trainers, and cheaper in the long run" is what she writes. The only numbers are 2.5 days vs. 5 days. The other business benefits include a high-quality solution and strengthening of the PricewaterhouseCoopers brand.

The final section of the proposal, Investment Decision, lays out the three phases of the project (including implementation as phase 3) and their time and cost requirements. She compares her costs with the alternatives she had discussed previously, and includes a graph showing that her solution has a fixed cost, whereas the other solutions all have variable costs, increasing perpetually with more learners.

THIS IS THE COST ANALYSIS FORM PAULA YOUNG USED
(REPRODUCED BY PERMISSION).

PricewaterhouseCoopers
Learning Technologies
Cost/Benefit Analysis

Project:

Direct cost of e-learning program

Initial investment   **Lump sum to secure before starting**
Prog. development/acquisition   a Self-build, contract out or buy off the shelf
Hardware acquisition/upgrade   b Don't forget any network enhancements
Establishing infrastructure   c Staff training, space, refurb, storage, wiring etc etc
                                         d=a+b+c

Recurring costs   **Annual costs to deliver the training**
Learner support   e People to start learners off & help them when stuck
Technology support   f People & systems to keep the technology going
Consumables   g Learner materials, heat, light, power
Revenues [enter as a negative]   h Sales, rentals, royalties, learning centre bookings
                                         i=e+f+g-h

Shelf life   j **Years training will remain current**

Total recurring costs   k=i×j

Total costs   l=d+k

Lifetime audience   m **Learners during shelf life**

Cost per learner   n=l÷m

*Savings over any existing taught alternative**

Learner costs   **Differential costs per learner***
Learning time   o Value of time saved [negative if MM is slower†]
Travel & accommodation   p Costs that can be avoided by using multimedia
                                         q=o+p

Event costs   **Differential costs per event***
Instructor time   r Value of instructor time saved
Venue costs   s Costs that can be avoided by using multimedia
                                         t=r+s

Learners per event   u **Average no. of learners per existing event**

Saving per learner   v=q+(t÷u)

Net cost/saving

Per Learner   w=n-v

Total   x=m×w

The proposal concludes with three options: fund the whole thing, fund the design and then seek approval for next phase, or do nothing.

There is not an ROI in sight in this proposal designed for the funders, although Young did do a cost analysis, on the form shown above, for the main sponsoring partner and the training partner.

Young's team received over $1 million in hard dollars. *Think strategically!*

8. Overcome Objections

There will always be objections. In his *Thiagi Game Letter,* Thiagi published two articles on reducing resistance to the use of games, first among executives and second among users.[9] In the first article, he recommends building a CASE for games, CASE being an acronym for Compatibility, Adaptability, Simplicity, and Effectiveness. Your project should be compatible, he says, with the organizational and cultural values of your company. You should make sure that your approach lends itself to changing content and group sizes. You should make your concept easy to communicate, understand, and use. And you should address relevant goals and produce effective results. Of all of these, I would especially highlight communication. By showing your prototype (and, even better, having your champion show it) to as many people in the organization as possible, you begin not only to enlist supporters, but also to flush out the objections you will have to overcome.

Thiagi's second point is also important: users may have concerns as well. We have already spoken of creating user focus groups and of having users on the team. But Thiagi reminds us that anything new and involving change, such as Digital Game-Based Learning, can either be embraced or resisted. Good communication, as well as attention to what Thiagi calls the "six stages of change"—ignorance, anxiety, curiosity, readiness, acceptance, disillusionment—is important to reducing any resistance and increasing the chances of its being embraced by the widest possible group.

When I first read the article, I was curious myself about his last point. Why disillusionment? What he means is that when users finally try Digital Game-Based Learning (or anything else that works) they often want more of it—and fast. Understanding that you may be unleashing a tidal wave of demand is also important. (This is usually referred to as a "good" problem.)

To executives who object that they are not in favor of games, you might cite these comments from Mark Bieler, former executive vice president and long-time head of HR at Bankers Trust:

> I don't have an enormous track record of being necessarily an early adopter and I don't think it's necessarily in my nature as a businessman to reach for the latest toy because it's a toy. But my career started in the training and development side of things, so my knowledge of the field is not theoretical, but real and practical. And I'd also spent a lot of time getting to know the unique population of young people and felt that I had a reasonable feel about how they were motivated, and what kinds of people they were, and how they were made up psychologically. As an HR director, I was in a uniquely clear position about the power and effectiveness of all of this. Both from a pedagogical point of view and a clinical point of view in terms of understanding this kind of population, honestly, this just seemed like a particularly powerful way to proceed.[10]

I wish you all could have bosses and sponsors like Mark Bieler. But even with executives predisposed to be favorable, you will still have to answer the question about Digital Game-Based Learning that is probably the biggest objection of all—"Does it work?" I take this up in the next chapter.

14
Evaluating Effectiveness
Does It Work?

Very effective and a lot of fun.
— Society for Technical Communications

In terms of motivation, in terms of getting time to spend time, and forgetting, not watching the clock, but suspending their sense of time and becoming deeply absorbed in it, and in terms of competition, it's really amazing how effective this is.
— Don Johnson, the Pentagon

It's out there, it's working.
— Joe Costello, CEO, think3

THE NAYSAYERS

Yeah, we know. Learning first, fun second.
— Bob Filipczak, *Training* Magazine

It is fair to say that Digital Game-Based Learning—even when presented as *only one way* to learn—has its share of skeptics. The skeptics include self-defined heretics such as Clifford Stoll,[1] educational psychologists such as Jane Healey,[2] instructional technologists such as David Merrill,[3] and a variety of other academics.

The arguments of the naysayers fall into a few categories. On the one hand, are the *supertraditionalists*. These are people who have a strong internalized model of what learning and education should look like: teacher as expert, students as receivers; logical exposition; one thing at a time; hard work. For this group, games, in almost any form, have no place in the formal learning, schooling, or training process. Count Clifford Stoll among these people.

Next, there are the *reviewers and reinforcers*. This group thinks that it is important to inject some fun in the learning process, and that games are an OK way to do it—just not to teach. Games cannot teach—only telling can teach. But at the end of a traditional teaching session (in classroom or online) games are a good way to review and to have the learners review what they have learned. Games are *not* the test, mind you; the test is formal and private, and certainly not fun. But they are good for review and reinforcement. Count the *Jeopardy!* folks among these people. Even Lightspan is in this camp.

A third group of naysayers is the *nothing there* group. This group argues that the proportion of educational content versus entertainment content in Digital Game-Based Learning is so small that it is not worth the time and effort to either create it or use it. This is Professor David Merrills' "gobs of frosting and precious little cake" argument.

A fourth group is the *I'm afraid* group. They see some positives but many more negatives and often cite a lack of research on long-term effects of technology and learning. Dr. Jane Healy represents this group ably.

A fifth argument I sometimes hear against Digital Game-Based Learning comes from the other direction altogether, from the *idealists*. Their argument is that only the truly complete integration of content and game into an extraordinary intrinsic simulation will work, and that unless or until we can do this, we are wasting our time. I count Michael Allen[4] as one of these.

Finally, there are the *passivists*. These are people, including many in the games industry itself, who see people generally as more passive than active, and who therefore think that *any* active learning methodology, of which Digital Game-Based Learning is only one, are doomed if not to failure, at least to a niche position. Scott Miller[5] represents their position.

Now let's discuss their points of view. Whenever possible, I will try to present examples of Digital Game-Based Learning that refute their perspectives.

A confirmed traditionalist, Clifford Stoll's book *High Tech Heretic: Why Computers Don't Belong in the Classroom*[6] is full of pithy comments intended to incite. For example:

- "A computer can't replace a good teacher."
- "How about computers replacing bad teachers? Again nope: Bad teachers ought to be replaced by good teachers."
- "The enjoyment of scholarship has nothing to do with making learning fun."
- "Most learning isn't fun. Learning takes work."
- "Teaching machines substitute quick answers and fast action for reflection and critical thinking."
- "Turning learning into fun denigrates the most important things we can do in life: to learn and to teach." (Guess what profession Stoll is in?)
- "Many subjects aren't fun. Plenty of jobs aren't fun either."
- "An inspiring teacher doesn't need computers; a mediocre teacher isn't improved by one."

Leaving aside the fact that there just *aren't* that many good teachers in Stoll's sense of good, and certainly not enough to go around, Stoll, like most of the traditionalists, either misses or chooses to ignore the fact that today's learners have changed. If only, the traditionalists argue, we could get rid of all this newfangled, unhelpful technology, stop trying to entertain, and get back to doing what we've always done, things would be fine. I've tried to show in this book that fun *helps* learning, rather than hurting it, and that that the "way things were always done" is not only relatively recent, but is related to a particular social and communications structures that are now in the process of change. It is these changes in structure that Stoll and his allies are *really* complaining about, and that is something I suspect that they can't do anything about.

But to me the real shame in Stoll's position (which I suspect he takes mainly for effect and possibly for profit) is that he is in an excellent position to improve things by creating Digital Game-Based Learning that works in all the ways he suggests. Stoll is an astronomer, a programmer, and—if his own self-assessments are to be believed—an excellent teacher. Because I am a city boy who sees a clear, moonless, star-filled sky maybe one night a year, I for one would *love* a game that taught me to identify and remember constellations and other things that I don't know about astronomy. I have used many "traditional" techniques (including having the constellations pointed out to me live) to no avail. Stoll writes that "no multimedia computer will help a student develop analytic abilities," and "no online astronomy program can engender the same sense of awe as first seeing the rings of Saturn through a telescope." Furthermore, Stoll writes, "show me the computer program that encourages quiet reflection." I would humbly suggest that Stoll is extremely capable of writing an astronomy learning game that will do all of that and more, should he choose to do so, and I would be happy to help him. For models, I would suggest he look at *Strategy Co-Pilot* for analysis, *Riven* for awe, and computer *Chess* and *Go* for quiet reflection.

The second group, the "review and reinforcement" naysayers, typically think that to "teach" a subject, *only* a logical explanation, provided by either a teacher or a book (or possibly read from the screen) will do, thus, the best a game can do is review. Clearly, *how* to teach through games (and especially digital games) is not something intuitively obvious to most of today's trainers, teachers, and educators. But the point of view that games *can't* teach is not only incorrect, but it is especially unfortunate in that it discourages experimentation on how best to do it. For good examples of how people can learn for the first and only time by using a game, I refer you to *Objection!, In$ider, The Monkey Wrench Conspiracy,* and numerous other examples in this book.

As for the "not enough edu" group, their complaint is not so much with the process as with the execution. "I'm not categorically against games," writes Professor M. David Merrill,[7] "but most of the educational games that I see use inappropriate principles of gaming and lose their educational value." "The problem with edutainment," he says, "is that there is often too much -tainment and not enough edu-." It's kind of a nutritional argument—some foods are clearly higher in nutrition ("edu") and most "experts" advise us to eat them. But most of us prefer to eat whatever appeals to us. The consequences of doing so may be less than optimal, but generally keep us alive and well. When Merrill talks about the "amount of learning per hour of play" he is certainly making this type of argument, even though Merrill has helped to design games with nutritional ratios more to his liking. The underlying assumption behind the "nutritional" argument is that *learning itself* motivates people. "Learning something new is the most powerful motivator we have," Merrill writes. Therefore, the "tainment" such as "games, themes, and settings that are irrelevant to the knowledge and skill being taught" is irrelevant and even counterproductive at times. This is an argument heard widely from academics for whom pleasure in learning is no doubt true. But the rest of us, I suspect, prefer as much *tainment* as we can get with our *edu*, particularly for things we'd rather not learn. That is why I argued in Chapter 6, that in creating Digital Game-Based Learning we must work to optimize *both* the motivation and the learning aspects at the same time. How many of us can stick for very long to a diet that's 100 percent wholesome?

The fourth group of naysayers—the "I'm afraid" group—is, to me, the most insidious, because I think they draw the wrong conclusions from the facts they cite. Dr. Jane Healy, an educational psychologist, a former teacher and elementary school principal, and the author of *Failure to Connect*,[8] has a thesis that computers aren't helping kids, especially younger kids, learn, and are even hurting the process. She cites many first-hand examples of computers being used in unproductive ways. To her credit, these are balanced by a good number of positive examples of computers, and even games, enhancing learning. But Healy gives the examples that do "work" (which, she claims, were "hard to find") almost no credence at all in her arguments, which almost always boil down to potential dangers unknown to us because of a lack of research. "No one knows if too many computer games will make children more subject to depression or affect their immune systems," she writes in italics, "because no research has considered such questions. Yet it is just one of many that should make us approach any new medium judiciously." If Merrill uses the "nutritional" argument, Healy's argument is the "genetically altered food."

Dr. Healy and others who share her views could be really helpful to the successful evolution of Digital Game-Based Learning by saying, "Here's what works, here's what doesn't, let's do more of the former." Instead, Healy proposes banning computers from the classroom until the age of 8, based on her feeling that kids need other things besides what computers were providing in many classrooms at the time she wrote the book. Of course, they do. Although Healy worries a lot about what computers will do to young children, her real arguments come down to the fact that much of the software out there is not doing what she thinks needs to be done, and most teachers don't have much of an idea of how to teach using software. Claiming that it takes "5 to 6 years" for teachers to change their teaching habits,[9] she prefers to stick her finger in the dike rather than to say, "so let's get started." She even sets herself up as a martyr, asking in response to the argument that familiarity with computers will help kids get jobs, "Do I risk being stoned in the public marketplace if I suggest that the purpose of education is not to make kids economically valuable, but rather to allow them to develop intellectual and personal worth as well as practical skills?" If Healy and her supporters should be intellectually stoned it is not for that, but rather for being alarmists and not working to make it easier and better for kids to learn in the language of their own times.

A fifth group of naysayers to much of Digital Game-Based Learning comes from the completely opposite direction—from a vision of perfection that is not being attained. "It is unfortunate that edutainment has traveled the course it has," writes Michael Allen, renowned creator of *Authorware* a multimedia authoring language and self-professed perfectionist.[10] "Intrinsic games—those in which learning is a component of success and in which success is not just a game score but personal growth transferable to real life. . .are perhaps the most noble and worthwhile applications of technology in the learning field. . . ." The problem, of course, as Allen is the first to admit, is that there aren't a whole lot of those yet; we're just getting started. Also, as I pointed out in Chapter 6, there are many different approaches—some intrinsic, some not—that are appropriate for different learning situations. As much as I admire the idealists, I think to dismiss alternative approaches and efforts that are taking us down the road of making learning more fun is counterproductive. Although perhaps not perfect, some pretty good examples of intrinsic learning games, can be seen in *Joint Force Employment*, *In$ider*, and *Strategy Co-Pilot*.

Finally, come the "passivist" naysayers to gaming's becoming really important. Many of these naysayers, oddly enough, are avid gamers and game creators themselves. But, like Scott Miller of Apogee Entertainment, they "don't believe that interactive entertainment will dominate other forms of entertainment this coming century." "I think," says Miller, "for the most part, people prefer passive entertainment, like TV, watching sports, and attending movies, where you can veg out and just enjoy what's in front of you. But there's little doubt that digital gaming will continue to grow."[11] Might that be true for Digital Game-Based Learning as well? We'll soon see.

THE EVIDENCE:
WHAT'S THE "IT" WE ARE TALKING ABOUT?

A metric isn't very good if a dead person qualifies.
— Clark Aldrich, the Gartner Group

As we examine and evaluate the evidence to answer the question "Does it work?", we need to decide what "it" is. Is "it" *all* Digital Game-Based Learning? There are a thousand instances, each a little different. Is "it" *individual examples?* If so, then to answer the question precisely, we would have to evaluate each example. Only a few have been evaluated, the results of which I will present in a minute. But are those results transferable?

I think we can best deal with the question of "Does it work?" by taking a variety of approaches:

1. We can ask whether fun, play, and games *in general* aid learning. This we have done. The answer is absolutely.

2. We can take data from one area (children's' learning) and extrapolate it to another (adult training.) We will do this with games from Lightspan, Click Health, and Scientific Learning. We will do it for young adults with games from Will Interactive.

3. We can define "ideal" Digital Game-Based Learning as the best approaches of technology-based learning put into a more engaging package. This allows us to use effectiveness of technology-based training as our criterion, assuming increased engagement will only improve the results.

4. We can listen to the people who have done the most Digital Game-Based Learning, namely the military, as well as others who have used or evaluated it, and hear what they say.

5. We can look at the few formal evaluations of specific examples of adult Digital Game-Based Learning that are available: *Darwin, Electro Adventure,* and *HIV Interactive Nights Out.*

6. We can ask the people who paid for it whether they think they got their money's worth.

All of the above will point us in the direction that Digital Game-Based Learning really does work, although some academics might still call this "unproven." We should remember though, that there are many levels of proof, some of which, while not perfect (e.g., statistical analysis), are often good enough for us to continue. As Einstein read every day on his office wall, "not everything that counts can be counted."

1. Evaluating the Value of "Fun," "Play," and "Games" for Learning

If you are not convinced by now, please go back and read Chapter 5.

2. Evaluating the Learning in Digital Game-Based Learning for Children

There are many who criticize children's learning games, and there is much there to criticize. "Edutainment" seems to have turned off many educators in the same way the early computer-based training turned off students. But if some games don't produce learning it is *not* because they are games, or because the concept of edutainment is faulty. It is because *those particular games are badly designed.* There is much evidence that children's learning games that *are* well designed *do* produce learning, and lots of it, by and while engaging kids.

Some people refer to the "game" part of Digital Game-Based Learning as "sugar coating," giving that a strongly negative connotation. I disagree that this is negative, and, in fact, think just the opposite—that it is often a big help. In schools, as in training, we're often talking about things people don't want to learn. There is no reason that I can see why a little (or even a lot) of "sugar" is not good if it helps digest other things, and if the whole package doesn't harm you. After all, that is exactly how we make bad-tasting medicine go down. For some reason this idea, though, gets many "serious" educators upset. And not only educators. *The Wall Street Journal* reported that Richard Fisher, deputy United States trade representative, derided Japanese *i-mode* Internet phones as "sugar, not substance," even though among the services they provide, in addition to Web access, are daily English lessons. David Wessel, the *Journal* reporter, asks rhetorically, "Who says mobile phones shouldn't entertain as well as inform?"[12] Who says learning shouldn't either?

I would actually maintain that *all* good education is, and has always been, edutainment. *Great education is edutainment that has gotten the mix right.* To condemn edutainment for not being effective is to condemn books, plays, or movies based on the very true fact that most of them are bad. No rational person condemns the genre; we speak of good books, good plays, and good movies as those that stand the test of time.

Some of this, of course, is just quibbling about proportions. An observation that John Kernan of The Lightspan Partnership made when I first met him really stuck with me. When you strip out the recesses, the lunch, and the in-between times, elementary school kids actually get about 3 hours of instruction time in their typical nine-to-three day.[13] Now assume that Lightspan's reinforcement games are only 50 percent "cake" (to use Professor Merrill's term). If you can get kids to use the Lightspan games for 6 hours over a weekend, you've effectively added a day a week to school! Six hours is actually far less than that student would typically spend over that weekend watching TV and playing video games. The trick, though, is to make the learning games compelling enough to actually be used in their place. Hence the need for "frosting."

Lightspan's numbers back this up. They sent me a CD filled with so many studies that when it's printed out they call it the "telephone book."[14] Studies were conducted in more than 400 school districts and a meta-analysis was done by Dr. William Stock, retired professor Arizona State University. In study after study, district after district, the numbers show scores on standardized tests with Lightspan being higher than the control group. The overall finding is that for every 100 students in the control group setting scoring above the fiftieth percentile, there were 128 successful Lightspan students, an almost 30 percent increase in the number of successful students over the control group. When broken down further, the vocabulary and language arts increases over the control groups were 24 and 25 percent, respectively, while the math problem solving and math procedures and algorithms scores were 51 and 30 percent higher. Who says that practice games don't help? Of course, Lightspan provides lots of professional development to teachers about how to integrate the programs with the curriculum, but the primary reason for the increased performance is use in the home to extend learning time, which is exactly why *-tainment* works.

But back to the part about the mix. *Is* there an optimal mix to make Digital Game-Based Learning work? I've not found any data on this, but my sense is no; that the right mix depends very heavily on context.

Lightspan, which is basically "doing the curriculum" tries to make its mix of "edu" to "tainment" higher than, say, Disney, does in its edutainment products, according to Winnie Wechsler, who moved from Disney Interactive to Lightspan in 1999 to run their Internet business.[15] But that doesn't necessarily mean kids don't learn from Disney's mix; the learning is just being provided in *different dosages*. My strong sense is that edutainment designers are getting better and better at mixing interesting learning with entertainment, and that the most innovative approaches, just like in Digital Game-Based Learning, are not coming from the traditional *edu* or instructional design side.

Personally, I think it would be great if *every* learning program in the world had a little slider control, always sitting in the same place like a car's temperature controls, which let each user (or trainer, or teacher, or parent) set the mix of *edu* and *tainment* for themselves. My guess is that in time this will happen and be readily accepted, just like almost all games today have controls for setting the difficulty level. Perhaps separate controls for game difficulty and learning difficulty (kind of like bass and treble) might work even better.

Lightspan's numbers are not the only ones that show Digital Game-Based Learning works with kids. Click Health, the company that makes games to help kids self-manage their diabetes and asthma, did clinical trials funded by the National Institutes of Health and found that in the case of diabetes, kids playing their games (as compared to a control group playing a pinball game) gained in self-efficacy, communication with parents, and diabetes self-care. More importantly, urgent doctor visits for diabetes-related problems declined 77 percent in the treatment group.[16] Again, this was attributable to repeated usage of the game by the kids. The subjects played the game 34 hours during the 6 months of the study. This was the same amount that the control group played the pinball game; only the Click Health group learned something!

And we're not done yet. Scientific Learning conducted National Field Trials of its *Fast ForWard* game-based program for retraining kids with reading problems, using sixty independent professionals at thirty-five sites across the United States and Canada. Using standardized tests, each of the thirty-five sites reported conclusive validation of *Fast ForWard's* effectiveness, with 90 percent of the children achieving significant gains in one or more tested areas including auditory word discrimination; the ability to follow spoken directions; listening and speaking fundamentals; auditory processing speed; speech discrimination; language processing; grammatical comprehension; and overall language comprehension.[17] In *Fast ForWard* kids play the games *a lot*—roughly 100 minutes per day for 5 to 10 weeks.

Repeatedly, it's the same simple story. Practice and time spent on learning *works*. Kid's don't like to practice. Games capture their attention and make it happen. And, of course, they must be practicing the right things, so *design* is important.

3. Evaluating Technology-Based Training in General

Because so much has been written elsewhere on evaluating technology-based learning I will not dwell on it here. Almost all studies—and there have been hundreds if not thousands by now—have shown that test scores and consistency improve, and time to deliver the same material is cut by 30 to 50 percent when compared with comparable tell-test classroom instruction.[18] Many of the studies come from the military.[19] Dexter Fletcher, a Ph.D., who has done military research, has established a "Rule of Thirds." The rule states that the use of technology-based instruction reduces costs by about one-third and *either* reduces instruction time by about one-third *or* increases effectiveness of instruction by about one-third,[20] says Don Johnson at the Pentagon, who comes from an education specialist community that is very interested in a scientific, systematic, approach to doing things. At the Pentagon, they have a whole field of inquiry called training effectiveness evaluation. They document requirements, build something, and then test it and see how well it works. "In DOD, we probably have done more studies of learning technology than you will find anywhere," says Johnson. "We've proven to ourselves that technology works. We've proven it academically, but more importantly, we've proven it operationally."

4. Evaluating Digital Game-Based Learning "Operationally"

What does Johnson mean by "operationally?" The Gulf War gave the military an opportunity to evaluate *in action* the effectiveness of training its tank crews in SIMNET networked tank simulators. During one particular battle known as 73 Easting—the flanking maneuver where our tanks sped around the Iraqi forces that were blinded and came at them from the West—a tank platoon led by an officer named McMaster encountered Iraqi tanks that were dug in. Military doctrine said that when you encounter forces that are dug in you need a 3 to 1 advantage in order to be successful and prevail. But McMasters' three or four tanks caught the Iraqis by surprise, rolling right over them and wiping out all 20 or 30 tanks that were dug in. When they were interviewed afterwards and asked, "How did you do this? It was against doctrine." McMaster said, "We'd done it before—we did it in simulation."[21] "This made everybody's hair kind of stand up," says Johnson, "because this was proof that the technology actually works. We've seen it time and time again in flying airplanes, and in our mission simulators."[22]

What's really important to the military leadership is not what academics think, but what war fighters think. If they've tried the technology out and they see that it works operationally in the field, then they typically don't require an academic study to prove to them that it works.

This practical perspective of the Department of Defense contrasts sharply with that of those educators who say, "We don't *know* that educational technology works, we need to do some more studies."[23] "We have a completely different perspective at DOD," says Johnson. "We *know* the technology works, we've proven it over and over again, and we are doing everything we can to expand and accelerate its use. It saves time, it saves money, and it saves lives. It allows military personnel to do training that is too dangerous or not possible in any other environment. There's *no question* in our minds that it works and is cost-effective."[24]

The areas where questions remain are primarily on the other side—can Digital Game-Based Learning replace the current, very expensive, large-scale simulations involving dozens to hundreds of participants? Johnson feels that Digital Game-Based Learning tools such as *Joint Force Employment* are going to be much more cost-effective than many of the multimillion dollar approaches and live simulations they have now. His hope is to test this with side-by-side comparisons.

Michael Parmentier, Johnson's boss, points out that students typically get to ask a question in a classroom only once every 10 hours,[25] but if they're interacting with a computer game "it's a constant Socratic dialog of Q&A." He cites studies showing that tutors—average tutors—can increase the learning speed and retention of students by two standard deviations and make them learn better than 98 percent of the students in a classroom environment.[26] Parmentier's group's goal has been to see if they can use technology to move people in the direction of the kind of performance they get from a tutor. "The answer that we found is that in some cases we can," Parmentier says. "In many cases, we're getting one standard deviation already—cognitively sound technology-based learning."

5. Evaluating Specific Examples of Digital Game-Based Learning

While not a lot of studies have been done on specific examples of Digital Game-Based Learning other than "smile tests," there have been a few. Let us look at them.

When Ameritrade created its *Darwin, Survival of the Fittest* Digital Game-Based Learning program for options trading, its intention from the very beginning was to evaluate its effectiveness. In 1998, it commissioned a study by Wiese Research Associates that consisted of a questionnaire administered by telephone to 141 people (129 men and 12 women) who had used the game.[27] They found that over half of the people (51 percent) reported their knowledge of options to be greater than before, with the program receiving a mean score of 3.86 out of 5 as to its "value" (30 percent gave it a 5 and 38 percent a 4). When the respondents were asked whether they had "little or no more understanding" or "much more understanding" of seventeen specific skills (e.g., how to buy an option; how to buy or sell a put or call; etc.), with nine "basic" skills, four intermediate skills, and four advanced skills, the average answers on the 5-point scales were all around 3—a little above for the basic and intermediate skills, a little below for the advanced skills. The standard deviations were relatively narrow (around 1.4), indicating that most felt that their understanding of all the skills in options trading had significantly increased as a result of the game, about halfway to the level of "much more." And remember—this was something customers chose to do *on their own*.

The Navy's *Electo Adventure* game also got evaluated, via test scores, against both classroom and computer-based training (CBT) instruction of the same material. In a test developed by the Naval Personnel Research and Development Center, the average scores for the classroom and game were slightly lower than the two CBT alternatives (68, 67, 75, 74) but on another test they were higher (89, 86, 84, 81).[28] Dr. Henry Halff, the game's designer, compares his 1991 product to the Wright Brothers at Kitty Hawk—he didn't know whether it would fly at all. "That it not only flew but carried the freight was both gratifying and unexpected," Halff says. To me, it is instructive that a first-generation Digital Game-Based Learning product did so well against the couple of generations that CBT has had and the multiple generations that classroom instruction has had to develop their approaches. Think of what will happen when we *really* get going!

HIV Interactive Nights Out, a Digital Game-Based Learning product from Will Interactive, was evaluated during an Army pilot study of its use in kiosks by 231 soldiers ages 19 to 29 years, more than half of whom voluntarily played it more than one time.[29] In interviews with twenty-nine of the soldiers (all they could get), the researchers found that the program reinforced already existing intentions to protect themselves against HIV infection; called into question previous risky behaviors that soldiers had not addressed but were now thinking about as a result of having played the game; made participants aware of their present risk for HIV and the behaviors linked to such risk that they needed to address now and in the future; and changed participants behavioral intentions (in a positive way) to protect themselves and their sex partners from exposure to HIV.

Contest 10: Do you know of any other data evaluating Digital Game-Based Learning projects? Email your entries to *Contest10@twitch speed.com*.

---

6. Did They Get Their Money's Worth?

Finally, companies have laid out some serious money for Digital Game-Based Learning. Do they think they got their money's worth?

Ameritrade spent over $1 million on *Darwin*. They were pleased with the results summarized above.

Joe Costello of think3 also spent close to $1 million on *The Monkey Wrench Conspiracy*. He feels it has been "*extremely* successful" in making it easy for people to learn 3D. "It's out there, and its working," he says.

PricewaterhouseCoopers spent close to $3 million, including salaries and implementation costs on *In$ider*. They are pleased as well.

One of the best indicators of success is the willingness of many of the companies cited, including PricewaterhouseCoopers, think3, Nortel, and others to share their products with their clients and to fund new Digital Game-Based Learning projects.

WHAT ABOUT OLDER GENERATIONS?

Much to our surprise, people in their seventies bought the game and played.
— Marc Robert, Monte Cristo

Can people *over* 39—who are not part of the Games Generations—also learn through computer games? Do they want to? Will Digital Game-Based Learning work for them?

There are several indications that it will, but not necessarily with the *same games* as for the younger folks. Sylvia Kowal of Nortel Networks[30] gave me some "pushback" about my initially speaking, when talking about Digital Game-Based Learning, of only younger people as the Games Generations. "A lot of us may not be chronologically from that generation, but we feel emotionally connected to it, and use all the technology," she said. Well maybe not *all* of the technology—Sylvia doesn't play twitch video games, or do instant messaging, or like her email responses to be interleaved, but she has a good point. She and I are what I called earlier "digital immigrants." We came to the technology (or rather it came to us) when we were adults. And although many of us like and enjoy the technology and are facile with it (and earn our livings from it), most of us did not use it early enough or long enough for our brains to get totally "wired" in the way the Games Generations' brains are. For us it's a "better way" to do things, but not "the way" (i.e., the way we grew up with, the way we know best.)

Having said that, as we saw in Chapter 8, increasingly adults *are* big gamers. One of the most interesting phenomena on the Internet is the rise of "old style" or "traditional" gaming. This includes *Bingo*, card games,

Chess, Checkers, trivia games, classic arcade games, and others. These games can be found on dozens of Web sites, including AOL, thestation.sony.com, and many others. One reason for these games' popularity on the Internet is that they generally require partners, which the Web can readily provide. People are online playing 24 hours a day, 7 days a week. The important underlying message is that older people *want* to play the games online—they find them engaging.

Can these "traditional" online games be turned into learning tools that will engage the people who play them? Or can new Digital Game-Based Learning games be designed specifically to these generations' style and tastes? We know *Jeopardy!* works. But can we get beyond *Jeopardy!*? We can and we are. Nortel Networks had such strong response to its first online Digital Game-Based Learning venture with employees of all ages, that it is undertaking another companywide Digital Game-Based Learning project in conjunction with its next strategic move.[31]

Digital Game-Based Learning is now being designed for audiences of all ages. From email and trivia games, to games for doctors and lawyers, to continuing education games, to process simulation games to detective games, most everyone can and does play. "I know what you're thinking," writes one reviewer of the legal game *Objection!* "'I'm too old for computer games.' You're wrong!"[32]

WHAT ABOUT NONGAMERS?

We are not here for fun. There is no reference to fun in any act of Parliament.
— A. P. Herbert

What about people who don't like, don't play, don't care about, and don't want to be involved with games in any way, shape, or form for learning or anything else? *Not a problem.* No matter what it is you do, in learning or anywhere else, there will be people who don't like it. My view is that it is important to do either of two things for these people. First, provide them with an alternative where they don't *have* to play—they can do the learning in some other, more traditional way, such as tell-test. It is relatively easy to build this into any Digital Game-Based Learning program.

A second, somewhat more complicated approach in terms of programming, but one that pays off well in the long run, is to let them switch back and forth. Many people who say they don't want to play may change their minds when no one is watching them and there is no loss of face. So, give them alternatives, let the game peek out and entice them, but basically, "don't ask, don't tell."

OVERCOMING SOME OTHER BARRIERS

Of course, you might ask, "If it works so well, then why hasn't Digital Game-Based Learning taken a bigger hold in the training world?" There are a number of barriers that come up repeatedly and that are worth discussing.

The first—and we've heard about it enough—is the purchaser vs. trainee/student generation gap. Many people who buy training today don't believe games are good for learning, even though their learners do. This barrier will disappear with time.

But this is far from the only barrier. For even in many places where Digital Game-Based Learning *has* been accepted, where noble experiments and extremely well-received projects have been done, it often doesn't "take"; come back 2 years later and it's gone, and things are back the way they were. What happened?

I've heard and seen a couple of things with surprising consistency.

1. *People move on.* We are a very mobile business world. The executive who championed a Digital Game-Based Learning project today might be in another company tomorrow. Or be a consultant, like my former boss at Bankers Trust. Or may have retired, like my former boss at Boston Consulting Group (consultants retire early). The person who did the project may have left the company, as I did and several others have to move up or start their own ventures, leaving no one to push for and support day-to-day a Digital Game-Based Learning project. The IT folk supporting the application have almost certainly turned over, and unless there is strong demand from important people, IT has probably let maintenance of learning games slip in favor of more pressing technical priorities. Even if an outside vendor provides the Digital Game-Based Learning, the people who bought it from that vendor have probably left. And because people typically use training one time only, there is no mass of highly

satisfied users clamoring to use it again. So *creating continuity* is a real challenge.

How do you overcome this? *By creating infrastructure.* Make sure when a project is done, that as part of the implementation process it has a permanent home, and people who will maintain it, *especially in IT.* You actually need to monitor this through personnel changes and, if *you* leave, make sure that job goes to someone else. If you remain but new bosses arrive, you may have to do an internal selling process all over again. But once something becomes part of the permanent fabric of a place, it tends to remain, and responsibility for it gets passed on as a regular thing.

2. *People who have the expertise to do Digital Game-Based Learning are put off by working in the corporate setting.* I have been on both sides of this issue, both as a "vendor" and as a corporate buyer. There were valid issues on both sides.

Vendors' and contractors' complaints about working with large corporations include that:

- Decision making takes forever
- Getting timely sign off is often next to impossible
- Features expand while budgets stay fixed
- Personnel changes often
- Independence gets lost
- Creative ideas are often rejected because the client already has an idea, or the idea is not "PC" enough
- Contracts taker forever and corporate lawyers want too much
- Getting paid takes *longer* than forever.

While corporate-side complaints about working with vendors include:

- They aren't flexible enough to change as our needs change (or as we learn more about our needs from our own line people)
- They want every single thing in writing
- They charge us for each little change
- They want to own and reuse stuff (code, graphics), whereas we want work-for-hire

- We need worldwide 24x7x365 support, preferably available in less than 5 minutes
- The corporation will pay them eventually, so what are they complaining about

Some of these complaints are just time-honored relationships between traditional training companies and their clients, which both sides have learned to live with. But games creators are typically *not* traditional training companies. They are either companies used to a publishing world, or individuals used to a much more freewheeling structure.

Marc Robert of Monte Cristo tells the story of being called by L'Oreal, a very important company in France, to do a customized version of one of its products.[33] "They said 'could you do something like that for us?' And we said 'no, we don't customize it.' They said, 'What, we're L'Oreal, we're calling you, and you're not going to do a game for us? What is this?' They didn't understand it, they called all over the market, they called Electronic Arts, and everybody said no. They had a hard time understanding it."

To make Digital Game-Based Learning, large and small companies are going to have to work together as a team. But a lot of the give, maybe more than 50 percent, needs to come, I think, on the corporate side. It is much too easy for corporate types, who are paying the bills and used to getting their way, to stomp on small companies, often without meaning to, cutting off in the process the very creativity that they want to get. I have done it; and I have had it done to me. People who know how to make good games have more options every day. If you want them to work with you, you'd better be easy to work with. As John Cleese says, "If you want creative workers, give them enough time to play."[34] That applies in spades for Digital Game-Based Learning contractors and vendors.

CROSSING THE CHASM

In his book *Crossing the Chasm*,[35] Geoffrey Moore speaks of early adopters, mainstream users, and the "chasm" between them. Despite everything I have said so far, the truth is that Digital Game-Based Learning is still in the early adopter stage. People are willing to build or use it piecemeal, as needed, to deal with specific problems or populations. But it is not part of the mainstream infrastructure and corporate approach to learning.

How can we make that happen? In Moore's terms, how can we cross the chasm?

I don't have any firm answers here, just a suggestion. Those of us who create Digital Game-Based Learning will have to get better and bigger at what we do. Moore says that the key to crossing the chasm is to have a "whole product," not just a piece of it that works only for some things.

Almost no one has this yet in elearning and the infrastructure is not fully in place. But it soon will be. And we must begin thinking, like those in the military, of large-scale projects that involve a lot of money and creative effort. Convincing some of the big players will help too—as soon as a Sony or a big training vendor gets on the Digital Game-Based Learning bandwagon it will move a lot faster. In the meantime, all of us who believe this is the way of thew future should be out there pulling and pushing.

What's a good way to do this? Invent a great learning game! Which brings us to the next chapter.

15

So You Have an Idea . . .

I had the idea in my head.
— Paula Young, PricewaterhouseCoopers

I've got a scenario of a game that I think would teach algebra.
— Ashley Lipson, Creator of *Objection!*

I used to tell people I was going to do a game about city planning. They'd just look at me, roll their eyes, and say "Oh good, Will, you go do that."
— Will Wright, Creator of *Sim City*

THE MODEL

When one considers all the Digital Game-Based Learning projects described in this book, a surprisingly consistent model arises of how they get done. This model has much in common with the way many creative projects happen, but it also has some specific elements to training and education. I will now attempt to describe this model and give a number of examples, so that you, should you be so moved, can follow in the footsteps of those who have successfully gone before. There is also a second model, used less frequently, that I will mention as well.

The main model works as outlined in the chart on the facing page.

Here are some examples of the model in action:

- Will Wright, software developer, wanted to do a game about urban planning. Result: *Sim City*.[1]

THE MODEL FOR CREATING
DIGITAL GAME-BASED LEARNING

A person (the "teacher") typically with *deep knowledge of a subject area,* thinks "you know, I could make this into a game." This happens either on his or her own, or because someone ("the producer") has brought the possibility to their attention.

The teacher *reflects on and thinks about the game for some time,* figuring out elements that might or might not work. Increasingly they turn to commercial consumer games — designed for adults or kids — for models, ideas and inspiration.

The teacher *makes a prototype,* either by him or herself, or by enlisting the help of others to do so. The prototype goes through several *iterations,* strengthening and improving the idea.

The teacher, often working with a producer, *gets funding* and builds the game.

If the game works, it *gets sold* to other customers outside the creating organization. It may be eventually sold to a distributor. It often spawns a host of extensions of the original idea into new content areas. It also spawns imitators, some who merely copy and some who improve on the concept.

The game is *continually upgraded,* as each wave of new game and hardware technology leads to an upgrade in the product's "look and feel." Given these upgrades, a good initial concept can last a long time.

- Ann McCormick, teacher, wanted to make a game to teach reading skills. Result: *Reader Rabbit.*[2]
- Jan Davidson, teacher, wanted to create a game to encourage math practice. Result: *Math Blaster.*[3]
- Greg Carlston, software developer, wanted to do a game about geography. Result: *Where in the World Is Carmen Sandiego?*[4]
- Myo Thant, MD, wanted to do a game about how surgery is done, and took his initial ideas to Software Toolworks. Result: *Life and Death.*[5]
- Ashley Lipson, law professor, thought there was a gamelike way to teach lawyers trial skills. Result: *Objection!*[6]
- Tom Levine, engineer, had an idea for a game about railroads. Result *Train Dispatcher.*[7]

- Dan Rawistch, student teacher, wanted to make a game to show his students how hard it was to cross the United States in the 1840s. Result: *The Oregon Trail*.[8]
- Mark Bieler, executive vice president of human resources, thought a game could be used to teach derivatives policies. Result: *Straight Shooter!*[9]
- Joe Costello, CEO, wanted a game about learning computer-assisted design (CAD). Result: *The Monkey Wrench Conspiracy*.[10]
- Jerry DelMissier, derivatives trader, wanted a game to teach clients about managing risks. Result: *HEDGEManager*.[11]
- Paula Young, training director, wanted to make a game about managing risk with derivatives. Result: *In$ider*.[12]
- Tom Hout, George Stalk, and Bob Wolf, consultants, thought they could make a game illustrating time-based competition. Result: *Time Out!*[13]
- Roger Bohn, college professor, wanted to make a game to teach process control. Result: *Kristen's Cookies*.[14]
- Richard Barkey, strategy consultant, wanted to capture the process of strategy in a game. Result: *Strategy Co-Pilot*.[15]
- William Massey, retired Stanford University professor and administrator, wanted to make a game about running a university. The result: *Virtual U*.[16]

The good news about this model is this: *If you know something well (or you know someone who does), then you can become a Digital Game-Based Learning creator.* There is lots of room and opportunity, especially because we are at the very beginning of the industry. Many, if not most, subjects do not have digital learning games, or if they do, there is probably room for a different or better one. Remember that Digital Game-Based Learning is really only about 20 years old. Twenty years into movies, the talkies had not been invented, and all the good stories were yet to be made.

As the text-and-bullet-slide training and education worlds slowly metamorphsize and disappear, what is going to replace them? (Remember that people already are not showing up for training classes and kids are dropping out or skipping college altogether so that they can be doing and playing rather than reading textbooks.) To a large extent, Digital Game-Based Learning can do so, *if we are clever enough to invent it!*

Compare the movie industry's history.. The movies are just over 100 years old (Edison invented the Cinematograph in 1889, and the first movie was shown publicly—in Paris—in 1895).[17] The first movies were black and white, silent, and lasted 10 minutes. No one thought you could tell a story. The *Great Train Robbery*, in 1903, was the first to do so. The first movie that anyone considers "art," *Birth of a Nation*, didn't appear until 1915. Music and dialog didn't arrive until the late 1920s, color arrived in the 1930s, and the great storytellers in the medium arrived in the 1940s and after. But even after the movies were with us for 100 years, Lucas, Spielberg, and Cameron, who had grown up on movies since their infancy, still came up with newer and more exciting ways to use the medium effectively, reaching literally hundreds of millions of people.

Commercial books are 400 to 500 years old.[18] But J. R. Rowling found a way in the Harry Potter books to redo the children's book in a new way that reached an enormous number of people, young and old. Of course, the Harry Potter movie and video games are already on the way!

HOW TO LEAVE US YOUR MIND

One of the great comments I remember my friend and fellow musician Laurie Spiegel saying about Bach, is that "he left us his mind."[19] In addition to putting together not only his great works of so many kinds, he created his own kind of "learning games" in *The Well Tempered Clavier* and *The Art of the Fugue*, in which he showed, starting from the simplest to the most complex, exactly what was required.[20] Students and teachers have been playing the "how did he do it?" game in music classes for hundreds of years.

One of the great promises made about electronic learning, regardless of how it is delivered, is that students would be taught by "the world's greatest instructors." But how best to do this? Make videotapes? *Boring.* Have an online session or chat with millions of people? *Unfeasible.* Make a multimedia piece where the "great one" comes on and delivers his message in little "chunks"? *Come on!*

How *can* a great practitioner, thinker, doer, best leave us his mind?

One way is via his books, of course, but in the case of, say, a Peter Drucker, that's a good 10,000 pages to get through.

Put it all online, say some. We'll have search! And chat! And plenty of video clips of the great man himself! Useful for research, maybe, but not especially useful to learn from.

"Knowledge-mine" say others. Find out what questions the great one has tried to answer. Ask him about the heuristics, or rules of thumb that he or she employs in his or her work. Look at lots of cases, and capture on videotape many little vignettes of what they did and why. Now connect those in some sort of expert system/case-based reasoning/learning by failure/searchable database. Better, but not necessarily engaging.

Here's my approach. Engage the expert with the following creative dialog: "Think of whatever it is you do—business, surgery, law—as a game at which you are the very best. Next, imagine that as a computer game that others could play and master. What game—including any projects, situations, challenges, people, and so on—could you create so that if someone did well in the game you would feel comfortable that they knew how to operate in your world as you do?" Offer him or her lots of great game examples for them to look at and maybe draw ideas and inspiration from. Tell them their goal with this game is to hold and capture the attention of people, to the point of addiction.

Fantasy? No, it's already happening. As we saw in Chapters 9 and 10, top derivatives traders, top law professors, top writers, top educators, top business people, and top military officers (among others) have all designed their own computer learning games to teach people about their own fields. And many of them are excellent!

Remember Robert Frost's quote, "I'm not a teacher, I'm an awakener." What a wonderful concept, to awaken the poet in all of us. How did he do this? I would guess he read his and other's poetry, for one thing. Then he had students try to create their own, for another. And then he had them share their creations with each other, for a third.

What about a game? Could Frost have created a game to help "leave us his mind" and awaken us to poetry? Is such a thing even possible?

Not only is it possible, but there's at least one poetry creation game already on the market. It even exists in a version on the computer. It's called the *Magnetic Poetry Kit*.[21] It comes with lots of interesting, image filled, evocative "poetic" words, that you put together on a magnetic board (or a filing cabinet) to make poetry. Does this mean any players' poetry will be Robert Frost-like? Of course not. But Frost didn't design the game, and it's only the earliest of beginnings. It might, however, inspire some people to make some interesting verses.

But here's the next step in making Robert Frost's approach to teaching into Digital Game-Based Learning. I ask Frost, "How do you make your poems?" (I'm imagining this, obviously.) He says (I'm making this up), "I observe things. I think about them. Images and sounds come into my mind, and I work with them."

So, we build a prototype of a game that generates images and sounds, possibly in response to waves coming from the brain (this part is not far-fetched. Brain waves—alpha, beta, and theta—are already used today to control all sorts of things on computers) that lets you "work with them." Frost works with us to iteratively improve the prototype, helping the program fit different kinds of word structures around these images until it produces something with which he is comfortable as approximating his own mental processes.

You get the idea. I'm not, of course, suggesting that we write poetry by computer, but that we *can* find a way to capture an expert's (artist's, scientist's, practitioner's) mental processes, not just through an "expert system" of heuristics, cases, and rules, but *through a game that feels to them like what they do.* A game that they, with their abilities, can master easily, but that others have to play long and hard to get better at. And where the game play is fun at the same time. Can this be done? Check out *Objection!*

Contest 11: What's your great idea for a Digital Game-Based Learning project and why? Email your entries to *Contest11@twitchspeed.com.*

A SECOND MODEL—BUILDING TOOLS OR ENGINES

In this less-frequently-used but also powerful model, the "producer" sees a way to create a Digital Game-Based Learning "engine," "shell," or "template" into which a large number of "teachers" can insert their content.

Examples include the *Living Books* series, *Reader Rabbit*, the *Blaster* series, as well as templates from LearningWare and games2train. Pretty much all the edutainment companies and games companies build and internally repurpose "engines" with different content. (This is not so different than the "for Dummies"-type books—where every book has the same structure, but a different author and content.)

In the long-run, building an "engine" is the best road to take for any Digital Game-Based Learning product that works well in one area and has applicability other areas, such as in a different industry. I strongly recommend that developers of Digital Learning games take into account when developing their first game that it *might* have multiple uses. By separating the "content assets" from the "engine" as much as possible from the beginning they can make the process of reusing the engine in other contexts much, much easier.

So now you've made your Digital Game-Based Learning masterpiece. How do you distribute it?

DON'T COUNT ON THE TRAINING COMPANIES

What about all those training companies that have grown so fast and moved to the Web? What do they think of Digital Game-Based Learning? I spoke with two CEOs to get their perspectives. Both, it turned out are personally in favor of learning through games. But neither saw it as a road to riches for their organizations. As practical heads of companies, they saw their business not as innovators but as providing whatever the market says it wants. And at least for now, both thought that adding "gamelike elements" to their products—such as simulations and scoring—was about as much games as the market would go for.

Pete Goettner, CEO of Digital Think, describes himself as a "big avid fan" of video games in general and of all kinds of simulations.[22] He feels that learning can "absolutely" be done through games. "But you have to remember," he says, "that Digital Think is a corporate elearning company and we are teaching professionals. There is a fine line where you have to be careful where you could offend people by making it too fun, by making it too whimsical." Goettner thinks that when you're training an engineer on how to program in Java, there's a limit to how many games you really want to put into that course. I, of course, think the opposite is true.

Goettner feels the corporate side is not going to have a lot of gaming for two reasons. The first is economic. Because games may cost more, he is not sure that the economics of Digital Game-Based Learning make sense. The second is that because people are not used to seeing games in training courses, "people maybe won't believe in it as much. If I walked into a CEO's office and said 'our philosophy around instructional design and content is to provide games,' I don't think that would sell."

Click2learn's CEO Kevin Oakes has spent time with games companies, such as Hyperbole, creators of the *X-files* game.[23] He thinks that there's a lot of things that the training companies could really learn from them. Oakes tells of receiving an email from one of his engineers after the engineer watched his mom play a game online simultaneously with 3,000 people. The engineer wrote that much of the content Click2learn is aggregating and providing is boring, page-turning text, without video or audio, and wouldn't it be fantastic if we used a lot more gaming activities. Oakes' reply to him was that he worries that senior executives, who "already have a biased perception about training" will see Digital Game-Based Learning as "a little fluffy rather than something they should spend serious money on." But Oakes does think that will start to change as corporations view the games as being a little more professional in nature, rather than just "fun-time" games. "As technology, tools, and processes get cheaper and cheaper and cheaper I think you'll start to see more emphasis on a better learning experience," said Oakes.

So, maybe we will see Digital Game-Based Learning in their future; on the other hand, we may never see it, if you believe these guys. When Digital Game-Based Learning takes off, it is unlikely to be because the training companies are pushing it. It will have to come from the creative efforts of people like those cited above (and hopefully you) who create really compelling Digital Game-Based Learning that generates unstoppable demand.

WHAT ABOUT THE GAMES COMPANIES?

But, you might ask, why aren't the games companies into this? They have the know-how; they have the technology. Here's a big new market for them— corporate learning. Seems like a natural. They should be dying to build Digital Game-Based Learning, right? When I first got started in the field, I thought my task would be just that simple. I'd go around to each games company, describe how they could use their game engines for business learning, and they would rush in to be my partners. I was definitely wrong.

Games companies have their own business model and their own sales problems. They are focused relentlessly on the consumer—the *entertainment* consumer. Their business is very competitive and they don't want to be distracted. Their goal is to keep ahead of the technology and produce megahits—they're a hits business just like the movies. This reaction from Trip Hawkins, CEO of game company 3DO, original founder of Electronic Arts, and one of the most forward-thinking pioneers on the business side of gaming, is typical: "We are in totally different markets both in terms of customer as well as marketing/distribution."[24]

At least one games company that tried to move in a corporate direction later regretted it. Maxis held off for a long time before finally taking on some corporate projects. According to Will Wright, it was very hard for a small company like it (at the time) to deal with big corporations. Maxis eventually spun off its corporate division.[25]

Demand, however, is again putting its siren song into the games makers ears. Harry Gottlieb president of Jellyvision, creators of the highly successful games *You Don't Know Jack* and *Who Wants to Be a Millionaire?*, says that it has been approached over and over again by companies wanting training versions of its games. "In the past," he says, "we always refused." However, they have had so many requests that they are now considering this seriously.[26]

WHAT ABOUT THE EDUTAINMENT COMPANIES?

They have their own problems. The Learning Company did not make Mattel richer, but just the opposite. "The problem with educational software," says Paul Saffo of the Institute for the Future in Palo Alto, California, who is generally a very good predictor of what's coming, "is that nobody has figured out how to make money doing it." [27]

When Lucas Interactive spun off Lucas Learning to make learning games, it had a lot of trouble positioning its initial game, *Droidworks*. Should it go on the games shelf? On the education shelf? This difficulty in positioning was actually very detrimental to sales, according to Collette Michaud, the project leader.[28] Imagine if they had an *adult* learning game? Where would they put that?

SO, WHAT IS THE ANSWER?

There are several potential solutions. A few companies appear to be in an excellent position to make a move in this area. One is Sony. They have all the ingredients: computers, game console with Internet links, handhelds, experience with education via Lightspan, and even a training subsidiary, Career Development International. Everyone I have contacted at Sony, from chairman Hideki Idei on down, has been tight-lipped, and despite the fact that they told PlayStation developers at the game developers conference that they "didn't want anything educational,"[29] they have positioned their latest game console as a portal to the Internet. Sony is a company that I would watch.

Two interesting efforts begun in 2004 are the Serious Games Initiative from the Woodrow Wilson Center in Washington, D.C., and the Education Arcade Initiative from MIT. I wish these efforts well, and we will see how far they get.

In addition there are numerous portals and Web sites that are fostering Digital Game-Based Learning. The Web sites for this book, *www.socialimpactgames.com* and *www.twitchspeed.com*, are two; *www.watercoolergames.org* and *www.seriousgames.org* are others. Hopefully, we will see more of these.

Finally, there are the users themselves. When Elliott Masie first suggested a Napsterlike peer-to-peer exchange for training programs,[30] I had to laugh. The reason Napster is so successful is, of course, that people *want* the music. Maybe trainers want to exchange lots of tell-test courses, but it's doubtful that learners do. However, I later thought, what if the learning was Digital Game-Based Learning, and really engaging and fun? Peer-to-peer might work, then, if the financial aspects could be worked out. Perhaps, in the *Key Commando* model (see Chapter 9), new learning games could even be given out free, with a charge for various content sets.[31]

We will find a way.

16

The Future
Where Do We Go From Here?

Opponents are everywhere.
— Sign at the entrance to Sega's booth at E3

I'm afraid he's on the Holodeck again, sir.
— *Star Trek, the Next Generation*

In 25 years your "typical gamer" will be everybody.
— Gabe Newell, Valve Entertainment

Where is the United States, technologically, at the start of the third millennium? Most business workers and a large percentage of our students and schools have—or have easy access to—networked multimedia computers. These computers are daily getting smaller, faster, and more multiuse. Devices that you can hold in your hand play video, place calls, connect with the Internet, determine your exact position on earth, and play a variety of games, alone and with others. You can use them to shop, bank, to vote, and even to get dates.[1] And in some cases, you can even use them to learn, although we are just at the beginning.

So, what does this all mean? In the words of game designer Justin Chin, "It means we all must start thinking a little bit differently, and that there are things out there that demand our creative attention."[2]

I believe that Digital Game-Based Learning, in our roles as business people, teachers, educators, parents, and *especially* trainers, is one of those things that *really demands* our creative attention. We have new generations—Games Generations—to educate and train, and we're just not going to get it done the old way. We are clearly at the very beginning of the Digital Game-Based Learning phenomenon—slightly past the Wright brothers, perhaps, but not much more. We're the airline industry of 1910. But with our creative attention and the technology now becoming available, we can, *in a very short time*, get from the bi-wing to the stealth bomber and way beyond.

Digital Game-Based Learning is a BIG IDEA. It works. It goes where no learning has gone before. We should all work together to create its future.

To think about that future, it is helpful to consider four of its elements:

- The future of digital learning
- The future of digital games
- The vision for their combination
- The creative challenges that it creates

One of our biggest challenges is clearly to "cross the chasm" into mainstream training and education. No matter how good Digital Game-Based Learning is or becomes in isolated instances and projects, it's future is not assured until that happens. Once it does, we can begin to *really* fly!

So, let us look at each of these futures in turn:

THE FUTURE OF DIGITAL LEARNING

Judging learning technology by what is out there today is probably unfair; we are going through a huge "building and construction" phase technologically, and what is out there is considerably less than the visions of many educators. What is that vision? Some of it, as we know by now, is just more boring tell-test online, with a few new twists. But parts of the vision are exciting.

We have infrastructure being built, components being integrated, companies being built up and consolidated, communities being formed. We are seeing willingness on the part of many corporations and schools to explore and embrace alternatives or additions to classroom learning. We see more and more content in courses, and hundreds, even thousands, of courses online. We see simulation starting to take on a larger and larger role in the online training process. We see colleges and universities rushing online.

What we don't yet see, percentage-wise, is much fun or joy in the online learning process. But that will come. It's as inevitable as the fact that the Games Generations will one day be in control. Training and education will become more learner-centered as learners demand it. Just as the Web led to "permission marketing," where people only want messages that they ask for and invite,[3] so the coming of Digital Game-Based Learning will lead to "permission training," where if training is not delivered in a form that is enjoyable and fun, it will be rejected.

THE FUTURE OF DIGITAL GAMES

Meanwhile, where is the games industry going? Because it is such a young business in such a rapidly changing and creative environment, it is impossible to say with any certainty. But based on the state of current research and development, the inevitable speeding up of the hardware and the thinking of top games designers,[4] here are some of the things future games are likely to be.

1. *Games will be much more realistic, experiential, and immersive.* We are very close to being able to create photorealistic 3D at will. Tomorrow's games will have the same and better special effects as today's movies, but they will be generated on the fly, from whatever perspective is desired. New displays, both huge and miniature, will allow players 360-degree vision, so players will be totally immersed in their game's 3D virtual worlds. Additional senses, such as smell and touch, will be stimulated as well. The "physics" of the way things look move and react will become more lifelike. Players will truly be inside the world of the game.

2. *Games will be fully online, wireless, and massively multiplayer.* Games will be played mostly online, with increasingly broadband capabilities, using portable and handheld devices with wireless access. Game worlds will allow thousands and eventually millions of players, who can play in single-player, one-on-one, and multiplayer modes. There will be worldwide games of all sizes and shapes going on 24/7/365.

3. *Games will include more and better storytelling and characters.* New, easier-to-use tools will allow writers artists and authors from

the Games Generations to begin to design and create games. Game subjects will be expanded. Better methods of combining story and interaction will be invented. A wider range of emotions will become involved. Improved artificial intelligence will allow the creation of more lifelike characters and interactions. Games will begin to produce classics with the lasting power of great movies and novels.

4. *Games will be more about people and human interaction.* Most games will involve playing a role in which you become involved with others emotionally, and that can last over many experiences (imagine yourself in a soap opera or a war.) We will see our friends and ourselves in our games however we want to look. The games will adapt effortlessly to our preferences, abilities, and needs, so we are always in the "flow state" as we play them. Although people are much harder to simulate than things, there will be characters in our games that express emotion, react believably to what we do, move and talk realistically, learn about us, and generally fun to play with. It will become harder and harder, in many situations, to tell an artificial intelligence (AI) character from a live one.

5. *Communication and cooperation will become more important elements.* We will communicate with other players via voice, privately or to all simultaneously. Games will be played around the world online, and by teams in the same room or arcade. Online sports and other competitions will become commonplace. Game relationships will be made and broken. Cooperation will become as important as competition.

6. *We will create the games we want.* We will have the ability to set enormous numbers of parameters, from who we are, to where the game happens, to who the players and opponents are, to how much challenge we want that day. In addition, the games will learn about us as we play, and adapt on the fly to what we enjoy. We will be able to take any perspective and viewpoint we choose. We will be able to share game elements that we create, and obtain them from others. We will input our own individuality and creativity into our games as we do into our houses and clothes. In this sense, we will all design our own games.

7. *We will have new game forms and subject matters.* As eye candy maxes out and people focus more on the game play and the interac-

tive entertainment experience, new forms of interaction and interactivity will emerge. As the Games Generations mature, we will see more and more universal themes expressed in the game medium. New genres will appear. Subject matter will take on the variety of books and movies. Games appealing to every demographic will be commonplace. Games will increasingly give us new types of experiences that we cannot get elsewhere.

8. *Mass entertainment types of games will become common.* Gaming and participation, where you, rather than someone else, are the protagonist, will become a new part of the home entertainment and TV experience. The boundaries between TV shows and multiplayer games will blur, as participation becomes the norm. Budgets will increase dramatically.

9. *Games will be higher quality.* As more and more people learn of how satisfying interactive entertainment is, the quality level demanded will rise. Games will have the same quality demands that we make on movies and other consumer products.

10. *Games will become even more engaging.* If you think people are hooked on games today, watch out for the future. All the techniques described above are designed to hook the player into the experience. "EverCrack" will become increasingly real, which is one important reason why we have to make these experiences *useful* as well as compelling. Certainly, whatever is coming will be a lot better and make today's best games seem as primitive as early movies.

THE VISIONS FOR DIGITAL GAME-BASED LEARNING

All these game advances will become part of Digital Game-Based Learning as it, too, gets better and better.

There are several "holy grails" for Digital Game-Based Learning. Perhaps the holiest is to create the equivalent of the holodeck of the *Star Trek* TV series. This is a place where the simulation becomes so real that characters appear to come alive and interact with you, and you experience yourself as being truly in the middle of another world. As Chris Crawford observed in his essay, "Thoughts on the Holodeck,"[5] it is interesting to see how the vision evolved over the life of the *Star Trek: The Next Generation* series from *object* game-based to *character* game-based.

One project to create the holodeck is already on its way—courtesy of the United States military. As we saw, the Army has given $45 million to the University of Southern California (USC) for precisely that mission—*to create the holodeck*. Hollywood directors and creators are working with a crack team of USC scientists to combine the latest state-of-the-art technologies with compelling stories, in order to provide immersive pre-mission environments.[6] These types of fully immersive environments, in huge warehouses, or through headmounted devices such as glasses, will have an impact on nonmilitary Digital Game-Based Learning as well. Virtual colleagues will come more slowly, but they will come.

Another exciting Digital Game-Based Learning vision is to have games and learning so integrated that the hottest new game on the market immediately becomes a learning tool. Because the distinction between the consumer market and the education market is still strong, this vision is further away. But signs of change exist. Some companies are creating learning game shells and selling engines.[7] Others market their learning games, from *SimCity* to *Start-up*, as consumer, rather than educational products.[8] Still other companies own both games and learning divisions.[9]

A third Digital Game-Based Learning vision is to have all teachers and learners hooked up to massive, persistent, multiplayer games where learning can be constantly happening, revisions input, students evaluated, and scores compared and tabulated. This is happening as well.[10] Persistent massively multiplayer games resembling *EverQuest*, *Asheron's Call*, *Ultima Online*, and *Star Peace* will merge with the new learning management systems to create just these sorts of Digital Game-Based Learning environments.

When will we get there? How soon? What will the online learning evolve into? What changes will universal broadband make? What will learning look like in the mid-twenty-first century, and after?

THE CHALLENGES

Computer games are still in their infancy—the whole industry is less than 30 years old, compared to over 100 years for the movies and hundred of years for novels. In the words of Warren Spector of Ion Storm, "All of us here today are witnessing the birth of a new medium. A hundred years ago, it was the movies, then radio, then television, now us."[11]

We can certainly expect games to evolve and mature just as those creative media did. A key difference, though, is speed. On the technology side, games are evolving at twitch speed and at the exponential speed of Moore's Law.[12] In only a few years, we have gone from *Pong* to *Quake II*, *Golden Eye*, *The Sims*, and sports games that are only a few pixels from absolute realism. Console games are already entering their sixth generation.[13]

Mass education and training—a few hundred years old, and much slower developers—are beginning their pimply adolescence, and are really uncomfortable in their own skin. They are sprouting a few technology whiskers, but have not yet decided what to do with them.

If the two are to really combine, it is not the technology, but rather the *people who are able to harness and use the technology for new inventions of their imagination* who will truly move the process forward. In movies, we can list all the technologies from the silents to the talkies to color to special effects, but what we care about and go to see are the films of Eisenstein, Capra, Truffaut, Kurosawa, Lucas, Spielberg, and Cameron. Although people are still attracted by technical breakthroughs, the movies have evolved to the point that technology alone cannot make a movie successful. At the Oscars, the best director Oscar is handed out just before the best picture, whereas the technical achievement awards are handed out in an untelevised ceremony the day before. Games now need great artists more than they need great technologists. Yet today, even among gamers, very few game artists, as we have seen, are known by name.

The same holds true even more for Digital Game-Based Learning—we need artists who happen to be teachers. The technology of the games industry can allow us to do marvelous, incredible things. But if learning games continue to be designed by people with a "teaching" perspective only, rather than by creative artists who grew up with and really know how to use the medium of games and fun, and who also happen, like Ashley Lipson, to be teachers, it won't happen. What we are waiting for is for the great teacher-designers to step forth, the people with the vision to harness this technology in the name of fun learning. They will certainly come.

In the meantime, Digital Game-Based Learning is clearly picking up steam. To move forward even more quickly we need several things and to meet several challenges:

- *From business* we need champions, who can provide both investment dollars and opportunities to help Digital Game-Based Learning "cross the chasm." *The challenge for business is to understand its changing work force and keep funding larger and larger initiatives in tune with a changing learner population.*
- *From teachers and trainers* we need willingness to try a style that perhaps isn't theirs by birth, but which works for their learners. *The challenge for teachers and trainers is to combine the old content with the new approaches.*
- *From schools* we need requests for more learning games that speak to the entire range and depth of the things that we want our kids to know, so that schools and school districts will buy and use them. *The challenge for schools is to not run back to the past, but to embrace the future, and to learn to shape it and to control it.*
- *From parents* we need as much interaction with their kids as possible around Digital Game-Based Learning, so parents can find what works for their kids and get them more of it. *The challenge for parents is to make the time to work with their kids and not just throw their kids the fanciest box on the shelf.*
- *From training companies* we need a willingness to take the risks to create the kinds of learning that they *know* works better for learners. *The challenge for training companies is to convince the buyers and sell Digital Game-Based Learning.*
- *From vendors* we need easier-to-use creation tools, so that trainers and teachers can create the games that they know will work without having to be programmers. *The challenge for vendors is to go far beyond the current generation of "authoring systems" to something much more powerful.*
- *From games companies* we need their managements to recognize that learning is important, whether or not education and training are big and potentially lucrative markets initially, because they will be lucrative markets in the long run. *The challenge for games companies is to understand that their skills and knowledge are valuable for learning, and that they have the ability to better educate their own kids and future generations of kids and adults.* It is truly sad when Nintendo uses a board game, rather than its own powerful technology, to teach its own employees about business.[14]

- *From academics* we need new experiments and assessments of the tools of today, rather than the theories of yesterday. *The challenge for academics is to work with those producing the new tools to validate them and make their effectiveness known.*
- *From learners,* at all levels, we need confirmation, through their time and success, that this is what they want and what works for them. *The challenge for learners is to get hold of the Digital Game-Based Learning that is out there and use it.*

If we can meet many or most of these challenges, Digital Game-Based Learning is assured an opportunity to make a huge difference in our companies', our nation's, and even our world's future.

So go ahead—fire up the old console or PC and slip in your favorite game. And as you unwind along those familiar and challenging paths, pause for a minute and reflect—"You know, I could be learning something *useful!*"

NOTES

PART ONE: INTRODUCTION / BACKGROUND

Introduction

1. Thomas Watson, Sr., chairman of IBM, 1953. This is quoted widely on the Internet and elsewhere, but no one gives a source. The quote may be apocryphal.
1. According to Ogilvy, this was included in a slide presentation.
2. Malcolm Gladwell, *The Tipping Point: How Little Things Can Make a Big Difference*, Little Brown & Company, 2000.
3. Merrill Lynch, in its 2000 report *The Knowledge Web*, estimates the worldwide education market at $2 trillion, including recruiting. eduventures.com estimates that the $750–800 billion U.S. market represents one-third of the world total, bringing the world figure to between $2.2 and 2.5 trillion.
4. I heard this at a talk Berners-Lee gave in New York in 1998.
5. Quoted by Edward, Duke of Windsor, *A King's Story*, Putnam, 1951.

Chapter 1

1. The *Hollywood Reporter* reported the 1999 U.S. film box office as $7.5 billion. PC Data reports 1999 retail game sales as $7.4 billion.
2. The U.S. Bureau of Labor Statistics' U.S. Population Survey estimates the 1999 median age of the workforce as 39.
3. Roger Schank, *Virtual Learning: A Revolutionary Approach to Building a Highly Skilled Workforce*, McGraw-Hill, 1997, p. xii
4. George Bernard Shaw, "A Treatise on Parents and Children," Preface to *Misalliance*, 1909.
5. Henry Louis Mencken (1880–1856) *A Mencken Chrestomathy* [1949]: "Travail," p. 308.
6. Burck Smith of Smarthinking.com at the Education Industry Finance and Investment Conference, Church Falls, VA, May 8–9, 2000.
7. "Bill Byham says what keeps him awake is how to get people to stick with Web training long enough to learn something." *Training & Development* magazine, March 2000.
8. Guy Kawasaki, *Rules for Revolutionaries*, Harper Business, 1999, p. 23.
9. See Chapter 1, note 1.

10. Merrill Lynch, in its 2000 report *The Knowledge Web*, estimates corporate plus government training at $110 billion.
11. See Introduction, Note 3.
12. Merrill Lynch, in its 2000 report *The Knowledge Web*, estimates a compound annual growth rate of 79 percent.
13. Including motion pictures, music, television, theater, publishing, gambling and sports.
14. The U.S. Bureau of Labor Statistics' U.S. Population Survey estimates the 1999 median age of the workforce as 39.
15. American Federation of Teachers.
16. *Online News*, November 1999.
17. In "Does Easy Do It? Children Games and Learning," in *Game Developer* magazine, June 1998.
18. For the full story, see Nicholas Negroponte, *Being Digital*, Vintage Books, 1996, p. 196.
19. This attribution of the term to Crockford comes from Noah Falstein.
20. Through programs such as *Sesame Street Letters, Jumpstart Learning Games ABC's*, and *Jumpstart Phonics, Toddlers*, and *Pre-school*.
21. The Lightspan Partnership. See Chapters 7 and 14.
22. Art Fazakis, "A Look at Chess in the Public Schools," online at *www.zone.com/kasparov/chessinschool.asp*
23. *New York Times*, December 31, 1998.
24. AOL's *President '96* and *Reinventing America* created by Crossover Technologies and funded by the Markle Foundation.
25. *Straight Shooter!* See Chapter 9.
26. *Sim Health*. See Chapter 9.
27. Training simulation from Andersen Consulting; *Sim Refinery* for Chevron from Thinking Tools.
28. *The Monkey Wrench Conspiracy*. See Chapters 1 and 9.
29. For example, SIMNET tank simulators. See Chapter 10.
30. Sarah Fister, "CBT Fun and Games," *Training*, May 1999.
31. Articles about *Straight Shooter!* appeared in *Training*, August 1997, *Securities Industry News*, August 24, 1998, *Future Banker*, July 1998, *Derivatives Strategy*, June 1998, *Training & Development*, September 1998, *Fast Company*, September 1998, and *Newsweek*, November 30, 1998.
32. Quoted in Christine Solomon, *Developing Applications with Microsoft Office*, p. 495.
33. From *The Monkey Wrench Conspiracy*.
34. Posted on The Monkey Wrench Zone on think3's website *www.think3.com*.
35. According to Paula Young, PricewaterhouseCoopers.
36. Financial Accounting Standards Board (FASB) Statement of Financial Accounting Standards No. 133, *Accounting for Derivative Instruments and Hedging Activities*, was issued on June 16, 1998, effective for fiscal years beginning after June 15, 1999.

Chapter 2

1. The U.S. Bureau of Labor Statistics' U.S. Population Survey estimates the 1999 median age of the workforce as 39.
2. Gladwell, op. cit., p.100.
3. David S. Bennehum, *Extra Life, Coming of Age in Cyberspace*, Basic Books, 1998, p.15.
4. J. C. Herz, *Joystick Nation: How Videogames Ate Our Quarters, Won Our Hearts and Rewired Our Minds*, Little, Brown & Company, 1997, p. 26.
5. Sony alone had sold over 150 million Walkmans by 1995, according to its website. Clones and imitators would surely double that number.
6. Telephone interview.

7. "Television in the Home, 1998: Third Annual Survey of Parent and Children," Annenburg Policy Center, June 22, 1998, gives the number as 2.55 hours. M. Chen, in *The Smart Parents Guide to Kid's TV* (1994) gives the number as 4 hours per day.

8. PricewaterhouseCoopers says that more than 25 percent of teens stay on more than an hour per visit. Jupiter communications cites 303 minutes per month for teens and 656 minutes for young adults.

9. "Interactive Video Games" *Mediascope*, June 1996.

10. 365 days per year x 3 hours per day x 21 years = 22,995 hours.

11. 365 days per year x 1.5 hours per day x 18 years (give them a few years to get started) = 9855 hours.

12. There are roughly eighteen 30-second commercials during a television hour. 18 commercials per hour x 22,995 hours (above) = 413,910 commercials.

13. Eric Leuliette, a voracious (and meticulous) reader who has listed online every book he has ever read (www.csr.utexas.edu / personal / leuliette / fw_table_home.html), read about thirteen hundred books through college. If we take 1300 books x 200 pages per book x 400 words per page, we get 10,400,000,000 words. If the books were read at 400 words per minute, that would give 260,000 minutes of reading per year, or 4333 hours. This represents a little over 3 hours per book. Although others may read more slowly, most have read far fewer books than Leuliette.

14. Cited by Don Tapscott in *The Digital Economy: Promise and Peril in the Age of Networked Intelligence*, McGraw-Hill, 1998.

15. Don Tapscott, *Growing Up Digital: The Rise of the Net Generation*, McGraw-Hill, 1998, p. 1.

16. Phone interview. Dr. Ray Perez, cognitive psychologist, works for the Department of Defense.

17. J. C. Herz, *Joystick Nation*, op. cit.

18. Don Tapscott, *Growing Up Digital*, op. cit., p. 2.

19. Marshall McLuhan and Quentin Fiore, *War and Peace in the Global Village*, Hardwired, 1997 (first printing 1968), p. 7.

20. Otto Lowenstein, *The Senses*, quoted by Marshall McLuhan in *War and Peace in the Global Village*, op. cit., p. 11.

21. Marshall McLuhan in *War and Peace in the Global Village*, op. cit., p. 36.

22. Ibid., p. 98.

23. *Newsweek*, January 1, 2000.

24. Paul Perry in *American Way*, May, 15, 2000.

25. *Newsweek*, January 1, 2000.

26. Marian Diamond, *Enriching Heredity: The Impact of the Environment on the Anatomy of the Brain*, The Free Press, 1988, p. 2.

27. Renate Numella Caine and Geoffrey Caine, *Making Connections: Teaching and the Human Brain*, Addison Wesley, 1991, p. 31.

28. Quoted in Frank D. Roylance "Intensive Teaching Changes Brain," SunSpot, Maryland's Online Community, May 27, 2000.

29. Dr. Mriganka Sur, *Nature*, April 20, 2000.

30. Sandra Blakeslee, *New York Times*, April 24, 2000.

31. Leslie Ungerlieder, National Institutes of Health.

32. James McLelland, University of Pittsburgh.

33. Cited in *Inferential Focus Briefing*, September 30, 1997.

34. Virginia Berninger, *American Journal of Neuroradiology*, May 2000.

35. Reported in *USA Today*, December 10, 1998.

36. *Newsweek*, January 1, 2000.

37. Alexandr Romanovich Luria (1902–1977), Soviet pioneer in neuropsychology. Author of *The Human Brain and Psychological Processes* (1963).

38. Quoted in Erica Goode, "How Culture Molds Habits of Thought," *New York Times*, August 8, 2000.

39. Ibid.

40. John T. Bruer, *The Myth of the First Three Years*, The Free Press, 1999, p. 155.

41. Roylance, op. cit.

42. *Time*, July 5, 1999.

43. Anthropologist Richard Potts of the Smithsonian Institution, quoted in *Inferential Focus Briefing*, September 30, 1997.

44. *The Economist*, December 6, 1997.

45. Quoted in Robert Lee Hotz "In Art of Language, the Brain Matters " *Los Angeles Times*, October 18, 1998.

46. Ibid.

47. Peter Moore, *Inferential Focus Briefing*, September 30, 1997.

48. Quoted in Moore, *Inferential Focus Briefing*.

49. Patricia Marks Greenfield, *Mind and Media: The Effects of Television, Video Games and Computers*, Harvard University Press, 1984.

50. This and the following references are from Greenfield, *Mind and Media*.

51. Patricia M. Greenfield and Rodney R. Cocking, Eds., *Interacting with Video*, Ablex Publishing, 1996.

52. Moore, op. cit.

53. McLuhan and Fiore, *War and Peace in the Global Village*, op. cit., p. 152.

54. Although the term *digital immigrants* may be mine, I am not the first to use the immigrant metaphor. Douglas Rushkoff, author of *Playing the Future: How Kid's Culture Can Teach Us to Thrive in an Age of Chaos*, is quoted as saying "kids are natives in a place where most adults are immigrants" (Elizabeth Weil, "The Future Is Younger Than You Think," *Fast Company*, May 1997).

55. Greenfield, *Mind and Media*, op. cit., p. 101.

56. Tapscott, *Growing Up Digital*, op. cit., p. 3.

57. Janet H. Murray, *Hamlet on the Holodeck:, The Future of Narrative in Cyberspace*, MIT Press, 1997.

58. Quoted in Geoff Keighley, *Millenium Gaming*, GameSpot, *www.gamespot.com /features/ btg_y2k*.

59. Ibid.

60. Greenfield, *Mind and Media*, op. cit., p. 102.

61. Quoted in Tapscott, op. cit., p.109

62. Quoted in Gladwell, op. cit., p. 110.

63. Personal conversation.

64. Susan Gilbert, "Gains in Diagnosing Hyperactivity," *New York Times*, June 20, 2000.

65. See J. F. Lubar, "Neurofeedback Assessment and Treatment for Attention Deficit/Hyperactivity Disorder," in J. R Evans and A. Abarnel, eds., *Quantitative EEG and Neurofeedback*, Academic Press 1999, pp. 103–143, and Monastra, V, "Assessing Attention Deficit Hyperactivity Disorder via QEEG," *Neuropsychology*, 1999, No. 13, pp. 424–433. This research is being used by East3, a biofeedback company that modifies video games, to show children what it feels like to move from theta- to beta-intensive mode.

66. Gladwell, op. cit., p. 100.

67. Ibid.

68. Gladwell, op. cit., p. 101.

69. Telephone interview.

70. Stoll, op. cit., p. 13.

71. Jane M. Healy, *Failure to Connect: How Computers Affect out Children's Minds— and What We Can Do About It*, Simon & Schuster, 1998, p. 32.

NOTES

415

72. *New York Times*, December 30, 1997.
73. Private communication.
74. Greenfield, *Mind and Media,* op. cit., p. 112.
75. Peter Moore, op. cit.
76. Ibid.
77. Tapscott, op. cit., p. 103.
78. Marshall McLuhan and Quentin Fiore, *The Medium Is the Massage: An Inventory of Effects*, Bantam Books, 1967, p. 63.
79. Dean Meyer, reported in Tapscott, op. cit., p. 104.
80. Patrticia M. Greenfield, "The Cultural Evolution of IQ," in U. Neisser, ed., *The Rising Curve: Long Term Gains in IQ and Related Measures* (pp. 81–123), American Psychological Association.
81. Stephen S. Hall, "Fear Itself," *New York Times Magazine*, February 28, 1999.
82. August 27, 2000.
83. Telephone interview.
84. Telephone interview.
85. Telephone interview.
86. The 2000 Pew Internet & American Life project found that 32 percent of Americans, or 31 million people, say they "definitely will not go" online, and an additional 25 percent say they "probably will not" venture on to the Internet. Of those who say they'll never go online, 81 percent are over the age of 50.
87. Tapscott, op. cit., p. 36.

Chapter 3

1. Jane M. Healy, *Endangered Minds: Why Children Don't Think and What We Can Do About It*, Simon & Schuster, 1990, p. 27.
2. Stan Davis and Jim Botkin, *The Monster Under the Bed*, Simon & Schuster, 1994, p. 32.
3. National Institute for Literacy (*www.NIFL.gov*).
4. Peter T. Kilborn "Learning at Home, Students Take the Lead," *New York Times*, May 24, 2000.
5. Davis and Botkin, op. cit.
6. Schank, op. cit., p. 7.
7. Quoted by Peter Applebome in "Two Words Behind The Massacre," *New York Times*, May 2, 1999.
8. Ward Cannel and Fred Marx, *How to Play the Piano Despite Years of Lessons: What Music Is and How to Make It at Home*, Crown & Bridge, 1976.
9. Telephone interview. Luyen Chou is CEO of Learn Technologies Interactive, Inc. See Chapter 7.
10. Telephone interview.
11. Elliott Masie, "The "e" in E-Learning Stands for 'E'xperience," The MASIE Center, Special Report, October 20, 1999.
12. John Holt, *How Children Fail*, Dell, 1964, p. 151.
13. Tapscott, op. cit., p. 129.
14. Telephone interview.
15. Trademarked by Learn2.com.
16. Roger C. Schank, "What We Learn When We Learn By Doing," The Institute for the Learning Sciences, Technical Report No. 60, October 1994, p. 1.
17. Neil Postman, *Amusing Ourselves to Death: Public Discourse in the Age of Show Business*, Penguin Books, 1985, p. 33.

18. Telephone interview.
19. Seth Godin, *Permission Marketing: Turning Strangers into Friends and Friends into Customers*, Simon & Schuster, 1999, p. 91.
20. Frank Smith, *The Book of Learning and Forgetting*, Teachers College Press, 1998, p. 63.
21. I heard Ferren express these ideas at United Digital Artists' *Edgewise 99* conference.
22. Ibid.
23. Religions of the World Organization Website: *www.religions.hypermart.net.*
24. Davis and Bodkin, op. cit., p. 151.
25. *Training*, April 2000.
26. *USA Today*, October 7, 1998.
27. Telephone interview.
28. Tapscott, op. cit., p. 36.
29. U.S. Department of Education, Digest of Education Statistics, National Center for Education Statistics, 1999, Table 2, p. 11.
30. National Institute for Literacy, *www.NIFL.gov.*
31. Telephone interview.
32. Telephone interview.
33. See Chapter 3, Note 29.

Chapter 4

1. McLuhan and Fiore, *War and Peace in the Global Village*, op. cit., p. 149.
2. See Chapter 3, Note 21.
3. Davis and Botkin, op. cit., p. 33.
4. Telephone interview.
5. "Computer Gaming in America," report commissioned by *Computer Gaming World* 1998, and Johhny Wilson, "Not Just for Kids," *Computer Gaming World*, May 1996.
6. Motion Picture Association of America.
7. Personal communication from Jason Robar.
8. Scott McCloud, *Understanding Comics*, Kitchen Sink Press, 1993.
9. In a talk in London, 2000. Reported by Paula Young.
10. Ashley S. Lipson, "The Inner Game of Educational Computer Games," self-published paper, no date.
11. Telephone interview.
12. Matt Richtel, "A Video Game Maker Hits Reset: Electronic Arts Is Betting on the Internet for the Future of Video Games," *New York Times*, August 21, 2000.
13. Quoted in Geoff Keighley, op. cit.
14. Ibid.
15. Ibid.
16. In "Does Easy Do It? Children Games and Learning," in *Game Developer* magazine, June 1998.
17. Eve Tahmincioglu, "To Shirkers, The Days of Whine and Roses," *New York Times*, July 19, 2000.

PART TWO

Chapter 5

1. *Microsoft Encarta World English Dictionary, North American Edition, www.dictionary.msn.com.*
2. *Oxford English Dictionary*, Second Edition, Oxford University Press, 1989.
3. Telephone interview.

4. Herz, op. cit., p. 40.
5. Johan Huizinga, *Homo Ludens*, The Beacon Press, 1955, p. 3.
6. Negroponte, op. cit., p. 196.
7. Christian Bisson and John Luckner, "Fun in Learning: The Pedagogical Role of Fun in Adventure Education," *Journal of Experimental Education*, Vol. 9, No. 2, 1996, pp. 109–110.
8. Ibid.
9. Colin Rose and Malcolm J. Nicholl, *Accelerated Leaning for the 21st Century*, 1998, p. 30.
10. Rose and Nicholl, op. cit., p. 63.
11. Bisson and Luckner, op. cit., p.109: "Research and reflections of the concept of fun/enjoyment have induced authors [cited in text] to directly relate intrinsic motivation with fun."
12. Huizinga, op. cit.
13. Roger Caillois, *Man, Play, and Games*, Free Press, 1961.
14. Huizinga, op. cit., p. 13.
15. Caillois, op. cit., p. 9.
16. Address to the Computer Games Developers Conference, March 2000.
17. Diane Ackerman, *Deep Play*, Random House, 1999, p.11.
18. Chris Crawford, *The Art of Computer Game Design*, 1982.
19. Cited in the *New York Times*.
20. Alison Gopnik, Andrew N. Meltzoff, and Patricia K. Kuhl, *The Scientist in the Crib: Minds, Brains, and How Children Learn*, William Morrow and Company, 1999, pp. 8–9.
21. See Note 16.
22. Quoted by Dale Russakoff in "Mind Games for Tech Success: You've Got to Play to Win," *The Washington Post*, May 8, 2000.
23. *Observer*, January 15, 1950.
24. William H. Starbuck and Jane Webster, "When Is Play Productive?," in *Accounting, Management and Information Technology*, Vol. 1, No. 1, 1991, p. 86.
25. Michael Schrage, *Serious Play: How the World's Best Companies Simulate to Innovate*, Harvard Business School Press, 2000.
26. William M. Bulkeley, "Business War Games Attract Big Warriors," *The Wall Street Journal*, December 22, 1994.
27. *Inside Technology Training*, April 2000, p. 14.
28. *Thiagi Game Letter*, Vol. 1, Number 5, August 1998, p. 1.
29. Ibid.
30. Eric Jensen, *Brain-Based Learning*, The Brain Store, 2000, p. 125.
31. Caine and Caine, op. cit., pp. 69–70.
32. William H. Starbuck and Jane Webster, "When Is Play Productive?," in *Accounting, Management and Information Technology*, Vol. 1, No. 1, 1991.
33. Tapscott, op. cit., p. 10.
34. Dale Russakoff in "Mind Games for Tech Success: You've Got to Play to Win," *Washington Post*, May 8, 2000.
35. Starbuck and Webster, op. cit., p 85.
36. From the article "Sports: Sociological, Psychological and Physiological aspects," *www.brittanica.com*. Used by permission.
37. Personal communication.
38. Telephone interview.
39. Quoted in Bob Filipczak, "Training Gets Doomed," *Training*, August 1997.
40. Telephone interview.
41. Telephone interview.
42. Telephone interview.

43. See Mihaly Csikszentmihalyi, *Flow: the Psychology of Optimal Experience*, Harper & Row, 1990.

44. Music Mouse is available at *www.dorsai.org/~spiegel/ls_programs.html*.

45. Telephone interview.

46. Chapter 3, Note 21.

47. "Electronic Storytelling and Human Immersion," position paper at Modeling and Simulation: Linking Entertainment and Defense Conference, 1996.

48. Telephone interview.

49. Telephone interview.

50. Telephone interview.

51. Caillois, op. cit., pp. 11–36.

52. Chris Crawford, *The Art of Computer Game Design*, 1982, (online at *www.erasmatazz.com*)

53. Address to Computer Game Developers Conference, March 2000.

54. Geoff Keighley, op. cit.

55. *Next Generation* magazine, July 97, pp. 41–49.

56. Jellyvision, Chicago, IL, *www.jellyvison.com*.

57. Telephone interview.

58. Quoted in Geoff Keighley, op. cit.

59. Quoted by Steve Lohr, *New York Times*, March 5, 1998.

60. Ibid.

61. Various speeches.

62. Nancy Malitz "Invasion of the Girls Surprises Video-Game Makers," *New York Times*, December 21, 1995.

63. Ibid.

64. According to PC Data, Barbie titles were ranked numbers 2, 7, and 14 in U.S. retail game sales in December 1998. In December 1999, a Barbie title was ranked number 5.

65. Malitz, op. cit.

66. Herz, op. cit., p. 172.

67. Ibid.

68. Greenfield, *Mind & Media*, op. cit., p. 102.

69. The code, taught to me by Russell Phelan, age 9, is "How do you turn this on."

Chapter 6

1. This is the premise of *The Monkey Wrench Conspiracy*, set out in a opening, 3-minute animated sequence created by Dub Media, a commercial game design house.

2. Internal presentation, results to be published.

3. *Thiagi Game Letter*, Vol. 1, No. 1, March 1998.

4. Thomas W. Malone, "What Makes Computer Games Fun?," *Byte*, December 1981.

5. See Chapter 6, Note 2.

6. Ashley S. Lipson, op. cit.

7. Telephone interview.

8. Schank, *Virtual Leaning*, op. cit., p. 30.

9. Quoted in Filipczak, op. cit.

10. Filipczak, op. cit.

11. Various speeches.

12. Gordon Dryden and Dr. Jeanette Vos, *The Learning Revolution: To Change the Way the World Learns*, The Learning Web, 1999, p. 34.

13. Thomas W. Malone, "Towards a Theory of Intrinsic Motivation," *Cognitive Science*, No. 4, 1981, pp. 333–369.

14. Personal communication.

15. Telephone interview.
16. *President '96* was a multiplayer online game, designed by Crossover Technologies, which ran concurrently with the 1996 election. It was hosted by America Online, Time Warner's Pathfinder, and CNN.
17. In *Star Peace: The Parallel Domain*, hundreds of players at a time create huge, *Sim City*–style cities, forming ongoing economies and political structures, complete with elections for mayors, ministers, and presidents.
18. Len Strazewski, "And Now for Training Completely Different," AV Video and Multimedia Producer, September 1996, p. 50.
19. Telephone interview.
20. Scott McCloud, op. cit.
21. Telephone interview.
22. Telephone interview.
23. Telephone interview.
24. Chapter 3, Note 21.
25. The paper case and spreadsheet for *Kristen's Cookies* are available from the Harvard Business School Case Clearing House. See also Chapter 8.
26. See Chapter 10.
27. *Telesim*, a simulation designed to teach managers about running their businesses more independently and competing in an era of deregulation, was created by Coopers and Lybrand and Maxis Business Systems (Later Thinking Tools) for Pacific Telesis and NYNEX.
28. Telephone interview and slide presentation, "Gaming in Education," Influent New Media Conference, 1998.
29. Telephone interview.
30. For example, from Nokia, NTT DoCoMo, and Motorola.
31. According to a Nintendo press release, June 15, 2000, "shipments of Nintendo's portable Game Boy will surpass 100,000,000 on June 16. Since its launch in 1989, Game Boy worldwide has sold continuously at an average rate of more than 1,000 systems per hour for 11 years to reach the 100 million number."
32. Personal interview.
33. Personal interview.

Chapter 7

1. Data from Nielson Home Technology Report; Jupiter Communications; Alliance for Converging Technologies; FIND/SVP, compiled in Tapscott, op. cit., p.22.
2. See Chapter 3, Note 29.
3. Anthony G. Oettinger, *Run Computer, Run: The Mythology of Educational Innovation*, Harvard University Press, 1969.
4. Apple Classrooms of Tomorrow (ACOT) was a ten-year research and development collaboration among public schools, universities, research agencies, and Apple Computer, Inc., set up to study the effects of the use of technology on teaching and learning outcomes. It concluded in 1998, but the results of this project and ongoing research conducted by Apple can be found on the Web site *www.apple.com/education/k12/leadership/acot/*
5. Jack Connick, "... And Then There Was Apple," Call-A.P.P.L.E., October 1986, p. 24.
6. Dr. Steven Weyhrich.
7. The two founders were Bill Bowman and David Seuss.
8. "The Learning Revolution," *Business Week*, February 28, 1994.
9. Biography of Ann Hathaway McCormick at *www.learningfriends.com/annresume.htm*.

10. Will Wright, telephone interview.
11. IDC.
12. Telephone interview.
13. *US News and World Report*, September 13, 1999.
14. *New York Times*, June 3, 1999.
15. Quoted in *US News and World Report*, September 13, 1999.
16. Jane Healy is the author of *Endangered Minds* and *Failure to Connect* (op. cit.). Clifford Stoll is the author of *High Tech Heretic* (op. cit.). I discuss their ideas in Chapter 14.
17. This is a "guesstimate," but the direction is, I'm sure, correct.
18. Quoted in Filipczak, op. cit.
19. Joe Costello "Let's Get Radical: Put Video Games in Classrooms," *Mercury Center*, January 29, 2000.
20. The Lightspan discussion is based on personal and telephone interviews.
21. Telephone interview.
22. The LTI discussion is based personal interviews with Luyen Chou..
23. According to the National Center for Education Statistics, in the fall of 1999, 95 percent of public schools were connected to the Internet. They expect 100 percent to be connected by 2000.
24. See Chapter 1, Note 22.
25. *New York Times*, December 31, 1998.
26. Both *President '96*, a multiplayer online game on America Online and *Reinventing America*, a multiplayer simulation on Time-Warner's Pathfinder, have been used.
27. Telephone interview and company information.
28. *www.clickhealth.com*.
29. Debra A. Lieberman, "Health Education Video Games for Children and Adolescents: Theory, Design and Research Findings," paper presented at the annual meeting of the International Communications Association, Jerusalem, 1998.
30. Telephone interview.
31. Debra Galant, "Schools Scramble to Find More Space," *New York Times*, July 4, 1999.
32. "Our Research," TERC website, *www.terc.edu / mathequity / gw / html / papers.html*.
33. Telephone interview. Dr. Chipman works for the Office of Naval Research.
34. Wyndhaven is a project of Intermetrics, and is part of the Computer Aided Education and Training Initiative (CAETI).
35. TERC, an education consulting company, can be found at www.terc.edu. The "Through the Glass Wall Project" can be found at *www.terc.edu / mathequity / gw / html / gwhome.html*.
36. Peter DeLisle, Whoola!'s co-founder, is professor of education at the University of Illinois, Urbana-Champaign. See www.whoola.com.
37. I experienced this case first in its spreadsheet form as a Harvard Business School student, and later helped to turn it into Digital Game-Based Learning.
38. Filipczak, op. cit.
39. An early interactive videodisc program, Dexter is now apparently defunct. Sharon Sloane, President of Will Interactive, worked on the team that created it.
40. Dr. Will Peratino, Director of Technology at Defense Acquisition University, was one of the designers.
41. As far as I know, Bushnell's ambitious vision was never realized.

Chapter 8

1. *New York Times*, July 14, 2000.
2. Jack Olsen, *The Mad World of Bridge*, Holt, Rinehart & Winston, 1960.

3. According to a 1999 Gallup poll, 57 percent of American adults had bought a lottery ticket in the past 12 months. *Gallup Poll Social Audit Survey on Gambling in America*, reported in July 8, 1999 poll release at *www.gallup.com/poll/releases/pr990708.asp*.

4. IDSA.

5. *Time Digital*, August 2000.

6. Russakoff, op. cit.

7. *New York Times Magazine*, November 1, 1998, p. 42.

8. Telephone interview.

9. Telephone interview.

10. Telephone interview.

11. Ron Zemke, "When Is a Game Not a Game and a Cigar Just a Smoke?," *Training Forum*, September 10, 1997.

12. Telephone interview.

13. *Online News*, November 1999.

14. *Jeopardy!* spokesperson.

15. *Jeopardy!* website, *www.spe.sony.com/tv/shows/jeopardy/*

16. *Jeopardy!* spokesperson.

17. These are not "real" *Jeopardy!* They don't use the name or the reverse question approach but do use the grid-type style.

18. Paul Ventmiglia, a developer of computer-based training at Ford Motor Company.

19. Personal communication.

20. *Jeopardy!* spokesperson.

21. Sony public relations spokesperson.

22. *Game Week*, June 19, 2000.

23. Telephone interview.

24. Telephone interview.

25. "Drama is life with the dull bits left out."

26. Telephone interview.

27. In a position paper at Modeling and Simulation: Linking Entertainment and Defense Conference, 1996, Jacquelyn Ford Morie reports that there is a sign on an airplane simulator invented by Edwin Link in 1930 at the U.S. Air Force Armament Museum in Pensacola, Florida, that states that it was originally designed as an entertainment device. This "Blue Box" was sold to amusement parks until 1934, when Link, a pilot himself, met with the Army Air Corp to sell the corp on the concept of pilot training with his device.

28. Telephone interview.

29. David R. Pratt, Department of Defense's Joint Simulation Systems/Joint Program Office.

30. See Chapter 10.

31. *Thiagi Game Letter*, Vol. 1, No. 9, January 1999, p. 7.

32. Ibid.

33. Telephone interview.

34. MiSSILE program. See Chapter 10

35. Telephone interview.

36. *Life and Death*, published by The Software Toolworks.

37. Personal communication.

38. Telephone interview.

39. Quoted in Geoff Keighley, op. cit.

40. Telephone interview.

41. The information on Monte Cristo is based on a personal interview with Marc Robert, Director of Marketing.

42. According to PC Data, the biggest selling games in 1999 were *Sim City 3000* and *Roller Coaster Tycoon.*
43. Michel Marriott, "I Don't Know Who You Are but (Click) You're Toast," *New York Times,* October 29, 1998.
44. Telephone interview.
45. Telephone interview.
46. Over 100 million units have been sold and the category is driving industry growth, accoring to *GameWEEK* magazine, August 11, 1999.
47. *Wall Street Journal,* August 3, 2000.
48. *www.ClickHealth.com.*

PART THREE
Chapter 9

1. According to *Training* magazine "Industry Report 1999" (October 1999), total dollars budgeted for training by U.S. organizations was $62.5 billion.
2. Dory Bertsche, Christopher Crawford, and Stephen E. Macadam, "Is Simulation Better Than Experience?," *McKinsey Quarterly,* No. 1, 1996.
3. Godin, op. cit., pp. 206–208.
4. Personal communication.
5. George Stalk and Thomas M Hout, *Competing Against Time: How Time-Based Competition Is Reshaping Global Markets,* Free Press, 1990.
6. This section is based on a personal interview with Klein.
7. DelMissier is currently at Barkleys Bank.
8. According to a Pilot spokesperson.
9. The description of the situation was provided by Mark Bieler, former Executive Vice President and Head of HR at Bankers Trust.
10. Telephone interview.
11. *Derivatives Strategy; Executive Edge; Future Banker; Newsweek.*
12. Gene Kim, former derivatives trader, Bankers Trust.
13. Kurt Copenhagen in the *Harvard Law Record.*
14. Joshua Kaufman in *Washington Lawyer* magazine.
15. Hugh R. Marshall in the *Detroit Legal News,* October 18, 1994.
16. Telephone interview.
17. Ashley S. Lipson, op. cit.
18. Based on a telephone interview with Ed Heinbockel.
19. *Workforce 2000,* Hudson Institute, 1987.
20. According to Lockheed Martin director of ethics communication and training Tracy Carter Dougherty, in 1997 and 1998 Lockheed used the Dilbert and Dogbert characters in videos and an "Ethics Challenge" board game that were part of their ethics training for their 175,000 employees.
21. *Wall Street Journal,* May 25, 2000.
22. Ibid.
23. Burger King corporate communications spokeperson.
24. WADs and MODs are game "zones" made up of spatial architectures and wall textures, which can be created by users with "editor" software. They enable advanced players to create new "places," or "levels," within a game.
25. These cleverly designed devices are manufactured in Germany and are sold in the United States by a small distributor in Florida.
26. This description is based on an article by Tanya Schevitz, "Video Game Simulates University Administration," *SF Gate, San Francisco Chronicle,* January 14, 2000.
27. Ibid.

28. Description by a spokesperson for U.S. Council of Mayors.
29. Epic, the maker of the *Unreal Tournament* game, for example, will allow for free "commercial exploitation," with original MODs, but without changing the game code, according to a spokeperson. Licensing the game's source code can cost up to $500,000.
30. From the Powersim Web site: *www.powersim.com / sim_resource / case_study / training_agriculture_0 l.asp*
31. Sarah Fister, op. cit.
32. "Zed's Diner," a game for learning requirements analysis, is described in Roger Schank, *Virtual Learning*, op. cit., p. 69.
33. From the 1998 Asymetrix Interactive Awards Web site at *www.simutech.on.ca / products / awards.htm* and the Telematrix Web site at *www.telematrix.com*.
34. Comment reported in *Inside Technology Training*, April 2000, p. 14.

Chapter 10

1. The Readiness and Training Unit reports to the Deputy Undersecretary of Defense for Readiness, who reports to the Undersecretary of Defense for Personnel and Readiness.
2. The military's training mission includes approximately eight hundred thousand civilian employees and all military dependents
3. Department of Defense, Office of Readiness and Training.
4. Ibid.
5. This is printed on the game box.
6. Personal interview with Donald Johnson and colleagues.
7. See Chapter 8, Note 27.
8. Herz, op. cit., p. 197.
9. Major Peter Bonanni, in a position paper at Modeling and Simulation: Linking Entertainment and Defense Conference, 1996.
10. Modeling and Simulation:Linking Entertainment and Defense report,1996.
11. Learning Ware's *Game Show Pro* is used by several branches.
12. Donald Johnson is a member of the Readiness and Training Unit and a Team Leader of the Advanced Distributed Learning project.
13. Filipczak, op. cit.
14. Telephone interview.
15. See *www.stricom.army.mil*.
16. According to Paul Asplund of the Institute for Creative Technology.
17. From *America's Army PC Game: Vision and Realization*, a pamphlet produced by The US Army and The MOVES Institute, Jan 2004.
18. Personal interview with Mike Zyda.
19. Telephone interview.
20. See Chapter 6, Note 5.
21. See Victor H. Vroom, *Work and Motivation*, John Wiley & Sons, 1964, reprinted by Jossey Bass (Jossey Bass Management Series), 1994.
22. See Chapter 6.
23. *www.cnet.navy.mil / microsim /*
24. Described in Henry M. Halff, "Adventure Games for Technical Education," Mei Technology Corporation, San Antonio TX, no date.
25. *Modeling and Simulation: Linking Entertainment and Defense* report, 1996.
26. See Chapter 10, Note 9.
27. Telephone interview with Professor Merrill.
28. Modeling and Simulation:Linking Entertainment and Defense report,1996.
29. Filipczak, op. cit.

30. Telephone interview.
31. Personal communication.
32. Telephone interview. Mark Oehlert is on the staff of the Office of Readiness and Training.
33. The QDR is a once-every-four-year budget review.
34. Personal interview.
35. *Modeling and Simulation: Linking Entertainment and Defense,* op. cit.
36. Ibid.
37. Ibid.
38. Ibid.
39. Telephone interview.
40. Telephone interview.

PART FOUR
Chapter 11

1. Created in HyperCard on the Macintosh.
2. Each of the game makers, such as Id (*Quake II Engine*) and Epic (*Unreal Engine*) has its own MOD building software as well.
3. According to a Yahoo! spokesperson.
4. Telephone interview
5. *www.learningware.com*
6. These can be used to "get a feel" for the Digital Game-Based Learning and whether it will work in your context. Such demos are available from several vendors discussed in this book. See *www.twitchspeed.com.*
7. Casket U was to be a project of the Batesville Casket Company, a part of Hillenbrand Industries. Unfortunately the project died. (Its "demise" is discussed in an article in by Gregory L. Ferris, "Avoiding the Hazards on the Corporate University Road," *Corporate University News,* November 1995.)

Chapter 12

1. Benjamin Franklin High School in East Harlem, since renamed.
2. MicroMentor, no longer in business.
3. *Pleasantville,* a New Line Cinema Production, written, produced and directed by Gary Ross, starring Tobey McGuire, Jeff Daniels, Joan Allen, William H. Macey, J.T. Walsh, Don Knotts, and Reese Witherspoon.
4. Myers & Briggs created a widely used personality test, related to Jung's theory of personality styles, that divides people into 16 "types."
5. Fister, op. cit.
6. Video Arts, which created numerous training films starring Cleese, including "Meetings, Bloody Meetings," has repurposed many of those films into more "interactive" presentations on CD ROM and the Web.
7. See Chapter 9, Note 20.
8. Telephone interview.
9. The "learning loop," which has been conceptualized in different language by David Kolb, Kurt Lewin, John Dewey, W.E. Deming, and others, consists of some variation of Doing, Observing, Reflecting, Abstracting Concepts, and Testing and Planning, before beginning to "do" again and repeating the loop. Whatever language one uses, the loop emphasizes the need to reflect on what one does and observes.
10. James G. Lengel, *Building the Future,* Apple Computer, Inc., no date.
11. B.S. Bloom, "The Two Sigma Problem: The Search for Methods of Group Instruction as Effective as One-to-One Tutoring," *Educational Researcher,* Vol. 13, Nos. 4-6, 1984.

12. The *Scout Law (SLAW) Game*, written by Pete and Hank Hufnagel using the Klik-n-Play game creation program, is designed to help Boy Scouts memorize the Scout Law ("A scout is trustworthy, loyal...") See *http://users.penn.com/~bsa51/scoutlaw.html*.

Chapter 13

1. Telephone interview.
2. Paula Young, personal interview.
3. Polaroid created a $3 million CD-ROM-based program on Total Quality Management.
4. Lexus Created *Lexus Labs*, a multi-million-dollar CD-ROM project.
5. FedEx spent millions with several vendors.
6. Ford spent roughly $10 million to train its plant workers.
7. IBM spent millions to make this happen.
8. The Joint Command spent over $3 million.
9. *Thiagi Game Letter*, Vol. 2, Nos. 7 and 8, October and November/December 1999.
10. Telephone interview.

Chapter 14

1. Stoll, op. cit. Stoll is an astronomer and professor at the University of California, Berkley.
2. Healy, op. cit. Healy is an educational psychologist and former elementary school principal.
3. David Merrill is a professor of instructional design at Utah State University.
4. Michael Allen is the CEO of Allen Interactions and the creator of the Authorware authoring tool.
5. Scott Miller is a founder of Apogee/3D Realms, creators of the computer game *Duke Nukem*.
6. Stoll, op. cit.
7. M. David Merrill, "What Motivates the MTV Generation?: Some Comments on Motivation" unpublished paper.
8. Healy, op. cit.
9. Healy, op. cit., p. 87
10. Telephone interview.
11. Quoted in Geoff Keighley, op. cit.
12. *Wall Street Journal*, August 3, 2000.
13. Telephone interview.
14. "Evaluation of Lightspan. Research Results from 403 Schools and Over 14,580 Students," February 2000, CD ROM.
15. Telephone interview.
16. Lieberman, op. cit.
17. Scientific Learning Corporation, *National Field Trial Results* (pamphlet). See also Merzenich, Jenkins, Johnston, Schreiner, Miller and Tallal, "Temporal Processing Deficits of language-Learning Impaired Children Ameliroated by Training" and Tallal, Miller, Bedi, Byma, Wang, Nagarajan, Schreiner, Jenkins and Merzenich, "Language Comprehension in Language Learning Impaired Children Improved with Acoustically Modified Speech," both in *Science*, Vol. 271, January 5, 1996, pp. 27–28, 77–84.
18. IDC, "Internet Futures Spending Model 1997-2002: Business Gears Up for E-Commerce."
19. Research.conducted and sponsored by the Department of Defense.

20. Dexter Fletcher, Ph.D. is a Senior Research Scientist at the Institute for Defense Analyses in Alexandria, Virginia.
21. Telephone interview.
22. Ibid.
23. See, for example, Jane M. Healy, *Failure to Connect*, op. cit.
24. Telephone interview.
25. Research conducted by the Office of the Secretary of Defense.
26. B.S. Bloom, "The Two Sigma Problem: The Search for Methods of Group Instruction as Effective as One-to-One Tutoring," *Educational Researcher*, Vol. 13, No. 4-6, 1984.
27. Weise Research Associates, St. Louis, MO. Private Study for Ameritrade.
28. Described in Halff, "Adventure Games for Technical Education," op. cit. The first test was a single experiment in an AV "A" school, which pitted the game against stand-up instruction and two other computer-based instruction systems. The game developers had access to the testing instrument during the game's development. The second test was developed by the same team that developed the competing computer-based instruction lessons.
29. Dr. Dooley Worth, "A Pilot Study of a Brief, Interactive HIV Prevention Intervention in the United States Army, Final Report," December 1999. Prepared for the U.S. Military HIV Research Program, Walter Reed Army Institute of Research and the Henry M. Jackson Foundation for the Advancement of Military Medicine.
30. Telephone interview.
31. Nortel Networks used the "Pick-it" Internet/intranet shell from games2train to create an intranet game in support of its new strategy initiative.
32. Paul S. Gillies, *Vermont Bar Journal & Law Digest*, February 1996.
33. Telephone interview.
34. Quoted on numerous websites.
35. Geoffrey A. Moore, *Crossing the Chasm: Marketing and Selling Technology Products to Mainstream Customers*, Harperbusiness, 1995.

Chapter 15

1. Geoff Keighley, "SIMply Divine, the Story of Maxis Software," on Gamespot, *www.gamespot.com / features / maxis /*
2. See Chapter 7, Note 9.
3. See Chapter 7, Note 8.
4. Telephone interview with Will Wright.
5. Personal communication from Walt Bilofsky, founder, The Software Toolworks.
6. Telephone interview.
7. Telephone interview.
8. The Learning Company.
9. Telephone interview.
10. Telephone interview.
11. I led the team that created this.
12. Telephone interview.
13. Telephone interview.
14. I was the project manager on this project.
15. Telephone interview.
16. Tanya Schevitz, op. cit.
17. The History of the Movies, at *www.aetsa.net / ~milaja / History.html*
18. By 1500, approximately thirty-five thousand books had been printed, some 10 million copies. The Media History Project Timeline, *www.mediahistory.com / time / 1400s.html*

19. Personal communication.

20. The *Well-Tempered Clavier* demonstrates how all the chromatic key signatures can be used, and the *Art of the Fugue* (unfortunately never finished) demonstrates all the nuances of how fugues are written from simple to complex.

21. The original "magnetic poetry kit" ((c) 1993 by Dave Kapell, PO Box 14862, Minneapolis, MN 55414), is an assortment of over 400 words and word fragments handily printed on little tiny magnets. Fridgedoor.com offers over 60 different "Magnetic Poetry ..." kits of 400+ words each in multiple languages. There is also a "Virtual Magnetic Poetry Kit," that works on your computer screen, online at *http://prominence.com/java/poetry.*

22. Telephone interview.

23. Telephone interview.

24. Personal communication.

25. Personal communication.

26. Telephone interview.

27. John Blossom and Collette Michaud, "LucasLearning's Star Wars DroidWorks," Postmortem, *Game Developer* magazine, August 1999.

28. Personal communication from Ashley Lipson.

29. Personal communication from Jeff Snipes.

30. Elliott Masie's TechLearnTRENDS #178, August 4, 2000. Published by The MASIE Center.

31. See Chapter 9.

Chapter 16

1. Almar Latour "Cell Phones Play Games and Find Dates Overseas," *Wall Street Journal*, May 30, 2000.

2. Quoted in Geoff Keighley, op. cit.

3. Godin, op. cit.

4. Interviewed by Geoff Keighley, op. cit.

5. Chris Crawford, "Thoughts on the Holodeck," *Journal of Computer Game Design*, Vol. 1, 1988, online at *www.erasmatazz.com.*

6. Run by the Institute for Creative Technology.

7. Digital Game-Based Learning engines can be licensed from LearningWare and games2train. First-person 3D game engines can be licensed from Epic (the Unreal Engine) and Id (the Quake II engine).

8. Maxis, Monte Cristo, and others.

9. For example, Havas and Sony.

10. The military, for example, is beginning to conduct some of its training this way.

11. Keighley, *Millenium Gaming,* op. cit.

12. Moore's Law, first proposed by Gordon Moore of Intel, states that the number of transistors on a chip doubles roughly every 18 months. It has come to be used a metaphor for exponential speed.

13. Although there are different ways of counting, generations of game consoles are often counted by the number of bytes their microprocessor can handle at once. We have seen the 4, 8, 16, 32, 64, and 128 byte generations so far.

14. The board game *Zodiak*, from Paradigm Learning, has been used by Nintendo.

FURTHER READING

The following books and articles are suggested to those who would like to do further reading on the topics treated in this book, along with a newsletter and some Web sites and suggested games.

Books

Ackerman, Diane, *Deep Play*, Random House, 1999.

Bennehum, David S., *Extra Life, Coming of Age in Cyberspace*, Basic Books, 1998.

Bruer, John T., *The Myth of the First Three Years*, The Free Press, 1999.

Cannel, Ward, and Fred Marx, *How to Play the Piano Despite Years of Lessons: What Music Is and How to Make It at Home*, Crown & Bridge, Publishers, 1976

Caine, Rennate Numela and Geoffrey Caine, *Making Connections: Teaching and the Human Brain*, Addison Wesley, 1991.

Cassell, Justine, and Henry Jenkins, Eds., *From Barbie to Mortal Kombat: Gender and Computer Games*, MIT Press, 1998.

Crawford, Chris, *The Art of Computer Game Design*, 1982.

Csikszentmihalyi, Mihaly, *Flow: The Psychology of Optimal Experience*, Harper & Row, 1990.

Davis, Stan, and Jim Botkin, *The Monster Under the Bed*, Simon & Schuster, 1994.

Diamond, Marian, *Enriching Heredity: The Impact of the Environment on the Anatomy of the Brain*, The Free Press, 1988.

Gladwell, Malcolm, *The Tipping Point: How Little Things Can Make a Big Difference*, Little, Brown & Company, 2000.

Godin, Seth, *Permission Marketing: Turning Strangers into Friends and Friends into Customers*, Simon & Schuster, 1999.

Gopnick, Alison, Andrew N. Meltzoff, and Patricia K. Kuhl, *The Scientist in the Crib: Minds, Brains, and How Children Learn*, William Morrow and Company, 1999.

Greenfield, Patricia M., *Mind and Media: The Effects of Television, Video Games and Computers*, Harvard University Press, 1984.

Greenfield Patricia M., and Rodney R. Cocking, Eds., *Interacting with Video*, Ablex Publishing Corporation, 1996.

Healy, Jane M., *Endangered Minds: Why Children Don't Think and What We Can Do About It*, Simon & Schuster, 1990.

Healy, Jane M., *Failure to Connect: How Computers Affect Our Children's Minds and What We Can Do About It*, Simon & Schuster, 1998.

Herz, J. C., *Joystick Nation, How Videogames Ate Our Quarters, Won Our Hearts and Rewired Our Minds*, Little, Brown and Company, 1997.

Huizinga, Johan, *Homo Ludens*, Beacon Press, 1955.

Jensen, Eric, *Brain-Based Learning*, The Brain Store, 2000.

McCloud, Scott, *Understanding Comics: The Invisible Art*, Kitchen Sink Press, 1993.

McLuhan, Marshall, and Quentin Fiore, *War and Peace in the Global Village*, Hardwired, 1997 (first printing 1968).

McLuhan, Marshall, and Quentin Fiore, *The Medium Is the Massage: An Inventory of Effects*, Bantam Books, 1967.

Modeling and Simulation: Linking Entertainment and Defense, National Academy Press, 1997.

Murray, Janet H., *Hamlet on the Holodeck: The Future of Narrative in Cyberspace*, MIT Press, 1997.

Negroponte, Nicholas, *Being Digital,* Vintage Books, 1996.

Papert, Seymour, *The Children's Machine: Rethinking School in the Age of the Computer*, Basic Books, 1994.

Postman, Neil, *Amusing Ourselves to Death: Public Discourse in the Age of Show Business*, Penguin Books, 1985.

Schank, Roger, *Virtual Learning*, McGraw-Hill, 1997

Smith, Frank, *The Book of Learning and Forgetting*, Teachers College Press, Columbia University, 1998.

Stoll, Clifford, *High Tech Heretic: Why Computers Don't Belong in the Classroom and Other Reflections by a Computer Contrarian*, Doubleday, 1999.

Tapscott, Don, *Growing Up Digital: The Rise of the Net Generation*, McGraw-Hill, 1998.

Articles, Reports, and Papers

Bisson, Christian, and John Luckner, "Fun in Learning: The Pedagogical Role of Fun in Adventure Education," *Journal of Experimental Education*, Vol. 9, No. 2, 1996.

Bloom B. S., "The Two Sigma Problem: The Search for Methods of Group Instruction as Effective as One-to-One Tutoring," *Educational Researcher*, Vol. 13, Nos. 4-6, 1984.

Filipczak, Bob, "Training Gets Doomed," *Training*, August 1997.

Fister, Sarah, "CBT Fun and Games," *Training*, May 1999.

Keighley, Geoff, *Millenium Gaming*, GameSpot, *www.gamespot.com / features / btg_y2k*

Lieberman, Debra A., "Health Education Video Games for Children and Adolescents: Theory, Design and Research Findings," paper presented at the annual meeting of the International Communications Association, Jerusalem, 1998.

Lipson, Ashley S., "The Inner *Game* of Educational Computer Games," self-published paper, no date.

Malone, Thomas W., "Towards a Theory of Intrinsic Motivation," *Cognitive Science 4*, 1981, pp. 333–369.

Malone, Thomas W., "What Makes Computer Games Fun?," *Byte*, December 1981.

Masie, Elliot, "The "e" in e-learning stands for "E"xperience," *TechLearn TRENDS*, Special Report, October 20, 1999.

Schank, Roger C., "What We Learn When We Learn by Doing," The Institute for the Learning Sciences, Technical Report #60, October 1994.

Starbuck, William H., and Jane Webster, "When Is Play Productive?," in *Accounting, Management and Information Technology*, Vol. 1, No. 1, 1991,

Papert, Seymour, "Does Easy Do It? Children Games and Learning," in *Game Developer Magazine*, June 1998.

"Television in the Home, 1998: Third Annual Survey of Parent and Children," Annenburg Policy Center, June 22, 1998

Newsletter

Thiagi Game Letter

Web Sites

www.twitchspeed.com
www.games2train.com
www.mbagames.com
www.objection.com
www.erazmatazz.com
www.learningware.com
www.imparta.com
www.montecristo.com
www.ninthhousenetworks.com
www.visualpurple.com
www.thiagi.com
www.think3.com
www.monkeywrench.think3.com
www.shrike.depaul.edu

Games

These are some suggestions for consumer PC-based games to look at. Remember that state-of-the-art gaming is a moving target, and always look for the latest versions.
Age of Empires
Alpha Centuri
Asheron's Call
Baldur's Gate
Black and White
Command and Conquer
Deus Ex
EverQuest
Riven
Roller Coaster Tycoon
Sim City 3000
The Sims
StarPeace
Start-Up
Ultima Online
Unreal Tournament
Wall Street 2000
Warcraft

INDEX

INDEX

ABOUT THE AUTHOR

Marc Prensky is the founder, CEO and Chief Creative Officer of Games2train and Corporate Gameware LLC. He is also founder of The Digital Multiplier, an organization dedicated to helping eliminate digital divides worldwide, and is the creator of the Web sites *www.socialimpactgames.com*, *www.dodgame community.com*, and *www.gamesparentsteachers.com*.

Marc earned a BA from Oberlin College, an MBA from the Harvard Business School (with distinction), and masters degrees from Middlebury and Yale. Before attending business school, he taught math and reading in New York City's East Harlem neighborhood and spent several years as an actor and musician, where he performed on Broadway and at Lincoln Center.

After earning his MBA, Marc spent six years at the Boston Consulting Group, where he was a consultant and later that firm's first product development director. He then joined a Boston-based software company, where he developed the first multimedia learning applications for Harvard Business School, JP Morgan, The Boston Consulting Group, and many other clients. Prior to launching Games2train as an independent company, Marc was a vice president at the global financial firm Bankers Trust, where he founded Corporate Gameware, the predecessor to Games2train, as an internal startup.

Marc has been featured in articles in the *New York Times* and the *Wall Street Journal* and has contributed to a number of business publications. His article "Twitch Speed," was a cover story of the Conference Board's magazine, *Across the Board*. Much attention has been given to his work, including a cover story in *Training* magazine and numerous articles in *Fast Company*, *Time Digital*, and *Newsweek*. He has appeared on television on CNBC, CNN/*fn*, and on the PBS show *Computer Currents*. More information, including further writings, speeches and speaking availability, can be found at *www.marcprensky.com*.